'Home-Grown' Jihad

Understanding Islamist Terrorism in the US and UK

DRILL HALL LIBRARY
MEDWAY
WITHDRAWN FROM UNIVERSITIES AT MEDWAY LIBRARY

3059715

‘Home-Grown’ Jihad

Understanding Islamist Terrorism in the US and UK

Sam Mullins

George C. Marshall European Center for Security Studies, Germany
& University of Wollongong, Australia.

ICP

Imperial College Press

Published by

Imperial College Press
57 Shelton Street
Covent Garden
London WC2H 9HE

Distributed by

World Scientific Publishing Co. Pte. Ltd.

5 Toh Tuck Link, Singapore 596224

USA office: 27 Warren Street, Suite 401-402, Hackensack, NJ 07601

UK office: 57 Shelton Street, Covent Garden, London WC2H 9HE

Library of Congress Cataloging-in-Publication Data
Mullins, Sam (Professor of counterterrorism), author.
"Home-grown" jihad : understanding Islamist terrorism in the US and UK / Sam Mullins.
pages cm
Includes index.
ISBN 978-1-78326-803-0 (hc : alk. paper) -- ISBN 978-1-78326-486-5 (pbk : alk. paper)
1. Terrorism--United States--Prevention. 2. Terrorism--Great Britain--Prevention.
3. Terrorism--Religious aspects--Islam. 4. Terrorists--Recruiting--United States.
5. Terrorists--Recruiting--Great Britain. 6. Jihad. I. Title.
HV6432.M857 2015
363.3250941--dc23

2015030485

British Library Cataloguing-in-Publication Data
A catalogue record for this book is available from the British Library.

Copyright © 2016 by Imperial College Press

All rights reserved. This book, or parts thereof, may not be reproduced in any form or by any means, electronic or mechanical, including photocopying, recording or any information storage and retrieval system now known or to be invented, without written permission from the Publisher.

For photocopying of material in this volume, please pay a copying fee through the Copyright Clearance Center, Inc., 222 Rosewood Drive, Danvers, MA 01923, USA. In this case permission to photocopy is not required from the publisher.

In-house Editors: Tasha D'Cruz/Dr. Sree Meenakshi Sajani

Typeset by Stallion Press
Email: enquiries@stallionpress.com

Printed by FuIsland Offset Printing (S) Pte Ltd Singapore

'There are things that we don't want to happen but we have to accept, things that we don't want to know but we have to learn'

— Hasna Shaheen Salam, mother of Abdul Moeed Abdul Salam, American al-Qaeda operative killed in Pakistan, December 2011.[1]

[1] Chris Brunmit and Gene Johnson, 'Why Did Boarding School Graduate Join al-Qaida?' *NBC News*, January 18 2012, available at http://www.nbcnews.com/id/46037238/ns/us_news-life/t/why-did-boarding-school-graduate-join-al-qaida/, accessed January 18, 2012.

Acknowledgments

First and foremost I must thank my parents, without whose help and encouragement I would not be where I am today. I will also be forever grateful to my friend and mentor, Adam Dolnik, who taught me almost everything I know about terrorism, and to Nick Pratt, who taught me the rest. I wish to thank everyone at ICP for their support throughout the publication process, as well as the University of Wollongong (where this project started) and the George C. Marshall Center (where it has ended). Last, but certainly not least, a special thanks to my wife for her undying patience and support.

Table of Contents

Introduction

A little more than a decade ago, relatively few people in the West had heard of Osama bin Laden or al-Qaeda, and when the attacks came on September 11, 2001 the world was truly shocked. Now, not only are we well aware that foreign terrorists adhering to distorted versions of Islam are intent on repeating such atrocities, but we have come to realize that the threat is also home-grown. Young men born and bred in Europe, North America, and Australia are radicalizing at home and pursuing violent jihad, either in conflicts overseas, or increasingly, in the countries where they grew up.

Large-scale successful attacks by home-grown terrorists such as in Madrid in 2004 and London in 2005 have been mercifully rare, thanks to the vigilance of our security services. Indeed, reports of disrupted terrorism plots have become such a steady and seemingly never-ending stream that we barely blink an eye at the latest raids or arrests. Nevertheless, smaller attacks carried out by autonomous groups and individuals inspired by the likes of al-Qaeda, but often lacking organizational support, continue to cause damage and distress (see Table 1.1, pp. 12–13). Individuals like Nidal Malik Hasan (the Fort Hood shooter), Roshonara Choudhry (who stabbed a British Member of Parliament), and Arid Uka (who murdered two US servicemen at Frankfurt airport) have not managed to inflict the kind of devastation we have seen in the past. Yet they are stark reminders of the existence of an internal enemy, intent on taking up the banner of violent jihad against the West.

Indeed, bin Laden may be dead, but his 'cause' lives on, as was demonstrated in dramatic fashion by the bombing of the Boston marathon in April 2013, and the brutal slaying of an off-duty British soldier on the streets of London the following month. As if this was not bad enough, we must also now contend with the so-called 'Islamic State' (IS), which rose to prominence amidst the chaos of the conflicts in Syria and Iraq and for the time being appears to have eclipsed al-Qaeda as the preeminent jihadist organization. It too, has indicated its intent to strike against the West and is inspiring home-grown extremists to carry out attacks on its behalf.

Home-grown Islamist terrorism (HGIT) has become an undeniable part of life in the West, yet it is still something that is often poorly understood. Contrary to popular belief, this phenomenon did not suddenly spring up after 9/11, even though this was a key turning point in the 'global jihad'. Indeed, the historical development of Islamist terrorism in different Western countries and the way in which this has helped shape the contemporary threat are often underappreciated. What is more, there are still confused notions about what motivates home-grown jihadis, and — with some notable exceptions[1] — still relatively little in the way of systematic research that would give us a clear understanding of the range of HGIT activity in any given country.

Relying on open source material (mainly press reports and legal documents), this book is based upon more than seven years of painstaking research examining the development over time and the contemporary manifestation of Islamist terrorism in two of the most prominent countries in the Global War on Terror — the US and the UK. By systematically collecting and analyzing data on all publicly identified cases of Islamist terrorism involving citizens or residents of these two countries, this book adds to and sometimes challenges existing research aimed at understanding who the terrorists are, how they operate, and how they are being dealt with by the security services.

Case-studies of individual countries are the first step in this process. Cross-comparison of results then adds another level of understanding. For example, it is widely believed that the home-grown threat in America has been significantly less than in Europe, yet there has been relatively little effort to *measure* this apparent difference. Moreover, popular explanations for this have tended to rely upon superficial description of Muslim populations, with little consideration for the historical development of militant infrastructure during the 1980s and 1990s, which laid the groundwork for developing jihadi subcultures. Similarly, explanations for the apparent rise in HGIT in the US in recent years pointed to continued American military operations overseas, with scant regard for the mechanisms of radicalization on the domestic stage. The detailed comparison of Islamist terrorist activity in the US and UK within this book is an attempt at illuminating the true nature of differences between these two countries, and provides in-depth, empirically supported, and theoretically relevant explanation. Ultimately, the more we understand the problem, the better equipped we will be to solve it.

Analytical Method

The aim of this research was to identify and analyze all publicly documented cases of Islamist terrorist activity relating to the Global Salafi Jihad (GSJ) committed by anyone from, living or offending in the US and UK.[2] This included citizens and residents of either country, whether they offended at home or abroad, as well as temporary visitors who committed a terrorist offense on American/British soil.

In order to be able to capture historical development over time, the sample includes individuals active from the 1980s through to September 11, 2013. The aim was to be as inclusive as possible and this therefore includes people who were:

- convicted of terrorist and/or relevant non-terrorist offenses at home or abroad;
- facing related legal allegations;
- subject to 'special' administrative sanctions such as financial asset freezing, deportation, detention without trial, and control orders;
- killed during the course of alleged terrorist activity;
- involved in terrorism by their own admission;
- publicly alleged to have been involved in terrorism.

For the US, this includes 365 individuals (198 cases, 2 repeat offenders) and for the UK it includes 427 individuals (242 cases, 7 repeat offenders).[3] This represents one of the largest combined samples of Western jihadi terrorists anywhere in the world to date and although the quantitative analysis is limited until September 2013, more recent developments are discussed throughout and given special consideration in relation to findings in the final chapter. It is also worth highlighting here that the chosen methodology (in particular the inclusion of people who are very clearly alleged to be involved in terrorism but have not been convicted, and the analysis of changes over time) becomes crucial when comparing results to other, similar studies and can significantly alter our understanding of the threat.

Nevertheless — and in common with the vast majority of comparable research — by relying on open source materials it is an unavoidable fact that we are likely to be missing many cases that never make it into the public eye, for example where authorities utilize disruption tactics rather than pursuing prosecutions. Indeed, when dealing with such clandestine activity the reality is that we can never know the *full* picture. Despite this, by taking an exhaustive approach to data collection and by including *all* publicly known individuals that fit our criteria, this research makes a significant contribution to our understanding of the overall threat.

The primary sources of data were press reports and legal or other official documents such as indictments and press releases from law enforcement agencies.[4] These were obviously not constructed for research purposes and are of course prone to inaccuracies and missing information. In particular, there seems to be a tendency towards 'positive reporting' in the media, i.e. only mentioning 'interesting' factors, such as being married or having gone to university, when they are present, but neglecting to mention them if absent. Such flaws in the data necessarily limit the degree of confidence in the findings. This is a common problem in the study of terrorism; however, the assumption (made by most terrorism researchers) is that there is enough accurate information that makes it into the public domain to point us in the right direction. As long as the reader remains cognizant of the limitations of open source data, the chances of treating findings with an unwarranted level of confidence are reduced. Indeed, while it may be frustrating to find that substantial amounts of data are missing and that definitive answers are sometimes elusive, analysis of what *is* available — especially when measuring change over time and differences between countries — can still prove to be valuable by raising questions and highlighting new topics for further research.

Another methodological detail that is important to bear in mind relates to the way that percentages are reported in this book. If researchers have a large enough sample and there is not too much missing information, they tend to report percentages as a function of the number of people that they do have data for (% n). For this study, however, the samples are not especially large mathematically speaking and information was sometimes missing for more than 50% of people on a given variable. On top of this, different variables have different probabilities which could be distorted or overlooked by using % n.[5] For example, university qualifications are statistically less likely, meaning that most of the missing information on that variable would be a negative. Using the % n method of reporting could therefore artificially inflate the proportion of people who appear to have such qualifications. The method used in this research was therefore to report all variables as a percentage of the total US/UK sample and to include the percentage of people for whom data were missing wherever relevant. This is important when comparing the results of this research to others where the % n method was used.

Five additional points must be made. First, as touched on above, a deliberate choice was made to utilize a relatively broad definition of terrorism to include people accused or convicted of a range of sometimes non-violent terrorism-related activities, including a limited number of criminal opportunists and others on the fringe of terrorism proper. Although we might not choose to call each and every individual included in the overall sample a *terrorist*, examining the full spectrum of violent and non-violent behavior gives a more complete understanding of the overall phenomenon. As discussed at length in Chapter 7, it also highlights international differences in terms of what is proscribed as a terrorism offense.

A second, related point is that the terms 'terrorist', 'militant', 'jihadi', and 'offender' will be used interchangeably to describe the individuals in this book (see Glossary for definitions of key terms).

Thirdly, the focus throughout is upon Islamist terrorists inspired by the vision of a global jihad against the US and its allies, as championed by al-Qaeda and subsequently taken up by a variety of violent Salafi-jihadi organizations and individuals with ostensibly global ambitions. It is important to bear in mind that such individuals represent only the tiniest proportion of the wider Muslim population and the findings within are not intended to reflect upon any segment of society beyond the militants themselves. Fourth, irrespective of the status of named individuals, this book is an analysis of existing, publicly available information. No new allegations are made at any point and this research has no bearing on legal judgments in any of the cases described. Fifth and finally, the threat that we are facing is dynamic in nature and is constantly evolving. The picture presented here is thus a snapshot of two countries during a particular period in time, which should be constantly reassessed in light of new developments.

Layout of the Book

We begin by examining the historical development of HGIT in the West in general. Chapter 2 explores the various motivations of Western jihadis and proposes a motivational model for understanding how these different factors fit together. Specifically, the model differentiates between pre-disposing risk factors, necessary conditions, and direct motivators. Chapters 3 and 4 provide a historical overview of HGIT in the US and UK respectively. The quantitative analysis is then presented in Chapters 5 through 7, including a systematic comparison of each country and how they have developed over time. The analysis in Chapter 5 includes a statistical summary of each sample and addresses the question of who becomes a jihadi terrorist and how? Chapter 6 focuses on operational behaviors — in other words, what exactly American and British jihadis have been doing; and Chapter 7 examines how they have been dealt with by law enforcement, including investigatory practice and legal outcomes. Findings are summarized in Chapter 8, followed by a discussion of theoretical and practical implications in light of recent developments in relation to Syria and Iraq.

Notes

[1]Of particular relevance to this research are: Robin Simcox, *Control Orders: Strengthening National Security* (London: The Centre for Social Cohesion, 2010), available at: http://www.socialcohesion.co.uk/files/1301651552_ 1.pdf, accessed December 20, 2010; Robin Simcox and Emily Dyer, *Al-Qaeda in the United States: A Complete Analysis of Terrorism Offences* (The Henry Jackson Society, 2013), available at: http://henryjacksonsociety.org/wp-content/uploads/2013/02/Al-Qaeda-in-the-USAbridged-version-LOWRES-Final.pdf, accessed April 7, 2013; Robin Simcox, Hannah Stuart, and Houria Ahmed, *Islamist Terrorism: The British Connections* (London: The Centre for Social Cohesion, 2010).

[2]For the sake of brevity, individuals in the sample will be referred to as being 'in' or 'from' the US/UK, and will be collectively referred to as the American or British sample.

[3]See online Appendices for the full list of individuals included in each sample. A further 191 (US) and 258 (UK) persons of interest were ultimately excluded from the final analysis either because their involvement in the GSJ could not be confirmed, or because they did not belong in the American or British samples according to the sampling criteria.

[4]Personally collected by the author over a seven year period beginning in 2007 and stored, organized, and analyzed using Microsoft Excel.

[5]For similar reasons, inferential statistics were not used for this study.

Chapter 1

Islamist Terror in the West: The Emergence of the Home-Grown Threat

Origins

In the aftermath of 9/11, one of the most striking findings of the investigation was that three of the four pilots, including the operational leader, Mohamed Atta, had radicalized in Hamburg, Germany. Intelligence agencies had been aware of thriving militant networks in Europe in particular but had largely underestimated the threat that they posed.[1] The fact that individuals were becoming radicalized within the West and were also willing to attack their host countries had not been fully appreciated. In reality, not only had the home-grown threat been gradually on the increase since the 1980s, but Westerners had been quick to embrace militant jihad and had even been involved in the very first attacks against the US and France. Militant networks developed during the 1980s and 1990s contributed to localized, pro-jihadi subcultures which set the scene for the mobilization of a new generation of recruits after 9/11.

Multiple factors contributed to the spread of militant Sunni Islamism to the West, chief among them the 1979–1989 Soviet occupation of Afghanistan. This was widely seen as a legitimate, defensive jihad against a foreign aggressor, and thousands of volunteers from around the world flocked to the aid of their Afghan brothers. The Egyptian and Saudi regimes in particular encouraged young men to go and fight, with additional support from the Pakistani intelligence services and the US.[2] Osama bin Laden and his mentor, Abdullah

Azzam, helped organize the foreign *mujahideen* (Islamic fighters) by setting up the Makhtab al-Khidemat (MAK) or Service Bureau in 1984, which operated in some 35 countries to raise funds and recruit volunteers for the Afghan jihad.[3]

The ideas that spawned al-Qaeda and the ideological shift from targeting the near to far enemy (i.e. the US and its allies) gathered pace following the withdrawal of the Soviets and the assassination of Azzam in 1989.[4] US military presence in Saudi Arabia for the 1990 Gulf War and then in Somalia for Operation Restore Hope in 1992 galvanized this shift and reinforced the image of America as the Great Satan and an enemy of Islam. Meanwhile, the fledgling al-Qaeda headquarters moved temporarily to Sudan, with paramilitary training camps maintained in Afghanistan, among other locations.[5] At the same time, many of the *mujahideen* sought refuge in Europe — and to a lesser extent in North America — in order to avoid crackdowns on Islamists back in their home countries.[6] Whilst not appreciated at the time, this dispersal of militants represented the first seeds of home-grown Islamist terrorism (HGIT).

The more-or-less simultaneous flare-up of ethno-nationalist conflicts involving Muslim populations around the world during the early 1990s added fuel to the belief that there was a conspiracy against Islam. Conflicts in Kashmir, Kosovo, Chechnya, Bosnia, and Algeria not only reinforced the global jihad worldview, but also served to sustain and expand the Arab–Afghan veteran network. Footage from the combat zones, often depicting atrocities inflicted upon Muslim civilians, acted as a hugely effective form of propaganda, inspiring a new wave of volunteers driven to defend their co-religionists. Individuals were able to gain training and combat experience, thereby developing the tradecraft of terrorism. They were, of course, also furnished with tales from the battlefield, which elevated their status among their peers, inspiring others to follow in their footsteps.

The expansion of the jihadi networks into Europe was further facilitated by the flow of refugees, immigrants, and asylum seekers from the conflict zones, and individuals who established themselves among the diaspora were instrumental in supporting the jihad and sending new recruits to fight. Extensive networks dominated by North Africans were established, with hubs of activity located in major cities across the UK, Spain, France, Italy, Germany, and elsewhere. In addition to widespread publication of propaganda and recruitment, militants engaged in fundraising, criminal activities such as forgery, and logistic support and planning for operations overseas.[7] As we shall see in Chapter 3, these activities took place in the US as well, with individuals close to bin Laden maintaining homes on American soil; likewise, substantial networks existed in Canada (most notably in Montreal) and jihadists from South East Asia had been present in Australia since the early 1980s. However, the scale and significance of the networks in these more distant locations were dwarfed in comparison to Europe.

First Attacks in the West

Whilst bin Laden continued to narrow his focus on the US and its allies as a target for attack, others were advancing similar plans. February 26, 1993 marked the first significant instance of an Islamist terrorist attack in the West when a powerful bomb was detonated in the underground car park beneath the World Trade Center in New York City, killing six and injuring over a thousand.[8,9] Just four months later, a group of individuals linked to the bombers was arrested for planning to carry out follow-up attacks on a number of New York landmarks and to assassinate visiting Egyptian President Hosni Mubarak.[10]

The majority of conspirators involved in the 1993 network had come from the Middle East; they had received financial assistance from abroad and had ties to a number of terrorist organizations (including the Egyptian Islamic Group, Islamic Jihad, Hamas, and the Sudanese National Islamic Front).[11] It was, at face value, very much a case of imported terrorism. However, there were home-grown elements even then. Several individuals had been living in the US for more than a decade and had seemingly radicalized there, rather than entering the country as terrorists. A number of them were naturalized US citizens and three were Americans by birth (Abdul Rahman Yasin, Clement Rodney Hampton-El, and Victor Alvarez).[12] Other

Americans were involved in the wider support network (see Chapter 3) and even the operational leader of the World Trade Center bombing, Ramzi Yousef, had been educated in the West before beginning his career as a terrorist.[13]

At the same time as America was being confronted by embryonic global jihadis from the Middle East, Algerian terror networks began gaining momentum in Europe. In 1993, Armed Islamic Group (GIA) support networks — established following the dissolution of the Islamic Salvation Front (FIS) the previous year — became evident in France, which was targeted because of its enduring, post-colonial involvement in Algerian affairs. GIA operations, including attacks on French citizens in Algeria, were facilitated by members active on Western soil.[14] Then, on December 24, 1994,[15] four GIA members hijacked a plane at Algiers airport, eventually landing in Marseilles where they were killed by a French terrorism intervention squad.[16] The following July, the GIA assassinated FIS founder Imam Abdelbaki Sahrawi at Myrha Street mosque in Paris; then from July 25 to October 14, 1995, executed a series of bombings around Paris and Lyon, leaving 10 dead and over 180 wounded.[17]

Behind the attacks were transnational networks, directed from Algeria and supported by militants in the British capital. Rachid Ramda of the GIA had been based in London in the early 1990s and was eventually extradited to France where he received separate convictions for conspiring towards and financing the 1995 bombings.[18] However, Ramda was far from alone in the UK. This period marked the integration of Algerian networks with Islamist veterans of the Afghan jihad who were settling throughout Europe.[19] There was sustained social contact, collaboration, and exchange of ideas between North African and Middle Eastern militants engaged in propaganda, support, and operational activities in the West.

The attacks in France also included terrorists who had been born and/or raised there. The alleged cell leader Khaled Kelkal[20] — who was killed in a televised shootout with police on September 29, 1995 — had come to France from Algeria at the age of two and had begun his journey into radical Islam whilst in prison, beginning in 1991.[21] In 1997, 40 militants were brought to trial in France charged with providing instrumental support to Kelkal's campaign[22] and 36 were convicted of belonging to a terrorist organization.[23] Amongst them was Safé Bourada, who admittedly recruited Kelkal and was likewise a French national of Algerian descent.[24] There were also French converts to Islam involved, including Joseph Jaime, David Vallat, and Alain Celle.[25]

European converts to Islam further demonstrated their dedication and violent potential the year after Kelkal's death. Christophe Caze and fellow French convert Lionel Dumont had formed the Roubaix Group after returning to France from fighting alongside the *mujahideen* in Bosnia in the early 1990s.[26] Their group performed a number of armed robberies before attempting a car-bomb attack to coincide with a G7 summit in Lille in March 1996.[27] These cases demonstrate that from its earliest days in the West, Islamist terrorism was able to attract Western citizens. Their willingness to participate in violence is indicative of how quickly militant Islam took root and began to incorporate home-grown elements.

Al-Qaeda Takes Center Stage

Meanwhile, the al-Qaeda network (or rather, what would later become known as al-Qaeda) continued to develop as its members dispersed and jihadi ideology took root around the globe.[28] Concern began to grow after an assassination attempt on Hosni Mubarak in Ethiopia on June 26, 1995, and bin Laden's name came up following the bombing of a National Guard base in Saudi Arabia on November 13 of the same year.[29] In 1996, bin Laden and his associates were forced to leave Sudan as the government came under increasing international pressure for harboring terrorists. Al-Qaeda subsequently relocated its base of operations back to Afghanistan just as the Pakistani-supported Taliban were coming to power.[30] From this point up until the end of 2001, the organization and related wider movement went from strength to strength. In August 1996 bin Laden published his *Declaration of War against the Americans Occupying the Lands of the Two Holy Places*[31] and 18 months later, on February 23, 1998, he issued a *fatwa* along with four cosignatories under the name of the World Islamic Front against Jews and Crusaders.[32] In it they declared that:

> ...to kill the Americans and their allies — civilians and military — is an individual duty for every Muslim who can do it in any country in which it is possible to do it, in order to liberate the al-Aqsa Mosque and the holy mosque [Mecca] from their grip, and in order for their armies to move out of all the lands of Islam, defeated and unable to threaten any Muslim.[33]

Although such bold, antagonistic actions caused considerable unease amongst the Taliban, the relationship on the whole remained one of protective, tolerant hosts and resourceful, outspoken, guests.[34] This continued even after al-Qaeda bombed the US embassies in Kenya and Tanzania on August 7, 1998, killing 240 people including 12 Americans.[35] Yet the response from Washington was limited — a missile strike on Afghan training grounds on August 20, followed by sanctions against the Taliban in 1999.

The West as a Primary Target

As al-Qaeda was allowed to grow in strength, Islamist terrorists increasingly turned their sights to the West. Investigations of Algerian terrorists operating in France in the early 1990s uncovered a vast network of militants interspersed throughout Europe, with links to the Far East and Canada.[36] The Canadian network was run by Fateh Kamel, who had fought in Bosnia and maintained contact with the Roubaix Group.[37]

Kamel's network was involved in document forgery and theft in support of *mujahideen* around the globe with direct links to al-Qaeda. They had come to the attention of the French authorities in 1996 and were under Canadian surveillance. Kamel himself was extradited to France in April 1999 where he was sentenced to eight years imprisonment for charges relating to the 1995 bombings and his dealings with Caze and Dumont.[38]

However, the potency of militant networks in Canada was underestimated until December 14, 1999. Ahmed Ressam of Algeria was arrested at the Canadian/US border trying to enter the US with more than 50 kg of explosives intended for detonation at Los Angeles LAX airport.[39] Ressam had spent some time living in France before traveling on false documents to Montreal in 1994, where he was swiftly absorbed into the militant diaspora subculture. He received paramilitary training in al-Qaeda camps in Afghanistan in 1998–99 and enlisted the help of others in Montreal before arranging to meet up with a contact in New York who would assist him with his mission.[40] Ressam also maintained communication with Islamist militants in Pakistan and London. Chief among them was Amar Makhlulif, better known as Abu Doha, who played a major coordinating role for al-Qaeda operations from his home in the UK.[41]

At around the same time, an Algerian terror cell had been established in Frankfurt, Germany, with plans to launch an attack in Strasbourg, just across the border in France.[42] Yet again, the investigation revealed that London-based militants working under Abu Doha had played a significant coordinating role.[43] Four members of the Frankfurt cell — who had met each other during training in Afghanistan[44] and had spent time in the UK[45] — were arrested on December 25, 2000 and received prison sentences ranging from ten to twelve years.[46] Following on from these arrests, police in the UK raided several London flats in February 2001 and arrested nine militants including Mustafa Labsi (who had been a close confederate of Ressam's) and the radical cleric Abu Qatada.[47] Two weeks later, Abu Doha was also arrested trying to leave the country and 'it became clear that the whole plot had been conceived, directed, and funded in England'.[48] In addition to being wanted by the Germans and French for the Strasbourg conspiracy, Abu Doha was wanted by the US for his role in the failed millennium plot. He was also implicated by the Italians regarding an aborted plot detected in January 2001 to attack the US embassy in Rome involving North African terrorists with links to the Islamic Cultural Institute (ICI) in Milan.[49]

By the late 1990s into the new millennium, Islamist extremists had become entrenched within European countries which served as breeding grounds for the increasingly globalized movement. Training and combat zones such as Afghanistan and Chechnya continued to stand out as beacons of jihad to aspiring *mujahideen*. However,

Afghanistan in particular often represented a way-station for volunteers where they would graduate to the next level in their path towards terrorism. Whilst training abroad in al-Qaeda-run camps, they would also network with peers before returning to Europe to proselytize, undertake fund-raising and support activities, or in some cases, to plan attacks. Radical mosques became hives of activity within transnational, fluid networks, allowing jihadis to move between locales as necessary. Of crucial importance is the fact that fledgling terrorists were becoming radicalized within the West through contact with experienced *mujahideen*, and that militant networks were continually expanding.

It was within this context, beginning around 1996, that the Planes Operation (which became 9/11) was conceived and developed by Khalid Sheikh Mohammed with the help of bin Laden and others.[50] Those who became the muscle hijackers were primarily of Saudi Arabian origin and entered the US a few months before the attack took place. However, it is now well-known that three of the four pilots, who also played vital planning roles, radicalized in Germany and came to America more than a year in advance of the operation.[51] The fourth pilot, Hani Hanjour, had lived in the US for around four years during which time he learned to fly before training for the mission in Afghanistan in 2000.[52]

The devastation caused on September 11, 2001 marked a turning point in the history of al-Qaeda and Islamist terrorism in the West. Aside from being the most destructive terrorist attack in history, causing nearly 3,000 fatalities, it was instrumental in popularizing the jihadi cause and inviting the US-led Global War on Terror. In consequence, Westerners became widely conscious of al-Qaeda and its cause, simultaneously causing widespread condemnation of their tactics but also increasing the number of sympathizers and potential recruits. At the same time, al-Qaeda's ability to coordinate and execute terrorist operations around the globe was severely disrupted as a result of worldwide punitive measures, spearheaded by Operation Enduring Freedom launched on October 17, 2001. The rule of the Taliban in Afghanistan had been cruel and lacking legitimacy, and as support from Pakistan also wavered, al-Qaeda's ally was unable to withstand the heavy military assault.[53] Within nine weeks the Taliban regime crumbled, terrorist training camps were destroyed and many militants were captured or killed. Al-Qaeda's sanctuary had been compromised.

Al-Qaeda as a 'Brand Name' and the Growth of HGIT

The world had awoken to the threat from Islamist terrorism and authorities began to realize that Western countries were an integral part of the terrorists' operations. Counterterrorism measures were revamped and enhanced, including new, far-reaching legislative powers and increased surveillance of known radicals, extremist mosques, and militant Islamist preachers, making it more difficult for the terrorists to communicate, travel, and coordinate activities. Numerous al-Qaeda leaders and operatives were captured or killed and significant amounts of bin Laden's assets were frozen, which further debilitated al-Qaeda's organizational capacity to fund terrorism.[54]

However, heightened counterterrorism measures did not prevent Islamist extremists from attempting further attacks. Several al-Qaeda-linked plots were underway and nearing completion in the direct aftermath of 9/11. On September 13, 2001, Belgian police arrested a Tunisian, Nizar Trabelsi, who was part of a cell planning to carry out a suicide attack on the Kleine Brogel airbase and was linked to a French–Algerian named Djamel Beghal who had been planning to attack the US embassy in Paris.[55] Trabelsi and Beghal had both attended Finsbury Park mosque in London, where they are believed to have met with Zacarias Moussaoui (later sentenced to life in prison as a co-conspirator in the 9/11 attacks) and Richard Reid, a British-born convert who on December 22, 2001 attempted to detonate a bomb hidden in his shoes onboard American Airlines Flight 63.[56]

The significance of early plots in the West was, however, poorly appreciated. Likewise, successful attacks by Islamist terrorists in Tunisia, Yemen, and Bali in 2002, and in Saudi Arabia, Morocco, and Turkey in 2003 were soon forgotten. The US State Department declared in January 2004 that al-Qaeda was 70% destroyed and that its days were 'numbered'.[57]

However, opinions began to change on March 11, 2004, when a network of mostly Spanish-based Moroccan terrorists bombed four trains in Madrid, killing 191 people.[58] It became widely acknowledged that whilst core elements of the al-Qaeda organization had indeed suffered in the aftermath of 9/11, the al-Qaeda 'brand name' had grown in stature. Affiliated organizations and like-minded jihadis the world over were thus inspired to carry on the fight.[59]

In the words of terrorism expert Bruce Hoffman (writing in 2004):

> [A] stunning transformation of Al Qaeda [took place], from the more or less unitary, near bureaucratic entity it once had been to something more akin to an ideology... an amorphous movement tenuously held together by a loosely networked transnational constituency rather than a monolithic, international terrorist organization with either a defined or identifiable command and control apparatus. The result is that today there are many al-Qaedas rather than the single al-Qaeda of the past. It has become a vast enterprise — an international movement or franchise operation with like-minded local representatives, loosely connected to a central ideological or motivational base, but advancing their common goal independently of one another.[60]

The realization that Islamist terrorism had very much become a home-grown problem still did not truly sink in for many until after the London bombings on July 7, 2005 in which 52 people were killed in addition to the four suicide bombers. The fact that three of the four perpetrators had been born in Britain, and all four had grown up there, was a shocking revelation. For the British public, the martyrdom video testimonies of Mohammed Siddique Khan and Shehzad Tanweer were just as haunting for their regional British accents as for the content of their words. Yet far from being an anomaly, the 7/7 bombers are illustrative of broader trends. Indeed, the seeds of HGIT, planted more than a decade before, have continuously borne fruit in the years since 9/11. There has been a proliferation of Islamist terrorist activity on Western soil and it has become increasingly apparent that the terrorists are often long-term residents or citizens of the West (including second or third generation immigrants as well as converts to Islam) as opposed to recent immigrants from the Middle East or North Africa.[61]

AT MEDWAY LIB

Since 2001 there have been well over 100 alleged terrorist plots to carry out attacks in as many as 15 different Western countries spanning Western Europe, North America, and Australia. At the time of writing, at least 40 attacks have been completed without any prior intervention taking place and 16 of these have resulted in fatalities, not including perpetrators (see Table 1.1 below).[62]

Historically, Islamist terrorism was not perceived to be a homegrown problem within the West. It was generally understood that foreign terrorist organizations (FTOs) were to blame and that terrorists operating in the West would thus be financed and directed from abroad. These assumptions have been increasingly eroded and replaced by the realization that the majority of Islamist terrorists active in the West are likely to have radicalized at home and to be largely self-organized with varying, but often limited or even completely lacking organizational support. Numerous attacks have also been committed by so-called 'lone wolves' — individual attackers who are largely removed from wider militant networks, are not supported by a foreign terrorist organization, and who have acted alone in their pursuit of violent jihad.[63] Indeed, all of the attacks highlighted in bold in Table 1.1 are believed to have been orchestrated and executed by lone, untrained individuals. Although these attacks have resulted in fewer casualties, they are clearly more likely to slip through the counterterrorism net (and as right-wing extremist Anders Breivik demonstrated in Norway in 2011, lone actor terrorists are also potentially capable of inflicting mass casualties). Moreover, these attacks have become more common in recent years, to the extent that more jihadi terrorism attacks were completed in Western countries in the past five years compared to the previous nine.

The surge in HGIT was undoubtedly inspired by the 9/11 attacks, which served as an incredibly effective form of 'propaganda by the deed' and acted as a catalyst for the transformation of the global jihadi movement. More people than ever before became aware of al-Qaeda and its mission, and although most people of course condemned the attacks this new exposure instantly increased the pool of sympathizers and potential terrorists. At the same time, existing radical Islamists with subcultural status and connections to terrorists

Table 1.1. Completed Islamist terrorist attacks in the West, December 2001–December 2014. Attacks highlighted in bold were committed by individuals acting alone, based on current information. Numbers of fatalities do not include perpetrators.

Date	Location	Event
Dec 2001	France/US	Attempted shoe-bombing of American Airlines Flight 63
Jan 2002	**US**	**Suicide plane attack on American Bank building, Tampa**
Jan 2003	**UK**	**Murder of DC Stephen Oake in Manchester (1 dead)**
Mar 2004	Spain	Madrid train bombings (191 dead)
Mar 2004	**Italy**	**Suicide car-bombing at McDonald's, Brescia**
Nov 2004	**Netherlands**	**Murder of Theo van Gogh (1 dead)**
Jul 2005	UK	7/7 London bombings (52 dead)
Jul 2005	UK	21/7 attempted London bombings
Mar 2006	**US**	**SUV attack at University of North Carolina**
Mar 2006	**Germany**	**Attempted murder of Die Welt newspaper editor, Berlin**
Jul 2006	**US**	**Seattle Jewish Centre shooting (1 dead)**
Jul 2006	Germany	Attempted bombing of two trains
Jun 2007	UK	London/Glasgow attempted bombings
May 2008	**UK**	**Attempted suicide bombing of Exeter restaurant**
Jun 2009	**US**	**Shooting at Little Rock army recruiting centre (1 dead)**
Oct 2009	Italy	Attempted suicide bombing of military barracks, Milan
Nov 2009	**US**	**Fort Hood shooting (13 dead)**
Dec 2009	Netherlands/US	Attempted bombing of North West Airlines Flight 253
Jan 2010	**Denmark**	**Attempted murder of Kurt Westergaard**
May 2010	US	Attempted bombing of Times Square in New York
May 2010	**UK**	**Attempted murder of MP Stephen Timms**
May 2010	Sweden	Arson attack at home of Lars Vilks
Sep 2010	**Denmark**	**Premature explosion in Copenhagen hotel**
Oct–Nov 2010	**US**	**Shootings on Virginia military installations**
Dec 2010	**Sweden**	**Stockholm suicide bombing**
Mar 2011	**Germany**	**Frankfurt airport shooting (2 dead)**
Mar 2012	France	Toulouse/Montauban shootings (7 dead)
Dec 2012	Germany	Attempted bombing of Bonn train station
Feb 2013	**Denmark**	**Attempted murder of Lars Hedegaard**
Apr 2013	US	Boston bombing & murder of police officer (4 dead)

(*Continued*)

Table 1.1. (*Continued*)

Date	Location	Event
May 2013	**France**	**Stabbing of a gendarme, Roussillon, Isère**
May 2013	UK	Murder of British soldier, Woolwich, London (1 dead)
May 2013	**France**	**Stabbing of a soldier, Paris**
Apr–Jun 2014	US	3 shooting incidents in WA and NJ (4 dead)
May 2014	Belgium	Shooting at Jewish Museum, Brussels (4 dead)
Sep 2014	**Australia**	**Stabbing of 2 police officers in Melbourne**
Oct 2014	**Canada**	**Two Canadian soldiers run over in Quebec (1 dead)**
Oct 2014	**Canada**	**Shooting attack at Parliament Hill, Ottawa (1 dead)**
Oct 2014	**US**	**Axe attack on NYPD officers, NYC**
Dec 2014	**Australia**	**Hostage incident, Sydney (2 dead)**

overseas were moved to praise bin Laden and to further promote their cause. The London-based group, al-Muhajiroun, for example, had published just nine press releases from 1999 to 2001, compared to almost fifty in the next two years alone.[64] Even after 9/11, extremists have been able to exploit Western commitment to human rights and freedom of speech, and governments have struggled to implement effective legislation for dealing with this new wave of militancy.[65]

Just as the shift from near to far enemy was facilitated by simmering global conflicts, so home-grown terrorism has been enflamed by military occupations and war. The invasion of Afghanistan was of course framed as an attack on Islam, but even more significantly, the March 2003 invasion of Iraq incensed a new generation of jihadi recruits. This was at first promoted as being not only a blow against a murderous dictator suspected of developing weapons of mass destruction (WMD) but also an opportunity to quell the tide of Islamist terrorism. As then US President George W. Bush declared: 'We are fighting them there so we don't have to fight them here'.[66] However, such arguments have now been 'patently discredited'.[67] The false grounds of the invasion instead caused Iraq to become a symbolic source of outrage and a rallying point for terrorists.[68] As Aymen al-Zawahiri remarked in September 2003:

> We thank God for appeasing us with the dilemmas in Iraq and Afghanistan. The Americans are facing a delicate situation in both

> countries. If they withdraw they will lose everything and if they stay, they will continue to bleed to death.[69]

The situation in Iraq was thus viewed by al-Qaeda as 'a means to influence and radicalize Muslim public opinion worldwide and as a magnet to draw in as many recruits as possible'.[70] In line with this assessment, a variety of terrorist networks involved in sending foreign recruits to Iraq from the Middle East, Europe, North Africa, Asia, and the Caucasus were discovered. As the US State Department pointed out, these 'networks were strategically significant in their own right, because they pose an enduring threat to their parent societies after the immediate conflict in Iraq has diminished'.[71] This reflected fears that events surrounding Iraq might follow the same pattern as in Afghanistan, where veteran *mujahideen* were instrumental in exporting the terrorist threat after leaving the country.[72]

However, from 2003 until around 2012 Iraq appears to have been of less practical importance overall, rather more of symbolic value for Western jihadis who while clearly outraged were not present inside Iraq itself in large numbers. Nevertheless, it was another crucial turning point in the evolution of HGIT. As former CIA officer and counterterrorism consultant Marc Sageman has observed, there were three waves or generations of Islamist terrorists prior to 2008.[73] The first wave consisted of mainly Egyptian veterans of Afghanistan; the second wave was dominated by Saudis and North Africans who joined the jihad in the 1990s and trained at camps in Afghanistan; and the third wave consisted of a large number of European born-and-raised Muslims who joined the jihad after Iraq was invaded.

Similarly, Norwegian analyst Petter Nesser identified three stages of violent jihad in Europe.[74] From 1994 to 1996 Europe functioned as an 'arena for local jihad', i.e. a base of operations and occasional target for Algerian Islamists; from 1998 to 2003/2004 Europe functioned as an 'arena for global jihad', i.e. a base of operations for terrorists linked to al-Qaeda, targeting US and Israeli interests, and to a lesser extent, France; finally in the third period, 2003/2004–present, Europe has emerged as a target for global jihad, whereby Western-based jihadis 'motivated principally by European participation in the invasion of Iraq' are attacking their home countries.[75] Islamist terrorists throughout the West confirmed this as they consistently cited Iraq as a major source of motivation even after the withdrawal of Western combat troops.

Since then, a number of other developments have added fuel to the fire. The 2005 publication of derogatory cartoons of the Prophet Muhammad in the Danish newspaper *Jyllands Posten* (which were subsequently reprinted numerous times) resulted in increased terrorist activity in Scandinavia in particular, with plots to attack the newspaper and the cartoonists responsible continuing to surface. Beginning in 2006, there was also a spike in militant activity among the Somali diaspora in response to the Ethiopian invasion of Somalia, which inspired a wave of volunteers to join what was initially seen as a legitimate, defensive jihad but turned into an ongoing recruitment drive for al-Shabaab.

The death of Osama bin Laden in Pakistan in May 2011 did not have a discernible impact on the willingness of Westerners to pursue violent jihad. The Arab Spring, initially thought to be a significant blow for Islamist terrorists, also clearly failed to undermine the appeal of their cause. Instead, political instability and 'ungoverned' spaces have created new potential opportunities for jihadis to exploit. Prior to the French intervention in January 2013, affiliates of al-Qaeda in the Islamic Maghreb (AQIM) were able to seize control of a vast expanse of territory in the north of Mali, and although they appear to have been temporarily defeated, the region is far from stable. In Yemen, AQIM's sister organization, al-Qaeda in the Arabian Peninsula (AQAP), likewise remains a viable threat despite wildly optimistic claims that 'final victory' against the group had been achieved in the summer of 2012.[76] Meanwhile, although al-Shabaab — now an official branch of al-Qaeda for some time — has been struggling militarily in Somalia, it remains resilient and increasingly active in the region, as demonstrated by the Westgate mall attack in Nairobi in September 2013 and the assault on Garissa University in April 2015. Jihadists are also wreaking havoc in northern Nigeria thanks to Boko Haram, and continue to pose a significant threat in Libya and in Egypt's Sinai Peninsula. Most recently, the announcement of al-Qaeda in the Indian Subcontinent (AQIS) signifies yet another potential hotspot of activity, and of course there is still the question of what will happen in Afghanistan as international troops withdraw.

Perhaps the most significant developments since 9/11, however, have been the outbreak of civil war in Syria in 2011 and the renewal of insurgency in Iraq soon afterwards. These two conflicts soon merged with one another and have become synonymous with the rise of IS, which split from al-Qaeda in 2013 and declared the formation of the 'Caliphate' in June of the following year. By early 2015 an estimated 15–20,000 foreign fighters from approximately 80 different countries around the world had gone to Syria/Iraq, most of them joining IS or its rival — and al-Qaeda's official representative in Syria — Jabhat al-Nusra (JN).[77] This is thought to include somewhere between 2,000 and 5,000 jihadi fighters from Western countries including perhaps 100 or more American and as many as 700 British nationals.[78] By all accounts these numbers are unprecedented in the history of global jihad and the impact of this will surely be felt around the world for years to come (for more on this, see Chapter 8).

Syria and Iraq especially, but each of these zones of instability (like Algeria, Bosnia and Chechnya before them) represents a lifeline for the Global Salafi Jihad and provides opportunities for volunteers from the West and elsewhere to gain terrorist training and combat experience.

Overseas developments, from Afghanistan to Syria, continue to play a role in HGIT in the West. The spread of global jihadi ideology and the expansion of the movement have also been facilitated by the growth of the Internet. The enabling influence of the World Wide Web and related changes in media and communication have been integral to the decentralization of al-Qaeda and the growth of a violent Islamist social movement. It has resulted in the 'virtualization' of jihad.[79] In other words, 'the ideological and organizational development of jihadist networks and individuals is increasingly taking place on or with the help of the Internet'.[80]

Islamist terrorists are able to make use of online communication and intelligence gathering, allowing dispersed networks of otherwise unconnected individuals to share information, coordinate activities and plan attacks.[81] Furthermore, jihadi propaganda has become increasingly accessible via the Internet. In turn this has made the movement more inclusive, seeming to unite people from around the world, and a more diverse array of individuals are able to identify with the idea of being a global Islamic warrior. This has been instrumental in the ongoing development of HGIT in the West, where the Internet is highly accessible and largely uncensored. Moreover, increasing use of the Internet is thought to be a crucial factor in changing jihadi profiles. Evidence that the average age of Islamist terrorists has decreased somewhat may thus be a reflection of greater usage of the Internet among teenagers and young adults.[82]

The accessibility of the Internet has also meant that more females (such as Colleen LaRose, otherwise known as 'Jihad Jane', or Roshonara Choudhry) are gradually getting involved in this traditionally heavily male-dominated arena.[83] The freedom of expression which the Internet allows also facilitates innovative adaptations of the Salafi, jihadi message. Al-Qaeda ideology is thus sometimes combined (with no sense of irony) with elements of hip-hop, making it 'cool' to be a jihadi 'terrorist'.[84] Violent Islamism has thus found a form of expression that is at once palatable to Western youth, and no doubt alien to the founders of the movement.

Yet despite the importance of the many facilitating circumstances after 9/11, it is crucial to realize that the mobilization of home-grown terrorists did not begin in 2001. Many of those who seemingly sprang into action after the attacks on the US, even some of those who waited until after the invasion of Iraq, had radicalized during the 1990s and had been involved to varying extents in militant networks. Scholars have tended to explain the apparently lower rates of HGIT in the US as compared to Europe primarily in socioeconomic terms — American Muslims are better off and therefore have less reason to turn to terrorism.[85] Putting aside the possibility that HGIT in America may have been underestimated (and appears to have increased in recent years) these explanations of differences on either side of the Atlantic, whilst still relevant, largely ignore the differential histories of jihad. The facilitating role of broad immigration and asylum policies in

Europe has been noted, but the implications of such factors are rarely expanded upon.

The jihadi immigrants of the 1980s and 1990s got Westerners involved in the movement. They distributed propaganda; they promoted their cause; they socialized with others around them and shared their ideas. A key difference is that seemingly greater numbers of *mujahideen* settled in Europe as compared to North America, creating jihadist social networks on a larger scale. Moreover, as discussed in Chapter 3, early jihadi networks established in the US (as substantial as they were) were dealt a significant setback in the 1990s after they moved to attack their host nation. Meanwhile, across the Atlantic, militant jihadi subcultures were able to flourish, thus laying the foundations for the apparent 'epidemic' of home-grown terrorism shortly after 9/11.[86]

Now, with the benefit of hindsight, it is apparent that the development of HGIT in the West was an almost inevitable outcome of the deliberate expansion of jihadi networks, which accelerated following the collapse of the Soviet campaign in Afghanistan. To the extent to which there have been differential rates of HGIT in Europe and North America since 2001, it is crucial to recognize that Europeans essentially had more of a head start in terms of a greater social and logistical base which could facilitate their involvement.

In the post-9/11 era, although the old militant networks were largely dismantled, numerous factors have combined to facilitate the continued growth of jihadi subcultures. It would be naive to think that any Western country is immune to HGIT, least of all those which have played lead roles in the Global War on Terror. The key to combating this problem will be to develop an informed and accurate understanding of who the terrorists are, how and why they become involved, and what exactly they are doing.

Notes

[1] A possible exception to this was France where authorities were quick to grasp the home-grown nature of the threat (see Frank Foley, *Countering Terrorism in Britain and France: Institutions, Norms and the Shadow of the Past* (Cambridge: Cambridge University Press, 2013) Kindle Edition.

[2]Olivier Roy, *Globalized Islam: The Search for a New Ummah* (New York: Colombia University Press, 2004), 290–325.

[3]Rohan Gunaratna, *Inside Al Qaeda, Global Network of Terror* (Carlton North: Scribe Publications, 2002), 4.

[4]Marc Sageman, *Understanding Terror Networks* (Philadelphia: University of Pennsylvania Press, 2004), 25–59.

[5]Sageman, *Understanding Terror Networks.*

[6]Sageman, *Understanding Terror Networks*; Alison Pargeter, *The New Frontiers of Jihad: Radical Islam in Europe* (Philadelphia: University of Pennsylvania Press, 2008).

[7]Pargeter, *The New Frontiers of Jihad*; Lorenzo Vidino, *Al Qaeda in Europe: The New Battleground of International Jihad* (New York: Prometheus Books, 2006).

[8]The Islamist element of the 1993 WTC bombing was significant enough to regard it as a direct predecessor of more recent terrorist attacks, although references to religion appear to have been far less pronounced than they are now. In a letter accredited to one of the perpetrators, Nidal Ayyad, posted to the *New York Times* four days after the bombing, responsibility for the attack was claimed in the name of the 'Liberation Army Fifth Battalion', with stated demands that 'the United States stop "all military, economical and political aids to Israel"'; that it end diplomatic relations with Israel, and that it refrain from interference "with any of the Middle East countries interior affairs."' (Alison Mitchell, 'Letter Explained Motive in Bombing, Officials Now Say', *The New York Times*, March 28, 1993, available at: http://query.nytimes.com/gst/fullpage.html?res=9F0CEEDD1E31F93BA157 50C0A965958260, accessed December 26, 2007). Religious, as opposed to strictly nationalistic or other motives are apparent based upon the group's involvement with the 'Blind Sheikh' Omar Abdel Rahman – leader of the Egyptian, jihadist Gamaa' Islamiyah organization – as well as their associations with several Islamist terrorist groups (see 'Liberation Army Fifth Battalion' MIPT Terrorism Knowledge Base, available at: http://www.tkb.org/Group.jsp?groupID=4113, accessed December 26, 2007). It has also been reported that group members excluding the mastermind Ramzi Yousef expressed religious motivations. However Yousef 'appears to have been a secular terrorist who mobilized others by playing on their religious zeal' (John Parachini, 'The World Trade Center Bombers (1993)', 203, cited in Jonathan Tucker (Ed.), *Toxic Terror: Assessing Terrorist Use of Chemical and Biological Weapons* (Cambridge, MA: MIT Press, 2000), 185–206).

[9]Dave Williams, 'The Bombing of the World Trade Centre in New York City' (1998), *International Criminal Police Review*, 469–471; reproduced in *Politics of the 'War on Terrorism'*, available at: http://www.learnworld.com/COURSES/P72/P72.2002.Q4.ReaderOne.pdf, accessed December 11, 2007.

[10]See *United States of America v. Rahman et al.* United States Court of Appeals for the Second Circuit, 189 F.3d 88, August 16, 1999, available at: http://www.

texascollaborative.org/SilverblattModule/US-v-Rahman.pdf, accessed December 15, 2007.

[11]Steven Emerson 'The Other Fundamentalists', 40, cited in Parachini, 'The World Trade Center Bombers (1993)', 196; Parachini, 'The World Trade Center Bombers (1993)', 197; Ralph Blumenthal, Robert Hanley, Alison Mitchell, Joseph Treaster and Mary Tabor 'The Bombing: Retracing the Steps — A Special Report; Fitting the Pieces of Terrorism-Accounts Reconstruct Planning of Trade Center Explosion' *The New York Times,* May 26, 1993, available at: http://query.nytimes.com/gst/fullpage.html?res=9F0CE5DA163CF935A1575 6C0A965958260, accessed June 6, 2008.

[12]Joseph Fried, 'Sheik Sentenced to Life in Prison in Bombing Plot', *The New York Times,* January 18, 1996, available at: http://query.nytimes.com/gst/fullpage.html?res=9D0DE4DF1E39F93BA25752C0A960958260&sec=&spon=&pagewanted=all, accessed June 23, 2008; Jeanne Hovanec, 'One of FBI's Top Suspects from Indiana' *University Wire*, October 22, 2001, available at: http://www.highbeam.com/doc/1P1-47673190.html, accessed January 15, 2012; Jo Thomas and Ralph Blumenthal, 'Rural Muslims Draw New, Unwanted Attention', *The New York Times*, January 3, 2002, available at: http://www.nytimes.com/2002/01/03/us/rural-muslims-draw-new-unwanted-attention.html?pagewanted=all, accessed June 23, 2008; *United States vs. Rahman et al.*

[13]David Kocieniewski, 'An Enigmatic Personality Whose Mission Was to Punish America', *The New York Times*, September 6, 1996, available at: http://www.nytimes.com/1996/09/06/nyregion/an-enigmatic-personality-whose-mission-was-to-punish-america.html?pagewanted=all&src=pm, accessed July 22, 2011.

[14]Philippe Migaux, 'The Roots of Islamic Radicalism' in Gérard Chaliand and Arnaud Blin (eds.) *The History of Terrorism: From Antiquity to Al-Qaeda* (Berkeley: University of California Press, 2007), 314–348.

[15]The same date that Ramzi Yousef, of the first World Trade Center attack, detonated a bomb on board an aircraft flying from Manila to Tokyo, killing a Japanese passenger (Philippe Migaux, 'Al Qaeda', 322, in Chaliand & Blin (Eds), *The History of Terrorism*, 314–348).

[16]Migaux, 'The Roots of Islamic Radicalism'.

[17]Migaux, 'The Roots of Islamic Radicalism'. Note, however, that the exact number of bombs and casualties varies slightly according to the source (see for example Jeremy Shapiro and Bénédicte Suzan, 'The French Experience of Counter-Terrorism' (2003), *Survival*, 45(1), 67–98).

[18]Jon Boyle, 'France Convicts Algerian of Paris Bombings', *The Herald Sun*, October 27, 2007, available at: http://www.news.com.au/heraldsun/story/0,21985,22657149-5005961,00.html, accessed June 13, 2008.

[19]See Migaux, 'The Roots of Islamic Radicalism'.

[20]Kelkal was directly aided in the attacks by two Algerians: Boualem Bensaid and Smain Ait Belkacem (convicted in 1998 and again in 2002). The plot was financed by Rachid Ramda, based in London (convicted in 2006 and 2007) and some 36 others provided logistical support under Ali Touchent, also known

as 'Tarek' (Craig Whitney, '40 on Trial in Paris on Charges of Aiding '95 Algerian Bombers', *The New York Times*, November 27, 1997, available at: http://query.nytimes.com/gst/fullpage.html?res=9906E6DD153AF934A1575 2C1A961958260, accessed June 6, 2008; Alan Riding, 'French Court Sentences 2 for Role in 1995 Bombings That Killed 8', *The New York Times*, November 1, 2002, available at: http://query.nytimes.com/gst/fullpage.html?res=9B06EFDD1E3FF932A35752C1A9649C8B63, accessed June 13, 2008; Boyle, 'France Convicts Algerian of Paris Bombings').

[21]Nick Fraser, 'How to Kill an Arab' (1998), *Critical Quarterly*, 40(3), 2–19.

[22]Whitney, '40 on Trial in Paris on Charges of Aiding '95 Algerian Bombers'.

[23]'36 Islamic Militants Sentenced in France', *The New York Times*, February 19, 1998, available at: http://query.nytimes.com/gst/fullpage.html?res=980CE FDD123FF93AA25751C0A96E958260&n=Top/Reference/Times%20Topics/Subjects/S/Sentences%20(Criminal), accessed June 23, 2008; Riding, 'French Court Sentences 2 for Role in 1995 Bombings That Killed 8'.

[24]Riding, 'French Court Sentences 2 for Role in 1995 Bombings That Killed 8'.

[25]Riding, *ibid.*

[26]Craig Whitlock, 'Trial of French Islamic Radical Sheds Light on Converts' Role', *The Washington Post*, January 1, 2006, available at: http://www.washingtonpost.com/wp-dyn/content/article/2005/12/31/AR2005123101056.html, accessed June 13, 2008.

[27]Whitlock, 'Trial of French Islamic Radical Sheds Light on Converts' Role'.

[28]The name 'al-Qaeda' was not chosen by bin Laden and his colleagues, rather it was a name seemingly imposed upon them by the FBI during the investigation of the 1998 east African embassy bombings (Jason Burke, 'Think Again: Al Qaeda', *Foreign Policy*, May 1, 2004, available at: http://www.foreignpolicy.com/articles/2004/05/01/think_again_al_qaeda?page=full, accessed January 16, 2008). The name is used here for the sake of continuity.

[29]Sageman, *Understanding Terror Networks*, 44–45; Steven Emerson, *American Jihad: The Terrorists Living Among Us* (New York: The Free Press, 2002), 127–158.

[30]See, for example, William Maley, *The Afghanistan Wars* (Houndmills: Palgrave Macmillan, 2002); Philippe Migaux, 'Al Qaeda'; Walter Laqueur, *No End to War, Terrorism in the Twenty-First Century* (New York: Continuum Publishing), 49–70.

[31]Osama bin Laden, 'Declaration of War against the Americans Occupying the Lands of the Two Holy Places' (1996). Reproduced in 'Bin Laden's Fatwa' (undated) PBS Online NewsHour, available at: http://www.pbs.org/newshour/terrorism/international/fatwa_1996.html, accessed May 12, 2008.

[32]Ayman al-Zawahiri, emir of the Jihad Group in Egypt, Abu-Yasir Rifa'i Ahmad Taha of the Egyptian Islamic Group, Sheikh Mir Hamzah, secretary of the Jamiat-ul-Ulema-e-Pakistan, and Fazlur Rahman, emir of the Jihad Movement in Bangladesh.

[33]Osama bin Laden, Ayman al-Zawahiri, Abu-Yasir Rifa'I Taha, Sheikh Mir Hamza, and Fazlur Rahman 'Jihad against Jews and Crusaders', *World Islamic Front Statement*, February 23, 1998, available at: http://www.fas.org/irp/

world/para/docs/980223-fatwa.htm, accessed January 4, 2009.

[34]The Taliban consistently ignored requests by the US to hand bin Laden over, incurring heavy international sanctions in 1999, ultimately, in consequence, falling from power following the invasion of Afghanistan in 2001 (Maley, *The Afghanistan Wars*, 248–250).

[35]Edward Mickolus and Susan Simmons, *Terrorism, 1996–2001: A Chronology, Vol.1* (Westport, Connecticut: Greenwood Press, 2002), 137.

[36]Jean-Louis Bruguière, 'Terrorism: Threat and Responses', Occasional Paper Series, No.31, October 2001, available at: http://www.ciaonet.org/wps/brj03/brj03.pdf, accessed June 13, 2008.

[37]See Sageman, *Understanding Terror Networks*, 99–103.

[38]Sageman, *Understanding Terror Networks*; Graeme Hamilton, 'Passport Order Infringes Rights of Former Terrorist: Court', *The National Post,* March 13, 2008, available at: http://www.canada.com/topics/news/national/story.html?id=2d443a84-fb4d-45ba-8afd-f11cd6bf65d3&k=30863, accessed January 5, 2009.

[39]For full details of Ressam's path into terrorism and how the 'Millenium Plot' developed, see Hal Bernton, Mike Carter, David Heath, and James Neff, 'The Terrorist Within: The Story Behind One Man's Holy War Against America', *The Seattle Times*, June 23–July 7, 2002, available at: http://seattletimes.nwsource.com/news/nation-world/terroristwithin/, accessed October 27, 2007.

[40]Note that by this time the main Algerian Islamist terrorist organization was the GSPC, which had been formed in 1998 following the descent of the GIA into seemingly unfocused violence and criminality. The GSPC maintained links to al-Qaeda, and as always, individuals affiliated with these and other organizations were able to interact and accommodate each other in numerous countries around the world.

[41]See *United States of America v. Abu Doha,* United States Southern District of New York, Complaint, July 2nd, 2001, available at: http://news.corporate.findlaw.com/hdocs/docs/abudoha/usabudoha70201cmpt.pdf, accessed January 5, 2009; Sean O'Neill, 'Architect of Terror Held in British Jail Cell', *The Telegraph,* January 9, 2003, available at: http://www.telegraph.co.uk/news/uknews/1418311/Architect-of-terror-held-in-British-jail-cell.html, accessed January 5, 2009; John Burns, 'UK Releases 2nd Suspect Linked to bin Laden', *International Herald Tribune*, July 3, 2008, available at: http://www.iht.com/articles/2008/07/03/europe/terror.php, accessed January 5, 2009.

[42]As part of his cooperation under arrest, Ressam later claimed to know that the Strasbourg-based Algerians intended to attack US, French, and Israeli targets outside Germany (Vidino, *Al Qaeda in Europe*, 154).

[43]See Vidino, *Al Qaeda in Europe*, 147–170.

[44]Petter Nesser, 'Jihad in Europe: Recruitment for Terrorist Cells in Europe' (2006) in Paths to Global Jihad: Radicalisation and Recruitment to Terror Networks (Proceedings from a Norwegian Defence Research Establishment seminar, Oslo, March 15, 2006), 2–21, 14, available at: http://www.investigative-project.org/documents/testimony/41.pdf, accessed May 26, 2009.

[45]Peter Taylor, 'A Jihad Warrior Living in London', *The Guardian*, February 9, 2004, available at: http://www.guardian.co.uk/world/2004/feb/09/alqaida.terrorism, accessed June 6, 2011.

[46]The cell-leader, Mohammed Bensakhria, also known as 'Meliani', was captured much later and sentenced along with nine others facing terrorism charges in December 2004 (Vidino, *Al Qaeda in Europe*, 147–170).

[47]Vidino, *Al Qaeda in Europe*.

[48]Vidino, *ibid.*, 157.

[49]Vidino, *ibid.*, 157–158.

[50]See *The 9/11 Commission: Final Report of the National Commission on Terrorist Attacks Against the United States: Official Government Edition* (Washington DC: US Government Printing Office, 2004).

[51] *Ibid.*

[52]*Ibid*, 225–227.

[53]Maley, *The Afghanistan Wars*, 251–283.

[54]Between September 2001 and June 2002, approximately $115 million of suspected terrorist assets had been seized worldwide, although the terrorists continue to be resourceful in raising funds ('Financing Islamist Terrorism' (2003), *Strategic Comments*, 9(10), 1–2).

[55]Alain Grignard, 'The Islamist Networks in Belgium: Between Nationalism and Globalisation' in Rik Coolsaet (ed.), *Jihadi Terrorism and the Radicalisation Challenge in Europe* (Aldershot, Ashgate, 2008), 85–93; Zachary Johnson, 'Chronology: The Plots', *Frontline*, available at: http://www.pbs.org/wgbh/pages/frontline/shows/front/special/cron.html, accessed June 18, 2008.

[56]Vidino, *Al Qaeda in Europe*, 190.

[57]Bruce Hoffman, 'The Changing Face of Al Qaeda and the Global War on Terrorism' (2004), *Studies in Conflict and Terrorism*, 27(6), 549–560, 549.

[58]See Nesser, 'Jihadism in Western Europe After the Invasion of Iraq'; Vidino, *Al Qaeda in Europe*, 291–335.

[59]See, for example, Hoffman, 'The Changing Face of Al Qaeda and the Global War on Terrorism'; Steven Emerson, *Jihad Incorporated: A Guide to Militant Islam in the US* (New York: Prometheus Books, 2006); Marc Sageman, *Leaderless Jihad: Terror Networks in the Twenty-First Century* (Philadelphia: University of Pennsylvania Press, 2008), 29–46.

[60]Hoffman, 'The Changing Face of Al Qaeda and the Global War on Terrorism', 552.

[61]See AIVD, *Violent Jihad in the Netherlands: Current Trends in the Islamist Terrorist Threat* (The Hague: General Intelligence and Security Service, 2006); Mitchell Silber and Arvin Bhatt, *Radicalization in the West: The Homegrown Threat* (New York: New York City Police Department, 2007).

[62]The precise number of attacks depends upon what we define as 'terrorism'. The key is to determine whether or not the actions in question were viewed by the perpetrators as acts of violent jihad (which does not rule out additional, personal motivations). Nevertheless, this is sometimes a difficult judgment to make. There are cases which are included here that some may disagree with,

and there are a few additional cases which have been excluded, for which there was insufficient information to be able to make a classification. Among those excluded are Muhammad al-Khatib, who killed himself exploding his car outside a synagogue in Modena, Italy on December 11, 2003, and Alton Nolen, who beheaded a women in Oklahoma on September 24, 2014.

[63]There is a continuing tendency to use the term 'lone wolf' to refer to any autonomous terrorist group that is lacking connections to a foreign terrorist organization (FTO). This confuses the point of the term, which is meant to convey the fact that it is especially out of the ordinary for *individuals* to become involved in terrorism by themselves. Indeed, group interaction (even without connections to an FTO) often plays an important role in radicalization, hence the distinction between groups and individuals is important for analyzing and understanding how and why they get involved. Furthermore, while both groups and individuals may be autonomous, they present quite different prospects for counterterrorism (the latter being far more difficult to detect). Genuine 'lone wolves' (or lone actor terrorists) have varying levels of connections to other extremists; however, they have largely radicalized alone, are self-organized, and act alone when conducting attacks.

[64]Quintan Wiktorowicz, *Radical Islam Rising: Muslim Extremism in the West* (Lanham: Rowman and Littlefield, 2005), 151.

[65]See Foley, *Countering Terrorism in Britain and France*; Vidino, *Al Qaeda in Europe*, 103–131.

[66]Cited in Hoffman, 'The Global Terrorist Threat: Is Al-Qaeda on the Run or on the March?', 53.

[67]Hoffman, *ibid.*, 53.

[68]Sageman, *Leaderless Jihad*, 91.

[69]Ayman al-Zawahiri cited in Anonymous, *Imperial Hubris: Why the West Is Losing the War on Terror* (Alexandria, VA: Brassey's, 2004), xxi.

[70]Office of the Coordinator for Counterterrorism, *Country Reports on Terrorism 2005* (Washington DC: United States Department of State, 2006), 13.

[71]*Ibid*, 14.

[72]See Kathryn Haahr, 'New Reports Allege Foreign Fighters in Iraq Returning to Europe' (2006), *Terrorism Focus*, 3(20), 2–3.

[73]Sageman, *Leaderless Jihad*, 48–50, 125–146.

[74]Petter Nesser, 'Chronology of Jihadism in Western Europe 1994–2007: Planned, Prepared and Executed Terrorist Attacks' (2008), *Studies in Conflict & Terrorism*, 31(10), 924–926.

[75]Nesser, 'Chronology of Jihadism in Western Europe 1994–2007: Planned, Prepared and Executed Terrorist Attacks', 925.

[76]'Yemen Claims Victory Over Al-Qaeda', *Janes Intelligence Weekly*, June 27, 2012.

[77]Peter Neumann, 'Foreign Fighter Total In Syria/Iraq Now Exceeds 20,000; Surpasses Afghanistan Conflict in the 1980s' (International Centre for the Study of Radicalisation), January 27, 2015, available at: http://icsr.info/2015/01/

foreign-fighter-total-syriairaq-now-exceeds-20000-surpasses-afghanistan-conflict-1980s/, accessed January 28, 2015; Michael Noonan, '15,000-plus for Fighting: The Return of the Foreign Fighters', *War on the Rocks*, October 8, 2014, available at: http://warontherocks.com/2014/10/15000-plus-for-fighting-the-return-of-the-foreign-fighters/, accessed October 8, 2014.

[78]Ken Dilanian and Eileen Sullivan, 'FBI: About a Dozen Americans Fighting in Syria', *Associated Press*, September 25, 2014, available at: http://m.apnews.com/ap/db_355780/contentdetail.htm?contentguid=_n8liAPTv, accessed September 25, 2014; Noah Rayman, 'U.S. Intel Chief: Roughly 40 Americans Have Returned From Syria', *Time*, March 2, 2015, available at: http://time.com/3729295/u-s-intel-chief-roughly-40-americans-have-returned-from-syria/, accessed March 8, 2015; Tom Whitehead, 'Up to 700 Britons Feared Fighting in Syria', *The Telegraph*, April 24, 2014, available at: http://www.telegraph.co.uk/news/uknews/law-and-order/10785316/Up-to-700-Britons-feared-fighting-in-Syria.html, accessed April 24, 2014.

[79]AIVD, *Violent Jihad in the Netherlands.*

[80]AIVD, *ibid.*, 44.

[81]See Emerson, *Jihad Inc*, 466–484.

[82]AIVD, *Violent Jihad in the Netherlands*; Sageman, *Leaderless Jihad*, 111.

[83]AIVD, *ibid.*, 39, 47; Sageman, *Leaderless Jihad*, 111–113.

[84]See Lorenzo Vidino, 'Current Trends in Jihadi Networks in Europe' (2007), *Terrorism Monitor*, 5(20), 8–11; Michael McCaul, 'Islamic State is Recruiting America's 'Jihadi Cool' Crowd', *The Wall Street Journal*, September 11, 2014, available at: http://www.wsj.com/articles/michael-mccaul-islamic-state-is-recruiting-americas-jihadi-cool-crowd-1410478638, accessed September 12, 2014.

[85]See Robert Leiken, *Bearers of Global Jihad? Immigration and National Security After 9/11* (Washington, DC: The Nixon Centre, 2004); Sageman, *Leaderless Jihad*; Silber and Bhatt, *Radicalization in the West.*

[86]Note that whilst this is true of Europe in general, it is still necessary to examine each individual country in detail.

Chapter 2

Understanding Motivations: From Pre-Disposing Risk to Direct Motivators

As the threat from HGIT has steadily become more apparent, Western society has struggled to come up with convincing answers for why it is happening. Why would someone born and raised in the West choose to blow themselves up in order to kill complete strangers? What is it that they hope to achieve? Moving beyond simple, knee-jerk responses ('they hate us'/'they hate freedom'...) it soon becomes clear that there is no simple answer. Rather, there are multiple, interacting factors which combine together in certain situations to create a lethal mix.

The challenge in trying to make sense of HGIT is first to be able to distinguish between factors which do and do not seem to contribute to individual involvement in terrorism. From there, it is necessary to understand *how* the various active ingredients combine and what relative contribution they each make. Taking a pragmatic approach to this problem, six areas of explanation will be examined: 1) individual explanations; 2) conditions in the West; 3) Western foreign policy; 4) the influence of the 'Islamic World'; 5) the role of religion, and 6) group dynamics.[1] Once these different elements have been analyzed individually, a composite model of motivations for HGIT will be proposed which distinguishes between pre-disposing risk factors (both general and specific) and direct motivators (divided into process drivers and ideological goals). The model also specifies necessary conditions which represent the bottom line for involvement in HGIT.

Individual Explanations

Given the levels of violence involved in terrorism and what seems like sheer pointlessness — since little is apparently achieved — the natural assumption to make is that terrorists must be somehow mentally unstable. The reality, though, is that terrorism is most often a group activity and mental illness could compromise group function and jeopardize the need for secrecy.[2] In support of this, evidence strongly disputes that psychopathology is a common causal factor behind terrorism.[3] Sageman's seminal studies of Islamist terrorists from around the world found that only around 1% of individuals showed any evidence of mental health issues.[4]

Studies of home-grown Islamist terrorists in Europe and Australia have found similarly low rates of psychopathology — seeming to occur in no more than about 5% of terrorist offenders.[5] The smaller sample numbers in these studies (compared to Sageman's) may have artificially inflated the percentages, and in fact several of those who were suffering from mental health problems became ill *after* their arrest as a result of incarceration. Of course, as the numbers indicate, there are exceptions. For example, Nicky Reilly, who attempted to blow himself up in a restaurant in Exeter in the UK in May 2008, was suffering from Asperger's syndrome and learning difficulties.[6] Indeed, it seems that psychopathology may be of greater relevance to understanding the actions of lone actor terrorists like Reilly.[7] However, outliers should not be considered disproof of general patterns; the first rule of terrorism studies is that there are no universal rules. Furthermore, where individuals are known to be suffering from mental health problems, this is often considered a potential mitigating factor *against* classifying their actions as terrorism even if they are still held legally responsible. Such cases are indicative of the complexity of human behavior and the fact that there are almost infinite pathways into the same type of activity. Some paths, however, are more well-traveled than others.

Although underlying psychopathology clearly fails as a general explanation for terrorism, an alternative possibility is that home-grown terrorists have been somehow traumatized. In conflict zones such as Palestine and Chechnya, suicide bombers have often experienced loss of family members at the hands of security forces, and may frequently be driven by grief and a desire for personal revenge. In the West, it is common for Islamist militants to have viewed propaganda videos of Muslims being tortured and killed in various settings around the world, and these moral shocks have been described as 'secondary traumatization'.[8] Moral shocks do, indeed, seem to play an important role, with Western jihadis often expressing outrage along with altruistic desires to defend 'their people' or simply to seek revenge against their oppressors. Sometimes the emotional response can be a profound experience. For instance, Syed Haris Ahmed (who was convicted in the US for conspiring to undergo terrorist training), was apparently moved to tears by the hardship and injustice endured by Muslims around the world.[9] As bin Laden himself once put it, the suffering of Muslims 'send[s] shivers in the body and shake[s] the conscience'.[10]

The problem with this explanation though, is that individuals are not directly traumatized and it is doubtful whether vicarious experiences can be considered a form of trauma. Certainly the individuals involved do not obviously suffer from impaired mental or physical functioning, and just because emotions are strongly experienced does not mean that some barrier has been crossed into the realm of mental instability. It could equally be argued that Western jihadis are desensitized to violence and gore by way of repeated exposure to footage of atrocities. Even more importantly, Sageman's 'problem of specificity' applies.[11] That is to say that many people are exposed to Muslim suffering and are equally outraged and upset, but they do not turn to terrorism. The traumatization argument thus appears limited in the context of the West.

So if home-grown terrorists are not mentally ill, and if they are not traumatized, is there anything else about them that might help explain their behavior? Research has revealed an incredibly broad demographic profile: they are generally young males (although female participation is increasing); often they are second- or third-generation immigrants from a wide variety of ethnic backgrounds, but also including a significant minority who are converts to Islam;

most have at least high school education, with up to a third of some samples having obtained a university degree; they are more often lower or middle class; significant numbers are married and also have children; they are more likely to be working or enrolled in full-time education than to be unemployed; and finally, up to a quarter of individuals have some form of criminal record, often for relatively minor and varied offenses, although few are life-long criminals.[12] Of course, this a rather general description to which there are many exceptions and the situation varies between nations and across time. For instance, Robin Simcox and colleagues found that jihadis in the US had a higher socioeconomic profile than those in the UK, while recent reports have found significantly higher rates of unemployment, criminality, and other indicators of marginalization among German, Australian, and Swedish jihadis.[13] Meanwhile, despite longstanding concern that prisons may be acting as incubators of terrorism in France, a study by the *Centre de Prévention Contre les Dérives Sectaries Liées á l'Islam* published in November 2014 found that 67% of their sample of French jihadis were middle class.[14] Ultimately, the fact remains that Western jihadis continue to come from all walks of life and there is no unique demographic profile which systematically distinguishes them from the rest of the population.

If, however, we delve a little deeper beneath the surface, there is still a lingering impression that significant numbers of home-grown jihadis are somehow troubled young adults who have experienced such adversities as facing racism, overcoming drug-habits, or coping with the loss of family members.[15] The experience of life crises of varying types can result in cognitive openings whereby individuals question their existing beliefs and become open to alternative ideas.[16] Individual receptivity to jihadi ideology can thus be enhanced through experiencing any manner of unrelated adversity, from losing a job to feeling socially or politically excluded, going through a family break-up or being imprisoned. Home-grown jihadis are also often described as experiencing more personal crises of identity. Newly arrived immigrants may feel socially and spiritually isolated in Western society, while second and third-generation immigrants (the bulk of home-grown Islamist terrorists) may be torn between their Muslim heritage and secular life in the West. Converts, meanwhile, are those who consciously reject their Western identity, sometimes for political or religious reasons, or simply because they somehow failed to fit in.[17]

What each of these very different individuals finds in radical Islam is a sense of belonging and a strong, unambiguous, and righteous identity — a straightforward way of viewing the world that does away with confusion, draws a line between good and evil, and brings certainty to their lives. In no other case is this kind of transformation of identity more apparent than that of Mohammed Siddique Khan, the operational leader in the 7/7 bombings. Before becoming a hardcore jihadi, willing to die for his cause, he had gone through a phase of calling himself 'Sid' and wearing cowboy boots and a leather jacket.[18]

Whether or not these kinds of efforts at reinventing oneself are spurred on by crises of identity is debatable, since this implies panic. Thus, a more appropriate term might be 'identity dissonance' (referring to mental tension or discomfort).[19] Whatever label we choose to apply, research has shown that experiencing isolation or a sense of threat to one's identity can indeed cause individuals to seek affiliation with others as a way of overcoming that threat.[20] Viewed in this light, identity dissonance not only fosters cognitive openings but can lead individuals to actively seek out an alternative identity.

As will become clear, issues of identity cut to the very core of what terrorism is about; however, as with moral shocks and experiences of adversity, the problem of specificity again applies. If everyone who felt somehow isolated or ill-at-ease in Western society turned to terrorism, we would have a rather more significant problem to deal with. At the same time, it is not clear that all terrorists have experienced these sorts of difficulties. Eighty percent of Bakker's European sample of Islamist terrorists radicalized in their country of residence, 'not far from their families and friends, and in many ways were at home in the countries of recruitment'.[21] Alienation and adversity may indeed play an important role for some individuals, but varying life crises cannot explain involvement in terrorism by themselves.

Conditions in the West

The realization that Islamist terrorism is now undeniably home-grown raises the question as to what it is about Western society that might be contributing. This has resulted in increasing attention being paid to the socioeconomic situation of Muslim populations in the West, since the vast majority of Islamist terrorists emerge from within this broader category (although they of course represent only a tiny minority).

By examining societal conditions, we are essentially searching for root causes of HGIT. Assumed root causes usually include such factors as State oppression, restricted civil liberties, social upheaval, poverty, or lack of educational and occupational opportunities.[22] The reasoning behind this is that deprivation leads to frustration and therefore aggression.[23] This is more likely when people are deprived of *expected* sources of gratification, and when they believe that their situation is deliberate and *unjust*.[24] The problem is that there is no clear relationship between deprivation and terrorism.[25] Indeed, extreme deprivation is likely to limit opportunities for engaging in terrorism, while higher socioeconomic status may result in greater political awareness, and possession of the skills and resources necessary to take part in this type of activity.

As the demographic profiles of Western jihadis demonstrate, they are not particularly deprived on the whole and in fact many are quite privileged. They have access to all of the benefits and trappings associated with life in the West and they are considerably better off than most of their counterparts in Asia, Africa, and the Middle East. It is therefore more plausible that Muslims in the West suffer from *relative* deprivation, i.e. compared to the majority population around them and their own expectations. For instance, Rabasa and Benard have noted that considerable numbers of Western jihadis appeared to be reasonably well educated and yet few were in skilled occupations befitting of their qualifications.[26] Jihadis in the West might also experience *vicarious* deprivation (similar to moral shocks in that a sense of empathy is felt for the plight of Muslims around the world).[27] This explains why even very wealthy individuals such as bin Laden can still feel outrage at the situation of 'their people'. Vicarious deprivation is certainly reflected in justifications for HGIT, which routinely draw attention to civilian casualties in places like Afghanistan, Iraq, and Syria. There is also a case to be made for relative deprivation of Muslims in the West, especially in Europe.

Notwithstanding substantial differences between individual countries, as well as variation within them, European Muslims are characterized as being poorly integrated and disadvantaged in a number of ways. Lax immigration policies allowed unskilled Muslim immigrants to enter countries like the UK under the 'guest-worker' programs which burgeoned during the 1950s. Then, under family reunification schemes, workers were joined by their families and Muslim communities took root.[28] However, integration into European societies is thought to have been limited by strong, exclusionary national identities, discriminatory labor markets and generous social benefit schemes.[29] This has contributed to lower average incomes compared to the general population and higher rates of unemployment and imprisonment among European Muslims. They are often described as living in socially deprived and 'ghettoized' urban areas, and are politically under-represented.[30] In the post-9/11 era the situation has been exacerbated by public backlash against Muslims, who feel demonized and unfairly targeted by counterterrorism activities.[31]

Clearly this depicts a situation that has the potential to foment frustration. What is more, Europe has suffered from higher rates of Islamist terrorism than the US, Canada, and Australia, whose Muslim populations have been viewed as better integrated and economically closer to their respective general populations.[32] Put simply, the poorer the circumstances of Western Muslims, the higher the rates of HGIT — or so the argument goes.

Estimates of differential rates of terrorist activity have varied wildly and have been based on extremely circumspect data. For instance, Sageman has suggested that there were 60 arrests in relation to Islamist terrorism in the US from September 11, 2001 until 2008, compared to 2,300 in Europe.[33] Pipes, on the other hand, claimed corresponding figures of 527 and 1,400 for the same period.[34] In fact, even different law enforcement agencies within the same country sometimes report different arrest rates for terrorism offenses and cannot always provide evidence to support their statistics.[35] Part of the problem is that cases sometimes begin as potential terrorism investigations only to result in an ordinary criminal charge, or even no charge at all. Arrest rates are ultimately both problematic and superficial and cannot be said to give an objective indication of rates of terrorism. Even terrorism conviction rates, which are a more reliable measure, have their problems. As discussed in Chapter 7, divergent legislation in different countries can make it difficult to make direct comparisons. Furthermore, studying convictions alone ignores many relevant terrorism cases that if overlooked can quite dramatically alter our understanding of the threat (a point which becomes salient when the current research is compared to studies which utilize more restrictive sampling).[36] Hence, the need for a more detailed and systematic comparison of specific countries.

The problem is compounded by unsubstantiated or generalized claims about Western Muslim populations. First, not all countries include religion in their national census and therefore details of the Muslim population in a number of cases (including the US) are educated approximations.[37] Second, the characterization of the US, Canada, and Australia as 'cultural melting pots' glosses over existing social problems. Muslims in Australia, for example, have been found to experience many of the same poor socioeconomic conditions as their European counterparts.[38] Likewise, although American Muslims have been described as 'middle class and mostly mainstream', 19% reported that discrimination, racism, and prejudice were a problem and 15% stated that they felt as if they were viewed as terrorists, confirming that Muslims in the US have also been subject to many of the same pressures reported in Europe.[39]

Third, it is important to recognize that Muslim populations are extremely diverse and as a result, international comparisons can be fraught with difficulty. For instance, Muslims born in the US were found to be more likely than their foreign-born counterparts and the general population to rate their personal financial situation as fair/poor (62%, 49%, and 50%, respectively) and were more likely to be dissatisfied with conditions within the US (77% compared to 45% of foreign-born Muslims and 61% of the general population).[40] Furthermore, 8% of US Muslims overall reported that they thought suicide terrorism was often or sometimes justified (compared to 7% of those who were asked a similar question in Germany, 15% in Britain, and 16% in France and Spain).[41] However, the figure was also 15% among 18–29 year olds in the American sample, indicating that youth, as well as place of birth, are important moderating variables and unless samples are matched it can be difficult to draw meaningful conclusions from such comparisons. Indeed, there is evidence to suggest that a larger proportion of the UK Muslim population is second or third generation compared to the US and that it also includes a larger number of young people.[42] Such factors may be equally important to socioeconomic conditions and yet are rarely considered.

A fourth point is that explanations of HGIT that revolve purely around socioeconomic conditions — which are relatively stable — do not seem sufficient to explain more rapid changes in rates of terrorism, as seems to have occurred in both the US and UK following the escalation of conflicts in Iraq, Somalia, and Syria. Finally, radical Islamists have been found to play upon domestic grievances as a way of finding common ground with prospective recruits[43] and there are instances of Islamist terrorists mentioning domestic policies as part of the reason for their actions.[44] However, the situation of Muslims in the West seems to play a subordinate role to the situation of Muslims in Afghanistan, Iraq, and elsewhere, at least as far as stated motivations go.

Ultimately, although the relative socioeconomic deprivation of Muslims in the West may contribute to differential rates of HGIT, it is 'only weakly related' to radicalization and is a very limited basis for theoretical explanation by itself.[45] Socioeconomic explanations overlook the differential historical development of the jihadi movement and as is the case with the vast majority of potential contributing variables, they cannot explain why it is only a very small minority of individuals that become terrorists despite experiencing the same broad environment.

Western Foreign Policy

Coping with various difficulties associated with life in the West, whether symbolic or pragmatic, represents a *general* form of predisposing risk in that it adds potential reason to be frustrated and angry. But it is not part of the core business of Islamist terrorism, which involves a persisting preoccupation with the activities of the US and its allies in relation to Muslim nations. Concern over Western foreign policy is closely related to moral shock (since Muslims often suffer in conflicts involving Western military) and it is a more specific form of risk in that it aligns directly with the concerns of jihadis around the world.

As detailed already in Chapter 1, the initial ideological shift from near to far enemy was based on the perception that apostate regimes in the Middle East and North Africa were being propped up by Western governments. Similarly, Western support for Israel has become ingrained as a symbol of injustice against Muslims (although global jihadis have been conspicuous by their general absence from the Palestinian conflict). Recent Western support for revolutions in the Arab world against the very regimes the West has been propping up has been perceived as yet more duplicity against largely Muslim populations, even though jihadis themselves have been calling for the overthrow of these governments.[46]

In addition to diplomatic foreign policy, Western military operations overseas have continuously fueled global jihadi ideology since the beginning of the movement and the list of perceived acts of aggression against Muslims continues to grow. Chief among these are the occupation of Afghanistan since 2001 and the 2003 invasion of Iraq, which has been noted for its significance in legitimizing attacks against the West in general. More recently, the NATO intervention in Libya in March 2011, the killing of Osama bin Laden by US Navy Seals in Abbottabad, Pakistan on May 2, 2011, the failure of Western governments to intervene in Syria, and the bombing of the 'Islamic State' (IS) have each been added to the list of grievances.

The significance of Western imperialism as a source of motivation for violent jihad was evident in bin Laden's 1996 *fatwa* in which he described the presence of 'the armies of the American Crusaders and their allies' in Saudi Arabia as 'the latest and greatest' act of aggression against Muslims.[47] These sentiments were repeated in the 1998 'World Islamic Front' statement, and home-grown jihadis throughout Europe, the US, Canada, and Australia have repeatedly demanded the withdrawal of Western troops from Muslim lands. In March 2004 the Madrid bombers made a videotaped claim of responsibility explaining that the attacks were 'a response to the crimes that you have caused in the world, and specifically in Iraq and Afghanistan.'[48] Shehzad Tanweer, one of the July 2005 London bombers, declared in his martyrdom video that:

> What you have witnessed now is only the beginning of a series of attacks which, *insh'Allah* [God willing], will intensify and continue until you pull all of your troops out of Afghanistan and Iraq, until you stop all financial and military support to the US and Israel, and until you release all Muslim prisoners from Belmarsh [prison] and your other concentration camps.[49]

Similarly, Faisal Shahzad, who attempted to bomb Times Square in May 2010, denounced '[t]he crusading US and NATO forces who have occupied the Muslim lands under the pretext of democracy and freedom',[50] while Zale Thompson, who attacked officers of the New York City Police Department with an axe in October 2014 had declared online that 'If the Zionists and the Crusaders had never invaded and colonized the Islamic lands after WW1, then there would be no need for Jihad!'[51]

Such is the emphasis among jihadis on trying to influence Western foreign policy that it swiftly emerges as paramount among the more tangible ideological goals across the movement. Max Abrahms has argued convincingly that al-Qaeda's primary objective is to drive the US and its allies out of the Muslim world, and yet the reverse has happened.[52] The Global War on Terror, designed to quell the rising tide of violent jihad against the West, is at the same time perpetuating the problem by inspiring new waves of Islamist terrorism. Thus, Pape and Feldman view the use of suicide tactics by home-grown terrorists as a response to vicarious occupation.[53] But anger at Western foreign policy is of course far from enough to create a terrorist. In a 2007 survey by the Pew Research Center, 48% of American Muslims reported that they believed the war in Afghanistan was wrong; 75% believed that the war in Iraq was wrong; and 55% felt that the Global War on Terror was insincere.[54] Perhaps even more revealingly, smaller but still substantial proportions of the general American population agreed with these sentiments.[55] Clearly, there are still pieces missing from our puzzle.

The Influence of the 'Islamic World'

Unraveling the mystery of HGIT rightly involves introspection, but foreign nations have also played a role and continue to do so. The 1979 Iranian revolution is significant because the establishment of a Shia theocracy provoked a response from Saudi Arabia. The Saudis felt inclined to more aggressively promote their brand of Sunni, Wahhabi Islam and they have since invested millions of dollars in establishing Islamic centers and mosques throughout the West.[56] This led to the rise of a form of Islam that many home-grown Islamist terrorists ostensibly subscribe to and facilitated entry to the West of extremist preachers with overtly militant agendas. As Laqueur observes:

> . . . in the 1980s, radicalization set in with the influx of a new generation of young radical preachers paid for mainly by Saudi money. . . In Britain alone, fifteen hundred new mosques were built and some five thousand Koran schools established, as well as cultural centres and radical students' associations.[57]

More directly, the arrival of *mujahideen* in the West following the Soviet–Afghan war was largely a consequence of the fact that they faced repression in their home countries. Militant activity in the West was initially focused upon events in the Islamic world and although Western nations themselves are now considered to be high-priority targets, overseas events and ties to the country of origin remain highly important for home-grown jihadis. Pargeter points out that even second and third generation immigrants to the West pay close attention to events back home and their heritage, which includes a long history of conflict with Western nations, helps to shape their lives as part of the diaspora.[58] These links have facilitated political theater between Islamic nations surrounding events in the West, resulting in increased levels of Islamist activism and acts of terrorism. The publication of *The Satanic Verses* by Salman Rushdie in Britain in 1988 first resulted in localized protests which gradually escalated as Islamic regimes learned of the affair, culminating with Iran issuing a *fatwa* calling for Rushdie's death.[59] In the post-9/11 world a similar pattern of events unfolded over disparaging cartoons of the Prophet Muhammad, first published in Denmark in 2005. Again, local activists pressed the issue and Middle Eastern and North African states competed in publicly demonstrating their outrage at what was quickly framed as part of a war on Islam.[60] Following the initial wave of protests and numerous death threats (including a *fatwa* against Danish troops in Iraq) there has been a notable increase in Islamist terrorist activity within Scandinavia and numerous plots have been detected involving plans to assassinate the cartoonists and/or attack the *Jyllands Posten* newspaper in particular. Of course, the Danes were not the only ones to publish such cartoons and the terrorists eventually got their revenge in January 2015 with the attack on the French satirical magazine *Charlie Hebdo* which left 11 people dead.

Although the Danish cartoon affair began in the West, the process of escalation and reverberation around the globe was facilitated by reactions in the wider Islamic world and seized upon by terrorists as a call to action. Events which originate and mostly take place in other regions can also have an impact in the West. For example, the 2006 Ethiopian invasion of Somalia, aimed at ousting the Union of Islamic Courts (UIC) from power, directly motivated young Somali men in the diaspora to return home in order to defend their country. In reality, for many this meant joining with al-Shabaab which was designated a Foreign Terrorist Organization (FTO) by the US in March 2008 and formally joined with al-Qaeda in February 2012. A number of Western recruits have since carried out suicide bombings for al-Shabaab in Somalia and although the organization has yet to conduct an attack outside of Africa it continues to attract international volunteers and has urged its followers in the West in particular to 'target the disbelievers wherever they are', even suggesting specific shopping centers in the US, Canada, and Britain.[61] In other cases, of course, instability abroad has had a much more direct impact on Western security.

Indeed, connections to jihadist organizations in conflict zones are a coveted prize and although it is often assumed that jihadis in the West are acting independently, this is not always the case. The London bombings are a well-known example but similar cases continue to surface. For example, three interlinked plots detected in the UK, US, and Norway in 2009 and 2010 all involved direction from al-Qaeda in Pakistan, while the aforementioned *Charlie Hebdo* attackers had trained with al-Qaeda in the Arabian Peninsula.[62] Making connections with foreign terrorists and undergoing training overseas may have become more difficult, but these elements have retained an important symbolic and practical value for aspiring home-grown terrorists. Western jihadis still sometimes succeed in making connections in places like Pakistan, Afghanistan, Yemen, and Somalia, and more recently Syria and Iraq have become the destinations of choice. For those who are successful, this not only validates their self-image as real *mujahideen*, but gives them access to weapons and explosives training that makes them a far more formidable threat.

It is important to recognize that although Islamist terrorism is indeed home-grown in the West, it does not occur in a vacuum. There are important historical, cultural, political, and practical connections to the Islamic world, which help shape the threat that we face.

The Role of Religion

The role of religion has probably been the most misunderstood of all aspects of Islamist terrorism. Muslims in the West have suffered from retaliatory attacks in the aftermath of acts of terrorism and 'Islamophobia' has undoubtedly swelled since 9/11. The burning of the Quran by pastors Terry Jones and Wayne Sapp in the US in March 2011, under the erroneous guise of freedom of speech, is a prime example of the ignorance which surrounds this issue. Not only does this display a complete lack of understanding of the role of religion, but it has only added to the ongoing violence: at least twelve people lost their lives in violent protests in Afghanistan related to this incident.[63]

The most important finding here, and one that is consistently repeated across different Western samples, is that home-grown jihadis have rarely lived their whole lives as observant Muslims.[64] Instead, the majority of these men and women appear to have lived distinctly Western lifestyles and have only become increasingly religious as a result of the process of radicalization. In this way spiritual curiosity can turn into religious misadventure. Mainstream teachings of Islam simply do not promote terrorism and greater levels of religious knowledge may even help protect against acceptance of jihadi ideology.[65] Islamist terrorists tend to focus on selective interpretation of certain contested concepts such as *jihad* and *takfir*, using cherry-picked quotes from the Quran and Hadith to support their views and referring to a narrow range of militant scholars for guidance. Although there is immense variation in levels of knowledge, this results in a comparatively limited understanding of religion. From the perspective of explaining involvement in Islamist terrorism, we are thus interested not so much in Islam in general, but in very specific, often highly politicized interpretations of the faith.

Some observers have downplayed the role of religious belief in Islamist terrorism to the extent that it is seen as entirely superficial. Olivier Roy argues that young men in the West are really attracted to Islamist terrorism because it gives them a chance to rebel against the system, and in this light HGIT appears to be a repackaged version of left-wing terrorism.[66] But while there is some validity to this perspective, it is a mistake to dismiss the religious element altogether. Just because home-grown terrorists tend to have limited religious knowledge does not mean that their beliefs are insincere. As Wiktorowicz has pointed out, religious beliefs (that individuals are doing God's will and that they will be rewarded in Heaven) make all the personal sacrifices worthwhile and therefore rational.[67]

The significance of religious beliefs can be seen in that they permeate every aspect of the terrorists' identity and swamp every aspect of their communication. More tangible, political goals are often lost within a torrent of references to select verses from the Quran and the language used is deliberately stylized to take on a religious bent. There is no doubt that Islamist terrorists see themselves as true Muslims and that they feel they represent an idealized *Ummah*, or worldwide Islamic community. This shared sense of identity is what ties together otherwise disparate networks of militants and enables home-grown jihadis to become part of the global movement. It is precisely because of this that al-Qaeda was able to transform itself from an organization with relatively finite boundaries into a sprawling, transnational franchise.

Not only does religion define how Islamist terrorists see and express themselves, bringing meaning to their lives, it also dictates behavior and contributes to ideological goals. The most extreme, and ultimately unrealistic, of these involves establishing the equivalent of a global empire governed by *sharia* (Islamic law). However, explicitly religious ambitions of Islamist terrorists have mostly been restricted to attempts at establishing *sharia* within specified Muslim nations or regions. Hence, Westerners such as Daniel Maldonado and Omar Hammami — both American converts who joined the Somali jihad — were drawn to the idea of 'fighting against all those who are against an Islamic state'.[68] More recently, the declaration of the 'Caliphate' in Iraq and Syria has managed to tap into these motivations by seemingly transforming the dream into reality. Just how long this will last is open to debate, yet despite a track record of self-defeating brutality the allure of a jihadist state remains a powerful attraction.

Specific, religious objectives are usually less clear within the West because even jihadis seem to realize that there is no realistic prospect of Islamist rule within the foreseeable future. Nevertheless, this has not stopped extremists living in Britain and other European countries from trying to enforce *sharia* within their neighborhoods[69] and as we have seen with the case of the Danish cartoon affair and the *Charlie Hebdo* attack in Paris, religious sentiments also give rise to more immediate and palpable operational goals. We must also not forget that attacks on Westerners — whether civilians or members of the security services — are seen to be justified precisely because they are *kuffar* or non-believers.

Regardless of the specific operational objective, and despite deeply flawed reasoning, jihadis believe that they are acting according to Divine imperatives. They do not sit back and evaluate alternative theological perspectives and they do not separate political and religious goals. They sometimes go through the motions of seeking religious approval for acts of violence that they want to carry out, but these acts are almost invariably approved. As UK-based ideologue Abu Hamza once declared:

> Anything that will help the *intifada*, just do it. If it is killing, do it. If it is paying, pay, if it is ambushing, ambush, if it is poisoning, poison. You help your brothers, you help Islam in any way you like it, anywhere you like it...They are all *kuffar* and can all be killed. Killing a *kuffar* who is fighting you is OK. Killing a *kuffar* for any reason, you can say it is OK, even if there is no reason for it.[70]

No matter how ill-informed or narrow-minded Islamist terrorists are, religion *as they see it* is an extremely important part of who they are and what they do. Gaining an appreciation of this adds another vital piece to understanding their motivations.

Group Dynamics

The chapter thus far has looked at *why* people become involved in HGIT. It is equally important to examine *how* this happens. Islamist terrorism is very much a group activity and, with a few exceptions, even lone actors tend to have significant (sometimes virtual) social connections which play a role in their radicalization. Generally speaking, initial involvement in jihadi subcultures appears to begin by way of a combination of routine association (friendships and/or family relations) and online exploration of radical websites and chatrooms.[71] Prisons have received a great deal of attention as potential starting points for pathways into extremism; however, whilst this may be the case for some, the majority of Islamist terrorists have not been to prison and their journeys begin in ordinary settings such as schools, youth clubs, gyms, or mosques where they meet with friends.

As groups become more extreme this is often reflected in their behavior. Though by no means inevitable, it is not uncommon for individuals to grow a beard and to start wearing traditional Muslim clothing. Many also express increasing intolerance of family, friends, or mosque officials whom they deem to be bad Muslims and over time they fall out with them. For groups that choose to pursue violent jihad, they are also likely to become increasingly secretive, withdrawing to more private settings, employing counter-surveillance measures, such as communicating in code, and engaging in physical training in preparation for combat.

But what is it that drives this process? Often we hear of terrorist masterminds or leaders who are held responsible for group activities and are seen as the primary influence over their companions. It does seem that more experienced, ideologically informed, and forceful personalities play a role within particular groups.[72] Individuals like Omar Khyam, who played a lead role in a 2004 plot to bomb civilian targets in the UK are good examples of this. Khyam had made contact with foreign militants twice before in 2000 and 2001 whilst still in his teens[73] and this experience and personal drive towards violent jihad appears to have afforded him a degree of personal influence. Numerous ideologues such as Abu Qatada, Abu Hamza, Abdullah el-Faisal, and Anwar al-Awlaki are also highly influential despite not necessarily being in direct contact with those they inspire. Al-Awlaki is of course now dead (killed in a missile strike in Yemen in September 2011) but his videos continue to circulate online, spreading his ideas.

At the same time there is little in the way of formal hierarchy within home-grown terrorist groups. Individuals are not generally following orders, they are voluntarily involved and there is a great deal of mutual influence among group members as they look to one another for support. The power of peer groups to influence beliefs and behavior is well documented and is reflected in theories of differential association,[74] social learning,[75] and offending as social exchange.[76] Friendships, which begin with geographic and social proximity, lead to shared knowledge and attitudes. Affective bonds provide powerful social rewards, such as acceptance, belonging, and status, which are the perfect remedy to life crises and which motivate individuals to preserve their group membership through conformity.[77] The process of radicalization itself can begin through external influence (some form of exposure to ideological propaganda) and/or the innovation of group members.

Providing that this initial step is accepted within the group, members can further self-radicalize one another through a process of one-upmanship as they compete to demonstrate their commitment to the cause and their willingness to turn words into action.[78] This is the 'bunch of guys' theory of Islamist terrorism, which finds support in psychological research into group dynamics. Under certain circumstances, groups have been found to make more extreme decisions than individuals and to become more extreme over time. Such tendencies are known to social scientists as 'groupthink' and 'risky shift'.[79] In particular, they can occur as a result of attitudinal conformity, inter- and intra-group competition, and support for leaders who drive the group in a certain direction. They are also exacerbated by such conditions as perceived external threats and social isolation. The perceptions that Islam is under attack from the West and that security services may be watching their every move thus contribute to increasing radicalization of budding jihadis. The more extreme that groups become, the more socially isolated they become. This removes them from more moderate or restraining influences and creates a cycle of radicalization.

Contrary to popular conceptions of this process, radicalization is not just about changes in ideology and thinking. It is an emotional, social and behavioral process largely driven by active participation in groups. In fact, changes in belief are likely to follow on from related behavior rather than to precede it. Individuals become caught up in the social momentum of increasingly radical groups and the more that they socialize with one another, reinforce each other's statements, and spend time absorbing and distributing Islamist propaganda, the more they gradually adjust their beliefs in order to maintain a consistent sense of self.[80]

What is also taking place here is a psychological shift in identity from individual to collectivist terms. This does not mean that individuals lose their sense of self (as originally conceptualized in deindividuation theory) but rather that they see themselves primarily in terms of their group membership.[81] This process is known as 'depersonalization' and means that individuals will adhere to group-level values and behavioral standards and are often empowered to act in ways that they would not when alone. It is ideologically encouraged but also facilitated by the social rewards from being part of the group and by the strong sense of empathy which arises through moral shocks. At a reasonably low level this results in 'diffusion of responsibility', whereby individuals feel insulated by the immediate group and feel less personally responsible for their actions. In the context of progressive Islamist militancy, groups come to define themselves not only as Muslims, but as *mujahideen* or soldiers. This self-conceptualization, which is reinforced by role-play in the form of paramilitary-style exercises, removes moral barriers to violence and is a vital determinant of behavior. In the most extreme cases of depersonalization individuals become willing to sacrifice themselves for the collective in martyrdom operations.

It is important to realize, however, that group dynamics do not inevitably create terrorists and only a minority of groups and individuals personally commit to violent jihad. This additional step (sometimes referred to as 'jihadization'[82] or simply mobilization) may depend on a number of different internal and external factors. The drive of individual leaders such as Khyam is likely important and sustained social support may be vital for keeping potential doubters involved. Emotional build-up resulting from group interaction and continued exposure to ideological propaganda also contributes, and in some cases there may be triggering events (such as the war in Iraq) that drive individuals over the brink. Ultimately though, personal commitment to violence may also come down to opportunity or circumstance and a lack of perceived or actual barriers. The Hamburg 9/11 group, for instance, allegedly established their initial connection to the camps in Afghanistan via a chance encounter.[83]

Social interaction and spontaneous group dynamics within ideologically oriented groups are the mechanisms of radicalization. For the vast majority of home-grown Islamist terrorists their involvement can be explained by a combination of sustained social and ideological exposure, often including online, in addition to face-to-face activities.

These are not sufficient conditions, since the outcome is far from inevitable, but they are as close to necessary conditions as can be identified. Furthermore, the significance of social interaction for the transmission of jihadi ideology adds weight to the argument that the greater influx of militants into Europe two decades ago has been a determinant of higher rates of terrorism over time (although of course this is not the *only* determining factor). This gives rise to the 'social transmission' hypothesis of HGIT.

> The presence of greater numbers of (and/or highly influential) Islamist militants in a given location will increase the likelihood of other violent Islamist extremists being found nearby over time as a function of localized social interaction, creating a subculture of militancy.

Given that proximity (next to similarity) is a major determinant of who interacts with whom, and that the more extreme a given counterculture is, the less likely it is to be adopted by outsiders, it follows that Islamist militancy will develop a natural center of gravity around its original distribution in social space. Of course individual mobility and the growth of militant ideology, imagery, and virtual interaction on the Internet, mean that extremism can spread in unpredictable ways. But according to the social transmission hypothesis there will always be a greater likelihood that the spread of Islamist terrorism will be geographically bounded according to its original distribution in any given country.

A Composite Model of Motivations for HGIT in the West

Having separately discussed the various factors which contribute to individual involvement in Islamist terrorism in the West, it is important to take a broader perspective. Bearing in mind that categories are not mutually exclusive and that motivations vary in significance for different individuals, Table 2.1 depicts the relative contribution of the different motivating factors behind HGIT.

Pre-disposing risk factors are widely experienced conditions and can be subdivided into 'general' and 'specific', based on their

Table 2.1. Motivating factors for HGIT in the West.

Pre-disposing risk			Direct motivators	
General	Specific	Necessary conditions	Process drivers & social goals	Ideological goals
Varying life 'crises' (disillusionment; dissatisfaction in life; openness to an alternative identity)	Identification with Muslims around the world	Ideological exposure	Belonging, acceptance, status, loyalty	To do God's will (as defined by jihadi ideology)
Discrimination in the West	Shared political grievances (e.g. anger at Western foreign policy)	Social contact	Group dynamics (groupthink/ risky shift)	To help other Muslims
Desire for adventure/ Fascination with violence	Empathy and altruism (moral shock at Muslim suffering)	Opportunity	Militaristic identity (mujahid)	To establish 'true' Islamic states
Desire for meaning/ significance	Geographic location		Desire to maintain positive group ID (group value, morality & distinctiveness)	To end Western interference in the Islamic world
			Desire for group survival	Revenge and violence

relevance to the jihadi cause. General pre-disposing risk factors are especially pervasive and although they potentially increase individual susceptibility to extremist ideology, by themselves they are of limited relevance. Experiencing discrimination in the West and varying life crises are so general that without a comprehensive understanding of processes of radicalization and an awareness of the concept of 'cognitive openings', they are of no obvious relevance. Equally, desire for adventure and an attraction to violence are both very common (especially in young males), but might be channeled in any number of different directions, as might a general desire for personal meaning or significance.

Identification with Muslims around the world straddles the general and the specific in that it is so widespread that in the absence of additional factors it is simply an indicator of faith; however, it is also specific in that it becomes a fundamentally important part of Islamist terrorist psychology. Even more specific pre-disposing risk factors (shared grievances — in particular anger at Western foreign policy — and moral shock at Muslim suffering) are also very widely experienced but are more directly aligned with jihadi ideology as compared to general pre-disposing risk factors. In essence, they create room for agreement and therefore add to potential risk for involvement. Being geographically located in an area where jihadi subcultures are thriving and terrorist recruiters are operating (being in the wrong place at the wrong time) also adds to this pre-disposing risk.

There do not appear to be any sufficient conditions for involvement in HGIT but generally speaking, the bottom line or necessary conditions for involvement are sustained ideological exposure and some form of social contact with likeminded individuals, combined with opportunity.[84] Without some form of exposure to jihadi ideology (however basic), people cannot know what it is about. It is the ideology — expressed through various forms of propaganda and social interaction — that gives specific direction and meaning to behavior. It provides narratives of grievance, distinguishes friends from enemies, and tells people how to speak, dress, and act. In short, ideology tells people what the global jihad is all about and what they need to do to get involved.[85] Meanwhile, peer groups provide a platform for ideological discussion and represent the primary gateway into homegrown Islamist terrorism. They facilitate radicalization and foster self-identification as *mujahideen*.

As with all general rules in the study of terrorism there are possible exceptions. 'Lone wolves' who are not part of immediate groups obviously question the necessity of sustained social interaction. However, they are outliers by definition and there are still important social processes at work.[86] They clearly see themselves in collective terms similar to most jihadis and they often interact, or at least try to interact with others as they seek social approval or validation.

Mohammed Reza Taheri-Azar (who ran students over in an SUV in North Carolina in 2006) was said to have been previously influenced by a family friend;[87] Andrew Ibrahim (who plotted to bomb a Bristol mall in 2008) came to the attention of police after he told Muslim acquaintances about his activities;[88] Nicky Reilly (the abovementioned failed suicide bomber) had been groomed online by two Pakistanis;[89] even Roshonara Choudhry (who stabbed an MP in London in 2010 and who did not apparently interact with anyone else) only decided to go ahead with an attack after listening to countless online sermons by Anwar al-Awlaki and watching a video in which Abdullah Azzam declared that females should also fight.[90] Social exposure to like-minded others clearly takes on a different form in these cases, but it is still an important part in understanding why they do what they do.

In addition to varying ideological and social exposure, groups/individuals must also have opportunity. Many people are radicalized but only a small minority within this larger pool of candidates actually commits to action. Although the reasons why some people take this additional step while others do not may be quite idiosyncratic, a key determining factor is simply whether or not a person is able to do so. If people do not have the right connections and at least a minimal level of resources available to them — or conversely if they are unable to relinquish other commitments in life — the doors to jihad will most likely remain closed.

Moving on to examine direct motivators for HGIT in the West, it is useful to distinguish between process drivers and related social goals on the one hand, and ideological goals on the other. Again, bearing in mind the special case of seemingly isolated individuals, processes of radicalization are generally driven by social rewards associated with being part of a group (belonging, acceptance, status, and loyalty) in addition to spontaneous group dynamics. Self-identification as a *mujahid* is also vital to the process of increasing militancy and represents a particular expression of underlying Muslim identity. Because of the positive aspects of being part of the group, there are also implicit, yet powerful social goals. These include an overarching desire to ensure the continued survival of the group, but also more specifically to maintain a positive sense of group value, subjective moral superiority over rivals, and distinctiveness compared to others.

These more specific social goals are derived from social identity theory (SIT) which provides a theoretical framework for understanding inter-group interaction and competition.[91] SIT underpins the concept of depersonalization and adds additional insight by helping us to understand the conditions which give rise to group conflict. When individuals feel that their group identity is threatened in some way, providing that they feel it is worth it, they are likely to respond by reaffirming their commitment to the collective and derogating a rival outgroup.[92] The scale of action taken against the perceived enemy — as with feelings of relative deprivation — is likely to be more severe when their actions are seen as deliberate and unjust.[93] Likewise, because the enemy is stereotyped they become dehumanized and the potential for violence is further enhanced. From this perspective, the various motivational factors at play in HGIT are important to the degree that they represent threats to identity and to the degree that they promote strong emotional responses and self-identification as a defender of the Muslim people.

The explicit ideological objectives which Islamist terrorists are fighting for are also tied to these social goals. To do God's will, to drive out or simply punish the West, to help other Muslims, and to establish 'true' Islamic states are combined attempts at reaffirming group value, morality, and distinctiveness. They are an integral part of the jihadi identity and merge into one another. The plausibility of actually achieving these goals is less important than simply expressing them, and home-grown jihadis are oblivious to how counterproductive their actions really are.

The Need for Further Research

Gaining an appreciation of the different motivating factors and the relative contribution they make in driving HGIT is vital for comprehending why and how people become involved. This knowledge in turn has the power to inform counterterrorism (CT) strategies in the search for more effective ways to curb and eventually neutralize the threat (see Chapter 8). What has been covered so far though has been little more than a general introduction to home-grown terrorism.

Although the body of empirical, evidence-based research into terrorism is gradually growing, there is a continuing need to expand and refine what we know. In particular there are still relatively few large, country-specific case-studies that can take us beyond generalizations and that will facilitate meaningful cross-comparison. Where such studies do exist there is still a need to replicate, update, and strive for innovation. Moreover, as the brief discussion above of differences between the US and Europe illustrates, there is still a great deal of conjecture involved. Descriptions of HGIT are still often based on broad descriptions which do not take into account unique contexts. Many questions remain for which we only have partial answers.[94] What are the real differences between the US and European countries such as the UK? Who becomes involved in different countries? Where are the 'hotspots' of radicalization, if any? Are there any differences in motivation or patterns of involvement? What precisely are home-grown terrorists in different countries doing? What roles exactly have the Internet and foreign terrorist organizations (FTOs) really played? And what differences are there in the CT response?

This book aims to add to previous research and provide empirically grounded answers to these questions, focusing on the US and UK. The unique development of HGIT in each country is examined individually, followed by a systematic and in-depth comparison of all publicly confirmed cases of Islamist terrorism from the 1980s to September 11, 2013.

Notes

---

[1]This chapter has been adapted from Sam Mullins, 'Iraq Versus Lack of Integration: Understanding the Motivations of Contemporary Islamist Terrorists in Western Countries' (2012), *Behavioral Sciences of Terrorism and Political Aggression*, 4(2), 110–133.

[2]For example, Rex Hudson, *The Sociology and Psychology of Terrorism: Who Becomes a Terrorist and Why?* (Washington DC: Library of Congress, 1999), 29, 48, available at: http://www.loc.gov/rr/frd/pdf-files/Soc_Psych_of_Terrorism.pdf, accessed January 15, 2008; Marc Sageman, *Understanding Terror Networks* (Philadelphia: University of Pennsylvania Press, 2004), 81–83.

[3]Arie Kruglanski and Shira Fishman, 'The Psychology of Terrorism: "Syndrome" versus "Tool" Perspectives' (2006), *Terrorism and Political Violence*, 18, 193–215; Jerrold Post, 'When Hatred is Bred in the Bone: Psycho-cultural Foundations of Contemporary Terrorism' (2005), *Political Psychology*, 26(4), 615–636; Charles Ruby, 'Are Terrorists Mentally Deranged?' (2002), *Analyses of Social Issues and Public Policy*, 15–16.

[4]Marc Sageman, *Leaderless Jihad: Terror Networks in the Twenty-First Century* (Philadelphia: University of Pennsylvania Press, 2008); Sageman, *Understanding Terror Networks.*

[5]Edwin Bakker, *Jihadi Terrorists in Europe: Their Characteristics and the Circumstances in Which They Joined the Jihad: An Exploratory Study* (The Hague: Clingendael Institute, 2006); Sam Mullins, 'Islamist Terrorism and Australia: An Empirical Examination of the "Home-Grown" Threat' (2011), *Terrorism and Political Violence*, 23(2), 254–285.

[6]'Man Admits Restaurant Bomb Attack', *BBC News*, October 15, 2008, available at: http://news.bbc.co.uk/2/hi/uk_news/7671138.stm, accessed July 6, 2010.

[7]Paul Gill, John Horgan, and Paige Deckert, 'Bombing Alone: Tracing the Motivations and Antecedent Behaviors of Lone-Actor Terrorists' (2013), *Journal of Forensic Sciences*, 59(2), 425–435.

[8]Anne Speckhard, 'De-Legitimizing Terrorism: Creative Engagement and Understanding of the Psycho-Social Processes Involved in Ideological Support for Terrorism' (2007), *Connections*, I, available at: http://www.annespeckhard.com/publications/Delegitimizing_Terrorism.pdf, accessed May 24, 2009.

[9]Bill Rankin, 'The Case of Syed Haris Ahmed: Suspect Coveted Jihad Life', *The Atlanta Journal-Constitution*, January 20, 2008, available at: www.newsbank.com, accessed June 8, 2010.

[10]Osama bin Laden, 'Declaration of War against the Americans Occupying the Lands of the Two Holy Places' (1996), reproduced in 'Bin Laden's Fatwa' (undated), *PBS Online NewsHour*, available at: http://www.pbs.org/newshour/terrorism/international/fatwa_1996.html, accessed December 15, 2007.

[11]Sageman, *Leaderless Jihad*, 20–23; Sageman, *Understanding Terror Networks*, 95–96.

[12]Yaner Altunblas and John Thornton, *Human Capital and the Supply of Home-grown Islamic Terrorists in the UK* (Bangor: Bangor Business School, 2009), available at: http://papers.ssrn.com/sol3/papers.cfm?abstract_id=1516490&download=yes, accessed May 15, 2011; Bakker, *Jihadi Terrorists in Europe*; William Banks, Laura Adams, Jason Cherish, Drew Dickinson, Richard Lim, Matthew Michaelis, Alyssa Procopio, and Joseph Robertson, *Jihadist Prosecutions Since 9/11 Database* (MPA Workshop: New America Foundation, 2010), available at: http://insct.syr.edu/uploadedFiles/insct/publications/MPA-NAF%20Workshop%202010%20final%20written.pdf, accessed May 15,

2011; Brian Jenkins, *Would-Be Warriors: Incidents of Jihadist Radicalization in the United States Since September 11, 2001* (Santa Monica, CA: RAND, 2010); Mullins, 'Islamist Terrorism and Australia'; Louise Porter and Mark Kebbell 'Radicalization in Australia: Examining Australia's Convicted Terrorists' (2010), *Psychiatry, Psychology and Law*, first published on June 11, 2010; Mitchell Silber and Arvin Bhatt, *Radicalization in the West: The Homegrown Threat* (New York: New York City Police Department, 2007); Robin Simcox and Emily Dyer, *Al-Qaeda in the United States: A Complete Analysis of Terrorism Offences* (The Henry Jackson Society, 2013), available at: http://henryjacksonsociety.org/wp-content/uploads/2013/02/Al-Qaeda-in-the-USAbridged-version-LOWRES-Final.pdf, accessed April 7, 2013; Robin Simcox, Hannah Stuart, and Houria Ahmed, *Islamist Terrorism: The British Connections* (London: The Centre for Social Cohesion, 2010).

[13]Simon Benson, 'Aussie Jihadists were on the Dole', *The Daily Telegraph*, February 21, 2015, available at: http://www.dailytelegraph.com.au/news/nsw/aussie-jihadists-were-on-the-dole/story-fni0cx12-1227233046278, accessed February 22, 2015; 'Germany's Jihadists: Young, Male, Losers', *The Local (Germany)*, September 11, 2014, available at: http://www.thelocal.de/20140911/germanys-jihadis-young-male-failures, accessed September 11, 2014; Magnus Ranstorp, Linus Gustafsson, and Peder Hyllengren, 'From the Welfare State to the Caliphate', *Foreign Policy*, February 21, 2015, available at: http://foreignpolicy.com/2015/02/23/from_the_welfare_state_to_the_caliphate_sweden_islamic_state_syria_iraq_foreign_fighters/, accessed February 23, 2015; Robin Simcox and Emily Dyer, 'Terror Data: US vs. UK', *World Affairs Journal*, July/August 2013, available at: http://www.worldaffairsjournal.org/article/terror-data-us-vs-uk, accessed December 10, 2013.

[14]Henri Astier, 'Paris Attacks: Prisons Provide Fertile Ground for Islamists', *BBC News*, February 5, 2015, available at: http://www.bbc.com/news/world-europe-31129398, accessed February 5, 2015; Dounia Bouzar, Christophe Caupenne, and Sulayman Valsan, *La Metamorphose Operee Chez le Jeune par les Nouveaux Discours Terroristes* (Centre de Prévention Contre les Dérives Sectaries Liées á l'Islam, 2014), available at: http://www.bouzar-expertises.fr/metamorphose, accessed April 3, 2015.

[15]Petter Nesser, *How Does Radicalization Occur in Europe?*, presented at the Second Inter-Agency Radicalization Conference, July 10, 2006, Washington, DC, 3, available at: http://www.mil.no/multimedia/archive/00080/DHS_foredrag_80480a.pdf, accessed February 18, 2008.

[16]Quintan Wiktorowicz, *Joining the Cause: Al-Muhajiroun and Radical Islam*, presented at The Roots of Islamic Radicalism Conference, May 10, 2004, Yale University, New Haven, available at:http://www.yale.edu/polisci/info/ conferences/Islamic%20Radicalism/papers/ wiktorowicz-paper.pdf, accessed February 7, 2009; Quintan Wiktorowicz, *Radical Islam Rising: Muslim Extremism in the West* (Lanham, Maryland: Rowman & Littlefield, 2005).

[17]Olivier Roy, *Globalized Islam: The Search for a New Ummah* (New York: Colombia University Press, 2004); Sageman, *Leaderless Jihad*; Sageman, *Understanding Terror Networks*; Michael Taarnby, *Recruitment of Islamist*

Terrorists in Europe: Trends and Perspectives (Copenhagen: Danish Ministry of Justice, 2005).

[18] Aidan Kirby, 'The London Bombers as "Self Starters": A Case Study in Indigenous Radicalization and the Emergence of Autonomous Cliques' (2007), *Studies in Conflict and Terrorism*, 30(5), 415–428.

[19] See Leon Festinger, *A Theory of Cognitive Dissonance* (Stanford, CA; Stanford University Press, 1957).

[20] Naomi Ellemers, Russell Spears, and Bertjan Doosje, 'Self and Social Identity' (2002), *Annual Review of Psychology*, 53, 161–186; Carlos Navarette, 'Death Concerns and Other Adaptive Challenges: The Effects of Coalition-Relevant Challenges on Worldview Defense in the US and Costa Rica' (2005), *Group Processes and Intergroup Relations*, 8(4), 411–427.

[21] Bakker, *Jihadi Terrorists in Europe*, 51.

[22] Edward Newman, 'Exploring the "Root Causes" of Terrorism' (2006), *Studies in Conflict and Terrorism*, 29(8), 749–772.

[23] See Tedd Gurr, *Why Men Rebel* (Princeton, NJ: Princeton University Press, 1970).

[24] Leonard Berkowitz, 'Frustration-Aggression Hypothesis: Examination and Reformulation' (1989), *Psychological Bulletin*, 106(1), 59–73.

[25] Jeff Burdette, 'Rethinking the Relationship Between Poverty and Terrorism', *Small Wars Journal*, June 9, 2014, available at: http://smallwarsjournal.com/printpdf/15779, accessed June 12, 2014; *Global Terrorism Index 2014: Measuring and Understanding the Impact of Terrorism* (Institute for Economics and Peace: 2014), available at: http://www.visionofhumanity.org/sites/default/files/Global%20Terrorism%20Index%20Report%202014_0.pdf, accessed November 19, 2014.

[26] Angel Rabasa and Cheryl Benard, *Eurojihad: Patterns of Islamist Radicalization and Terrorism in Europe* (New York, Cambridge University Press, 2015), Chapter 5, Kindle Edition.

[27] See Sageman, *Understanding Terror Networks*, 95–96; Sageman, *Leaderless Jihad*, 48–50.

[28] See, for example, Kylie Baxter, 'From Migrants to Citizens: Muslims in Britain 1950s–1990s' (2006), *Immigrants and Minorities*, 24(2), 164–192.

[29] Robert Leiken, *Bearers of Global Jihad? Immigration and National Security after 9/11* (Washington: The Nixon Centre, 2004); Robert Leiken and Steven Brooke, 'The Quantitative Analysis of Terrorism and Immigration: An Initial Exploration' (2006), *Terrorism and Political Violence*, 18(4), 503–521; Mitchell Silber and Arvin Bhatt, *Radicalization in the West: The Homegrown Threat* (New York: New York City Police Department, 2007); Marc Sageman, *Leaderless Jihad: Terror Networks in the Twenty-First Century* (Philadelphia: University of Pennsylvania Press, 2008); Lorenzo Vidino, *Al Qaeda in Europe: The New Battleground of International Jihad* (New York: Prometheus Books, 2006).

[30] *Ibid.*

[31] Serena Hussain and Tufyal Choudhury, *Muslims in the EU: Cities Report* (Open Societies Institute, 2007), available at: http://www.soros.org/initiatives/

home/articles_publications/publications/museucities_20080101/museucitiesuk_20080101.pdf, accessed May 17, 2011.

[32]Leiken, *Bearers of Global Jihad?*; Leiken & Brooke, 'The Quantitative Analysis of Terrorism and Immigration'; Silber and Bhatt, *Radicalization in the West*; Sageman, *Leaderless Jihad*; Vidino, *Al Qaeda in Europe*.

[33]Sageman, *Leaderless Jihad*, 90.

[34]Daniel Pipes, 'Which Has More Islamist Terrorism, Europe or America?', *The Jerusalem Post*, July 2, 2008, available at: http://www.danielpipes.org/ article/5723, accessed September 3, 2008.

[35]US Department of Justice, *The Department of Justice's Internal Controls Over Terrorism Reporting* (2007), Audit Report 07-20, available at: http: //msnbcmedia.msn.com/i/msnbc/sections/news/DOJreport.pdf, accessed September 3, 2008.

[36]See Chapters 5, 6, and 8 in particular.

[37]See Pew Research Center, *Muslim Americans: Middle Class and Mostly Mainstream* (Pew Research Center, 2007) 9–11, available at: http://pewresearch.org/assets/pdf/muslim-americans.pdf, accessed April 29, 2009.

[38]Amanda Wise and Jan Ali, *Muslim Australians and Local Government: Grassroots Strategies to Improve Relations between Muslim and Non-Muslim-Australians* (Sydney: Centre for Research on Social Cohesion, 2008), 21, available at: http://www.immi.gov.au/media/publications/ multicultural/grassroots/, accessed November 10, 2010.

[39]Pew Research Center, *Muslim Americans*, 36.

[40]*Ibid*, 2.

[41]Pew Research Center, *Muslim Americans* 5–6; Pew Research Center, *Europe's Muslims More Moderate: The Great Divide: How Westerners and Muslims View Each Other* (Pew Research Center, 2006), 4, available at: http: //pewglobal.org/reports/pdf/253.pdf, accessed May 4, 2009.

[42]Exact, comparable data are not available, however 35% of the US Muslim population was estimated by the Pew Research Center to be second or third generation in 2006, compared to 46% of UK Muslims in 2001, as reported by the Office for National Statistics (Office for National Statistics, *Focus on Religion* (2004), available at: http://www.statistics.gov.uk/downloads/ theme_compendia/for2004/ FocusonReligion.pdf, accessed April 17, 2013, 6; Pew Research Center, *Muslim Americans*, 5). The observed gap may be even wider taking into consideration the different points in time. With regards to age, 55% of the US Muslim population was aged 29 or under in 2006, while 71% of the UK Muslim population was aged 34 or under in 2001 (Office for National Statistics, *Focus on Religion Data: 02_Age&SexDistribution* (2004), available at: http://www.statistics.gov.uk/statbase/Product.asp?vlnk=13209, accessed April 17, 2013; Pew Research Center, *Muslim Americans*, 10).

[43]Wiktorowicz, *Radical Islam Rising*, 85–133.

[44]For example, see Magnus Ranstorp, 'Terrorist Awakening in Sweden?' (2011), *CTC Sentinel*, 4(1), 1–5, available at: http://www.dtic.mil/cgibin/GetTRDoc?AD=ADA536135&Location=U2&doc=GetTRDoc.pdf, accessed May 11, 2011.

[45]Rabasa and Benard, *Eurojihad,* Location 5487, Chapter 10, Kindle Edition.

[46]For example, see 'Abu Yahya al-Liby: "To Our People in Libya"', *NEFA Foundation*, March 12, 2011, available at: http://nefafoundation.org//file/ alLiby-0311.pdf, accessed March 14, 2011.

[47]Osama bin Laden, 'Declaration of War against the Americans Occupying the Lands of the Two Holy Places' (1996), 7. Reproduced in 'Bin Laden's Fatwa' (undated), *PBS Online NewsHour*, available at: http://www.pbs.org/ newshour/terrorism/international/fatwa_1996.html, accessed May 20, 2011.

[48]'Full Text: "Al-Qaeda" Madrid Claim', *BBC News*, March 14, 2004, available at: http://news.bbc.co.uk/2/hi/europe/3509556.stm, accessed May 21, 2011.

[49]As-Sahab Media, *Shehzad Tanweer Martyrdom Video*, aired on al-Jazeera TV, July 2006, available at: http://www.archive.org/details/wasiya24, accessed May 25, 2009.

[50]'Read the Faisal Shahzad Transcript', *The New York Post*, October 5, 2010, available at: http://www.nypost.com/p/news/local/manhattan/read_the_faisal_shahzad_transcript_zDoUXlGEMoqZMwzsIRrlkM, accessed May 21, 2011.

[51]Alexandra Klausner, Kieran Corcoran, David Martokso, and Sophie Jane Evans, 'Armed and Radicalized: Ranting "Self-Proclaimed Convert" New York Hatchet Attacker was a "Terrorist" Say Police', *The Daily Mail*, October 24, 2014, available at: http://www.dailymail.co.uk/news/article-2806731/Was-terror-attack-Police-probe-extremist-links-online-rants-New-York-hatchett-attacker-emerge-shot-dead-attack-group-cops-Queens.html, accessed October 24, 2014.

[52]Max Abrahms, 'Al Qaeda's Scorecard: A Progress Report on Al Qaeda's Objectives' (2006), *Studies in Conflict and Terrorism*, 29(5), 509–529.

[53]Robert Pape and James Feldman, *Cutting the Fuse: The Explosion of Global Suicide Terrorism and How to Stop It* (Chicago and London: University of Chicago Press, 2010).

[54]Pew Research Center, *Muslim Americans*, 5.

[55]29% believed the war in Afghanistan was wrong; 47% believed the war in Iraq was wrong; and 25% believed the Global War on Terror was insincere.

[56]Olivier Roy, *Globalized Islam: The Search for a New Ummah* (New York: Colombia University Press, 2004), 290–325.

[57]Walter Laqueur, *No End to War: Terrorism in the Twenty-First Century* (New York, Continuum International Publishing Group, 2003), 60.

[58]Alison Pargeter, *The New Frontiers of Jihad: Radical Islam in Europe* (Philadelphia: University of Pennsylvania Press, 2008).

[59]*Ibid*, 24–29.

[60]*Ibid*, 187–203.

[61]SITE, 'Shabaab Releases Video on Westgate Mall Raid, Names Western Malls as Targets for Lone Wolf Attacks', *INSITE Blog*, February 21, 2015, available at: http://news.siteintelgroup.com/blog/index-php/entry/363-shabaab-releases-video-on-westgate-mall-raid%2C-names-western-malls-as-targets-for-lone-wolf-attacks, accessed February 23, 2015.

[62]Yara Bayoumy and Mohammed Ghobari, 'Yemeni Security Officials: Brothers Behind Charlie Hebdo Attack Trained with Al Qaeda', *Reuters*, January 11, 2015, available at: http://www.uk.businessinsider.com/yemeni-security-officials-brothers-behind-charlie-hebdo-attack-trained-with-al-qaeda-2015-1, accessed January 11, 2015; Rafaello Pantucci, 'Manchester, New York and Oslo: Three Centrally Directed Al-Qa'ida Plots' (2010), *CTC Sentinel*, 3(8), 10–12, available at: http://www.ctc.usma.edu/sentinel/CTCSentinel-Vol3Iss8.pdf, accessed October 6, 2010.

[63]'Unrest Spreads in Afghanistan over Koran Burning', *Jane's Country Risk Daily Report*, April 4, 2011.

[64]Bakker, *Jihadi Terrorists in Europe*; Porter and Kebbell, 'Radicalization in Australia'; Sageman, *Leaderless Jihad*, 51–52.

[65]Sageman, *Leaderless Jihad*, 60.

[66]Olivier Roy, *Al Qaeda in the West as a Youth Movement: The Power of a Narrative* (Brighton: Microcon, 2008).

[67]Wiktorowicz, *Radical Islam Rising.*

[68]*United States of America v. Daniel Joseph Maldonado*, Complaint, United States District Court for the Southern District of Texas, Case No. CR-H-07-125M, February 13, 2007, 3, available at: http://nefafoundation.org/miscellaneous/FeaturedDocs/U.S._v_Maldonado_Complaint.pdf, accessed June 11, 2010.

[69]Note that this in itself falls short of the definition of 'terrorism'. Nevertheless, 'extremist' and 'terrorist' networks clearly overlap as the case of *al-Muhajiroun* continues to demonstrate. By way of example, Royal Barnes, who was convicted of disseminating terrorist publications and inciting murder, was also separately convicted for his role in the so-called 'Muslim Patrol' which sought to forcibly implement *sharia* on the streets of East London, and had previously been arrested for assaulting the caretaker of Finsbury Park mosque for allowing 'improperly dressed' tourists inside the house of worship ('Converts to Islam Jailed for Terrorising Streets as "Muslim Patrol" are Banned from Promoting Sharia Law for FIVE YEARS', *The Daily Mail*, February 14, 2014, available at: http://www.dailymail.co.uk/news/article-2559426/Converts-Islam-jailed-terrorising-streets-Muslim-Patrol-banned-promoting-Sharia-law-FIVE-YEARS.html, accessed February 14, 2014; Mary Dejevsky, 'Beyond the Veil: What Happened after Rebekah Dawson Refused to Take Her Niqab off in Court', *The Independent*, April 7, 2014, available at: http://www.independent.co.uk/news/uk/home-news/beyond-the-veil-what-happened-after-rebekah-dawson-refused-to-take-her-niqab-off-in-court-9244409.html, accessed April 7, 2014).

[70]Sean O'Neill and Daniel McGrory, *The Suicide Factory: Abu Hamza and the Finsbury Park Mosque* (London: HarperCollins, 2006), 56–57.

[71]See for example, Rabasa and Benard, *Eurojihad,* Kindle Edition; Scott Matthew Kleinmann, 'Radicalization of Homegrown Sunni Militants in the United States: Comparing Converts and Non-Converts' (2012), *Studies in Conflict and Terrorism*, 35(4), 278–297; Scott Helfstein, *Edges of Radicalization: Ideas, Individuals and Networks in Violent Extremism* (Combating Terrorism

Center at West Point, 2012), available at: http://www.ctc.usma.edu/wp-content/uploads/2012/02/CTC_Edges ofRadicalization.pdf, accessed May 3, 2012; Thomas Precht, *Home Grown Terrorism and Islamist Radicalization in Europe: From Conversion to Terrorism* (Danish Ministry of Justice: Copenhagen, 2007), available at: http://www.justitsministeriet.dk/fileadmin/downloads/Forskning_og_dokumentation/Home_grown_terrorism_and_Islamist_radicalization_in_Europe_-_an_assessment_of_ influencing_factors__2_.pdf, accessed April 14, 2009; Silber and Bhatt, *Radicalization in the West.*

[72]Daveed Gartenstein-Ross and Laura Grossman, *Homegrown Terrorists in the U.S. and U.K: An Empirical Examination of the Radicalization Process* (Washington, DC: FDD Press, 2009), available at: www.defenddemocracy.org/downloads/HomegrownTerrorists_USandUK.pdf, accessed May 26, 2009; Petter Nesser, *How Does Radicalization Occur in Europe?*, presented at the Second Inter-Agency Radicalization Conference, July 10, 2006, Washington, DC, available at: http://www.mil.no/multimedia/archive/00080/DHS_foredrag_80480a.pdf, accessed February 18, 2008; Silber and Bhatt, *Radicalization in the West.*

[73]'Profile: Omar Khyam', *BBC News*, April 30, 2007, available at: http://news.bbc.co.uk/2/hi/uk_news/6149794.stm, accessed June 24, 2010.

[74]Edwin Sutherland, *Principles of Criminology, fourth edition* (Philadelphia: Lippincott, 1947), cited in Ross Matsueda, 'Differential Social Organization, Collective Action and Crime, (2006), *Crime, Law and Social Change*, 46, 3–33.

[75]For example, Ronald Akers, *Deviant Behaviour: A Social Learning Approach, second edition* (Belmont: Wadsworth, 1977).

[76]Frank Weerman, 'Co-Offending as Social Exchange: Explaining Characteristics of Co-Offending' (2003), *British Journal of Criminology*, 43, 398–416.

[77]John Horgan, *The Psychology of Terrorism* (New York: Routledge, 2005).

[78]Sageman, *Understanding Terror Networks*; Sageman, *Leaderless Jihad.*

[79]Irving Janis, *Groupthink: Psychological Studies of Policy Decisions and Fiascoes, second edition* (Boston, MA: Houghton-Mifflin, 1982); Clark McCauley and Sophia Moskalenko, 'Mechanisms of Political Radicalization: Pathways Toward Terrorism' (2008), *Terrorism and Political Violence*, 20, 415–433; Andrew Silke, 'Holy Warriors: Exploring the Psychological Processes of Jihadi Radicalization' (2008), *European Journal of Criminology*, 5, 99–123.

[80]McCauley and Moskalenko, 'Mechanisms of Political Radicalization: Pathways Toward Terrorism'; Sam Mullins, 'Parallels Between Crime and Terrorism: A Social Psychological Perspective' (2009), *Studies in Conflict and Terrorism*, 32, 811–830; Silke, 'Holy Warriors'.

[81]Stephen Reicher, Russel Spears, and Tom Postmes, 'A Social Identity Model of Deindividuation Phenomena' (1995), *European Review of Social Psychology*, 6(1), 161–198.

[82]AIVD, *Violent Jihad in the Netherlands: Current Trends in the Islamist Terrorist Threat* (The Hague: General Intelligence and Security Service, 2006); Mitchell Silber and Arvin Bhatt, *Radicalization in the West: The Homegrown Threat* (New York: New York City Police Department, 2007).

[83] *The 9/11 Commission: Final Report of the National Commission on Terrorist Attacks Against the United States: Official Government Edition* (Washington DC: US Government Printing Office, 2004), 165–166.

[84] This is supported by recent research which concluded that radical networks, 'sustained by ideology' are 'critical to the progression from radicalization to terrorism' (Rabasa and Benard, *Eurojihad*, Location 5493–5501, Chapter 10, Kindle Edition).

[85] Note that this does not imply that all jihadi terrorists must be ideological or religious scholars. Even basic ideological concepts (core grievances and prescribed action) can be highly motivating.

[86] See Lars Erik Berntzen and Sveinung Sandberg, 'The Collective Nature of Lone-Wolf Terrorism: Anders Behring Breivik and the Anti-Islamic Social Movement' (2014), *Terrorism and Political Violence*, 26(5), 759–779.

[87] Jessica Rocha, 'Outburst Reveals "Other Taheri-Azar"', *News Observer.com*, March 6, 2007, available at: http://www.newsobserver.com/2007/03/06/89540/outburst-reveals-other-taheri.html, accessed June 10, 2010.

[88] 'Tip-off Saved Bristol Shoppers from Bombing', *Bristol Evening Post*, July 18, 2009, available at: http://www.thisisbristol.co.uk/news/Tip-saved-Bristol-shoppers-bombing/article-1177067-detail/article.html, accessed July 6, 2010.

[89] Duncan Gardham, 'Men who Groomed Exeter Bomber Still on the Loose', *The Telegraph*, January 31, 2009, available at: http://www.telegraph.co.uk/news/uknews/4401968/Men-who-groomed-Exeter-bomber-still-on-the-loose.html, accessed July 6, 2010.

[90] Vikram Dodd, 'Roshonara Choudhry: Police Interview Extracts', *The Guardian*, November 3, 2010, available at: http://www.guardian.co.uk/uk/2010/nov/03/roshonara-choudhry-police-interview, accessed November 4, 2010.

[91] Henry Tajfel and John Turner, 'An Integrative Theory of Intergroup Conflict' (1979), in W.G. Austin and S. Worchel (eds.), *The Social Psychology of Intergroup Relations* (Monterey, CA: Brooks/Cole), 33–47; John Turner, 'Social Categorization and the Self-Concept: A Social Cognitive Theory of Group Behavior' (1985), in E.J. Lawler (ed.), *Advances in Group Processes: Theory and Research, Vol.2* (Greenwich, CT: JAI Press), 77–122.

[92] Naomi Ellemers, Russell Spears, and Bertjan Doosje, 'Self and Social Identity' (2002), *Annual Review of Psychology*, 53, 161–186.

[93] See Miles Hewstone, Mark Rubin, and Hazel Willis, 'Intergroup Bias' (2002), *Annual Review of Psychology*, 53, 575–604; Stephen Reicher, Clifford Stott, Patrick Cronin, and Otto Adang, 'An Integrated Approach to Crowd Psychology and Public Order Policing' (2004), *Policing: An International Journal of Police Strategies and Management*, 27(4), 558–572.

[94] The previously cited, highly reputable studies by Simcox *et al.* indeed provide answers to many of these questions. However, this does not negate the need for replication and as will become clear in later chapters, the current research at times contradicts these findings on a number of significant points.

Chapter 3

Global Jihad and the Great Satan

Although the US has never experienced a domestic campaign of violence on the scale of Northern Ireland, it is no stranger to terrorism. Since 1970, there have been over 1,200 terrorism-related incidents in America perpetrated by more than 120 different groups and assorted individuals of varying ideological persuasions.[1] Among them have been white racists, black nationalists, left- and right-wing revolutionaries, Puerto Rican separatists, anti-Castro Cubans, anti-abortionists, animal rights extremists, environmentalists, Christians, Jews, Muslims, and people fighting for just about every other cause imaginable.[2] Whilst the rate of attacks declined from nearly 70 per year during the 1970s to 14 per year during the 2000s, and while the threat remains diverse, global jihadists have been responsible for 90% of fatalities, most of which were inflicted in the devastating, coordinated attacks of September 11, 2001.[3] Since then they have understandably dominated perceptions about terrorism. However, the roots of jihad in the US run much deeper than this. Before 9/11 there was of course the first World Trade Center attack in 1993, but this too was simply a milestone, a symptom of activities and events that had been gradually building for more than a decade.

Pre-1993

Early incidents of violence in the US inspired by politicized forms of Islam can be traced back to the 1970s.[4] However, these mostly involved African-Americans with links to the Nation of Islam — worlds apart from the future Global Salafi Jihad. Nevertheless, Saudi Wahhabism (a puritanical form of Islam which jihadists find some common ground with) had been gaining popularity in the US as early as the 1960s and a considerable number of African–Americans traveled to Saudi Arabia for the *hajj* or to study in Islamic universities.[5] During the 1980s, 'dozens of native-born Americans' then heeded the call to defend their fellow Muslims in Afghanistan against the Communist invaders of the Soviet Union.[6] At the same time, the ever-pragmatic *mujahideen* quickly recognized the vast potential that America had to offer and promptly sought to take advantage.

Not long after the Makhtab al-Khidemat (MAK) had been established in 1984 in Pakistan with the aim of supporting the Afghan jihad, international offices were opened in the US under the name of the Al-Kifah Refugee Center.[7] Beneath its charitable facade, in reality it was the 'precursor organization' to al-Qaeda.[8] Headquarters were initially located at the Islamic Center of Tucson (ICT) in Arizona, with offices dotted elsewhere around the country including in Brooklyn, Jersey City, Boston, Chicago, and Atlanta. Among other activities, Al-Kifah published a magazine called *Al-Jihad* which chronicled the exploits of the *mujahideen* and solicited donations, reaching thousands of people in the US as well as overseas.[9] The father of the Afghan jihad and founder of the MAK, Abdullah Azzam, and one of his most trusted confidantes, Sheikh Tamim al-Adnani, also visited the US on fundraising tours. From 1985 to 1989 they 'visited dozens of American cities, exhorting recruits to pick up the sword against the enemies of Islam. They raised tens of thousands of dollars and enlisted hundreds and hundreds of fighters and believers'.[10] According to Pakistani intelligence sources, around 400 Americans trained at jihadi camps in Afghanistan between 1989 and 2001 alone, discounting the previous decade of war.[11]

In the early years, the president of the ICT was a Saudi named Wael Hamza Julaidan.[12] From Tucson, he made his way to Peshawar in 1985 or 1986 where he united with Azzam and bin Laden and took part in one of the earliest meetings of what later became al-Qaeda on August 11, 1988.[13] Julaidan is believed to have fought in Afghanistan and was extensively involved with numerous charities which subsequently had their assets frozen for ties to terrorism before himself becoming a US- and UN-designated terrorist in 2002.[14] Also present at that fateful meeting in 1988 (and dutifully taking notes) was former Kansas City student and dual Syrian–US national, Mohammed Loay Bayazid, also known as Abu Rida.[15] Like Julaidan, Bayazid had spent time in Tucson[16] but was reportedly inspired to join the jihad after coming across a leaflet written by Azzam while living in Kansas in 1985.[17] He went on to become a key advisor to bin Laden in Sudan and was joined there by another member of the Tucson fraternity, Mubarak al-Duri, described by the 9/11 Commission as the 'principal [al-Qaeda] procurement agent for weapons of mass destruction'.[18]

The US served as the launching pad for many illustrious jihadi careers during this period. Bin Laden's personal secretary, a Lebanese–American convert named Wadih el-Hage, studied urban planning in South Louisiana in the late 1970s before cutting his teeth in Afghanistan.[19] He then spent four years living in Tucson from 1986 to 1990, followed by spells in Arlington, Texas and New York, before relocating to Sudan and Kenya to help plan the 1998 East African embassy bombings.[20] Another key planner of those attacks and a close confederate of both bin Laden and el-Hage was Ali Mohamed. A former Egyptian Army officer who had joined the Egyptian *Jihad* organization in 1981, Mohamed volunteered as an informant for the CIA in 1984 but the agreement was swiftly terminated after the agency realized he was not to be trusted.[21] Nevertheless, he was able to immigrate to the US a year later and went on to gain American citizenship.[22] Stationed at Fort Bragg in North Carolina, he served in the US Army for over three years, all the while acting as a double agent and a deeply committed jihadist, at one point even taking leave to fight against the Soviets in Afghanistan. Making full use of his American passport, he traveled extensively, including to supervise bin Laden's movements to and from Sudan in 1991 and 1996.[23] In the early 1990s he also began acting as an informer for the FBI at the same time as planning the attacks on the American embassies. He was equally active on US soil, however, having established a communications hub in Santa Clara, California operated by Khaled Abu el-Dahab. El-Dahab had been recruited by Mohamed back in Egypt in 1984, coming to the US two years later and, like his mentor, obtaining US citizenship.[24] From his home in Silicon Valley he would patch calls from militants in Egypt through to Afghanistan and Sudan, allowing the 'brothers' to communicate whilst avoiding unwanted attention. He performed other support duties when called upon (including training recruits in Afghanistan in how to use hang-gliders) in addition to handling money and recruiting others to the cause.[25]

On the other side of the country, New York and Jersey City were rapidly becoming the focus for Islamist terrorism in America.[26] The headquarters of Al-Kifah shifted from Tucson to Brooklyn after being incorporated under the name of the Afghan Refugees Services Center at the al-Farooq mosque in December 1987.[27] The Brooklyn Jihad Office, as it was known, was initially run by Mustafa Shalabi, assisted by Fawaz Mohammed Damrah and Ali Shinawy of the Abu Bakr mosque.[28] The area quickly became a hive of jihadi activity the likes of which America has not seen since. Numerous criminal enterprises were established in support of the jihad, including counterfeiting, forgery, and arms-dealing in addition to fundraising, recruitment, and providing opportunities for training and combat.[29]

Among those who made their way from Brooklyn to Afghanistan in the late 1980s was American-born Mohamed Zaky who went on to set up his own pro-jihadi 'charities' while living in San Diego and who fought in Bosnia before ultimately being killed in Chechnya in 1995.[30] Others included Jamal al-Fadl, a Sudanese immigrant who swore allegiance to bin Laden only to defect after stealing $110,000 from him in Sudan[31] and Ephron Gilmore, a former soldier in the US Army who also fought in Bosnia and used his skills to train the *mujahideen* in hand-to-hand combat and light weaponry.[32]

Recruits were also trained at home in the US. Gilmore provided martial arts instruction at al-Farooq[33] and El Sayyid Nosair, an Egyptian-American who had come to the US in 1981, organized weekend trips to a shooting range in Connecticut, which were advertised at the El-Salaam mosque in Jersey City.[34] Ominously, Ali Mohamed was called in to give specialized military instruction in the summer of 1989.[35] It was around this time that the Brooklyn jihad network first attracted the attention of the FBI and Nosair was photographed at Calverton shooting range on Long Island in July.[36] Also present were Clement Rodney Hampton-El, an American convert who had trained in Afghanistan with Zaky and Gilmore;[37] Mahmud Abouhalima, an Egyptian veteran of Afghanistan;[38] Mohammed Salameh, a Palestinian who had overstayed his tourist visa;[39] and Nidal Ayyad, then at Rutgers University studying chemical engineering.[40]

In today's environment it is quite possible that arrests would have ensued at this stage, but at the time there were insufficient grounds for persisting with the investigation and events continued to escalate. Back in Tucson, a controversial imam named Rashad Khalifa was murdered on January 31, 1990 — apparently punishment for his 'heretical' interpretation of the Quran.[41] It later emerged that Wadih el-Hage (who had been in contact with members of the New York network since at least 1988 and would later visit Nosair in jail) had hosted an unidentified individual from New York who conducted surveillance on Khalifa before his death.[42] Furthermore, two individuals convicted of conspiring to murder him were members of Al-Fuqra, a sect-like organization also known in the US as 'Muslims of the Americas', with which Hampton-El was also affiliated.[43]

July 1990 marked the arrival in New York and Jersey City of the 'Blind Sheikh', Omar Abdel Rahman. As the spiritual leader of the Gamaa' Islamiyah, or Egyptian Islamic Group (EIG), Rahman was a highly influential figure known for his venomous tirades against the enemies of Islam and he was already a suspected terrorist.[44] His presence upset the delicate balance of power that had been established and infused the network with a potent radicalizing force. Less than six months later, on November 5, Nosair (driven by Salameh and accompanied by Jordanian Bilal Alkaisi[45]) boldly walked up to the founder of the Jewish Defence League, Rabbi Meir Kahane, offered him his hand in an apparent greeting and then fatally shot him in the neck.[46] Then on March 1, 1991, Mustafa Shalabi was found murdered in his apartment. Although no-one was ever charged, Shalabi had earned the wrath of the Blind Sheikh for allegedly mishandling donations and it is believed that Rahman had issued a *fatwa* calling for his death.[47] Nidal Ayyad has reportedly since admitted that he was there when Salameh and Alkaisi carried out the execution, a story consistent with information provided by Nosair.[48]

With Shalabi out of the way, Rahman's power was uncontested. In the meantime, members of the network busied themselves with attending Nosair's trial and visiting him in jail after he was convicted. By the end of 1992 renewed efforts were being made to organize paramilitary training for volunteers to go to Bosnia, a task which had fallen upon Hampton-El.[49] More significant still was the arrival of Ramzi Ahmed Yousef in September.

1993–2001

An enigmatic individual educated in the UK, Yousef has been described as 'a secular terrorist who mobilized others by playing on their religious zeal'.[50] From the camps in Afghanistan he made his way to Peshawar and flew first class to the US with a single goal in mind — to bring down the Twin Towers. His traveling companion, a Palestinian named Ahmad Ajaj who had previously worked as a pizza delivery boy in Houston, was detained at JFK airport in possession of false passports and manuals on bomb-making.[51] Undeterred, Yousef made it past security by pretending to be an asylum seeker and made a beeline for Jersey City. Within just three months he had assembled a team from within the Al-Kifah/Rahman network to assist in his plans, including Mahmud Abouhalima, Salameh, and Ayyad. Also involved were American-born Abdul Rahman Yasin,[52] Eyad Ismoil (a boyhood friend of Yousef's who had been living in Dallas),[53] and Ajaj, who was kept in the loop despite being in prison.

The attack took place just after noon on February 26, 1993, a huge explosion ripping a hole 150 feet (45.7 meters) wide and 5 stories deep at the base of the World Trade Center complex, killing 6 people.[54] Remnants of the rental van used to transport the bomb provided a crucial link to the perpetrators and (with the exception of Yousef who evaded capture for another two years, and Yasin who remains at large) they were quickly rounded up and prosecuted. The World Trade Center attack also prompted the FBI to further investigate the remaining members of the network, utilizing an informant named Emad Salem to infiltrate their ranks. By this time another informant named Garret Wilson was already part of Hampton-El's

'Project Bosnia', which had begun to overlap with an emerging plan to carry out additional attacks in New York. Hampton-El had run several domestic training exercises in Pennsylvania with the assistance of two other American converts — a former US marine, Abu Ubaidah Yahya and Kelvin Smith.[55] Among those who attended was a Sudanese immigrant named Siddig Ibrahim Siddig Ali with whom Salem soon became close. It quickly emerged that Ali was planning additional attacks in New York, with Rahman playing the role of 'spiritual advisor' and several others, including Hampton-El, helping out in various ways. Towards the end of June, members of the group were filmed mixing explosives at a safe-house in Queens and multiple arrests ensued, leading to lengthy prison sentences.[56]

The dismantling of the New York network in 1993 was a watershed moment for jihad in America, yet there were indicators of things to come which were not fully appreciated at the time. Although it pre-empted bin Laden's public declaration of 'War against the Americans' by three-and-a-half years, Yousef's attack and Ali's thwarted plot were evidence of the ideological shift that was taking place overseas from the near to far enemy. Similarly, Rahman's role in sanctioning 'jihad . . . against God's enemies'[57] was a clear sign of the growing significance of religious ideology, despite the fact that justification for the World Trade Center attack was primarily expressed in nationalistic and political terms.[58] Furthermore (as noted in Chapter 1) the involvement of Americans and the otherwise quite extensive ties to the US of many of the plotters was indicative of how quickly the jihadi movement was able to plant roots in American soil. Indeed, the loss of the New York network was a setback, yet the US continued to serve as an important base of operations and elsewhere infrastructure continued to grow.

The month after the World Trade Center attack, one of bin Laden's closest associates and the leader of the EIG, Ayman al-Zawahiri, visited the US on one of several fundraising tours.[59] He had apparently already been to the US around the time that the Soviets were leaving Afghanistan and he would do so again in 1995, chaperoned by Ali Mohamed and el-Dahab who took him to several California mosques raising money in the name of 'charity'.[60]

Estimates of the amounts raised vary from a few hundred dollars to half a million. Regardless of the amount, the jihadis were unperturbed in their efforts to exploit their most hated enemy. Indeed, as the 1990s progressed and the US began to emerge as the preferred target for attacks, operatives based there — including Americans — formed an integral part of those plans. Ali Mohamed was first 'asked by bin Laden [in 1993] to conduct surveillance of American, British, French, and Israeli targets in Nairobi'.[61] The American embassies in Kenya and Tanzania were decided upon and over the next five years Mohamed and el-Hage worked tirelessly in bringing the attacks to fruition, all the while traveling on their American passports and maintaining contact with associates in the US.[62] Theirs was not the only American contribution either. In fact the satellite phone (plus continual airtime top-ups and a separate battery) used by bin Laden in the lead-up to the 1998 attacks were purchased in the US. Communicating via Khalid al-Fawwaz in London, the al-Qaeda leader requested the phone in 1996 and it was supplied by way of a Palestinian–American computing student at Columbia College called Ziyad Khaleel.[63] When bin Laden needed a replacement battery, Khaleel again did the purchasing and an Iraqi–American charity worker, Tarik Hamdi from Herndon, Virginia, personally delivered it just months before the attacks.[64]

American charities would continue to play an important role throughout the 1990s. In spite of the wave of arrests in 1993, offices of Al-Kifah continued to function around the country, although they were 'somewhat fragmented'.[65] The Boston branch of Al-Kifah was the only one to close down, but even then it was simply replaced. It had been run by a Libyan named Emadeddin Muntasser who had come to the US in 1981 and later established a successful furniture chain.[66] After the World Trade Center attack, Muntasser incorporated a charity called Care International which functioned as 'an outgrowth of, and successor to, the Al-Kifah Refugee Center . . . and was engaged in non-charitable activities involving the solicitation and expenditure of funds to support and promote the *mujahideen* and jihad'.[67] From 1993 to 1997, Care published *Al-Hussam*[68] ('The Sword'), a pro-jihadi newsletter which had previously been the work of Al-Kifah Boston. From 1993 to 2003, the charity collected donations to the tune of \$1.7 million and until 2001 was secretly funding Islamist militants overseas.[69]

Muntasser was assisted by Muhamed Mubayyid, a dual Lebanese–Australian national, and Samir al-Monla, an American citizen originally from Kuwait.[70] Al-Monla claimed to have trained in Afghanistan in 1995 and was close with a Boston cab driver named Bassam Kanj who went by the *kunya* or *nom de guerre*, Abu Aisha.[71] Kanj had come to the US from Lebanon as a student in the mid-1980s and married an American convert.[72] By the end of the decade he had made his way to Afghanistan where he met the al-Qaeda leadership and took part in combat. He would eventually be killed back in his homeland after playing a lead role in establishing an Islamist militia group, but he spent most of the 1990s living in Boston. From 1997 to 98 there was something of an al-Qaeda reunion in 'The Puritan City' after Kanj was joined by a trio of friends from the Afghan training camps who worked alongside him driving cabs. Mohamad Kamal Elzahabi was another Lebanese–American who obtained his US passport by paying a woman to marry him and had been living in Houston before joining the jihad.[73] By contrast, Raed Hijazi was born and raised in California and had found his way to Afghanistan from a mosque in Sacramento.[74] The final member of the group was Nabil al-Marabh from Kuwait, who divided his time between the US and Canada and was later alleged to have ties to the 9/11 hijackers.[75] Although many of the allegations against al-Marabh have never been proven, the credentials of Elzahabi and Hijazi (like Kanj) have been well established — Elzahabi as a sniper and Hijazi as part of a plot to attack Jewish and American targets in Jordan. Their individual pathways ultimately led in different directions, yet they shared a safe-haven in the US — a place of respite to recover from injuries, raise funds, obtain equipment for the *mujahideen* overseas, and to plan their next steps.

The Boston cab-drivers were not the only ones taking advantage of life in America. Mohammed Bayazid, who had been present when al-Qaeda was first conceived, returned to the US from about 1994 until 1998, serving as the president of the Illinois chapter of the

Benevolence International Foundation (BIF), another highly dubious charity.[76] From 1993 onwards the national director of BIF was another Syrian–American, Enaam Arnaout, who was a friend of bin Laden's from Afghanistan and had been living in the US since 1990.[77] BIF raised more than $17.5 million from 1993 to 2001 and (unbeknownst to donors) a significant portion of funds were siphoned off to support Islamist militants in Bosnia, Chechnya, and elsewhere.[78]

Similar to Bayazid, Mohamed Zaky also returned to the US during the 1990s to focus on fundraising. Based in San Diego, he established two charities, Save Bosnia Now (which was later renamed American Worldwide Relief (AWR)) and the Islamic Information Center of the Americas.[79] Zaky's enterprises were part of a much larger North American support network by virtue of his connection to Kifah Wael Jayyousi with whom he closely coordinated. Jayyousi had come to the US from Jordan in the late 1970s, studying engineering and spending three years in the Navy.[80] While living in San Diego in 1993 he established the American Islamic Group (AIG), which promoted jihad and solicited donations by way of *The Islam Report*.[81] He was also described as a 'supporter and follower' of Omar Abdel Rahman with whom he stayed in touch until at least 1995.[82] Other members of the network included Kassem Daher in Canada and Adham Amin Hassoun in Fort Lauderdale, Florida. Hassoun (a Palestinian computer programmer who overstayed his student visa) acted as the East Coast representative for Zaky and Jayyousi's charities and distributed *The Islam Report* along with an Australian jihadi magazine called *Nida'ul Islam*.[83]

Hassoun was also an active recruiter and in 1998 he helped arrange for former Chicago gang member Jose Padilla to travel to Cairo en route to Afghanistan where he trained in preparation for attacks in the US.[84] During the summer of 2001, Padilla was paired up with another al-Qaeda operative in a plan to blow up apartment buildings using gas. Remarkably, it was another former resident of Broward County in Florida who Padilla had met before — Adnan Gulshair El Shukrijumah.[85] Previously, Shukrijumah's father associated with the Blind Sheikh at al-Farooq mosque in Brooklyn before moving south, and Shukrijumah first trained in Afghanistan around late 1998/early

1999.[86] Although he and Padilla could not get along and the latter was arrested in 2002, Shukrijumah remained ghost-like in his elusiveness for more than a decade. It was widely reported that he rose through the ranks to become chief of al-Qaeda's external operations in charge of plots to attack the US homeland before he was eventually killed in a Pakistani military operation in December 2014.[87]

Perhaps the most prominent jihadi figure to emerge from the US during the 1990s however, was Adam Gadahn, who went on to appear in a number of promotional videos as the American spokesman for al-Qaeda. A former death-metal enthusiast, Gadahn converted as a teenager and soon fell under the influence of two vehement jihadists and veterans of the Bosnian conflict (both also US passport holders), Khalil Said Deek and Hisham Diab.[88] Deek and Diab had come to America separately during the 1980s, eventually settling in Orange County where in late 1992 they played host to none other than Omar Abdel Rahman, who was touring California spreading the word of jihad.[89] During the mid-1990s, they established yet another suspect, not-for-profit enterprise called 'Charity Without Borders' and ran Islamic study circles in Garden Grove which were attended by Gadahn.[90] Their eager young recruit left the US in late 1997 and by 2001 was embroiled with al-Qaeda, acting at first as a translator and later appearing in online videos issuing threats against his former country.[91] Deek left the US around the same time as Gadahn and became close with senior al-Qaeda operative Abu Zubaydah. In 1999 he was held in relation to the plot to attack Jewish and American targets in Jordan involving Raed Hijazi of Boston, but was eventually released and later reported dead under circumstances that remain unclear.[92] Diab departed America shortly before 9/11 and subsequently vanished.

Similar to events in Florida and California, a pattern of recruitment was being replicated around the country whereby outspoken jihadists, including veteran *mujahideen*, were settling (or re-settling) in the US and using their influence to radicalize a fresh wave of volunteers. In Falls Church, Virginia, a group of aspiring militants materialized at the Dar al-Arqam Islamic Center where a charismatic imam named Ali al-Timimi began preaching around the turn of the millennium. Although born and mostly raised in America, al-Timimi had spent two years living in Saudi Arabia during the late 1970s where he had come under the tutelage of Bilal Philips, a Canadian convert who oversaw Hampton-El's Project Bosnia in 1993.[93] By the end of the 1990s, al-Timimi was extolling the virtues of armed jihad, a message that was given added credibility in Falls Church by Randall Todd Royer, an American university dropout who fought alongside the *mujahideen* in Bosnia and worked for Islamic charities in the US.[94] Including al-Timimi and Royer, at least 11 individuals (6 of whom were Americans by birth) formed what later became known as the 'Virginia jihad group'[95] and by early 2000 (just as the second bout of war in Chechnya was igniting) they were practicing with live firearms in preparation for jihad overseas.[96] Prior to 9/11, several members of the group trained with Lashkar e-Taiba (LeT) in Pakistan and as late as 2003 assisted a senior, British LeT operative, Mohammed Ajmal Khan, in obtaining supplies in the US.[97]

Around the same time as the Virginia group was coming together, a similar chain of events was unfolding 400 miles north in Lackawanna, an old steel town on the outskirts of Buffalo. The recruiter in this instance was Kamal Derwish who was born locally but had grown up in Yemen and Saudi Arabia, returning to Lackawanna in 1998. Like so many others, his influence derived from a combination of impressive religious knowledge and the enhanced reputation of having first-hand experience in battle, having been to Bosnia during the mid-1990s.[98] A small group of young men (mostly American-born Yemenis) quickly gravitated to the former *mujahid* and by early 2001 were ready to follow in his footsteps. That April, shortly after a visit from one of Derwish's fellow combatants in Bosnia, Juma al-Dosari, they made their way to Afghanistan where they trained at the infamous al-Farooq camp and met with bin Laden.[99] For most of the Lackawanna group the experience proved to be something of a reality check and they simply returned home. Only Derwish and one other, Jaber Elbaneh, stayed on, eventually turning up in Yemen where in November 2002 Derwish was killed in a US missile strike, making him the first American to perish at the hands of his own government in the Global War on Terror.[100]

But at the time that Americans such as the Lackawanna group were radicalizing and traveling abroad with romanticized visions of becoming holy warriors, the war had not yet begun. Nevertheless, there was talk in the Afghan camps of an upcoming operation against the US and there had been numerous signs of this gathering intent to strike at the 'far enemy'. Of course, this was most evident in the string of attacks on American targets in Africa and the Middle East, but domestic events were moving in the same direction. Back in January 1993, a Pakistani immigrant named Mir Aimal Kasi had gunned down five CIA agents (killing two) in Langley, Virginia. Although he was not part of any organization, he claimed to be exacting revenge for US foreign policy in Muslim countries,[101] a justification offered by jihadis to this day. Two months later was the first World Trade Center attack, followed by the arrest of Sheikh Rahman and his acolytes. In July 1997 a Palestinian named Ghazi Ibrahim Abu Maizar was arrested in New York in possession of a pipe bomb that he intended to detonate on the subway. Like Kasi, he was seemingly acting alone and specifically wanted to kill Jews, yet he also demanded the release of Rahman and Yousef, declaring 'that the United States is at war against Islam'.[102] December 1999 saw the arrest of Ahmed Ressam, a Montreal-based al-Qaeda operative planning to bomb Los Angeles airport who enlisted the help of a petty New York crook, Abdelghani Meskini.[103] Then in the early months of 2001, two Florida-based college students (friends of Adnan El Shukrijumah) became involved in a fanciful plot to wage violent jihad against multiple domestic targets ranging from power stations to Mount Rushmore.[104,105]

Meanwhile, the 9/11 attacks had been in preparation since 1996 and the future hijackers had come to the US as early as January 2000 to develop the skills they would need at American flight schools.[106] The plot mastermind, Khalid Sheikh Mohammed (KSM), understood the value of American education all too well, having gained a degree in mechanical engineering in North Carolina in 1986 before going to take part in the Afghan jihad.[107] One of the pilots, Hani Hanjour, had also previously spent time in the US, learning to fly during the late 1990s while living in Arizona. During that time he associated with a number of extremists, some of whom had trained in

Afghanistan and who have since been the subject of counterterrorism investigations.[108]

Similarly, after the hijackers began to arrive in the US in the months leading up to the operation, their movements at times intersected with members of the local populace whose credentials invoke the specter of an American support network. Visits paid to a then relatively obscure American imam (and future 'key leader' of al-Qaeda in the Arabian Peninsula[109]), Anwar al-Awlaki, are particularly intriguing. Early in 2000, two of the original members of the hijacking team, Nawaf al-Hazmi and Khalid al-Mihdar, met with Awlaki at the Masjid Ar-Ribat al-Islami in San Diego shortly after moving there from Los Angeles. Then in April 2001 al-Hazmi, this time accompanied by Hanjour, visited him at the Dar al-Hijrah mosque in Falls Church and again moved into a nearby apartment.[110] Although the true nature of these connections will never be known, the notion that they were purely coincidental seems somewhat unlikely. Four years prior to the meeting in San Diego, Awlaki had encouraged at least one person to pursue violent jihad overseas whilst living in Denver[111] and from 1998–1999 he had served as vice president of the Charitable Society for Social Welfare (CSSW), which was founded by a future designated terrorist (the Yemeni Sheikh Abd al-Majid al-Zindani) and was later referred to as a 'front organization' in support of al-Qaeda.[112] In 1999 Awlaki was in contact with Ziyad Khaleel, bin Laden's procurement agent and a representative of CSSW's partner organization, the Islamic American Relief Agency (IARA), which was also designated by the US Treasury for supporting terrorism.[113] Early in 2000 — around the same time as he met with the 9/11 hijackers — the American cleric was visited by a close associate of Omar Abdel Rahman; then after 9/11 the phone number for Dar al-Hijrah was found in the Hamburg apartment of one of the main plot facilitators, Ramzi bin al-Shibh.[114]

Whatever the involvement of Awlaki or others that the hijackers came into contact with in the US, the plan as a whole was conceived, funded, and directed from overseas and was executed by foreign operatives who had come to America for the sole purpose of attacking it. After the devastation of September 11, 2001, a wave of panic washed over the country, quickly followed by a surge in patriotism and a desire for revenge.[115] Domestic leads were vigorously pursued but the primary focus of the response naturally fell upon bin Laden and his camps in Afghanistan. At the time it was practically inconceivable, but as the Global War on Terror raged overseas, many more Americans would be drawn to the idea of global jihad and would turn against their own country.

Post-9/11

In the years immediately following 9/11 the majority of jihadi terrorism cases which came to light involved people who had radicalized and were operational prior to those attacks. The network of charities which had been helping to finance the *mujahideen* was among the first casualties of the American response. A number of these organizations had been under investigation during the 1990s and several of them were shut down as designated financiers of terrorism. However, the difficulty in establishing terrorism financing in a court of law has produced mixed results in terms of prosecutions, which have generally relied upon the 'Al Capone' approach of charging people with lesser but more readily identifiable offenses such as tax evasion and fraud. MAK and Al-Kifah had their assets frozen within two weeks of the Twin Towers falling, but by this time they had gone underground and no criminal cases could be made.[116] The exception to this was Care International, which continued until 2003, but it was not until 2012 that the case against Muntasser and his confederates concluded, with final sentences of just a few months of home confinement.[117] Meanwhile, Enaam Arnaout's BIF was designated on November 19, 2001 and Arnaout was later sentenced to ten years in prison for defrauding donors by failing to disclose the fact that donations were going to militants.[118] In another case, the Global Relief Foundation (GRF) was shut down and its chairman Rabih Haddad was arrested in December 2001 amidst allegations of providing support to al-Qaeda.[119] Yet Haddad was detained and later deported simply for violating the conditions of his visa.[120] The most successful prosecution of jihadi fundraisers (beginning in 2002 and ending in 2008) was of Jayyousi and Hassoun, who had been subject to extensive wiretaps. However, the case against them only proceeded after the arrest of Jose Padilla and their convictions were for much broader terrorism offenses.[121]

Like Padilla, other Americans who had radicalized during the 1990s also surfaced during this period. Among them was the 'American Taliban', John Walker Lindh from California who was captured in Afghanistan in November 2001.[122] Early 2002 saw the arrest of Imran Mandhai and Shueyb Mossa Jokhan, the two Florida students who had talked about blowing up Mount Rushmore. Towards the end of the year, members of the Lackawanna group who had returned home were arrested and a similar group in Portland was dismantled at around the same time,[123] followed by the Virginia jihad group in June 2003. March 2003 saw the arrest of Iyman Faris, a naturalized US citizen living in Columbus, Ohio who trained with al-Qaeda in Afghanistan and had been tasked by KSM with plotting to bring down the Brooklyn Bridge.[124] Eight months later the FBI arrested another Columbus resident (and a friend of Faris), a Somali asylum seeker named Nuradin Abdi who had been toying with the idea of blowing up a shopping mall.[125] Later still it would transpire that both men were also friends with Christopher Paul, a native of Columbus who had formally joined al-Qaeda in the early 1990s and prior to 9/11 had been involved in a plot to attack American targets in Germany.[126]

Many other groups and individuals can of course be added to this list and as time has gone on, the pre-9/11 generation has been replaced by newer waves of recruits, many more of whom grew up in America and only radicalized after 2001. These post-9/11 jihadis began to emerge in particular after the invasion of Iraq in 2003 and many of them have been lacking the experience and connections to foreign terrorist organizations that their predecessors could boast. Worryingly, however, they have shown a greater willingness to harm their own country. Such cases have included Ryan Anderson, a young National Guardsman from Washington who was arrested in 2004 after attempting to supply military intelligence to individuals he thought were al-Qaeda operatives.[127] August of the same year saw the arrest of two New Yorkers, Shahawar Matin Siraj and James Elshafay, who were planning (along with an informant) to bomb the Herald Square subway station, although they lacked the capability to do so.[128] A more disturbing plot was exposed in June of 2005, when an armed robbery investigation in Los Angeles led to the discovery of a three-man terror cell acting on the orders of a charismatic inmate at Folsom State Prison named Kevin James.[129] The plan — to attack Israeli, Jewish, and US military targets — had come dangerously close to succeeding and the case remains perhaps the most concrete example of the potential dangers of radicalization within prison.

Amidst the procession of cases over the last decade, several others are noteworthy. In January 2006, for example, the FBI was alerted to the presence of a budding group of jihadists in New Jersey who went on to plan a paramilitary (now commonly referred to as 'Mumbai-style') assault on the nearby Fort Dix Army base.[130] Similar to many of the post-9/11 US cases, members of the group had been raised in America and were lacking connections to foreign terrorist organizations. Others, however, have indeed managed to establish such links and in some cases have even gone on to occupy senior positions. In particular, numerous Americans succeeded in making the journey to Somalia where they swelled the ranks of al-Shabaab. Beginning around 2007 something of a pipeline was established between Minneapolis and the Horn of Africa, a connection that has proven difficult to sever despite continued arrests. The reality in Somalia is exceptionally harsh though and many of these volunteers have simply been cannon fodder — among them America's first suicide bomber, Shirwa Ahmed, who drove a car packed with explosives into a government compound on October 29, 2008.[131] Yet the most prominent American to join the jihad in Somalia was a convert to Islam from Daphne, Alabama named Omar Hammami. Taking on the *kunya* Abu Mansour al-Amriki (Abu Mansour the American), he rose swiftly through the ranks of al-Shabaab after joining them in late 2006 and went on to enjoy several years in an apparently senior position, appearing in online recruitment videos and boldly threatening revenge for the death of bin Laden in May 2011. Shortly afterwards, however, Hammami's luck began to run out. Having become embroiled in an internal organizational dispute, the young American was eventually targeted for assassination by his former comrades.[132] In light of this experience (and the weakened condition of al-Shabaab), it is quite possible that Somalia has lost some its appeal for American jihadis. But of course this does not rule out other options.

A seemingly smaller number of individuals have sought and found jihad in the more traditional hotspot along the mountainous borders of Afghanistan and Pakistan. Bryant Neal Vinas, a former Catholic from Long Island was one of them. Arrested in Peshawar in November 2008, he had trained with al-Qaeda, fired on a US military installation on the Afghanistan–Pakistan border and provided his handlers with detailed information on the operation of the Long Island railroad system as a potential target for attack.[133] About the time that Vinas was arrested, three friends from Queens were independently establishing connections with many of the same contacts. Najibullah Zazi, Zarein Ahmedzay, and Adis Medunjanin later returned to the US and began to set in motion a plan to bomb the New York subway that was intercepted as it neared the final stages of preparation. One of the chief architects behind this plot was later identified as none other than El Shukrijumah, the erstwhile resident of Broward County, Florida and one-time training partner of Jose Padilla.[134]

Yet another American to join a major terrorist organization was David Headley. Born in the nation's capital as Daood Gilani, in 2001 he joined LeT and went on to conduct surveillance for one of the most dramatic terrorist attacks in history — the November 2008 assault on Mumbai, which lasted four days and left more than 160 people dead.[135] Perhaps even more significantly, Americans have also helped sustain and expand the global jihad through ideological contributions — none more so than the aforementioned Anwar al-Awlaki. Little was heard from Awlaki immediately following 9/11 but by 2006 he had begun to attract the interest of authorities in Yemen who held him for more than a year in relation to an alleged kidnapping plot before eventually releasing him without charge.[136] In the ensuing years his stature among Western jihadis grew exponentially, matched in equal measure by his growing infamy within counterterrorism circles. Speaking in a calm, measured tone and in perfect

English — worlds apart from the almost comical irate stylings of the likes of the Blind Sheikh — Awlaki released a steady stream of online videos offering an increasingly militant interpretation of the Quran. These were reinforced with inflammatory articles, also in English, including such pieces as '44 Ways to Support Jihad' in addition to contributions to the online magazine *Inspire,* an AQAP publication which first appeared in the summer of 2010 and was produced by Awlaki's side-kick — another American — Samir Khan.

These works have proven enormously popular with Western jihadis to the extent that they have become almost obligatory material for aspiring *mujahideen.* Of course Awlaki's endeavors did not end there and his increasing forays into the operational side of things have been well documented (including provision of 'spiritual advice' for Nidal Malik Hasan — responsible for the Fort Hood massacre in November 2009 — as well as a far more substantial role behind Umar Farouk Abdulmutallab's attempt to destroy an American airliner on Christmas Day using liquid explosives concealed in his underwear).[137] Awlaki was officially designated a terrorist by the US in June 2010 and the following January a Yemeni court sentenced him in absentia to ten years in prison for inciting murder.[138] Eight months later he was killed, along with Khan, in a US Predator drone strike.

Awlaki's death, although significant, is balanced by the fact that his recordings live on, imbued with the added mystique of having 'achieved' martyrdom. Indeed, despite such tactical successes for counterterrorism, the ideas which drive the global jihad continue to seduce new volunteers — including Americans — many of whom are intent on attacking the US. This reality, however, has been largely misconstrued, particularly regarding the domestic situation, where — until the Boston Marathon was bombed in April 2013 — a certain sense of complacency was allowed to creep in. Partly, this can be attributed to the long line of successful, pre-emptive arrests of terrorism suspects, who were little match for the seemingly omnipotent FBI. At the same time, the preference for sting operations in domestic counterterrorism has given rise to questions of entrapment and lingering doubt about the seriousness of the threat.

Admittedly, jihadis have largely failed to inflict significant damage on American soil since 9/11. Over a period of just over 13 years, 11 attacks have actually been completed in the US,[139] committed by individuals inspired by the global jihad (see Table 1.1, Chapter 1). All but one of these individuals were American citizens and the majority of them were acting entirely by themselves. Between them they managed to kill just 23 people (13 of whom lost their lives at Fort Hood). While tragic, these numbers are barely enough to trouble a nation of more than 300 million people where random killing sprees take place with alarming regularity. Furthermore, some of these attacks were borderline in terms of classification as acts of terrorism and were generally dismissed as the actions of mentally unstable loners.[140]

Luckily, even the more serious cases, which were orchestrated by foreign terrorist organizations, ultimately failed and thus did not have the same impact as the bombings in Madrid or London, despite the fact that they could have easily caused a similar number of deaths. In fact, there has been a long-standing tendency to superficially compare the experience in the US to what appears to be a more dangerous and widespread problem in Europe and this has added to the (mis)perception that there is no home for jihad in America. This is reinforced by the fact that the primary threat to the US often appears to be external, rather than generated from within. Abdulmutallab, for example, was neither an American citizen nor resident (and for the purposes of the analysis in this book, he is actually included in the UK sample, given that he radicalized in London).

Of course, the attack in Boston was a stark reminder that the US is not immune from terrorism. Indeed, America's fragile sense of complacency was shattered that day. Far fewer people were killed than at Fort Hood, but many more were injured and the nature of the attack made it a more effective act of terrorism. The use of explosives to attack ordinary civilians at a crowded, high profile event generated exactly the kind of fear and intense media coverage that the perpetrators intended. The ensuing manhunt and dramatic showdown with police four days later brought the city to a standstill, whipped the media into a frenzy, and immediately raised questions about possible failures of intelligence.

Yet there is still a very real possibility that important lessons from Boston have been overlooked. In line with the established inclination to assume that the only real threat of Islamist terrorism to America is external, much has been made of the fact that the bombers (brothers Tamerlan and Dzhokhar Tsarnaev) were ethnic Chechens. Certainly, this appears to have been an important part of their self-image. Moreover, we know that Tamerlan — the older brother and apparent plot leader — had previously been identified as a person of interest by Russian intelligence and allegedly met with a suspected militant during a six-month trip to the Caucasus in 2012.[141] However, it should not be forgotten that the Tsarnaevs had come to the US a decade before they decided to attack it, then aged just 16 and 8 years old and appear to have radicalized at home in Cambridge, just north of Boston.[142,143] Whilst some form of external direction or support for the attack cannot be ruled out at this stage, according to Dzhokhar (a naturalized American citizen), they were acting independently out of revenge for the wars in Afghanistan and Iraq, and had learned how to make bombs using *Inspire* magazine.[144] In this light, the Boston attack would appear to be a case of home-grown jihadi terrorism — a possibility that many seem reluctant to accept.

In the years since Boston, the problem has escalated as dozens of Americans (along with citizens of many other nationalities) have been drawn to jihad in Syria and Iraq, while others have carried out attacks at home. In May of 2014, 'all-American' suicide bomber Moner Mohammad Abusalha — born and raised in Florida — blew himself up in Syria.[145] Between April and June of the same year, Ali Muhammad Brown from Seattle is believed to have murdered four people in three separate shooting incidents in the US as 'vengeance...[f]or the lives, millions of lives ... lost every day...[in] Syria, Iraq, Afghanistan.'[146] Then in October, yet another convert with a history of online extremist activity named Zale Thompson attacked a group of New York City Police Department officers with an axe.[147] Although there are still questions as to whether these and other domestic incidents should be classified as acts of terrorism, they are nevertheless symptomatic of continued Islamist radicalization within the US which cannot be ignored.[148,149]

The flip-side to neglecting the continued appeal of violent jihad in the US has been to overemphasize its significance. Whether for political, ideological, religious, or personal reasons, those who seek to magnify and sensationalize the danger of home-grown Islamist terrorism in America often display extremely limited understanding of the issues at hand and tend to focus on religion as the supposed root of the problem. As discussed in Chapter 2, it is imperative to appreciate jihadis' understanding of religion and how it contributes to their identity, but the drivers and motivations for Islamist terrorism are far more complex than this. To conflate 'terrorism' with 'Islam' (or indeed, any singular factor) is to misdiagnose the problem and potentially exacerbate it.

Whilst different factions continue to disagree about the nature of the problem, American jihadis continue to engage in the entire range of terrorist activity (including distribution of propaganda, various forms of financing and recruitment, conducting training exercises at home, liaising with terrorists overseas, traveling to conflict zones, and planning domestic attacks). Hence, there remains a need for balanced, comprehensive, and empirically informed assessment of the nature of this ever-evolving threat.[150] This chapter has provided no more than an anecdotal overview of the American jihad. In subsequent chapters the available evidence will be examined in far greater detail and the situations in the US and UK systematically compared.

Notes

[1] Global Terrorism Database, *United States*, Study for Terrorism and Responses to Terrorism, available at: http://www.start.umd.edu/gtd/search/Results.aspx?country=217, accessed August 2, 2012.

[2] Christopher Hewitt, *Understanding Terrorism in America: From the Klan to Al Qaeda* (Oxon, Routledge, 2003).

[3] Global Terrorism Database, *United States*.

[4] Lorenzo Vidino, 'Homegrown Jihadist Terrorism in the United States: A New and Occasional Phenomenon?' (2009), *Studies in Conflict and Terrorism*, 32(1), 1–17.

[5] *Ibid.*, 4.

[6] David Kaplan, 'Made in the U.S.A.: Hundreds of Americans Have Followed the Path to Jihad. Here's How and Why', *U.S. News.com*, July 2, 2002, available

at: http://www.usnews.com/usnews/news/articles/020610/archive_021602.htm, accessed January 20, 2008.

[7]Steven Emerson, *American Jihad: The Terrorists Living Among Us* (New York, Free Press, 2002), 130–131.

[8]'Makhtab al-Khidamat/ Al Kifah', *United States Treasury — Office of Terrorism and Financial Intelligence*, November 13, 2007, available at: http://nefafoundation.org/file/FeaturedDocs/TreasuryDept_MAK.pdf, accessed February 20, 2010.

[9]Ibid, 131.

[10]Ibid, 129.

[11]Kaplan, 'Made in the U.S.A.'

[12]Len Sherman, 'Al Qaeda Among Us', *Arizona Monthly*, November 2004, available at: http://toyfj40.freeshell.org/Stories/AZnov4.html, accessed January 12, 2012.

[13]Lawrence Wright, *The Looming Tower: Al-Qaeda and the Road to 9/11* (New York: Alfred A. Knopf, 2006), 163, Kindle Edition.

[14]'Treasury Department Statement on the Designation of Wa'el Hamza Julidan', *United States Treasury*, September 6, 2002, available at: http://www.treasury.gov/press-center/press-releases/Pages/po3397.aspx, accessed January 12, 2012.

[15]Wright, *The Looming Tower.*

[16]*The 9/11 Commission: Final Report of the National Commission on Terrorist Attacks Against the United States: Official Government Edition* (Washington DC: US Government Printing Office, 2004), 521.

[17]Wright, *The Looming Tower.*

[18]*The 9/11 Commission*, 521.

[19]Oriana Zill, 'Portrait of Wadih El Hage, Accused Terrorist', *Frontline*, September 12, 2001, available at: http://www.pbs.org/wgbh/pages/frontline/shows/binladen/upclose/elhage.html, accessed October 10, 2008; *United States of America v. Usama bin Laden et al.* (1998), Indictment, United States District Court Southern District of New York, S (10) 98 Cr. 1023 (LBS), available at: http://cns.miis.edu/reports/pdfs/binladen/indict.pdf, accessed October 10, 2008.

[20]Zill, 'Portrait of Wadih El Hage'.

[21]Benjamin Weiser and James Risen, "The Masking of a Militant: A Special Report; A Soldier's Shadowy Trail in U.S. and in the Mideast', *The New York Times*, December 1, 1998, available at: http://www.nytimes.com/1998/12/01/world/masking-militant-special-report-soldier-s-shadowy-trail-us-mideast.html, accessed August 13, 2011.

[22]Peter Lance, *Triple Cross: How Bin Laden's Master Spy Penetrated the CIA, the Green Berets, and the FBI* (New York, Harper Collins), Kindle Edition.

[23]*Ibid.*

[24]Lance Williams, 'Bin Laden's Bay Area Recruiter/Khalid Abu-al-Dahab Signed Up American Muslims to be Terrorists', *San Francisco Chronicle*, November 21, 2001, available at: http://articles.sfgate.com/2001-11-21/news/17628171_1_laden-bin-terrorism-charges, accessed January 14, 2012.

[25] *Ibid.*

[26] According to Burr and Collins, el-Dahab relocated to Brooklyn and was responsible for initially establishing Al-Kifah there, but this is not substantiated (J. Millard Burr and Robert Collins, *Alms for Jihad: Charity and Terrorism in the Islamic World* (Cambridge, Cambridge University Press, 2006), 269–271).

[27] Elizabeth Sullivan, Amanda Garrett, and Joel Rutchick, 'Cleveland's Islamic Leader Helped Found, Lead Group Linked to Bin Laden', *The Plain Dealer*, November 6, 2001, available at: http://www.freerepublic.com/focus/f-news/564508/posts, accessed January 14, 2012.

[28] *Ibid.*

[29] J.M. Berger, *Jihad Joe: Americans Who Go To War in the Name of Islam* (Washington DC, Potomac Books, 2011), 37; Emerson, *American Jihad*, 28.

[30] Berger, *Jihad Joe*, 14, 85–86.

[31] Johanna McGeary, 'A Traitor's Tale', *Time*, February 11, 2001, available at: http://www.time.com/time/printout/0,8816,98939,00.html, accessed January 14, 2012.

[32] FBI interview of El Sayyid Nosair, December 27, 2005, available at: http://www.scribd.com/doc/35687185/FBI-302-El-Sayyid-Nosair-12-20-05, accessed January 14, 2012; FBI interview of Gamal Ahmed Mohamed Al-Fedel, November 10, 1996, available at: http://www.scribd.com/doc/16981234/T1-B24-Various-Interrogation-Reports-Fdr-11898-FBI-Investigation-Gamal, accessed January 14, 2012; *United States of America v. Omar Ahmed Ali Abdel Rahman et al.,* Testimony of Clement Hampton-El, United States District Court, Southern District of New York, S5 93 CR 181 (MBM) August 2, 1995, available at: http://hurryupharry.org/wp-content/uploads/2010/05/US-vs-Omar-Ahmad-Ali-Abdel-Rahman.pdf, accessed January 14, 2012.

[33] FBI interview of El Sayyid Nosair, December 27, 2005.

[34] *United States of America v. Rahman et al.*, Testimony of Khaled Ibrahim, S5 93 CR 181 (MBM) July 13, 1995, available at: http://www.investigativeproject.org/documents/case_docs/1664.pdf, accessed January 15, 2012.

[35] *Ibid.*

[36] Peter Lance, *1000 Years for Revenge: International Terrorism and the FBI — The Untold Story* (PerfectBound, 2003), 24, Kindle Edition; *United States of America v. Omar Ahmed Ali Abdel Rahman et al*, Opinion, United States Court of Appeals for the Second Circuit, 189 F.3d 88, August 16, 1999, available at: http://www.texascollaborative.org/SilverblattModule/US-v-Rahman.pdf, accessed January 15, 2012.

[37] Berger, *Jihad Joe*, 14–15; *United States v. Rahman et al.*, Testimony of Clement Hampton-El.

[38] Richard Behar, William Dowell, Nomi Morris, Jefferson Penberthy, and David Seideman, 'The Secret Life of Mahmud the Red', *Time*, October 4, 1993, available at: http://www.time.com/time/printout/0,8816,979338,00.html, accessed January 15, 2012.

[39]Rick Hampson, 'Bombing Suspect Beat Odds to Get Visa', *Albany Times Union*, March 10, 1993, available at: http://www.highbeam.com/doc/1G1-156700699.html, accessed January 15, 2012.

[40]'Chemical Engineer Held in N.Y. Blast; Mideast Immigrant Linked to Salameh', *Washington Post*, March 11, 1993, available at: http://www.highbeam.com/doc/1P2-936585.html, accessed January 15, 2012.

[41]Berger, *Jihad Joe*, 34–35; Emerson, *American Jihad*, 136.

[42]Berger, *ibid.*, 34; Emerson, *ibid.*, 135–137; Steven Emerson, *Jihad Incorporated: A Guide to Militant Islam in the US* (New York: Prometheus Books, 2006), 33.

[43]Emerson, *Jihad Incorporated*, 278.

[44]Robert Friedman, 'The CIA's Jihad', *The New Yorker*, March 17, 1995, available at: http://freedom4um.com/cgi-bin/readart.cgi?ArtNum=13902, accessed January 15, 2012.

[45]FBI interview of El Sayyid Nosair.

[46]'El Sayyed A. Nosair', *Federal Bureau of Investigation*, September 18, 1992, published by *Intelwire*, available at: http://intelfiles.egoplex.com/1992-xx-nosair-fbi-302s.pdf, accessed August 10, 2012.

[47]Emerson, *American Jihad*, 135.

[48]FBI interview of El Sayyid Nosair; Peter Lance, 'First Blood: Was Meir Kahane's Murder al-Qaida's Earliest Attack on U.S. Soil?', *Tablet*, September 1, 2010, available at: http://www.tabletmag.com/news-and-politics/44243/First-blood/print/, accessed January 16, 2012.

[49]Berger, *Jihad Joe*, 51–77.

[50]John Parachini, 'The World Trade Center Bombers (1993)', 203, cited in Jonathan Tucker (ed.), *Toxic Terror: Assessing Terrorist Use of Chemical and Biological Weapons* (Cambridge MA: MIT Press 2000).

[51]Laurie Mylroie, *The War Against America: Saddam Hussein and the World Trade Center Attacks: A Study of Revenge* (Harper-Collins E-Books, 2001), Kindle Edition.

[52]Jeanne Hovanec, 'One of FBI's Top Suspects from Indiana', *University Wire*, October 22, 2001, available at: http://www.highbeam.com/doc/1P1-47673190.html, accessed January 15, 2012; David Kohn, '60 Minutes: The Man Who Got Away', *CBS News*, May 31, 2002, available at: http://www.cbsnews.com/stories/2002/05/31/60minutes/main510795.shtml, accessed January 15, 2012.

[53]James McKinley, 'Suspect is Said to be Longtime Friend of Bombing Mastermind', *The New York Times*, August 4, 1995, available at: http://www.nytimes.com/1995/08/04/nyregion/suspect-is-said-to-be-longtime-friend-of-bombing-mastermind.html?pagewanted=all&src=pm, accessed January 15, 2012.

[54]Dave Williams, 'The Bombing of the World Trade Centre in New York City' (1998), *International Criminal Police Review*, 469–471, available at: http://www.learnworld.com/COURSES/P72/P72.2002.Q4.ReaderOne.pdf, accessed December 11, 2007.

[55]Luke Cyphers and Bruce Feldman, 'The Good Son', *ESPN Magazine*, September 3, 2002, available at: http://espn.go.com/magazine/vol5no19musa.html, accessed January 16, 2012; *United States v. Rahman et al*, Testimony of Clement Hampton-El.

[56]*United States of America v. Rahman et al*, Indictment, United States District Court Southern District of New York, S5 93 CR 181 (MBM) October 20, 1994, available at: http://www.investigativeproject.org/documents/case_docs/935.pdf, accessed January 16, 2012; *United States v. Rahman et al*, Opinion, August 16, 1999.

[57]*United States v. Rahman et al*, Opinion, August 16, 1999.

[58]Alison Mitchell, 'Letter Explained Motive in Bombing, Officials Now Say', *New York Times*, March 28, 1993, available at: http://query.nytimes.com/gst/fullpage.html?res=9F0CEEDD1E31F93BA15750C0A965958260, accessed December 26, 2007.

[59]Wright, *The Looming Tower*, 220–221 (Kindle Edition).

[60]Lance, *Triple Cross*, 4246–4299 (Kindle Edition); Lance Williams and Erin McCormick, 'Top bin Laden Aide Toured State: Special Report: Al-Zawahiri Solicited Funds Under the Guise of Refugee Relief', *San Francisco Chronicle*, October 11, 2001, available at: http://www.sfgate.com/news/article/Top-bin-Laden-aide-toured-state-SPECIAL-REPORT-2871023.php, accessed January 17, 2012.

[61]Emerson, *Jihad Incorporated*, 35; *United States v. Usama bin Laden et al.*

[62]*United States v. Usama bin Laden et al.*

[63]Mark Morris, 'Phone Used in bin Laden's Dealings Linked to Former Student', *Knight Ridder Tribune*, September 20, 2001, available at: http://www.highbeam.com/doc/1G1-78460499.html, accessed January 17, 2012.

[64]David Kane, 'Affidavit in Support of Application for a Search Warrant', United States District Court Eastern District of Virginia, 1:02 MG 140, March 13, 2002, available at: http://www.investigativeproject.org/documents/case_docs/800.pdf, accessed January 17, 2012.

[65]David Kaplan, 'Made in the U.S.A.: Hundreds of Americans Have Followed the Path to Jihad. Here's How and Why', *USA Today*, June 2, 2002, available at: http://www.usnews.com/usnews/news/articles/020610/archive_021602.htm, accessed March 5, 2009.

[66]Emadeddin Muntasser, 'Overview of Emadeddin Muntasser's Career', *Wordpress.com*, February 12, 2011, available at: http://emadeddinmuntasser.wordpress.com/2011/02/12/overview-of-emadeddin-muntasser%e2%80%99s-career/, accessed February 16, 2012; *United States of America v. Muhamed Mubayyid and Emadeddin Z. Muntasser*, Appeal, United States Court of Appeals for the First Circuit, Case No. 10-1094, September 1, 2011, available at: http://www.investigativeproject.org/documents/case_docs/1668.pdf, accessed February 16, 2012.

[67]'Former Officers of a Muslim Charity, Care International, Inc., Convicted', *Federal Bureau of Investigation*, January 11, 2008, available at: http://boston.fbi.gov/dojpressrel/pressrel08/care011108.htm, accessed January 16, 2012.

[68]See, for example, *Al-Hussam: Newsletter of Care International*, April 16, 1993, available at: http://www.investigativeproject.org/documents/misc/670.pdf, accessed February 16, 2012.

[69]'Former Officers of a Muslim Charity, Care International, Inc., Convicted'.

[70]Mark Jewell, 'Three Men Convicted in Muslim Charity Probe', *AP Worldstream*, January 11, 2008, available at:http://www.highbeam.com/doc/1A1-D8U3U7OG2.html, accessed January 16, 2012.

[71]Lee Hammel, 'Testimony: Care International Leaders Tied to Jihadists', *The Telegram and Gazette*, November 30, 2007, available at: http://www.highbeam.com/doc/1G1-171989225.html, accessed January 16, 2012.

[72]Gary Gambill and Bassam Endrawos, 'Bin Laden's Network in Lebanon' (2001), *Middle East Intelligence Bulletin*, 3(1), available at: http://www.meforum.org/meib/articles/0109_l1.htm, accessed January 16, 2012.

[73]*United States of America v. Mohamad Kamal Elzahabi*, Complaint, United States District Court District of Minnesota, June 28, 2004, available at: http://www.investigativeproject.org/documents/case_docs/758.pdf, accessed January 17, 2012.

[74]Judith Miller, 'Dissecting a Terror Plot from Boston to Amman', *The New York Times*, January 15, 2001, available at:http://www.nytimes.com/2001/01/15/world/dissecting-a-terror-plot-from-boston-to-amman.html?pagewant-ed=all, accessed January 17, 2012.

[75]Marc Santora, 'Early Sept. 11 Suspect is Ordered Jailed and Deported', *The New York Times*, September 4, 2002, available at: http://www.nytimes.com/2002/09/04/us/traces-terror-investigation-early-sept-11-suspect-ordered-jail-ed-deported.html, accessed January 17, 2012.

[76]Andrew Hermann, 'The FBI Links These Men to Benevolence International Foundation', *The Chicago Sun-Times,* May 1, 2002, available at: http://www.highbeam.com/doc/1P2-1443058.html, accessed January 12, 2012; *United States of America vs. Enaam Arnaout* (2003), Government's Evidentiary Proffer Supporting the Admissibility of Coconspirator Statements, 02 CR 892, January 31, 2003, available at: http://fl1.findlaw.com/news.findlaw.com/hdocs/docs/bif/usarnaout10603prof.pdf, accessed January 13, 2012.

[77]Stephen Franklin, Laurie Cohen, and Noreen Ahmed-Ullah, 'Arnaout Insists He Had No Personal Relationship With Bin Laden', *The Chicago Tribune*, October 12, 2002, available at: http://www.highbeam.com/doc/1G1-120058548.html, accessed June 1, 2010; *United States of America v. Enaam Arnaout*, Indictment, United States District Court, Northern District of Illinois, Eastern Division, Case No. 02 CR 892, April 2002, available at: http://fl1.findlaw.com/news.findlaw.com/hdocs/docs/terrorism/usarnaout10902ind.pdf, accessed June 1, 2010.

[78]Emerson, *Jihad Incorporated*, 326–333; 'Transcript of Attorney General John Ashcroft Regarding Guilty Plea by Enaam Arnaout, *US Department of Justice*, February 10, 2003, available at: http://www.justice.gov/archive/ag/speeches/2003/021003agenaamaranouttranscripthtm.htm, accessed June 1, 2010.

[79]Evan Kohlmann, *Expert Report – U.S. v. Muhamed Mubayyid, Emadeddin Muntasser, and Samir Al-Monla Criminal Action No. 05-40026-FDS. (2007)*, 5–54, available at: http://www.powerbase.info/images/9/93/Kohlmann's_Expert_Report_in_US_v._Muntasser_et_al.pdf, accessed January 17, 2012.

[80]David Ashenfelter, 'Ex-Detroiter Supported Despite Guilty Verdict', *Detroit Free Press*, August 17, 2007, available at: http://www.accessmylibrary.com/article-1G1-167688635/ex-detroiter-supported-despite.html, accessed January 17, 2012; *United States of America v. Adham Amin Hassoun, Kifah Wael Jayyousi and Jose Padilla*, Transcript of Proceedings, United States District Court Southern District of Florida, 04-60001-CR-COOKE, July 12, 2007, available at: http://docs.justia.com/cases/federal/district-courts/new-york/nywdce/1:2010cv00569/79861/386/1.pdf?ts=1338016190, accessed January 17, 2012.

[81]Kohlmann, *Expert Report — U.S. v. Muhamed Mubayyid.*

[82]Justine Redman, 'Former School Official Faces Terrorism Charges', *CNN*, March 31, 2005, available at: http://articles.cnn.com/2005-03-31/justice/ terror.suspect.arrest_1_public-schools-kifah-wael-jayyousi-criminal-complaint?_s =PM:LAW, accessed January 17, 2012.

[83]*United States of America v. Adham Amin Hassoun, Kifah Wael Jayyousi and Jose Padilla*, Superseding Indictment, United States District Court Southern District of Florida, 04-60001-CR-COOKE, November 17, 2005, available at: http://nefafoundation.org/miscellaneous/FeaturedDocs/U.S._v_Padilla_SpcIndictment.pdf, accessed January 17, 2012.

[84]*Ibid.*

[85]*Jose Padilla v. Commander C.T.Hanft, USN, Commander, Consolidated Naval Brig*, Declaration of Mr. Jeffrey N. Rapp, Director, Joint Intelligence Task Force for Combating Terrorism, United States District Court, District of South Carolina, Case No. 2:04-CV-2221-26AJ, August 27, 2004, available at: http://www.nefafoundation.org/file/FeaturedDocs/Padilla_JeffreyRappDeclaration. pdf, accessed January 17, 2012.

[86]Dina Temple-Raston, 'Al-Qaida Mastermind Rose Using American Hustle', *NPR*, October 11, 2010, available at: http://www.npr.org/templates/story/story.php?storyId=130434651, accessed October 13, 2010.

[87]Susan Candiotti and Ross Levitt, 'From Dishwasher to al Qaeda Leadership: Who is Adnan Shukrijumah?', *CNN*, August 6, 2010, available at: http://edition.cnn.com/2010/CRIME/08/06/terror.qaeda.leader/index.html, accessed August 8, 2010; Bill Roggio, 'Pakistani Taliban Confirms Death of al Qaeda Leader Adnan Shukrijumah', *The Long War Journal*, December 8, 2014, available at: http://www.longwarjournal.org/threat-matrix/archives/2014/12/pakistani_taliban_confirms_dea.php, accessed December 8, 2014.

[88]Raffi Khatchadourian, 'Azzam the American: The Making of an Al Qaeda Homegrown', *The New Yorker*, January 22, 2007, available at: http://www.newyorker.com/reporting/2007/01/22/070122fa_fact_khatchadourian?currentPage=all, accessed March 5, 2010.

[89]Nick Schou, 'So I Married a Terrorist... Saraah Olsons Strange Trip Through the US War on Terror', *OC Weekly*, April 19, 2007, available at: http://www.ocweekly.com/content/printVersion/53298/, accessed January 17, 2012.

[90]*Ibid.*

[91]Khatchadourian, 'Azzam the American'.

[92]Stephen Kinzer, 'Jordan Links Terrorist Plot to bin Laden', *The New York Times*, February 4, 2000, available at: http://www. nytimes.com/2000/02/04/world/jordan-links-terrorist-plot-to-bin-laden.html?pagewanted=all&src=pm, accessed January 17, 2012; Nick Schou, 'Where is OCs Missing Terrorist', *OC Weekly*, June 15, 2006, available at: http://www.ocweekly.com/2006-06-15/news/where-is-oc-s-missing-terrorist/, accessed January 17, 2012.

[93]'Ali Al-Timimi: A Life of Learning', *Ahlus Sunnah Wal Jama'ah Association of Australia,* 2004, available at: http://web.archive.org/web/20060819165800/http://www.iisca.org/articles/document.jsp?id=97, accessed January 18, 2012; Berger, *Jihad Joe*, 51–77.

[94]Karen Branch-Brioso, 'Islam Set Direction in Man's Life', *The St. Louis Post-Dispatch*, June 28, 2003, available at: http://cleveland.indymedia.org/news/2003/07/5419.php, accessed January 18, 2012.

[95]Also affiliated with the group was American-born Sabri Benkahla who trained with LeT in July 1999; however, he was acquitted of the original charges and tried separately for perjury (Matthew Barakat, 'Man Gets 10 Years for Lying in Terrorism Case', *The Virginian-Pilot*, July 25, 2007, available at: http://www.highbeam.com/doc/1G1-166790715.html, accessed January 18, 2012).

[96]*United States of America v. Randall Todd Royer et al*, Indictment, United States District Court Eastern District of Virginia, 03-CR-296, June 25, 2003, available at: http://www.investigativeproject.org/documents/case_docs/156.pdf, accessed August 8, 2009.

[97]*United States of America v. Ali Asad Chandia and Mohammed Ajmal Khan*, Indictment, United States District Court Eastern District of Virginia, 1:05 CR 401, September 14, 2005, available at: http://www.investigativeproject.org/documents/case_docs/1087.pdf, accessed August 8, 2009.

[98]James Sandler, 'Kamal Derwish: The Life and Death of an American Terrorist', *PBS Frontline*, October 16, 2003, available at: http://www.pbs.org/wgbh/pages/frontline/shows/sleeper/inside/derwish.html, accessed January 18, 2012; Dina Temple-Raston, *The Jihad Next Door: The Lackawanna Six and Rough Justice in the Age of Terror* (New York: PublicAffairs, 2007), Kindle Edition.

[99]Jason Felch, "The Closer": An Al Qaeda Recruiter in the United States', *PBS Frontline*, October 16, 2003, available at: http://www.pbs.org/wgbh/pages/frontline/shows/sleeper/inside/juma.html, accessed January 18, 2012; Temple-Raston, *The Jihad Next Door.*

[100]Sandler, 'Kamal Derwish'.

[101]'Kasi is Executed for CIA Deaths', *United Press International*, November 15, 2002, available at: http://www.highbeam.com/doc/1P1-69570118.html, accessed January 18, 2012.

[102] Joseph Fried, 'Defendant in Bomb Plot Tells of Plan to Kill Jews', *The New York Times*, July 21, 1998, available at: http://www.nytimes.com/1998/07/21/nyregion/defendant-in-bomb-plot-tells-of-plan-to-kill-jews.html?pagewan-ted=all&src=pm, accessed January 18, 2012.

[103] Sam Skolnik, 'Longtime Con Man Admits to Aiding Ressam in Bomb Plot', *Seattle Post-Intelligencer*, March 30, 2001, available at: http://www.highbeam.com/doc/1G1-72551570.html, accessed January 18, 2012.

[104] Richard Willing, 'Pursuit of al-Qaeda Keeps Coming Back to Fla.', *USA Today*, June 15, 2003, available at: http://www.usatoday.com/news/nation/2003-06-15-florida-usat_x.htm, accessed January 18, 2012.

[105] Other notable domestic attacks during this time period include shootings in March 1994 on the Brooklyn Bridge and in February 1997 at the Empire State Building. However, these attacks, like the shooting at LA airport in July 2002, appear to have been driven by a narrower set of anti-Semitic and personal motivations, showing less relation to the Global Salafi Jihad.

[106] *The 9/11 Commission*, 148–149, 159.

[107] *Ibid.*, 145–146.

[108] *Ibid.*, 226.

[109] 'Treasury Designates Anwar Al-Aulaqi, Key Leader of Al-Qa'ida in the Arabian Peninsula', *US Department of the Treasury*, July 16, 2010, available at: http://www.nefafoundation.org/miscellaneous/Treasury_AwlakiDesignation.pdf, accessed January 19, 2012.

[110] Susan Schmidt, 'Imam from Va. Mosque Now Thought to Have Aided Al-Qaeda', *The Washington Post,* February 27, 2008, available at: http://www.washingtonpost.com/wp-dyn/content/article/2008/02/26/AR2008022603267_pf.html, accessed January 19, 2012; *The 9/11 Commission*, 221.

[111] Bruce Finley, 'Muslim Cleric Targeted by U.S. Made Little Impression During Colorado Years', *The Denver Post*, April 11, 2010, available at: http://www.denverpost.com/commented/ci_14861059?source=commented-news, accessed April 12, 2010.

[112] Schmidt, 'Imam from Va. Mosque Now Thought to Have Aided Al-Qaeda'.

[113] Schmidt, 'Imam from Va. Mosque Now Thought to Have Aided Al-Qaeda'; 'Treasury Designates Global Network, Senior Officials of IARA for Supporting bin Laden, Others', *US Department of the Treasury*, October 13, 2004, available at: http://nefafoundation.org/file/FeaturedDocs/IARA_TreasuryDes.pdf, accessed June 25, 2008.

[114] Schmidt, 'Imam from Va. Mosque Now Thought to Have Aided Al-Qaeda'.

[115] Hewitt, *Understanding Terrorism in America*, 3–4.

[116] Kaplan, 'Made in the U.S.A.'

[117] Lee Hammel, '6 Months of Home Confinement Added to Sentence in Muslim Charity Tax Fraud Case', *The Telegram and Gazette*, May 29, 2012, available at: http://www.telegram.com/article/20120529/NEWS/120529428/0/, accessed August 10, 2012; Kevin Keenan, 'Analysts Say Fundraising for Terrorists Went on Without Notice', *The Telegram and Gazette*, September

11, 2006, available at: http://www.investigativeproject.org/146/analysts-say-fundraising-for-terrorists-went-on-without, accessed July 7, 2009.

[118]'New Sentence for Charity Director', *The New York Times*, February 18, 2006, available at: http://query.nytimes.com/gst/fullpage.html?res=9A01E6D7103 EF93BA25751C0A9609C8B63, accessed March 11, 2009; 'Transcript of Attorney General John Ashcroft Regarding Guilty Plea by Enaam Arnaout'.

[119]'Treasury Department Statement Regarding the Designation of the Global Relief Foundation', *US Department of the Treasury*, October 18, 2002, available at: http://www.ustreas.gov/press/releases/po3553.htm, accessed April 17, 2010.

[120]Rachel Swarns, 'U.S. Deports Charity Leader in Visa Dispute', *The New York Times*, July 16, 2003, available at: http://www.nytimes.com/2003/07/16/us/threats-and-responses-a-michigan-case-us-deports-charity-leader-in-visa-dispute.html, accessed April 17, 2010.

[121]'Jose Padilla and Co-Defendants Convicted of Conspiracy to Murder Individuals Overseas, Providing Material Support to Terrorists', *US Department of Justice*, August 16, 2007, available at: http://www.nefafoundation.org/miscellaneous/FeaturedDocs/U.S._v_Padilla_DOJPR_Convictions.pdf, accessed November 9, 2008.

[122]'Profile: John Walker Lindh', *BBC News*, January 24, 2002, available at: http://news.bbc.co.uk/2/hi/americas/1779455.stm, accessed June 3, 2010.

[123]'Two Admit to Being Part of Terror Cell', *The Washington Times*, October 16, 2003, available at: http://www.washingtontimes.com/news/2003/oct/16/20031016-104712-9055r/, accessed September 5, 2008.

[124]*United Stated of America v. Iyman Faris*, Statement of Facts, United States District Court for the Eastern District of Virginia, Case No. 03-189-A, May 2003, available at: http://www.investigativeproject.org/documents/case_docs/229.pdf, accessed June 3, 2010.

[125]'Ohio Man Indicted for Providing Material Support to al-Qaeda, Falsely Obtaining and Using Travel Documents', *US Department of Justice*, June 14, 2004, available at: http://nefafoundation.org/miscellaneous/FeaturedDocs/U.S._v_Abdi_DOJPRIndictment.pdf, accessed June 3, 2010.

[126]'Ohio Man Pleads Guilty to Conspiracy to Bomb Targets in Europe and the United States', *US Department of Justice*, June 3, 2008, available at: http://www.usdoj.gov/opa/pr/2008/June/08-nsd-492.html, accessed June 1, 2010.

[127]'Military Jury Convicts Soldier of Trying to Help Al Qaeda', *USA Today*, September 3, 2004, available at: http://www.usatoday.com/news/nation/2004-09-03-anderson_x.htm, accessed June 7, 2010.

[128]'Shahawar Matin Siraj Sentenced to Thirty Years of Imprisonment for Conspiring to Place Explosives at the 34th Street Subway Station in New York', *US Department of Justice*, January 8, 2007, available at: http:// nefafoundation.org/miscellaneous/FeaturedDocs/U.S._v_Siraj_DOJPRSentencing.pdf, accessed June 7, 2010.

[129]'Man Who Formed Terrorist Group that Plotted Attacks on Military and Jewish Facilities Sentenced to 16 Years in Federal Prison', *United States Attorney's Office, Central District of California*, March 6, 2009, available

at: http://www.nefafoundation.org/miscellaneous/FeaturedDocs/US_v_James_dojprsent.pdf, accessed June 7, 2010.

[130] 'Three Brothers Sentenced to Life Prison Terms for Conspiring to Kill U.S. Soldiers', *US Department of Justice*, April 28, 2009, available at: http://www.investigativeproject.org/documents/case_docs/842.pdf, accessed June 11, 2010.

[131] Andrea Elliott, 'A Call to Jihad, Answered in America', *The New York Times*, July 11, 2009, available at: http://www.nytimes.com/2009/07/12/us/12somalis.html?pagewanted=all, accessed June 11, 2010.

[132] J.M. Berger, 'Me Against the World', *Foreign Policy*, May 25, 2012, available at: http://www.foreignpolicy.com/articles/2012/05/25/me_against_the_world?page=full, accessed May 26, 2012; 'Somalia: Al-Shabaab Fighters Loyal to Godane Reportedly Kill Al-Amriki', *All Africa.com*, May 8, 2013, available at: http://allafrica.com/stories/201305090519.html, accessed May 9, 2013.

[133] Sebastian Rotella and Josh Meyer, 'A Young American's Journey into Al Qaeda', *The Los Angeles Times*, July 24, 2009, available at: http://articles.latimes.com/2009/jul/24/nation/na-american-jihadi24, accessed July 25, 2009.

[134] 'Charges Unsealed Against Five Alleged Members of Al-Qaeda Plot to Attack the United States and United Kingdom', *US Department of Justice*, July 7, 2010, available at: http://www.justice.gov/opa/pr/2010/July/10-nsd-781.html, accessed July 8, 2010.

[135] 'Chicago Resident David Coleman Headley Pleads Guilty to Role in India and Denmark Terrorism Conspiracies', *US Department of Justice*, March 18, 2010, available at: http://www.nefafoundation.org/miscellaneous/US_v_Headley_dojprguilty.pdf, accessed April 2, 2010.

[136] Schmidt, 'Imam from Va. Mosque Now Thought to Have Aided Al-Qaeda'.

[137] *United States of America v. Umar Farouk Abdulmutallab*, Government's Sentencing Memorandum, United States District Court Eastern District of Michigan Southern Division, Case No. 2:10-CR-20005, February 10, 2012, available at: https://s3.amazonaws.com/s3.documentcloud.org/documents/291667/abdulmutallab-sentencing-memorandum.pdf, accessed February 19, 2012.

[138] 'U.S.-Born Radical Cleric Added to Terror Blacklist', *Fox News*, July 16, 2010, available at: http://www.foxnews.com/us/2010/07/16/born-radical-cleric-added-terror-blacklist/, accessed July 17, 2010; Robert Worth, 'Yemen Sentences American-Born Cleric in Absentia', *The New York Times*, January 18, 2011, available at: http://www.nytimes.com/2011/01/19/world/middleeast/19awlaki.html?_r=1&emc=tnt&tntemail1=y, accessed January 19, 2011.

[139] Note that although the 'shoe-bomber' Richard Reid was targeting a US-bound flight, he attempted his attack outside of US airspace.

[140] For example, Charles Bishop's January 2002 attack on the American Bank Plaza building in Tampa, Florida is widely regarded solely as an act of suicide by a troubled teenager. However, whilst there is some validity to this explanation, it ignores the fact that Bishop left a note explaining that in his mind it was an attack inspired by bin Laden and al-Qaeda ('Teen Pilot's Suicide Note', *The Smoking Gun*, February 1, 2002,

available at: http://www.thesmokinggun.com/documents/crime/teen-pilots-suicide-note, accessed December 12, 2011). Given the context (shortly after 9/11) and the perpetrator (a 15-year-old Caucasian with no links to any terrorist organization) it is understandable that this was not seen as an act of terrorism at the time. However, Bishop's stated motivations and intentions (despite being delusional) are the key to classifying this as al-Qaeda inspired terrorism. Furthermore, although the perpetrator is much less important than the motivation, had the same act been committed by a Muslim youth, the sad truth is that fewer people would question this classification.

[141]Tom Parfitt, 'Canadian Boxer Had Links to Boston Bomber', *Sydney Morning Herald*, April 29, 2013, available at: http://www.smh.com.au/world/canadian-boxer-had-links-to-boston-bomber-20130429-2io3k.html, accessed April 29, 2013.

[142]Tamerlan arrived in the US approximately a year later than Dzhokhar.

[143]Alissa de Carbonnel and Stephanie Simon, 'Special Report: The Radicalization of Tamerlan Tsarnaev', *Reuters*, April 23, 2013, available at: http://www.reuters.com/article/2013/04/23/us-usa-explosions-radicalisation-special-idUSBRE93M0CZ20130423, accessed April 23, 2013.

[144]Pete Williams and Erin McClam, 'Boston Suspect: We Learned How to Make Bombs from Inspire Magazine', *NBC News*, April 23, 2013, available at: http://usnews.nbcnews.com/_news/2013/04/23/17877288-boston-suspect-we-learned-how-to-make-bombs-from-inspire-magazine#.UXbLI3fGsBA.twitter, accessed April 23, 2013; Scott Wilson, Greg Miller, and Sari Horwitz, 'Boston Bombing Suspect Cites U.S. Wars as Motivation, Officials Say', *The Washington Post*, April 23, 2013, available at: http://www.washingtonpost.com/national/boston-bombing-suspect-cites-us-wars-as-motivation-officials-say/2013/04/23/324b9cea-ac29-11e2-b6fd-ba6f5f26d70e_print.html, accessed April 23, 2013.

[145]Peter Bergen, 'The All-American Al Qaeda Suicide Bomber', *CNN*, July 31, 2013, available at; http://edition.cnn.com/2014/07/31/opinion/bergen-american-al-qaeda-suicide-bomber-syria/index.html, accessed July 31, 2014.

[146]Ashley Fantz, Pamela Brown, and Aaron Cooper, 'Police: Seattle Man's Hatred of U.S. Foreign Policy Motivated Killings', *CNN*, September 16, 2014, available at: http://edition.cnn.com/2014/09/16/justice/ali-brown-charges-killing-spree/, accessed September 16, 2014.

[147]'New York Axe Attack "Terrorist Act by Muslim Convert"', *BBC News*, October 25, 2014, available at: http://www.bbc.com/news/world-us-canada-29753347, accessed October 25, 2014.

[148]Notably, the beheading of a woman in Oklahoma by Alton Nolen in September 2014, which was apparently precipitated by an argument concerning the 'need' to stone to death women who violated Islamic law. This in itself is not necessarily intended to influence a wider audience and would therefore not classify as terrorism, and yet Nolen was also reported to have been clearly 'seduced by militant ideology' (Joanna Jolly, 'Alton Nolen: A Jihadist Beheading in Oklahoma?', *BBC News*, September 29, 2014, available at: http://www.bbc.com/news/magazine-29408139, accessed September 29, 2014).

[149]The key to this debate is whether or not the motives involved trying to influence a wider audience for political/religious ideals.

[150]The best effort to date, although an excellent piece of research, profiles 171 individuals convicted or killed during the commission of terrorism offenses in the US from 1997 to 2011 and thus utilizes a smaller sample and more narrow time-frame (see Robin Simcox and Emily Dyer, *Al-Qaeda in the United States: A Complete Analysis of Terrorism Offences* (The Henry Jackson Society, 2013), available at: http://henryjacksonsociety.org/wp-content/uploads/2013/02/Al-Qaeda-in-the-USAbridged-version-LOWRES-Final.pdf, accessed April 7, 2013).

Chapter 4

Londonistan

For decades the word 'terrorism' in the UK immediately brought to mind the Troubles — the long-running conflict in Northern Ireland. The region experienced close to 4,000 recorded attacks from 1970 to 2010, resulting in 2,840 known fatalities.[1] During the same period, Irish terrorist groups were responsible for nearly half of 606 recorded attacks on the UK mainland, the remainder of which are attributed to more than 50 other identifiable groups and unknown perpetrators with diverse ideological agendas.[2] Given such a long-standing and formidable threat, British authorities were understandably preoccupied with the Provisional Irish Republican Army (PIRA) and their contemporaries, and were slow to adjust to the emerging danger posed by Islamist terrorists.[3] It was not that the security services were unaware of the jihadi networks steadily growing in their midst, nor were they oblivious to their connections to militants overseas. But until 2004–2005, no-one truly grasped the extent to which these networks and their violent ideology were becoming ingrained in British communities and turning their venom against Britain itself.

Pre-9/11

As a country which prides itself on offering asylum to political dissidents, the UK allowed waves of Islamist activists, former *mujahideen* and active supporters of jihadist organizations to enter the country during the 1980s and 1990s. These guests — for the time being preoccupied with events overseas — happily exploited the British tradition of freedom of speech and busily endeavored to expand and strengthen their networks. Unobstructed, they were prolific in publishing propaganda, recruiting, fundraising, and even coordinating terrorist operations abroad.[4] At a time when politicized Islam was already on the rise following the Salman Rushdie affair of 1988, the UK thus became a hub of Islamist activism and militancy.

Among the pioneers of the movement in London was a Syrian-born preacher named Omar Bakri Mohammed who had been forced to flee his homeland and had been expelled from Saudi Arabia for involvement with Islamist extremists. On arriving in Britain in 1985 he was granted asylum and promptly founded the London branch of Hizb ut-Tahrir (HT), which quickly established a growing presence in mosques and on university campuses. Precisely how militant HT's ideas are is a subject of some debate but according to Ed Husain — a former member of the group in London during the 1990s — '[h]ome-grown British suicide-bombers are a direct result of HT disseminating ideas of jihad, martyrdom, confrontation, and anti-Americanism, and nurturing a sense of separation among Britain's Muslims'.[5] Bakri Mohammed was particularly controversial. During the 1990–1991 Gulf War he made headlines by allegedly declaring that then Prime Minister John Major was a legitimate target for assassination, and when war broke out in the former Yugoslavia he suggested that Bosnian Muslims should 'eat Serbs' rather than accept food aid from the West.[6] Eventually, in 1996 the 'Tottenham Ayatollah' as he would later become known, broke away from HT to form his own, more radical group named al-Muhajiroun (AM).

From its inception the group engaged in fundraising for jihadi groups in Palestine, Kashmir, and Chechnya and was openly anti-Western and anti-Semitic.[7] Yet for years AM was given the freedom to continue recruiting and when members transgressed the law it was treated as an individual offense rather than a problem relating to group affiliation. Among the early warning signs of the potential danger of AM was the December 1998 firebombing of a London military barracks by 19-year-old Amer Mirza following a protest against British troops in Iraq.[8] In October 2000, London Underground worker Iftikhar Ali and security guard Zaheen Mohammed were arrested for distributing AM leaflets calling on Muslims to murder Jews.[9] Then on Christmas Day, a student from Birmingham named

Bilal Mohammed blew himself up in Kashmir, killing six Indian soldiers and three Kashmiri students. While Jaish e-Mohammed (JeM) claimed responsibility for the attack, Bakri Mohammed admitted knowing the young man and added that he was 'not surprised by his actions. He [became] a martyr and that is the wish of every Muslim in order to go to paradise'.[10]

After 9/11, AM would court further controversy, testing the limits of the British legal system, but during the 1990s they could enjoy what Bakri Mohammed referred to as the 'covenant of security' — a tacit understanding that the jihadis would be generally left alone as long they did not break the law in Britain. Others with far more substantial ties to terrorism also exploited this policy, including several men with direct links to bin Laden and al-Zawahiri. Chief among them was a Saudi named Khalid al-Fawwaz, who had been a comrade of bin Laden's in Afghanistan before coming to the UK in 1994. In July that year he was tasked by bin Laden with running the Advice and Reformation Committee (ARC) based in Dollis Hill in Northwest London, which published anti-Saudi propaganda and according to US investigators effectively functioned as al-Qaeda's European headquarters.[11] Working alongside al-Fawwaz were two 'official' UK representatives of al-Zawahiri's Egyptian Islamic Jihad (EIJ), Adel Abdel-Meguid Bari and Ibrahim Eidarous.[12]

The London operatives kept in close contact with the al-Qaeda leadership and coordinated activities with network members in other countries, including the US. In fact, in its initial years, the ARC was closely tied to an obscure entity named the Action Committee for the Rights of Middle East Minorities (ACRMEM), based in Denver, Colorado. The ACRMEM was established in 1994 by the wife of another London Islamist, Muhammad al-Massari, who ran his own propaganda office in the UK called the Committee for the Defence of Legitimate Rights (CDLR). During the mid-1990s the Denver office was used to connect calls from Saudi Arabia to the ARC using a toll-free line that had been set up for US servicemen, an arrangement that bin Laden personally thanked al-Massari for.[13]

Transatlantic cooperation continued when in December 1995 al-Fawwaz received a personal visit from the American al-Qaeda agent

Wadih el-Hage, who was then putting plans in motion to attack the US embassies in East Africa.[14] Shortly afterwards (apparently frustrated with existing arrangements for communication) al-Fawwaz coordinated the acquisition and delivery of bin Laden's satellite phone. The money came from yet another London-based dissident named Saad al-Faqih, who in 1995 founded the Movement for Islamic Reform in Arabia (MIRA) which likewise functioned in support of al-Qaeda.[15] Meanwhile, the purchase of the phone itself was conducted in the US by Ziyad Khaleel, a college student affiliated with numerous Islamist charities in addition to al-Massari's CDLR.[16] Al-Fawwaz and bin Laden subsequently exchanged more than 200 phone calls and it is believed that the Londoners, including Bari and Eidarous, played a key support role in planning the embassy attacks.[17] At the least, the ARC was responsible for spreading al-Qaeda propaganda including the 1996 'Declaration of War', the February 1998 'World Islamic Front' *fatwa* and the claim of responsibility for the embassy bombings in August, which was faxed to London *before* the attacks took place.[18]

Soon afterwards the plug was pulled on the ARC and al-Fawwaz, Bari, and Eidarous were detained, facing a lengthy fight against extradition to the US. However, Saad al-Faqih continued to operate the MIRA in order to 'propagate support' and 'facilitate' al-Qaeda operations.[19] Similarly, Muhammad al-Massari maintained the CDLR and various other projects including the Global Jihad Fund (GJF), which was established 'to facilitate the growth of various jihad movements around the world by supplying them with sufficient funds to purchase weapons and train their individuals'.[20] The GJF operated via a website called the Islamic Gateway and was run on a day-to-day basis by an IT security specialist named Mohammed Sohail who would also meet with potential recruits. When the GJF was exposed in 1999, Sohail admitted that 'I work for two people, really. Mr. Massari and Osama bin Laden'.[21]

Another individual who had crossed paths with the al-Qaeda leader and al-Fawwaz, and who made a rather more substantial contribution to the growth of militant Islam in Britain, was Omar Mahmoud Mohammed Othman, better known as Abu Qatada. Like many others, the Palestinian-born cleric had left his home in Jordan to avoid persecution and had met bin Laden in Peshawar before making his way to Britain in 1993 where he was granted asylum.[22] Based at the Four Feathers Social Club in central London, Qatada became a highly respected figure in what rapidly developed into an extensive and well-connected web of militancy. Besides rubbing shoulders with al-Fawwaz, he was a 'close associate' of Amar Makhlulif aka Abu Doha, a former instructor at the Khalden training camp in Afghanistan and a key London-based al-Qaeda facilitator.[23] Another friend of Qatada's and a frequent visitor to the British capital was Imad Eddin Barakat Yarkas, alias Abu Dahdah, who would later be convicted for running al-Qaeda operations in Madrid.[24]

Even amidst such illustrious company Qatada's standing was significant. In recognition of his religious authority, numerous terrorist organizations referred to him for spiritual advice, including the ultra-violent Algerian Armed Islamic Group (GIA) and its successor, the Salafist Group for Preaching and Combat (GSPC).[25] Along with Rachid Ramda (later convicted for funding the 1995 metro bombings in Paris[26]), he co-edited the GIA newsletter *al-Ansar* and issued *fatwas* justifying all manner of violence and crime.[27,28] For example, in March 1995 he authorized the killing of wives and children of 'apostates' in Algeria, fueling the appalling escalation of violence; in December 1996 he legitimized the killing of Jews in Britain; and in October 1999 he declared that Jewish children could also be killed, and that there was no difference between Jews, Americans, or the English.[29]

Qatada also did what he could to bring in new recruits for the camps in Afghanistan, among them Djamel Beghal, who was later convicted for plotting to bomb the American embassy in Paris.[30] From 1999 to 2001 Qatada 'played a leading role in the UK in raising funds and providing logistic support and recruits for the Arab *mujahideen* in Chechnya'.[31] To this end he would travel around the country, entourage in tow, making speeches and taking collections.[32] According to Jordanian authorities at the time, Qatada's activities extended to plotting attacks for which he was convicted and sentenced *in absentia* to life imprisonment in April 1999, followed by another 15 years in September 2000 for his alleged part in a conspiracy to carry out attacks in Jordan at the turn of the millennium.[33,34] In the UK, events gradually began to catch up with him when in February 2001 his home was raided as part of the investigation into Abu Doha. Police discovered £170,000 in cash in mixed currencies, including an envelope marked for the Chechen *mujahideen*.[35] However, there was insufficient evidence to press charges and Qatada was set free. His time would finally run out only after 9/11, but by then much damage had been done. Tapes of Qatada's sermons were even found in the Hamburg apartment of 9/11 hijacker Mohammed Atta[36] and many others were inspired by his words. Of particular note was an Egyptian named Kamel Mustafa Kamel, whom he described as 'the best student he ever had'.[37]

Kamel would eventually rise to infamy as Abu Hamza, the 'hook-handed cleric', but before coming to Britain in 1979 he led a secular life. It was not until the mid-1980s, while studying civil engineering in Brighton, that he took a renewed interest in Islam and in 1987 (newly acquired British passport in hand) he went on the *hajj* to Mecca. On his travels he met Abdullah Azzam, the patriarch of the Afghan jihad, and from then on became increasingly immersed in militant Islam.[38] From 1991 to 1993 he and his family lived in Afghanistan, returning to the UK only after he lost an eye and both hands in an explosion, the true nature of which is surrounded by speculation. As fate would have it, this was the same year that Abu Qatada arrived in the UK and Hamza was soon taking lessons from him, absorbing his twisted interpretation of the Quran.[39]

A year later Hamza founded his own group, the Supporters of Sharia (SoS) and in 1995 he spent time in Bosnia before taking up a position at a mosque in Luton, a town which has struggled with Islamist extremism ever since.[40] But it was at Finsbury Park mosque in North London where he settled in 1997 that Abu Hamza made his mark as a leading figure in the Great British jihad. Under his leadership the mosque would serve as the focal point of Islamist extremism in the UK, attracting a veritable who's who of terrorists from far and wide. Among them were al-Qaeda facilitators and fundraisers, several prospective suicide bomb plotters, a mixture of aspiring and veteran *mujahideen*, jihadi preachers, criminals, murderers, and future Guantanamo detainees. Visitors included Abu Qatada; Abu Doha; Djamel Beghal; Parisian 9/11 conspirator Zacarias Moussaoui; Nizar Trabelsi from Tunisia (who 'begged' bin Laden for the chance to become a martyr[41]); shoe-bomb plotters Richard Reid and Saajid Badat; the virulent, Jamaican-born ideologue Abdullah El-Faisal, and many, many more. It was the hub of a bustling network where established and budding militants alike would come to listen to Abu Hamza's hate-filled sermons, to socialize and make connections. It was also awash with criminal activity and in particular functioned as a trading post in stolen goods, cloned credit cards, and forged identity documents.[42]

Like his mentor Qatada and other UK-based jihadi preachers, Abu Hamza's influence was not limited to London. He also conducted 'outreach', touring the country and lecturing on the need to fight the enemies of Islam, which earned him a ban from mosques in Burnley in 1998 after two young locals, Afrasiab Ilyas and Arshad Miaz, were subsequently killed in Afghanistan.[43] Nevertheless, Finsbury Park remained very much Hamza's base of operations and although he was best known for his rhetorical skills, he also utilized his position at the mosque to act as a facilitator of terrorist activities overseas. The first real signs of this began to emerge in October 1998 when the SoS newsletter featured a warning to the US and other 'unbelievers' to leave Yemen or suffer the consequences.[44] On December 23, a contingent of six individuals from Finsbury Park — including one of Hamza's bodyguards and his stepson — was arrested in Yemen in possession of a stockpile of firearms and explosives. The situation escalated five days later when sixteen Western tourists were kidnapped by a group calling itself the 'Islamic Army of the Aden' whose leader, 'Abu Hassan', demanded the release of the arrested men. Before taking the hostages Hassan had spoken with Abu Hamza by satellite phone and he continued to seek the cleric's advice as events unfolded.[45] The crisis ended messily the next day when Yemeni troops intervened but the saga continued when another four Finsbury Park regulars (this time including Hamza's son) were arrested in Yemen in January. Ultimately, it was revealed that prior to events in the Arabian Peninsula, Hamza had been organizing physical training exercises in the mountains of Wales but wanted to provide a more authentic experience involving actual firearms. He had sent the London operatives to receive 'real' training from Hassan and his men in exchange for payment and even supplied the satellite phone and airtime used in the kidnapping operation.[46] At the time of their arrest, Hamza's men had been in the final stages of preparing for a potentially deadly wave of terrorist attacks to take place on Christmas Day.[47] All involved in Yemen were convicted but UK authorities refused to extradite Hamza to stand trial and he continued to operate with impunity.

Towards the end of 1999 the irrepressible ideologue embarked on another scheme to find a suitable training ground for his recruits — this time in the US. The plan was hatched by a Seattle entrepreneur and convert to Islam named Earnest Ujaama who began visiting Finsbury Park around the time that the Yemeni project was falling apart. In November 1999 Hamza dispatched one of his star pupils, Haroon Rashid Aswat (originally from Dewsbury in West Yorkshire), along with Oussama Abdullah Kassir from Sweden, to assess the proposed training site in Bly, Oregon. The location was quickly deemed unsuitable and the plan abandoned, but before leaving, Hamza's men distributed bomb-making instructions and taught a small number of recruits in hand-to-hand combat.[48]

Undeterred by such failures, Hamza pressed on and a year later he sent Ujaama and a fresh British recruit named Feroz Abbasi to Northwest Pakistan to make contact with the Taliban. Whether the American achieved his mission (to curry favor with the militants by offering them cash[49]) is unclear. Abbasi on the other hand succeeded in crossing into Afghanistan where he trained at al-Qaeda's al-Farouq camp and volunteered to be a suicide bomber before being captured and taken to Guantanamo Bay.[50] It would later become apparent that Finsbury Park mosque was a springboard for many careers in Islamist terrorism, and that Abu Hamza played a substantial role in nurturing an environment in Britain where militant Islam could flourish. Along with Omar Bakri Mohammed, Abu Qatada, Abdullah El-Faisal, and others, he was instrumental in earning the

British capital its derogatory nickname 'Londonistan' and it is no exaggeration to say that combined, these four preachers exerted an ideological influence that affected practically every Islamist terrorist in Britain and many abroad for more than a decade.

As the 1990s drew to a close, Britons had already made a significant contribution to the global jihad. Numerous individuals had lost their lives in Bosnia, Chechnya, Afghanistan, and Kashmir, including at least two by suicide attack (the first being Khalid Shahid from Birmingham, who blew himself up in Afghanistan in 1996[51]). British residents had helped to facilitate the 1995 metro bombings in France; they helped coordinate the 1998 US embassy bombings in Africa; and from 1999 to 2001 Abu Doha and his associates oversaw plots to attack Los Angeles airport, a Christmas market in France, and the US embassy in Rome.[52] Furthermore, the UK itself was becoming a viable target. This became apparent in November 2000 when police arrested Moinul Abedin in Birmingham. Originally from Bangladesh but raised in the UK, Abedin (and an apparent accomplice who was later cleared) had been manufacturing the high explosive HMTD[53] and was in possession of a cornucopia of incriminating material in addition to a martyrdom note making reference to *mujahideen*.[54] Although this has since been referred to as al-Qaeda's first plot in the UK, details to substantiate this have never been made public and the significance of the event was almost certainly overlooked at the time. Nevertheless, the depth of British involvement in the global jihad would become increasingly clear in the aftermath of September 11, 2001.

2001–2005

It took just 48 hours after the attacks on America for an al-Qaeda operative with ties to the UK to be arrested. Nizar Trabelsi, a student of both Abu Qatada and Abu Hamza, and reportedly recruited in the UK by Djamel Beghal, was arrested in Brussels on September 13, 2001.[55] He would eventually be convicted (along with another Finsbury Park regular named Mohammed Amor Sliti[56]) of planning a suicide attack on a NATO airbase housing US soldiers in Belgium.

Information leading to Trabelsi's arrest had likely come from his mentor, Beghal, who had been detained in Dubai on his way back to Europe from Afghanistan in July. Next in line to fall was Kamel Daoudi, another student of Qatada's based in Paris who went on the run after hearing of Beghal's arrest. Police tracked Daoudi down to Leicester in the UK where they found him taking refuge with Brahim Benmerzouga and Baghdad Meziane, a pair of fellow Algerians and illegal immigrants who were running a fraud and terrorism facilitation network worth hundreds of thousands of pounds.[57] Following their arrests on September 25, Daoudi was extradited to France while Baghdad and Meziane became the first people in Britain to be convicted of terrorism offenses in support of al-Qaeda.[58]

The two Leicester-based operatives, by no coincidence, had also been in regular contact with Abu Qatada in London.[59] The cleric's reign, however, was swiftly coming to an end and in October 2001 his assets were frozen. He then went into hiding following the introduction of the Anti-Terrorism, Crime and Security Act in December, until being traced ten months later to an address in Bermondsey, South London. He was detained on grounds of national security pending deportation to his native Jordan and would spend the best part of the next decade in custody while his case was being fought in the courts.[60]

More disturbing still was the arrest of another of Beghal's recruits, the 'shoe-bomber' Richard Reid, who attempted to detonate explosives hidden in his trainers on board an American Airlines flight from Paris to Miami on December 22, 2001. Unsurprisingly, Reid's trail led yet again back to the Finsbury Park mosque. But the fact that he was a British-born convert, radicalized in London before becoming a suicide operative for al-Qaeda, was the clearest indication yet that Islamist terrorists were being home grown in the UK. This was seemingly confirmed by the successive capture of Britons in Afghanistan and Pakistan under highly dubious circumstances. Over a 12-month period beginning in late 2001, a total of 18 former residents of the UK (including 7 citizens by birth) were detained and subsequently transferred to Guantanamo Bay.[61] All would eventually be released without charge and some even received compensation, but this was primarily a result of the flawed legal basis of their detention rather than because they were exonerated. The truth of their actions will ultimately never be known but if the allegations against them are even partially true (as some appear to be), they are indeed further evidence of the British appetite for violent jihad. Abu Hamza's young recruit, Feroz Abbasi, remained defiant throughout his captivity and openly declared in 2004 that 'I actually left Britain to either join the Taleban [sic] or fight for the sake of Allah in Kashmir'.[62] Others made detailed confessions only to later retract them. For example, Binyam Mohammed, an Ethiopian who had spent time at Abu Qatada's Baker Street mosque, admitted (apparently under duress) to meeting with the 9/11 mastermind Khalid Sheikh Mohammed and being teamed up with American Jose Padilla to conduct attacks in the US.[63]

As the number of British jihadis arrested abroad continued to rise, UK authorities stepped up their efforts to dismantle the networks at home. On February 18, 2002, the radical cleric Abdullah El-Faisal was arrested and later convicted of stirring up racial hatred and soliciting murder after tapes of his sermons were discovered in which he repeatedly urged his audience to kill non-Muslims.[64] Ten months later, police received intelligence that a group of Algerians with ties to Finsbury Park mosque were planning a terrorist attack in Britain using homemade chemical weapons. A subsequent raid on a North London flat led to the discovery of detailed instructions for manufacturing poison and what appeared to be traces of the deadly toxin ricin.[65] The apparent ringleader, an illegal Algerian immigrant named Kamel Bourgass, had been sleeping at Abu Hamza's mosque the night that the flat was raided and disappeared the next day. He was found by chance in Manchester on January 14, 2003, but failing to realize the danger that he posed, police neglected to handcuff him while they searched the property. Desperate to avoid capture, Bourgass suddenly launched a violent assault, stabbing DC Stephen Oake to death with a kitchen knife before being subdued.[66] Six days later, police finally moved in on Finsbury Park mosque.

Inside the house of worship were found an array of knives, blank-firing guns, chemical protection suits, military paraphernalia, and hundreds of forged documents and credit cards.[67] Abu Hamza was relieved of his duties as imam but continued to preach on the streets outside, capitalizing on the added drama and publicity. However, it was not until May 27, 2004, pursuant to a US extradition request, that Britain's most infamous proponent of violent jihad was taken into custody. Soon afterwards British authorities brought their own charges against him and in 2006 Hamza was convicted (like El-Faisal before him) of inciting racial hatred and soliciting murder in addition to possessing an extensive manual of terrorism techniques, aptly titled the *Encyclopedia of the Afghani Jihad.*[68] He would remain in British custody until October 2012 when his extradition to the US was ultimately approved and in January 2015 he was sentenced to life in prison.[69]

The tide was also beginning to turn for Omar Bakri Mohammed and AM. The Syrian preacher had been more vocal and outspoken than ever since 9/11, and evidence of the group's subversive influence had been mounting. Besides the increasingly belligerent rhetoric at home, members of AM were actively involved in militancy abroad. At least five of their affiliates were killed in Afghanistan in 2001 and the group's office in Lahore appeared to function as a way-station for British recruits on their way to jihad (including a number of those detained in Guantanamo).[70] Indeed, members of the group openly acknowledged this at the time and according to one of them, who was interviewed in November 2001 following a bout on the front line, 'there were around 150 Al-Muhajiroun members, including support staff, in Afghanistan'.[71] Despite this, AM was allowed to continue operating and further ties to terrorism soon emerged. On April 30, 2003, Asif Hanif from Hounslow in West London blew himself up at a bar in Tel Aviv, killing three people. Hanif's would-be accomplice, Omar Khan Sharif from Derby, was found dead several days later and it soon came to light that both men had been students of Bakri Mohammed's, as well as visitors to Finsbury Park mosque.[72] A year after the attack they appeared in a pre-recorded video released by Hamas in which they vilified Israel and called on God to punish the leaders of America and Great Britain.[73]

Islamist anger at the British government came to a boil soon after troops set foot in Iraq and nascent plans to attack the UK were already underway by the time of Hanif's operation. Unsurprisingly, AM was again at the center of events, this time largely thanks to the initiative of an American named Mohammed Junaid Babar. Babar had joined AM in New York and re-located to Pakistan shortly after 9/11, traveling via the UK where he met with Bakri Mohammed.[74] He stayed at the group's office in Lahore until 2002 when he moved into his own house and embarked on a project to establish a militant training camp with a group of British jihadis led by Omar Khyam from Crawley. Members of Khyam's group had met one another at AM meetings and other venues on the outskirts of London and were already part of a UK-based terrorism facilitation network with links to senior al-Qaeda operative Abdul Hadi al-Iraqi.[75] However, they wanted a more active role. In the early part of 2003 members of the group decided that they wanted to conduct a terrorist attack at home in the UK and from June to August that year they trained with explosives, as arranged for by Babar, in Malakand in Northwest Pakistan. Back in the UK, Khyam *et al.* purchased 600 kg of ammonium nitrate fertilizer and discussed multiple possible targets for attack, including shopping malls and nightclubs, which would maximize the number of casualties. They maintained coded communication with Babar and other members of the plot and in late February 2004 things appeared to gather pace when they received a visit from Mohammad Momin Khawaja, a Canadian jihadist they had met in Malakand who had agreed to help by building a remote control detonator.[76] Unwilling to take any risks, security services switched the fertilizer for an inert substance and arrests were then made at the end of March before Khyam and his men could put their plans into action.

Despite the recurring discovery of AM activists involved in terrorism, the organization's role appeared to be ideological and indirect, rather than hands-on and operational. There were certainly never any allegations that the likes of Khyam were acting on AM's behalf, and Bakri Mohammed's ability to tread a fine line between inflammatory rhetoric and actively breaking the law undoubtedly contributed to the group's longevity. British authorities were also faced with more pressing concerns. Hot on the heels of the Khyam investigation, a second plot to attack the UK was discovered. On June

13, 2004, an al-Qaeda agent named Mohammed Naeem Noor Khan was arrested in Pakistan and an examination of his laptop revealed a highly detailed set of plans to conduct multiple, simultaneous bombings in the British capital.[77] The ensuing investigation led back to the UK where the plans had originated with a group of militants under the leadership of a veteran jihadist named Dhiren Barot. A former Hindu convert to Islam, Barot had come to the UK as an infant and had been involved in violent jihad from as early as 1995 when he attended a militant training camp in Kashmir. In the late 1990s he served as a lead instructor at a camp in Afghanistan and prior to 9/11 he was sent by Khalid Sheikh Mohammed to conduct surveillance of potential targets in New York and Washington DC.[78] After 9/11 Barot had decided that an attack in the UK was more feasible and with the help of his team, spent the next three years methodically casing targets and researching novel ways to cause as much death and destruction as possible. Discovery of the plot was largely a matter of luck after Barot had gone to Pakistan seeking the blessing of the al-Qaeda leadership and had handed out electronic copies of the group's plans.[79] Following an intensive surveillance operation, British police finally brought the conspiracy to an end on August 3, 2004.

By comparison, the coming months were relatively calm and in May 2005 the Joint Terrorism Analysis Centre (newly established in 2003) downgraded the terrorism threat to the country from 'severe-general' to 'substantial'. The sentiment was echoed by the Director General of MI5, Dame Eliza Manningham-Buller, who on July 6, 2005 reassured a group of senior MPs that there were no imminent attacks in the pipeline.[80] The next day four British jihadis blew themselves up on the London Underground and a double-decker bus in the center of the city, killing 52 people.

The bombers were quickly identified as Mohammed Siddique Khan, Shehzad Tanweer, Jermaine Lindsay, and Hasib Hussain, all British citizens who had radicalized and come together as a group while living in West Yorkshire. Furthermore, their lives had intersected at numerous times with those of known terrorists in the UK and Pakistan, and the security services had come agonizingly close to identifying them prior to the attacks. The ringleader, Khan, had been photographed (but not identified) at a domestic training exercise attended by approximately 40 suspected extremists back in January 2001.[81] That summer, he attended a training camp in Kashmir run by Harakat ul-Mujahideen (HuM) along with another British extremist from West Yorkshire named Waheed Ali.[82] Khan was also in contact with Asif Hanif and Omar Sharif[83] and in 2002 he reportedly paid a visit to Finsbury Park mosque looking for fellow Yorkshireman Haroon Rashid Aswat.[84] By 2003 he was in contact with Mohammed Qayum Khan, who was running the facilitation network in which Omar Khyam was involved.[85] Then in the summer of that year, Mohammed Siddique Khan was present at the training camp in Malakand[86] and in February and March of 2004 he and Shehzad Tanweer visited Khyam and his men in Crawley. By that time the Crawley plotters were under heavy surveillance but despite repeated efforts to identify Khan and Tanweer, there was no indication at the time that they were planning terrorist attacks of their own.[87]

In fact the decision to attack the UK was not seemingly made until during another trip to Pakistan from November 2004 to February 2005.[88] Details remain murky but it appears that there, a jihadi facilitator named Rashid Rauf (a fellow Brit who had left the UK in 2002) put Khan and Tanweer in touch with Abu Ubaidah al-Masri of al-Qaeda who convinced them to conduct a suicide attack and arranged for further training in explosives.[89] Before returning home, they recorded martyrdom videos at a house in Islamabad, supervised by Rauf. Then, once back in Britain they reconvened with Lindsay and Hussain and from there the plot moved quickly forward. Keeping in close contact with Rauf in Pakistan,[90] they rented properties in April and May which they used to mix the explosives and on June 28 they conducted a practice run of the operation.[91] Nine days later the plan went ahead and the UK finally awoke to the reality that had been festering within for years.

Post-7/7

The British government had of course taken significant steps to strengthen the country's counterterrorism (CT) capabilities well before the London bombings. However, the attacks had a galvanizing effect, which was compounded by the fact that just two weeks later an almost identical assault was attempted by a second group that had somehow managed to slip under the authorities' radar.[92] Within months, new legislation was passed making it an offense to encourage or glorify acts of terrorism, among other newly proscribed offenses, and renewed efforts were made to devise and implement a more comprehensive national CT strategy.

No doubt realizing that life in Britain was about to become more difficult, Omar Bakri Mohammed left the UK for Lebanon in August 2005 and the Home Secretary promptly announced that he was banned from returning 'on the grounds that his presence [was] not conducive to the public good'.[93] By this time Bakri Mohammed had already announced the official dissolution of AM but almost identical organizations sprang up in its place. Two of these new groups, al-Ghurabaa and the Saved Sect, were banned under the Terrorism Act of 2006 and subsequent reincarnations have likewise been outlawed, among them Islam4UK, Call to Submission, Islamic Path, London School of Sharia, and Muslims Against Crusades, as well as the original AM.[94] Despite this, AM's legacy lives on. Bakri Mohammed's followers remain active and, understanding that they now exist in a far more restrictive environment, over the years they have tried to adapt their message (at least in public) in an effort to remain within the provisions of the law.[95] Nevertheless, individuals affiliated with AM splinter groups continue to be involved in a variety of terrorist activities in Britain including incitement of terrorism, fundraising, domestic training, planning attacks, and murder. Indeed, as many as one in five terrorism convictions in the UK are reportedly linked to AM and Britain has yet to find an effective solution to Bakri Mohammed's enduring subversive influence.[96]

Others whose presence in the UK had previously been tolerated were likewise pursued with fresh enthusiasm after the London bombings and have been dealt with rather more decisively. The Libyan Islamic Fighting Group (LIFG) had been active in the UK since the 1990s and several members of the group had previously been identified as potential threats. For example, in May 2000 police in

Manchester discovered the now infamous 'al-Qaeda manual' at the abandoned home of Anas al-Liby, a key suspect in the 1998 East African embassy bombings.[97] Of equal concern, in 2004 it came to light that the former deputy *emir* of the LIFG (and sometime resident of London), Sami al-Saadi aka Abu Munthir, acted as a facilitator in the Operation Crevice case.[98] In fact the LIFG had been a designated terrorist organization since 2001[99] but had somehow still managed to construct a web of fundraising enterprises in Britain including a charity named the Sanabel Relief Agency and several property companies with offices in London, Manchester, Birmingham, Liverpool, and Middlesbrough.[100] Limited measures to contain the group had been taken in 2004 as UK relations with Libya began to thaw[101] but it was not until October 2005 that the LIFG was finally added to the list of proscribed organizations in the UK[102] and more concerted efforts were made to detain, prosecute, and deport the remaining ringleaders.

In addition to dealing with established networks of extremists, British security services have been faced with a new and ever more diverse range of cases involving individuals who largely mobilized after the invasion of Iraq. For many members of this newer generation, the Internet has taken on greater significance as a means of acquiring and sharing knowledge, and sometimes as a way of establishing connections with fellow 'virtual travelers' and even foreign terrorist organizations. The overlapping stories of Younis Tsouli and Aabid Khan are illustrative. Tsouli, a young Moroccan immigrant who came to London to study computing, began his criminal career as a hacker and was quickly swept into the world of online jihad. Calling himself '*Irhabi* [Terrorist] 007', he soon made a name for himself by facilitating the distribution of online videos made by al-Qaeda in Iraq, earning direct praise from their media wing which had been struggling to overcome the technical challenges involved.[103] His stature continued to grow as an administrator for a popular jihadi forum called 'At-Tibyan' which he ran along with Khan, a prolific online jihadist from Bradford who amassed one of the most extensive collections of jihadi propaganda and training materials ever found in Britain.[104]

At-Tibyan served not only as a jihadi resource library but also as a meeting place that — not unlike the Malakand training camp of 2003 — brought together aspiring jihadists from around the world. Khan in particular was active in nurturing connections with counterparts in North America who were looking for someone who could arrange training in Pakistan.[105] He met with a handful of individuals in person in Toronto in March 2005 followed by two separate (and ultimately fruitless) meetings in Pakistan with Syed Haris Ahmed from Atlanta and later with Jahmaal James from Toronto.[106] Tsouli, meanwhile, was working with Tariq al-Daour and Waseem Mughal in the UK in a highly lucrative online credit card fraud scheme which they were using to purchase website domains and equipment for *mujahideen* overseas.[107] However, it was Tsouli's connections to a Swedish–Bosnian jihadist named Mirsad Bektsevic living in Sarajevo that led to the unraveling of the network. Bektsevic and two others were planning suicide attacks in Europe and were arrested on October 19, 2005 in possession of explosives and firearms. An examination of the group's phone records in turn led investigators to an address in London.[108] Two days later police finally apprehended 'Terrorist 007'and by mid-2006 the remainder of the network was likewise in custody.

The discovery of the Tsouli/Khan network highlighted the growing potential of the Internet, both as a networking tool for jihadis and as an essential avenue of investigation for CT. Indeed, there is little doubt that the Internet plays an important role in sustaining the global jihad. Nevertheless, virtual networks have not entirely replaced those of a more physical nature, and one of the most striking features of Islamist terrorism in the UK has been the continued ability of individuals to establish physical contact with terrorists overseas, particularly in Northwest Pakistan. In fact, when Aabid Khan returned to Britain from his last trip there in June 2006 and was finally arrested, his clothes tested positive for traces of explosives, suggesting that he had personally taken part in some kind of training even if he did not arrange for others to do so. In other cases, connections to terrorists in Pakistan have been far more pronounced, among them perhaps the most ambitious terrorist plot worldwide since 9/11.

Operation Overt became a matter of public knowledge on August 9, 2006 when police conducted a wave of arrests across London, Buckinghamshire, and Birmingham, bringing to light a conspiracy to destroy as many as ten passenger planes in mid-flight using suicide operatives armed with liquid explosives. The ringleader of the plot, Abdulla Ahmed Ali, had been known to security services for some time as a result of his extremist associations (among them Muktar Said Ibrahim, the leader of the failed 21/7 bombings[109]). However, the true nature of his activities was largely unknown until the summer of 2006 when he was returning to the UK from Pakistan and a covert search of his luggage revealed a suspicious number of batteries and large amounts of a soft drink powder — items which in the wrong hands could be used for manufacturing explosives.[110]

Investigators were right to be suspicious. Sometime previously Ali had made contact with Rashid Rauf — the British-Pakistani operative who facilitated both of the 2005 London bomb plots.[111] Ali had been in Pakistan from August 2004 to January 2005, overlapping with time spent there by Mohammed Siddique Khan and Shehzad Tanweer as well as Muktar Ibrahim, who all received explosives training during that period. There is no evidence to show that that the respective plot leaders trained together. However, like the others, Ali was introduced by Rauf to Abu Ubaidah al-Masri, and like them he would learn how to make hydrogen peroxide-based bombs using organic material (in this case powdered soft drink) to fuel the explosion.[112] By the summer of 2006 (by which time two further trips to Pakistan had taken place) the liquid bomb plot was beginning to take shape.

While Britain was marking the first anniversary of the London bombings, Ali and his men were recording martyrdom videos and experimenting with explosives in an East London flat. As July gave way to August, Ali was in 'near constant' contact with Rauf in Pakistan.[113] On August 6, Ali and one of his most trusted lieutenants, Assad Ali Sarwar, met with a friend of Rauf's from Birmingham named Mohammed Gulzar, who had recently flown into Britain on a false passport and was suspected of having been sent to oversee the final stages of the plot.[114] Three days later Rauf was arrested in

Pakistan at the request of the US and, fearing that the investigation had been compromised, British authorities were forced to move in, eventually securing ten convictions including eight life sentences.

Since 2006, few terrorism cases in the UK have come close to the liquid bomb plot in terms of the sophistication and the scale of planned destruction. In part, this may be thanks to the fact that both of the primary facilitators of that conspiracy are now dead. Abu Ubaidah al-Masri is believed to have died from hepatitis in December 2007[115] and Rashid Rauf — who promptly escaped from jail in Pakistan — was reportedly killed in a drone strike in November 2008.[116] Indeed, Rauf's significance should not be underestimated. Not only did he provide a much-needed link between Western jihadis and al-Qaeda in the first place, but he clearly played an important advisory role in at least two of the three major bomb plots in Britain in which he was involved (perhaps even being the critical factor behind the success of the 7/7 bombings[117]). Moreover, prior to his death Rauf is known to have met with other Western volunteers seeking to join al-Qaeda in the Afghanistan–Pakistan border region (including Moez Garsallaoui from Belgium and Bryant Vinas from the US[118]), suggesting that he was intent on continuing his role as a facilitator of violent jihad against the West.

Nevertheless, the plan to destroy transatlantic airliners was certainly not the last terrorism case in the UK to show signs of foreign involvement and Rauf has not been the only British jihadi of consequence. Other notable cases have included, for example, Rangzieb and Habib Ahmed, a pair of experienced jihadists from Manchester with membership in both HuM and al-Qaeda. Rangzieb in particular had worked closely with senior members of al-Qaeda and before being captured in Pakistan in August 2006 (briefly sharing a prison cell with Rauf[119]) he had been entrusted with notebooks containing the contact details of other key operatives written in invisible ink.[120] In another case uncovered in January 2007, an individual from Birmingham named Parviz Khan had been running a supply network for militants in Pakistan before hatching a scheme to kidnap and behead a British Muslim soldier.[121] In April 2009, police disrupted what they believe was yet another al-Qaeda-directed plot to attack the UK, this time involving Pakistani nationals who had entered the country using student visas.[122] In December of the same year, a Jordanian 'triple agent' named Abu Dujana blew himself up at a CIA base in Khost, Afghanistan, killing eight people. Later it would emerge that the mastermind behind the attack had been a UK jihadi named Omar al-Brittani who was a member of the Tehrik e-Taliban Pakistan (TTP).[123]

As time has gone on, Islamist extremists from Britain have continued to demonstrate their ability to make contact with terrorists in Pakistan who can provide much-needed training with explosives. The Operation Pitsford group, arrested in Birmingham in September 2011 is another notable example. In accordance with a now-familiar pattern, the leaders of the plot spent several months abroad learning their deadly tradecraft before returning home to conduct attacks, with the goal of carrying out multiple suicide bombings. In a slight twist to the usual story, however, their handlers instructed them not only to murder and maim, but also to pass on their bomb-making skills so that others in the UK could do the same.[124] This is consistent with increasing encouragement from al-Qaeda for Western jihadis to be more self-reliant, rather than risking the security of the beleaguered core of the network. Even so, these pleas appear to have fallen on deaf ears to a large extent, and contact with foreign militants continues to be a highly sought reward.

International linkages, of course have not been restricted exclusively to South Asia, even if connections to other countries have been somewhat less developed. The insurgency in Iraq beginning in 2003 was a source of anger and inspiration for British jihadis, but generally much less accessible to them for operational purposes. Nevertheless, there was still a small number of suspected Iraqi fundraisers and recruiters active in Britain[125] and at least two suicide attacks in Iraq were perpetrated by former UK residents in 2003 and 2005.[126] Possible links to militants in Iraq also emerged in June 2007 following the attempted attacks in London and Glasgow by Bilal Abdulla and Kafeel Ahmed, a pair of doctors-turned-terrorists who had been working for the National Health Service. Both men had made 'wills' which referred to an unknown *emir*, and Abdulla (who was born in the UK but raised in Iraq) had written a tribute to the 'rewarding' time he claimed to have spent with Iraqi *mujahideen* in the summer of 2006.[127] Finally, Stockholm suicide bomber Taimour Abdulwahab al-Abdaly, who radicalized whilst living in Luton, is known to have visited the Middle East on several occasions and reportedly trained with al-Qaeda affiliates in Mosul.[128]

Somalia too has attracted its fair share of recruits from the UK, most notably Ahmed Hussein Ahmed, a 21-year old Somali asylum seeker living in London who blew himself up at a checkpoint in Baidoa in October 2007.[129] Numerous others are also known or suspected to have joined with al-Shabaab, including the widow of 7/7 bomber Jermaine Lindsay — a British-born convert to Islam named Samantha Lewthwaite who at the time of writing is on the run, having been charged with terrorism offenses in Kenya.[130]

Others still have been drawn to Yemen in search of al-Qaeda in the Arabian Peninsula (AQAP). Umar Farouk Abdulmutallab is a case in point. Having radicalized as a student living in London, the young Nigerian then spent seven months at the University of Wollongong in Dubai before making his way to Sanaa in August 2009.[131] Thereafter he met with Anwar al-Awlaki and trained with AQAP before embarking on his now infamous suicide mission to bring down an airplane over Detroit on December 25, 2009.[132] Two months later, in another case, police in the UK arrested Rajib Karim, a computer expert from Bangladesh who had enlisted Awlaki's help online in looking for ways to exploit his job with British Airways as a means of carrying out yet another airborne attack.[133] Such desire to forge ties with jihadis in Yemen corresponded with Awlaki's rise to ascendency as the dominant English-speaking voice of al-Qaeda. Nevertheless, British citizens have tried to make their way there even after the influential American was killed in September 2011 and his teachings continue to be found on the hard drives and cellphones of British terrorists.[134]

However, not all British jihadis have been in contact with foreign terrorist organizations. In many cases, connections to *mujahideen* overseas have been tenuous or lacking altogether and the level of foreign direction or support has been questionable. Indeed, British militants appear to be largely self-organized and self-financing, and in many cases their efforts have been decidedly amateurish. For instance, since the London bombings of 2005, there have been many planned attacks in the UK but only five have actually been completed as of early 2015, and only one of these was particularly successful.

The 21/7 bombings of course failed despite Ibrahim's training in Pakistan. The June 2007 attacks in London and Glasgow also failed, and although Bilal Abdulla may well have met with insurgents in Iraq, there is no evidence to suggest that he received any operational support from them. Next was the May 2008 attempted suicide bombing of a restaurant in Exeter. The perpetrator, Nicky Reilly, had apparently been influenced by two individuals in Pakistan whom he met online, but the attack was unsophisticated and ineffectual. Two years later, Roshonara Choudhry (who was acting entirely by herself) succeeded in stabbing MP Stephen Timms but was unable to kill him. The string of failures finally ended on May 22, 2013 when two British-born Nigerians, Michael 'Mujahid' Adebolajo and Michael Adebowale, ran over a soldier named Lee Rigby as he walked down the street in Woolwich, London before leaping from their car and hacking him to death. A former student of Bakri Mohammed's,[135] Adebolajo in particular was involved with Islamist extremists for several years prior to the attack and in 2010 he had been arrested in Kenya on suspicion of trying to join al-Shabaab.[136] Yet there are no indications that the attack was directed from abroad and the primitive *modus operandi* suggests a lack of such organizational support.

The Rigby murder thus appears to be indicative of an emerging trend among British jihadis, who seem to be increasingly willing to conduct attacks using whatever means are readily available even if it is likely to result in fewer casualties. This is consistent with a decreased ability to make the kind of connections with overseas militants that they would like, which in turn reduces their chances of being able to pull off large-scale, sophisticated attacks using explosives. Nevertheless, it is clear that even crude attacks can have significant repercussions. The savagery and brazenness of the Woolwich attack was enough to guarantee widespread publicity, but the fact that Adebolajo and Adebowale then stood waiting for armed police to show up, rather than fleeing the scene, gave them an ideal opportunity to further harness the power of media. By encouraging passersby to take their picture and record them offering justification for the attack, they ensured that their message would be broadcast around the world, thus magnifying the impact of their actions.

Just three days later a French soldier was stabbed in the neck in Paris in a suspected copycat attack[137] and before the week was out, a group of 'fanatical' Muslim prisoners, likewise believed to have been inspired by Rigby's murder, seriously assaulted a guard at a maximum security prison in Yorkshire.[138] Within Britain, there was also an immediate reaction from the far-right, including inflammatory marches by the English Defence League (EDL) and the vandalizing of several mosques. Indeed, right-wing backlash further reinforced the jihadi narrative that Islam is under attack in the UK and exposed a simmering sectarian rivalry that may yet come to the boil in explosive fashion.[139] This was narrowly avoided in June 2012 when a routine traffic stop led to the discovery of a group of jihadis from Birmingham who had set their sights on attacking the EDL using an improvised explosive device (IED) and an assortment of sawn-off shotguns and knives.[140]

The fact that such fall-out can be generated within a few days from such an unsophisticated attack is quite remarkable and there is a good possibility that others in the UK will yet try to emulate it. Certainly, this was on the mind of 19-year-old Brusthom Ziamani, who was arrested on the streets of London in August 2014 carrying a hammer and a knife wrapped in an Islamic flag.[141] Radicalized by former members of AM and apparently obsessed with Rigby's killers, he was later convicted for planning an almost identical assault.[142] At the same time, planned — and potentially deadly — 'spectacular' attacks are hardly a thing of the past and British police reportedly foil a plot on the scale of the 7/7 bombings every year.[143] Moreover, from 2011 to 2012, there was a 60% increase in terrorism-related arrests,[144] and as the conflicts in Syria and Iraq have mushroomed, so too has the number of UK residents becoming involved in terrorism. Hundreds of British jihadis have made their way to the Middle East and in 2014 alone more than 200 terror-related arrests were made, placing a massive burden on law enforcement.[145] Although most of these individuals have so far been focused on overseas activities, several domestic attack plots have also been uncovered and in August 2014 the UK terror alert level was raised to 'severe'. Domestic attack cases have so far included an alleged plot to assassinate former Prime Minister Tony Blair[146] and a plan hatched by four men — who had pledged allegiance to the 'Islamic State' (IS) — to murder British police officers and members of the armed services.[147]

These developments have unfolded despite vast investment aimed at broadening and strengthening the UK's ability to counter terrorism, including controversial punitive tools such as terrorism prevention and investigation measures (TPIMs)[148] as well as arguably one of the most advanced 'soft' CT strategies in the Western hemisphere. Whilst it would be naïve to expect a problem that took decades to develop to simply disappear overnight, such persistence in the face of adversity clearly signifies a need for improved understanding of the nature of the issue confronting us. Whilst some highly commendable studies have been conducted to this end,[149] there is still a need for further research and in particular greater attention to change over time as well as international comparison. In the chapters that follow, the US and UK will be analyzed and compared on several dimensions, including background variables, operational behaviors, and features of investigations, followed by the summary and conclusions.

Notes

[1]Global Terrorism Database, *Northern Ireland*, Study for Terrorism and Responses to Terrorism, available at: http://www.start.umd.edu/gtd/search/Results.aspx?country=233, accessed August 2, 2012.

[2]Global Terrorism Database, *Great Britain*, Study for Terrorism and Responses to Terrorism, available at: http://www.start.umd.edu/gtd/search/Results.aspx?country=216, accessed August 2, 2012.

[3]For an in-depth account of the evolution of British counterterrorism in relation to Islamist terrorism, see Frank Foley, *Countering Terrorism in Britain and France: Institutions, Norms and the Shadow of the Past* (Cambridge: Cambridge University Press, 2013), Kindle Edition.

[4]Mark Hollingsworth and Nick Fielding, *Defending the Realm: Inside MI5 and the War on Terrorism* (London: André Deutsch, 2003); Sean O'Neill and Daniel McGrory, *The Suicide Factory: Abu Hamza and the Finsbury Park Mosque* (London: HarperCollins, 2006); Alison Pargeter, *The New Frontiers of Jihad: Radical Islam in Europe* (Philadelphia: University of Pennsylvania Press, 2008); Lorenzo Vidino, *Al Qaeda in Europe: The New Battleground of International Jihad* (New York: Prometheus Books, 2006).

[5]Ed Husain, *The Islamist: Why I Became an Islamic Fundamentalist, What I Saw Inside, and Why I Left* (New York: Penguin, 2009), 119.

[6]O'Neill and McGrory, *The Suicide Factory*, 113.

[7]Quintan Wiktorowicz, *Radical Islam Rising: Muslim Extremism in the West* (Lanham, Maryland: Rowman & Littlefield, 2005), 62.

[8]Muhammad al-Shafi'i, 'Incendiary Device Thrown at Military Barracks in West London: Fundamentalists Demonstrate Opposite British Prime Minister's Office in Support of Iraq', *Al-Sharq al-Awsat*, December 18, 1998, available at: http://nl.newsbank.com, accessed May 19, 2010.

[9]'Man Distributed Race Hate Leaflet', *BBC News*, July 22, 2005, available at: http://news.bbc.co.uk/2/hi/uk_news/england/london/4709231.stm, accessed January 15, 2012; 'Muslim Guilty of Inciting Racial Hatred', *BBC News*, May 30, 2002, available at: http://news.bbc.co.uk/2/hi/uk_news/england/1966839.stm, accessed May 19, 2010.

[10]Ian Burrell and David Orr, 'Islamic Militant Backs "Martyred" Suicide Bomber', *The Independent*, December 29, 2000, available at: http://www.highbeam.com/doc/1P2-5115479.html, accessed May 19, 2010.

[11]O'Neill and McGrory, *The Suicide Factory*, 110–111; *United States v. Usama bin Laden et al.* (1998), United States District Court Southern District of New York, S(10) 98 Cr. 1023 (LBS), 22, available at: http://news.corporate.findlaw.com/legalnews/us/terrorism/cases/background.html, accessed May 20, 2010.

[12]Robin Simcox, Hannah Stuart, and Houriya Ahmed, *Islamist Terrorism: The British Connections* (London: The Centre for Social Cohesion, 2010), 426–431.

[13]Lou Kilzer, 'Al-Qaida Cell Dialed via Denver Phone System was Secret Conduit from Arabia to Britain', *Rocky Mountain News*, November 10, 2001, available at: http://www.highbeam.com/doc/1G1-80040625.html, accessed February 12, 2011.

[14]*United States v. Osama bin Laden et al.*, 23.

[15]'Treasury Designates MIRA for Support to Al Qaida', *US Department of the Treasury*, June 14, 2005, http://www.treasury.gov/press-releases/Pages/js2632.aspx, accessed January 17, 2012.

[16]Mark Morris, 'Phone Used in bin Laden's Dealings Linked to Former Student', *Knight Ridder Tribune*, September 20, 2001, http://www.highbeam.com/doc/1G1-78460499.html, accessed January 17, 2012.

[17]*United States v. Osama bin Laden et al.*

[18]*Ibid*, 33, 42, 45.

[19]'Treasury Designates MIRA for Support to Al Qaeda'.

[20]Steven Emerson, 'Fund-Raising Methods and Procedures for International Terrorist Organizations', testimony before the House Committee on Financial Services Subcommittee on Oversight and Investigations, February 12, 2002, available at: http://www.au.af.mil/au/awc/awcgate/congress/021202se.pdf, accessed March 3, 2012.

[21]Chris Hastings and Jessica Berry, 'Muslims in Britain Train for Bin Laden', *The Washington Times*, November 7, 1999, available at: www.nl.newsbank.com, accessed June 3, 2014.

[22]Sean O'Neill, '£180,000 is Discovered in Account of Radical', *The Telegraph*, October 18, 2001, available at: http://www.telegraph.co.uk/news/uknews/1359770/180000-is-discovered-in-account-of-radical.html, accessed May 19, 2010.

[23]Sean O'Neill, '"Architect of Terror" Held in British Jail Cell', *The Telegraph*, January 9, 2003, available at: http://www.telegraph.co.uk/news/uknews/1418311/Architect-of-terror-held-in-British-jail-cell.html, accessed May 19, 2010.

[24]Michael Burleigh and Tom Whitehead, 'Abu Qatada: The Evil Let Loose on Our Streets', *The Telegraph*, February 10, 2012, available at: http://www.telegraph.co.uk/news/uknews/terrorism-in-the-uk/9074335/Abu-Qatada-the-evil-let-loose-on-our-streets.html, accessed February 10, 2012.

[25]*Omar Othman aka Abu Qatada and Secretary of State for the Home Department*, Special Immigration Appeals Commission, Appeal No. SC/15/2005, February 26, 2007, available at: http://www.icj.org/IMG/QATADA.pdf, accessed May 19, 2010, 5–9.

[26]Simcox, Stuart, and Ahmed, *Islamist Terrorism: The British Connections*, 401–402.

[27]Pargeter, *The New Frontiers of Jihad*, 54–55.

[28]*Omar Othman aka Abu Qatada and Secretary of State for the Home Department*, 5–9.

[29]*Ibid.*

[30]*Ibid*, 12.

[31]*Ibid*, 13.

[32]*Jamal Ben Miloud Amar Ajouaou and Secretary of State for the Home Department*, Special Immigration Appeals Commission, Appeal No. SC/10/2002, October 29, 2003, available at: http://www.siac.tribunals.gov.uk/ Documents/outcomes/documents/sc102002ajouaou.pdf, accessed May 19, 2010.

[33]*Omar Othman aka Abu Qatada and Secretary of State for the Home Department*, 49–50.

[34]Qatada was subsequently acquitted of all charges in Jordan and released in 2014.

[35]*Omar Othman aka Abu Qatada and Secretary of State for the Home Department*, 13.

[36]*Ibid*, 7.

[37]O'Neill and McGrory, *The Suicide Factory*, 29.

[38] *Ibid*, 3–20.
[39] *Ibid*, 29.
[40] *Ibid*, 30–33.
[41] Simcox, Stuart, and Ahmed, *Islamist Terrorism: The British Connections*, 340.
[42] O'Neill and McGrory, *The Suicide Factory*, 66–75.
[43] *Ibid*, 59–60.
[44] *Ibid*, 164.
[45] *Ibid*, 156–157, 161.
[46] *Ibid*, 157–158.
[47] *Ibid*, 155–169.
[48] O'Neill and McGrory, *The Suicide Factory*, 185–200; *United States of America v. Mustafa Kamel Mustafa, Oussama Abdallah Kassir and Haroon Rashid Aswat*, Indictment, United States District Court Southern District of New York, Case No. S2 04 Cr.356 (JFK) February 6, 2006, available at: http://www.investigativeproject.org/documents/case_docs/507.pdf, accessed May 20, 2010.
[49] O'Neill and McGrory, *The Suicide Factory*, 196.
[50] Dipesh Gadher, 'From Croydon to Kandahar: A "Martyr's" Story', *The Times*, November 21, 2004, available at: http://www.timesonline.co.uk/tol/news/uk/article393619.ece?print=yes&randnum=1267606050088, accessed June 22, 2010; O'Neill and McGrory, *The Suicide Factory*, 201–214.
[51] O'Neill and McGrory, *The Suicide Factory*, 87.
[52] Lorenzo Vidino, *Al Qaeda in Europe: The New Battleground of International Jihad* (New York: Prometheus Books, 2006), 157–158.
[53] Hexamethylene triperoxide diamine.
[54] 'Martyr Note Found under Bed of Bomb Accused', *The Birmingham Post*, February 14, 2002, available at: http://www.highbeam.com/doc/1G1-82838170.html, accessed May 20, 2010.
[55] Simcox, Stuart, and Ahmed, *Islamist Terrorism: The British Connections*, 340–341.
[56] *Ibid*, 325–326.
[57] Steve Bird, 'Quiet Existence in Leicester Suburb Masked Complex Terrorist Network', *The Times*, April 2, 2003, available at: http://www.timesonline.co.uk/tol/news/uk/article1125944.ece, accessed June 22, 2010; Crown Prosecution Service, 'Joint Effort Convicts Fraudsters and Terrorists', *Leicestershire Annual Report 2002-2003*, 3, available at: http://www.cps.gov.uk/ publications/docs/areas/2003/ar2003leicestershire.pdf, accessed June 22, 2010.
[58] Matthew Wilkinson, 'Al Qaida Terrorists Jailed for Credit Card Fraud Fund', *The Birmingham Post*, April 2, 2003, available at: http://www.highbeam.com/doc/1G1-99485868.html, accessed June 22, 2010.
[59] Simcox, Stuart, and Ahmed, *Islamist Terrorism: The British Connections*, 13.
[60] Qatada was eventually deported from the UK to Jordan in July 2013.
[61] Only seventeen are included in the current analysis. Ahmed Errachidi is excluded because employment records from the time independently refuted the timing of the allegations against him.

[62]Paul Reynolds, 'Guantanamo: Anatomy of a Hearing', *BBC News*, March 4, 2006, available at: http://news.bbc.co.uk/2/hi/americas/4774566.stm, accessed June 22, 2010.

[63]'Recommendation for Continued Detention Under DoD Control (CD) for Guantanamo Detainee, ISN US9ET-001458DP (S)', *US Department of Defense*, December 26, 2008, available at: http://s3.documentcloud.org/documents/86269/isn-1458-binyam-mohamed-jtf-gtmo-detainee.pdf, accessed March 6, 2012.

[64]'Profile: Sheikh Abdullah El-Faisal', *BBC News*, May 25, 2007, available at: http://news.bbc.co.uk/2/hi/uk_news/6692243.stm, accessed June 23, 2010.

[65]'Killer Jailed Over Poison Plot', *BBC News*, April 13, 2005, available at: http://news.bbc.co.uk/2/hi/uk_news/4433709.stm, accessed June 23, 2010.

[66]O'Neill and McGrory, *The Suicide Factory*, 235–249.

[67]*Ibid*, 253–264.

[68]*Ibid*, 296–311.

[69]'Mustafa Kamel Mustafa, AKA "Abu Hamza," Sentenced in Manhattan Federal Court to Life Imprisonment', *US Department of Justice*, January 9, 2015, available at: http://www.justice.gov/opa/pr/mustafa-kamel-mustafa-aka-abu-hamza-sentenced-manhattan-federal-court-life-imprisonment, accessed January 10, 2015.

[70]Amardeep Bassey, 'Secret Tipton Links With Taliban Mr. Fix-It', *The Sunday Mercury*, February 3, 2002, available at: http://www.highbeam.com/doc/1G1-82474996.html, accessed January 21, 2012; Paul Harris, Martin Bright, and Burhan Wazir, 'Five Britons Killed in "Jihad Brigade"', *The Guardian*, October 28, 2001, available at: http://www.guardian.co.uk/world/2001/oct/28/terrorism.afghanistan3, accessed June 8, 2011; 'How Many More Are Out There?', *BBC News*, April 30, 2007, available at: http://news.bbc.co.uk/2/hi/programmes/newsnight/6607647.stm, accessed March 15, 2008; Martyn Leek, 'Taliban's Fixer Goes on the Run: Fear of Muslim Who Recruited Fighters in the UK', *The Sunday Mercury*, March 3, 2002, available at: http://www.highbeam.com/doc/1G1-83473420.html, accessed February 24, 2012.

[71]Amardeep Bassey, 'Taliban Scot: I'll Fight On: Blitz Victim Vows Revenge', *The Sunday Mirror*, November 11, 2001, available at: http://www.highbeam.com/doc/1G1-79940380.html, accessed January 16, 2012.

[72]Martin Bright and Fareena Alam, 'Making of a Martyr: From Passivism to Jihad', May 4, 2003, *The Guardian*, available at: http://www.guardian.co.uk/world/2003/may/04/terrorism.religion, accessed May 19, 2010.

[73]'Bomb Britons Appear on Hamas Tape', *BBC News*, March 8, 2004, available at: http://news.bbc.co.uk/2/hi/uk_news/3543269.stm, accessed May 19, 2010.

[74]Duncan Gardham, 'Hamza Follower Testifies Against Terror Suspects', *The Telegraph*, March 24, 2006, available at: http://www.telegraph.co.uk/news/uknews/1513838/Hamza-follower-testifies-against-terror-suspects.html, accessed June 5, 2010.

[75]'Regina vs Khyam *et al.*, Opening Statement: Prepared Text of the Crown's Opening Statement in the Trial of Seven Men Alleged to Have Plotted to Bomb London', *Canada.com*, March 23, 2006, available at: http://www.canada.com/ottawacitizen/news/story.html?id=408dc2ed-d950-4ee5-a4b7-392eb5faaf34&k=75162, accessed June 24, 2010.

[76]*Ibid*; *R. v. Mohammad Momin Khawaja*, Reasons for Judgement, 04-G30282, (Ontario Superior Court of Justice, October 29, 2008), available at: http://nefafoundation.org/file/FeaturedDocs/Khawaja_ReasonsforJudgment.pdf, accessed December 14, 2011.

[77]'Al Qaeda Briton Planned Dirty Bomb Attacks', *The London Evening Standard*, November 7, 2006, available at: http://www.thisislondon.co.uk/news/article-23373534-al-qaeda-briton-planned-dirty-bomb-attacks.do, accessed June 22, 2010.

[78]*The 9/11 Commission: Final Report of the National Commission on Terrorist Attacks Against the United States: Official Government Edition* (Washington DC: US Government Printing Office, 2004), 150.

[79]'Al Qaeda Briton Planned Dirty Bomb Attacks'.

[80]Ian Cobain, David Hencke, and Richard Norton-Taylor, 'MI5 Told MPs on Eve of 7/7: No Imminent Terror Threat', *The Guardian*, January 8, 2007, available at: http://www.guardian.co.uk/politics/2007/jan/09/july7.uksecurity, accessed February 21, 2013.

[81]The Rt. Hon Lady Justice Hallett DBE, *Coroner's Inquests Into the London Bombings of 7 July 2005*, (London: H.M. Coroner, 2011), 5, available at: http://7julyinquests.independent.gov.uk/docs/orders/rule43-report.pdf, accessed January 26, 2013.

[82]*Ibid*; 'Profile: Mohammad Sidique Khan', *BBC News*, March 2, 2011, available at: http://www.bbc.co.uk/news/uk-12621381, accessed February 22, 2013.

[83]Shiv Malik, 'My Brother the Bomber', *Prospect Magazine*, June 30, 2007, available at: http://www.prospectmagazine.co.uk/magazine/ mybrotherthebomber/, accessed February 22, 2008.

[84]O'Neill and McGrory, *The Suicide Factory*, 191.

[85]Kim Howells, *Could 7/7 Have Been Prevented? Review of the Intelligence on the London Terrorist Attacks on 7 July 2005* (London: Intelligence and Security Committee, 2009), 19, available at: http://www.cabinetoffice.gov.uk/media/210852/20090519_77review.pdf, accessed May 20, 2010.

[86]In addition to Khyam's group and Khan, at least three other British jihadis were present at the Malakand camp — Mohammed Shakil from Beeston and Londoners Kazi Nurur Rahman and Zeeshan Siddiqui.

[87]Howells, *Could 7/7 Have Been Prevented?*; Hallett, *Coroner's Inquests Into the London Bombings of 7 July 2005*, 7–10.

[88]Hallett, *Coroner's Inquests Into the London Bombings of 7 July 2005*, 14.

[89]Nic Robertson, Paul Cruikshank, and Tim Lister, 'Documents Give New Details on al Qaeda's London Bombings', *CNN*, April 30, 2012, available at: http://edition.cnn.com/2012/04/30/world/al-qaeda-documents-london-bombings/?c=&page=0, accessed April 30, 2012.

[90] *Ibid.*

[91] House of Commons, *Report of the Official Account of the Bombings in London on 7th July 2005* (London: The Stationery Office, 2006), 22, 24, available at: http://www.official-documents.gov.uk/document/hc0506/hc10/1087/1087.pdf, accessed October 26, 2007; Justice Hallett DBE, *Coroner's Inquests Into the London Bombings of 7 July 2005*, 14.

[92] There has been much speculation that the leader of the July 21 attempted bombings, Muktar Said Ibrahim, trained with Khan and Tanweer in Pakistan in late 2004/early 2005. This is indeed a possibility since their time there overlapped and Ibrahim shared the same handler, Rashid Rauf, who also introduced him to 'Haji', also known as Abu Ubaidah al-Masri. However, recently discovered documents believed to have been authored by Rauf do not indicate that they trained together, or that there were any operational links between the groups. Furthermore, in contrast to Khan and Tanweer, Ibrahim neglected to keep in contact with Rauf on returning to the UK and this was likely the crucial factor explaining the failure of the 21/7 attack (Robertson, Cruikshank, and Lister, 'Documents Give New Details on al Qaeda's London Bombings').

[93] Mark Oliver, 'Radical Cleric Banned From Britain', *The Guardian*, August 12, 2005, available at: http://www.guardian.co.uk/uk/2005/aug/12/politics.syria, accessed December 29, 2007.

[94] *Proscribed Terrorist Organisations*, (Home Office, November 23, 2012), available at: http://www.homeoffice.gov.uk/publications/counter-terrorism/proscribed-terror-groups/terror-groups-proscribed?view=Binary, accessed February 25, 2013.

[95] Jack Barclay, 'UK Extremists Sidestep Law', *Janes Terrorism and Security Monitor*, July 17, 2012.

[96] Tom Whitehead, 'Woolwich Attack: Al Muhajiroun Linked to One in Five Terrorist Convictions', *The Telegraph*, May 24, 2013, available at: http://www.telegraph.co.uk/news/uknews/terrorism-in-the-uk/10079827/Woolwich-attack-Al-Muhajiroun-linked-to-one-in-five-terrorist-convictions.html, accessed May 24, 2013.

[97] Michael Dobbs, 'Britain a Refuge for Mideast Dissidents; Some With Suspected Ties to Bin Laden Resist Extradition', *The Washington Post*, October 7, 2001, available at: http://www.highbeam.com/doc/1P2-475430.html, accessed January 9, 2012.

[98] Nick Hopkins, 'A Glimpse Into the World of 21st-Century Espionage', *The Guardian*, September 9, 2011, available at: http://www.guardian.co.uk/world/2011/sep/09/libya-papers-tripoli-mi6-cia, accessed March 17, 2012; 'Regina vs Khyam *et al* Opening Statement'.

[99] *Consolidated List of Financial Sanctions Targets in the UK* (HM Treasury, February 21, 2013), available at: http://www.hm-treasury.gov.uk/d/ sanctionsconlist.htm, accessed February 26, 2013.

[100] *Consolidated List of Financial Sanctions Targets in the UK* (HM Treasury, April 7, 2010), 29–30, available at: http://www.hm-treasury.gov.uk/d/sanctionsconlist.pdf, accessed April 12, 2010; 'QI.B.213.06. MOHAMMED

BENHAMMEDI', *United Nations Security Council Committee*, September 7, 2010, available at: http://www.un.org/sc/committees/1267/NSQI21306E.shtml, accessed April 6, 2012.

[101]Most notably prior to 2005, Khaled Abusalama and Abdul Bourouag were jailed for forgery offenses in May 2004. They were then re-arrested along with fellow LIFG member Ismail Kamoka in December 2005 when they were prosecuted for terrorism fundraising ('Sentence on Forgery Pair Welcomed', *BBC News*, May 13, 2004, available at: http://news.bbc.co.uk/2/hi/uk_news/england/west_midlands/3712235.stm, accessed April 30, 2010; 'Three Jailed Over Terror Funding', *BBC News*, June 11, 2007, available at: http://news.bbc.co.uk/2/hi/uk_news/6742645.stm, accessed May 3, 2010).

[102]*The Terrorism Act 2000: Proscribed Organisations* (House of Commons Library, January 7, 2013), available at: www.parliament.uk/briefing-papers/sn00815.pdf, accessed February 26, 2013.

[103]Evan Kohlmann, 'Expert Report on the AQCORPO Website', *NEFA Foundation*, August 2006, available at: http://nefafoundation.org/miscellaneous/FeaturedDocs/ekirhaby0108.pdf, accessed June 25, 2010.

[104]'Jail for Terror Document Cousins', *BBC News*, August 19, 2008, available at: http://news.bbc.co.uk/2/hi/uk_news/7570134.stm, accessed June 29, 2010.

[105]Tsouli and Khan were in touch with Syed Haris Ahmed and Ehsanul Islam Sadequee from Atlanta in the US, and with Fahim Ahmad and Jahmaal James of the 'Toronto 18' in Canada. Both the American and Canadian groups were later prosecuted for terrorism offenses.

[106]Evan Kohlmann, 'Anatomy of a Modern Homegrown Terror Cell: Aabid Khan et al (Operation Praline)', (2008) *NEFA Foundation*, available at: http://www.nefafoundation.org/miscellaneous/nefaaabidkhan0908.pdf, accessed June 29, 2010; Isabel Teotonio, 'The Battle of Toronto', *The Toronto Star*, 2010, available at: http://www3.thestar.com/static/toronto18/index.1. html, accessed August 14, 2011.

[107]Brian Krebs, 'Terrorism's Hook into Your Inbox', *The Washington Post*, July 5, 2007, available at: http://www.washingtonpost.com/wp-dyn/content/ article/2007/07/05/AR2007070501153_pf.html, accessed June 25, 2010.

[108]*Ibid.*

[109]'Liquid Bomb Plot: What Happened', *BBC News*, September 9, 2008, available at: http://news.bbc.co.uk/2/hi/uk_news/7564184.stm, accessed July 1, 2010.

[110]Duncan Gardham and Gordon Rayner, 'Airliner Bomb Trial: How MI5 Uncovered the Terror Plot', *The Telegraph*, September 9, 2008, available at: http://www.telegraph.co.uk/news/uknews/2709379/Airliner-bomb-trial-How-MI5-uncovered-the-terror-plot.html, accessed July 1, 2010.

[111]Robertson, Cruikshank, and Lister, 'Documents Give New Details on al Qaeda's London Bombings'.

[112]'Liquid Bomb Plot: What Happened'; Robertson, Cruikshank, and Lister, 'Documents Give New Details on al Qaeda's London Bombings'.

[113]Richard Greenberg, Paul Cruikshank, and Chris Hansen, 'Inside the Terror Plot that "Rivalled 9/11"', *MSNBC News*, September 14, 2009, available at: http://www.msnbc.msn.com/id/26726987, accessed July 1, 2010.

[114]Richard Edwards and Duncan Gardham, 'Airline Bomb Plot Chief Flew in to Britain under False Passport', *The Telegraph*, April 8, 2008, available at: http://www.telegraph.co.uk/news/uknews/1584357/Airline-bomb-plot-chief-flew-in-to-Britain-under-false-passport.html, accessed July 1, 2010.

[115]'Terror Planner Dies on Afghan Border', *The Washington Times*, April 10, 2008, available at: http://www.washingtontimes.com/news/2008/apr/10/terror-planner-dies-on-afghan-border/, accessed October 6, 2010.

[116]Dominic Casciani, 'Profile: Rashid Rauf', *BBC News*, November 22, 2008, available at: http://news.bbc.co.uk/2/hi/uk_news/7743339.stm, accessed October 6, 2010.

[117]See Robertson, Cruikshank, and Lister, 'Documents Give New Details on al Qaeda's London Bombings'.

[118]Nic Robertson and Paul Cruikshank, 'Belgian Court Convicts Three of Recruiting to Fight in Afghanistan', *CNN*, May 10, 2010, available at: http://afghanistan.blogs.cnn.com/2010/05/10/belgian-court-convicts-three-for-recruiting-to-fight-in-afghanistan/?iref=allsearch, accessed October 18, 2010; Sebastian Rotella and Josh Meyer, 'A Young American's Journey into Al Qaeda', *The LA Times*, July 24, 2009, available at: http://articles.latimes.com/2009/jul/24/nation/na-american-jihadi24, accessed June 13, 2010.

[119]'Testimony of Rangzieb Ahmed', Undated, *Cageprisoners*, available at: http://www.cageprisoners.com/downloads/RangziebAhmed.pdf, accessed June 29, 2010.

[120]Russell Jenkins, 'British Muslim, Rangzieb Ahmed, Convicted of Being al-Qaeda Mastermind in Landmark Trial', *The Times*, December 19, 2008, available at: http://www.timesonline.co.uk/tol/news/uk/crime/article5365911.ece, accessed June 29, 2010.

[121]Duncan Gardham, 'Fanatic "Hoped to Spread Fear with Beheading"', *The Telegraph*, January 29, 2008, available at: http://www.telegraph.co.uk/news/uknews/1576916/Fanatic-hoped-to-spread-fear-with-beheading.html, accessed June 28, 2010.

[122]Alex Carlile, *Operation Pathway: Report Following Review* (London: Home Office, 2009), available at: http://security.homeoffice.gov.uk/news-publications/publication-search/legislation/terrorism-act-2000/operation-pathway-report, accessed October 11, 2010.

[123]Steve Robson, 'British Terrorist Linked to CIA Suicide Bombing Which Killed Seven Agents in Afghanistan', *The Daily Mail*, February 16, 2013, available at: http://www.dailymail.co.uk/news/article-2279598/British-terrorist-linked-CIA-suicide-bombing-killed-seven-agents-Afghanistan.html?ito=feeds-newsxml, accessed February 16, 2013.

[124]Tom Whitehead, 'Al-Qaeda Wants Terror Knowledge Spread Throughout Europe to "Whack" People Here', *The Telegraph*, February 21, 2013, available at: http://www.telegraph.co.uk/news/uknews/terrorism-in-the-uk/9888499/Al-Qaeda-wants-terror-knowledge-spread-throughout-Europe-to-whack-people-here.html, accessed February 21, 2013.

[125] James Slack, 'Al Qaeda "Sergeant" Becomes Seventh Terror Suspect on the Loose After Snubbing Control Order', *The Daily Mail*, June 22, 2007, available at: http://www.dailymail.co.uk/news/article-463498/Al-Qaeda-sergeant-seventh-terror-suspect-loose-snubbing-control-order.html, accessed May 19, 2012.

[126] Wail Abdul Rahman al-Dhaleai had been living in Sheffield before blowing himself up in Iraq in late October/early November 2003, and Idris Bazis had been living in Manchester before doing the same in February 2005 (Nick Craven and Chris Brooke, 'Britain's Suicide Bomber', *The Daily Mail*, November 22, 2003, available at: http://www.highbeam.com/doc/1G1-110447935.html, accessed March 16, 2012; Daniel McGrory and Michael Evans, 'The Deadly Trail of a Mystery Bomber', *The Times*, June 23, 2005, available at: http://www.timesonline.co.uk/tol/news/uk/article536494.ece, accessed June 8, 2011).

[127] Andrew Alderson, Ben Leach, and Duncan Gardham, 'Bilal Abdulla: Doctor by Day, Terrorist by Night- the Secret Life of a New Breed of Terrorist', *The Telegraph*, December 20, 2008, available at: http://www.telegraph.co.uk/news/uknews/law-and-order/3867334/Bilal-Abdulla-Doctor-by-day-terrorist-by-night-the-secret-life-of-a-new-breed-of-terrorist.html, accessed July 5, 2010; Chris Greenwood, 'Terror Police "A Road Away From Stopping Bombers"', *The Independent*, December 16, 2008, available at: http://www.independent.co.uk/news/uk/crime/terror-police-a-road-away-from-stopping-bombers-1145074.html, accessed July 5, 2010.

[128] 'Stockholm Bomber "Trained in Iraq"', *The Daily Telegraph*, January 8, 2011, available at: http://www.dailytelegraph.com.au/stockholm-bomber-trained-in-iraq/story-fn6e1m7z-1225984021072, accessed January 9, 2011.

[129] Sean Rayment, 'British Muslims Recruited to Fight for "al-Qaeda" in Somalia', *The Telegraph*, February 18, 2012, available at: http://www.telegraph.co.uk/news/worldnews/africaandindianocean/somalia/9090606/British-Muslims-recruited-to-fight-for-al-Qaeda-in-Somalia.html, accessed February 18, 2012.

[130] Mike Pflanz, 'July 7 Bomber Widow Samantha Lewthwaite Charged With Planning Explosions', *The Telegraph*, May 11, 2012, available at: http://www.telegraph.co.uk/news/worldnews/africaandindianocean/kenya/9260206/July-7-bomber-widow-Samantha-Lewthwaite-charged-with-planning-explosions.html, accessed May 11, 2012.

[131] Sean O'Neill, 'Al-Qaeda "Groomed Abdulmutallab in London"', *The Times*, December 30, 2009, available at: http://www.timesonline.co.uk/tol/news/uk/article6971098.ece, accessed December 30, 2009.

[132] *United States of America v. Umar Farouk Abdulmutallab*, Government's Sentencing Memorandum, United States District Court Eastern District of Michigan Southern Division, Case No. 2:10-CR-20005, February 10, 2012, available at: https://s3.amazonaws.com/s3.documentcloud.org/documents/291667/abdulmutallab-sentencing-memorandum.pdf, accessed February 19, 2012.

[133] Duncan Gardham, 'British Airways Worker Planned Terrorist Attack on US-Bound Plane, Court Hears', *The Telegraph*, February 3, 2011, available at: http://www.telegraph.co.uk/news/uknews/terrorism-in-the-uk/8301449/

British-Airways-worker-planned-terrorist-attack-on-US-bound-plane-court-hears.html, accessed February 3, 2011.

[134]For example, Mahdi Hashi from London (who was charged in the US of providing material support to al-Shabaab) was arrested in Africa with two Swedish nationals in August 2012, believed to be en route to Yemen ('Three Supporters of Foreign Terrorist Organization Al Shabaab Charged in Brooklyn Federal Court, Face Life in Prison', *Federal Bureau of Investigation*, December 21, 2012, available at: http://www.fbi.gov/newyork/press-releases/2012/three-supporters-of-foreign-terrorist-organization-al-shabaab-charged-in-brooklyn-federal-court-face-life-in-prison, accessed December 21, 2012).

[135]Peter Walker, Shiv Malik, Matthew Taylor, Sandra Laville, Vikram Dodd, and Ben Quinn, 'Suspect's Journey from Schoolboy Football to Phonejacking and Jihad', *The Guardian*, May 23, 2013, available at: http://www.guardian.co.uk/uk/2013/may/23/suspect-michael-adebolajo-woolwich-jihad?CMP=twt_gu, accessed May 23, 2013.

[136]'Woolwich Murder Probe: Suspect Michael Adebolajo Arrested in Kenya in 2010', *BBC News*, May 26, 2013, available at: http://www.bbc.co.uk/news/uk-22673164, accessed May 26, 2013.

[137]'French Stabbing "Religiously Motivated": Prosecutor', *Reuters*, May 29, 2013, available at: http://www.reuters.com/article/2013/05/29/us-france-stabbing-statement-idUSBRE94S0EX20130529?feedType=RSS&feedName=worldNews, accessed May 29, 2013.

[138]Rosa Silverman and Tom Whitehead, 'Terror Police Called in After Prison Warden Stabbed in Attack "Inspired by Woolwich Murder"', *The Telegraph*, May 28, 2013, available at: http://www.telegraph.co.uk/news/uknews/terrorism-in-the-uk/10083899/Terror-police-called-in-after-prison-warden-stabbed-in-attack-inspired-by-Woolwich-murder.html, accessed May 28, 2013.

[139]See Andrew Gilligan, 'The Truth About the "Wave of Attacks" on Muslims Following Woolwich Murder', *The Telegraph*, June 1, 2013, available at: http://www.telegraph.co.uk/news/uknews/terrorism-in-the-uk/10093568/The-truth-about-the-wave-of-attacks-on-Muslims-after-Woolwich-murder.html, accessed June 2, 2013; Matthew Taylor and Haroon Siddique, 'Woolwich Murder: 200 Islamophobic Incidents Since Lee Rigby's Killing', *The Guardian*, May 28, 2013, available at: http://www.guardian.co.uk/uk/2013/may/28/woolwich-murder-200-islamophobic-incidences, accessed May 28, 2013.

[140]'Six Guilty of Plotting Attack on EDL Rally', *West Midlands Police*, April 30, 2013, available at: http://www.west-midlands.police.uk/latest-news/press-release.asp?ID=4658, accessed April 30, 2013.

[141]Justin Davenport, 'Man, 19, "Plotted Terror Attack and had a Hammer and Knife Wrapped in Islamic Flag"', *The Evening Standard*, August 21, 2014, available at: http://www.standard.co.uk/news/crime/man-19-plotted-terror-attack-and-had-a-hammer-and-knife-wrapped-in-islamic-flag-9683028.html, accessed August 21, 2014.

[142]Tom Whitehead, 'Brusthom Ziamani: The former Jehovah's Witness who was Radicalised within Weeks', *The Telegraph*, February 19, 2015, available at: http://www.telegraph.co.uk/news/uknews/terrorism-in-the-uk/11423156/Brusthom-Ziamani-The-former-Jehovahs-Witness-who-was-radicalised-within-weeks.html, accessed February 19, 2015.

[143]'Terrorism Plot Size of 7/7 Attacks "Foiled Every Year"', *BBC News*, March 21, 2013, available at: http://www.bbc.co.uk/news/uk-21878867#TWEET677065, accessed March 21, 2013.

[144]*Ibid.*

[145]'Terror-Related Crime "Stretches Police" — Scotland Yard', *BBC News*, October 17, 2014, available at: http://www.bbc.com/news/uk-29649010, accessed October 17, 2014.

[146]Victoria Ward and Gordon Rayner, 'Secret Terror Trial: Erol Incedal "Planned Attack on Tony Blair's House or Mumbai-Style Atrocity" Jury Hears', *The Telegraph*, October 14 2014, available at: http://www.telegraph.co.uk/news/uknews/terrorism-in-the-uk/11162989/Secret-terror-trial-Erol-Incedal-planned-attack-on-Tony-Blairs-house-or-Mumbai-style-atrocity-jury-hears.html, accessed October 14, 2014.

[147]'Four Men from London Charged over "Terror Plot", Police Say', *BBC News*, October 17, 2014, available at: http://www.bbc.com/news/uk-29662245, accessed October 17, 2014.

[148]TPIMs came into effect in January 2012 as a replacement for Control Orders, which were established in March 2005 (but were judged to be too restrictive). TPIMs, like Control Orders before them, enable authorities to restrict the movement and activities of terrorism suspects who cannot be prosecuted, based on evidence which remains secret.

[149]Most notably, Robin Simcox, *Control Orders: Strengthening National Security* (London: The Centre for Social Cohesion, 2010), available at: http://www.socialcohesion.co.uk/files/1301651552_1.pdf, accessed December 20, 2010; Simcox, Stuart, and Ahmed, *Islamist Terrorism: The British Connections.*

Chapter 5

Who Becomes a Jihadi Terrorist and How?

The historical experience of global jihad in the US and UK has clearly been quite different. However, in order to move beyond superficial observation it is necessary to examine the problem in greater detail. Quantitative analysis enables a much more systematic comparison of key variables of interest, which in turn allows us to make empirically informed judgments about the existence and nature of any differences between the two countries, as well any changes that have occurred over time (and at this point the reader is encouraged to review the notes on 'Analytical Method' in the Introduction). This chapter begins with an overview of each sample, including a comparison of the rates of Islamist terrorist activity, individual classifications, and the geographic distribution of offenders in both countries. This is followed by an examination of demographic profiles, processes of radicalization, and ideological commitment (see Tables 5.1 and 5.2 for summaries of the data throughout).

Statistical Summary

The scale of the apparent difference in rates of Islamist terrorism on either side of the Atlantic has been a hotly contested issue. The overall US sample of Islamist terrorists includes a total of 365 individuals (divided into 198 cases or groups),[1] as compared to the UK sample, which includes a total of 427 individuals (divided into 242 cases).[2] This translates into an average rate of 11.1 jihadi individuals per year for the US and 13.2 for the UK. In absolute terms, clearly more

Table 5.1. Statistical summary and background variable information of American jihadis beginning their careers before and after 9/11 (1980s–2013).

	Pre-9/11	Post-9/11
Statistical summary	143 individuals (66 cases); 6.6 individuals (3.0 cases) per year	222 individuals (132 cases); 18.3 individuals (10.8 cases) per year; 2 repeat offenders
Individual classifications*	48% domestic prosecutions; 3% overseas prosecutions; 2% legal allegations; 24% killed; 1% special sanctions; 7% offender admissions; 22% public allegations	73% domestic prosecutions; 4% overseas convictions; 14% legal allegations; 9% killed; 2% special sanctions; 3% offender admissions; 1% public allegations
Geographic distribution	21% based in NY; 19% NJ; 17% FL; 12% VA; 10% CA; 8% AZ	17% based in NY; 13% MN; 9% CA; 8% FL; 7% NC; 6% VA; 6% IL
Demographic profiles	Mostly males in late 20s/early 30s; 32% American as first nationality; 64% foreign (50% of which have permanent residency/US citizenship); 15% Egyptian; 13% Saudi; 10% Palestinian; Education mostly unknown (at least 24% completed university); 17% in skilled occupations; 13% students; 6% unemployed; 17% converts; 51% married; 13% criminal records; 3% history of mental health problems	Mostly males in late 20s; 42% American as first nationality; 58% foreign (72% of which have permanent residency/US citizenship); 17% of South Asian heritage; 16% Somali; Education largely unknown (at least 19% completed university); 8% in skilled occupations; 18% students; 13% unemployed; 22% converts; 30% married; 28% criminal records; 11% history of mental health problems
Radicalization	Little reliable information; Radicalization primarily driven by social processes	Available information indicative of social, virtual, and combined processes
Ideological classification	97% jihadists; 3% unknown	82% jihadists; 7% criminal opportunists; 7% unknown; 4% troubled individuals

*Sample divided by when offenses ended.

people from the UK have joined the global jihad compared to the US, but we must also take into account population sizes in order to grasp the relative scale of the difference. Allowing for changes in population size, from 1980 until September 11, 2013 there has been a yearly average of 0.4 jihadi terrorists per 10 million people in the US, compared to 2.1 jihadis per 10 million UK residents.[3] As a proportion of the overall population, the average yearly rate of Islamist terrorism

Table 5.2. Statistical summary and background variable information of British jihadis beginning their careers before and after 9/11 (1980s–2013).

	Pre-9/11	Post-9/11
Statistical summary	139 individuals (99 cases); 6.4 individuals (4.6 cases) per year	288 individuals (143 cases); 24.2 individuals (11.7 cases) per year; 7 repeat offenders
Individual classifications*	9% domestic prosecutions; 43% overseas prosecutions; 11% legal allegations; 21% killed; 11% special sanctions; 11% offender admissions; 4% public allegations	48% domestic prosecutions; 6% overseas prosecutions; 7% legal allegations; 9% killed; 29% special sanctions; 3% offender admissions; 8% public allegations
Geographic distribution	62% based in London; 18% West Midlands; 4% Greater Manchester; 4% Yorkshire	42% based in London; 15% West Midlands; 8% Greater Manchester; 6% Yorkshire
Demographic profiles	Males in late 20s/early 30s; 32% British as first nationality; 65% foreign (38% of which have permanent residency/UK citizenship); 25% Algerian; 25% of South Asian heritage; 12% Libyan; Education levels mostly unknown (at least 17% completed university); 7% in skilled occupations; 7% students; 14% unemployed; 9% converts; 40% married; 31% criminal records; 7% history of mental health problems	Mostly males in late 20s; 56% British as first nationality; 40% foreign (46% of which have permanent residency/UK citizenship); 49% of South Asian heritage; Education levels mostly unknown (at least 10% completed university); 3% in skilled occupations; 10% students; 18% unemployed; 12% converts; 32% married; 19% criminal records; 6% history of mental health problems
Radicalization	Little reliable information; Radicalization primarily driven by social processes	Available information indicative of social, virtual and combined processes
Ideological classification	99% jihadists; 1% unknown	91% jihadists; 7% unknown; 2% troubled individuals

*Sample divided by when offenses ended.

in the UK is thus 5.6 times higher than in the US.[4] This appears to confirm the given wisdom that the problem in the UK is far more substantial than that in the US. However, it is perhaps more meaningful to assess the number of Islamist terrorists as a proportion of respective Muslim population sizes — not because Muslims in general are associated with terrorism, but because Islamist terrorists are, of course, mostly Muslims. Although there is not enough information to be able to calculate yearly averages, recent figures suggest that there are currently around 2.6 million Muslims living in the US compared to 2.87 million in the UK.[5] When expressed as a percentage of current Muslim population sizes, the two sample totals thus represent 0.014% and 0.015% respectively. From this perspective, the rate of Islamist terrorism involving each country up until September 2013 has been practically identical. Naturally, this is not the final word on the subject though — there are many other elements that could be factored into the equation and the current samples include only those offenders who could be individually identified.[6] As a result, they do not take into account estimates of jihadi mobilization in response to the conflict in Bosnia, for example, which suggest that several hundred more British jihadis — but seemingly much fewer Americans — mobilized during the 1990s.[7] Likewise, these figures do not include the current wave of mobilization in response to the wars in Syria and Iraq, which again is strongly indicative of a much greater increase in the UK than the US (see Chapter 8). Nevertheless, it would appear that known (as opposed to estimated) rates of jihadi activity in each country prior to Syria have not been as vastly disparate as is often assumed.[8]

A more nuanced understanding of the similarities and differences between the two countries is made possible by comparing the occurrence of Islamist terrorist activity over time. Prior to 9/11, 143 individuals from/living/offending in the US are known to have begun their jihadi careers, compared to 139 individuals in the UK, equating to 39% and 32% of the respective samples. In the post-9/11 period up until September 11, 2013, a further 222 jihadi offenders were confirmed in the US plus 288 in the UK. Bearing in mind the ongoing problem of missing information, the current samples suggest that the average number of people getting involved in Islamist terrorism each year before and after 9/11 has effectively trebled in the US and quadrupled in the UK.

Nevertheless, the increases in terrorist activity over time have not followed a uniform or strictly linear progression, but have varied according to the unique positioning of each nation within the overall tapestry of the global jihadi movement. The graphs in Figures 5.1 and 5.2 illustrate the differential rates of Islamist terrorist activity

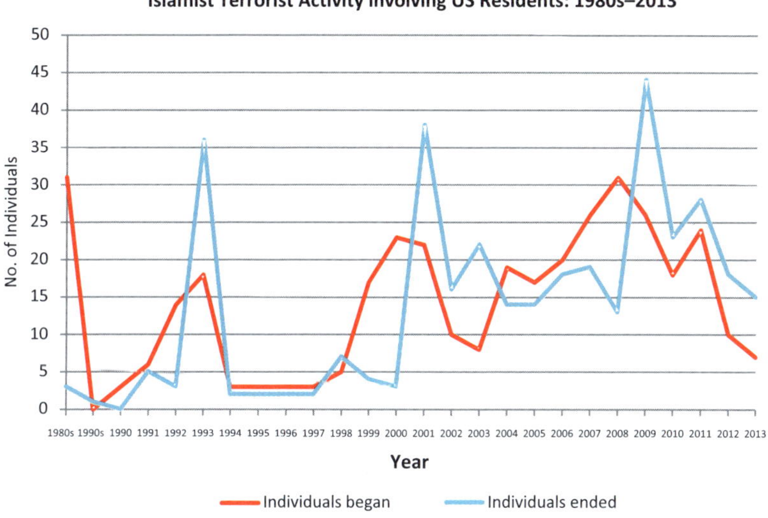

Figure 5.1. Numbers of American jihadis according to when they began and ceased offense behavior.[10]

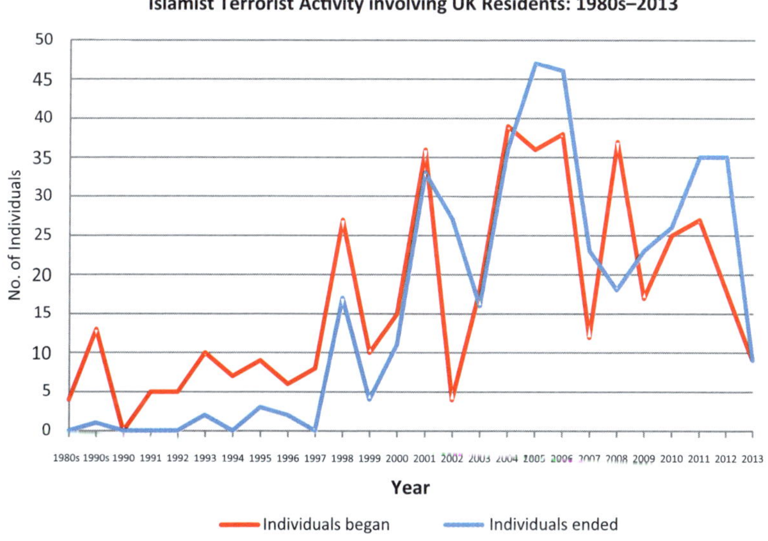

Figure 5.2. Numbers of British jihadis according to when they began and ceased offense behavior.

over the years, both in terms of when individuals began and ended their militant careers. Ordinarily, analysts tend to assess rates of terrorism based on the number of terrorists arrested, charged, killed, or prosecuted (i.e. endings). Whilst these things are easy to quantify, they (mis)direct attention to high-points in *counter* terrorism rather than terrorism. Furthermore, endings are often involuntary and tend to take place months or even years after an individual has radicalized and commenced operations. It is thus more instructive to focus on when individuals *begin* to offend (for example, their first known trip to a terrorist training camp) because it is more likely to reflect voluntary behavior and allows us to draw inferences about possible connections between wider contextual factors and varying levels of terrorism.[9]

The immediate spike in activity during the 1980s in the US (Figure 5.1) is reflective of the early networks (discussed in Chapter 3) which emerged during the Soviet occupation of Afghanistan and spawned numerous combat veterans, fundraisers, facilitators, and future planners of attacks against the US. The subsequent spike from 1990 to 1993 includes (among others) individuals involved in the first World Trade Center attack and the connected plot to attack multiple targets in New York City, led by Omar Abdel Rahman. Then prior to 9/11 there was a third uptick, beginning in 1998 and peaking in 2000. This spike in the number of people joining the global jihad is partly attributable to increasing levels of home-grown radicalization within the US itself (including Virginia, Lackawanna, and Portland). But a large proportion of the pre-9/11 surge also consists of the hijackers themselves, who of course came to the country with the *a priori* intention of attacking it.

By comparison, the pre-9/11 years in the UK followed a somewhat different trajectory. To begin with, Figure 5.2 suggests that the 1980s were a much quieter time for jihadi operations in Britain. If true this would be somewhat surprising and could potentially call into question the 'head start' hypothesis that seems to explain greater levels of militancy in Europe over time (see Chapter 1). But, without ruling out this possibility, it seems to be at least partially a product of missing data. Indeed, much of the information that we have about jihadi networks in the US during this period only came to light because of the investigation into the first World Trade Center bombing. It is almost certain that more jihadis than we know of were active in the UK during the 1980s but were simply not discovered because they remained focused on overseas events rather than attacking their home/host country (and hence there were no major investigations until later on).[11] Certainly as the 1990s progressed, militant support networks expanded dramatically and greater numbers of British residents joined the jihad (see Chapter 4). The apparent increase in activity in 1998 depicted in Figure 5.2 includes the 'Aden Ten' who were dispatched that year by Abu Hamza to wreak havoc in Yemen. The subsequent, even greater peak, from 2000 to 2001 is not dominated by any one group in particular, but is indicative of the increasing numbers of British militants who were being drawn to jihadi training camps and conflict zones, in particular Afghanistan. Among them were several individuals who went on to plan attacks against Western targets in addition to numerous others who were killed in combat or ended up in Guantanamo.

After 9/11, there was an immediate decrease in the number of people joining the jihad in both countries, followed by a resurgence of activity peaking in 2004. The post-9/11 lull in new recruits may have been largely for pragmatic reasons as existing networks were thrown into disarray by the overwhelming counterterrorism response. But — in the US in particular — it also suggests a period of shock and awe as even many extremists needed time to digest and interpret what they had seen on September 11. The recall to action in 2004 in both cases was driven at least in part by the radicalizing influence of the war in Iraq, but militants in the UK were quicker to respond and also did so in greater numbers, with 39 individuals moving to action that year compared to just 19 in the US. The somewhat more muted reaction in the US is perhaps related to greater levels of popular support for the war at the time. More fundamentally, it is a reflection of the comparative lack of established jihadi subcultures and networks which were playing such a radicalizing and facilitating role in the UK.[12]

In fact, the high-point in home-grown Islamist terrorism in America was not until 2008. By this time public opinion was turning both against the war in Iraq and in Afghanistan,[13] and a number of domestic terrorism plots began that year — most notably Najibullah Zazi *et al.*'s plan to bomb the New York subway. Moreover, at about the same time jihadis had found a new call to arms in Somalia where al-Shabaab had established itself as the focal point of a brutal insurgency against the Transitional Federal Government and allied Ethiopian forces. As a direct consequence, militant support networks sprang to life among the Somali diaspora and the Twin Cities of Minneapolis and Saint Paul in Minnesota became home to the largest terror network in the US since the early 1990s. Coordinated by a handful of recruiters and facilitators, at least 19 men from Minnesota made the journey to Somalia between 2007 and 2009 and at least 10 of them were killed there.[14]

2008 was also a big year for jihad in the UK, where — with the exception of an apparent lull in 2007 — jihadist activities had continued apace.[15] Of the 37 individuals who mobilized that year, several either went to Somalia or were involved in sending funds to those who did.[16] There was also a variety of domestic plots, including an attempted suicide bombing in Exeter in May. Since then, jihadi mobilization has certainly continued in both Britain and America, although looking at Figures 5.1 and 5.2 it would appear that there was a gradual decline in activity beginning in 2009. Some decline of course should be expected, since higher levels of activity cannot be maintained indefinitely. However, the seemingly continuous decrease from about 2012 onwards is really a reflection of the fact that there is a delay between the point in time that an individual mobilizes and when that information becomes public knowledge. In reality, there has been a dramatic increase in jihadist activity in both countries in response to Syria and Iraq, and especially so in the UK.

Individual Classifications

Prior to 9/11, the majority of individuals in the US sample were either subject to domestic prosecution (48%), were killed taking part in violent jihad (24%), or else were publicly alleged to have engaged in such activities but were not subject to any sanctions (22%). In the post-9/11 period, the percentage of domestic prosecutions rose to 73%, while another 14% were facing legal allegations in the US, and only 9% were killed.

In Britain, 43% of individuals in the earlier sample were prosecuted overseas[17] (compared to just 9% at home) and 21% were killed. After 9/11, 48% were prosecuted in the UK, with another 3% facing domestic legal allegations.[18] A further 23% were subject to 'special' domestic administrative sanctions in the absence of conviction, including control orders, detention, deportation and exclusion from the country, financial asset freezing, and revocation of citizenship. The percentage of people killed also decreased to 9%.

In both cases, there has been a substantial increase in the domestic prosecution of terrorism offenses. However, this was — and remains — much higher in the US than the UK due to the fact that the US was targeted for attack earlier, and because American jihadis appear to have been less active abroad over time (for more information see Chapter 6). By comparison, there has seemingly been a larger and more enduring international component to the activities of British jihadis. Moreover, UK legislation has allowed for a much greater application of special sanctions against British residents, meaning that there are relatively fewer prosecutions. Although both countries have responded differently to their respective problems, each has clearly become more proactive and effective in containing the threat.

Geographic Distribution of Individuals

The geographic distribution of American and British jihadis is depicted in Figures 5.3 and 5.4. The US states with the most Islamist terrorists prior to 9/11 were New York (mostly New York City; 21%), New Jersey (19%), Florida (17%), Virginia (12%), California (10%), and Arizona (8%). Four of these states also feature in the top seven after 9/11, with the largest numbers located again in New York (17%), followed by Minnesota (13%), California (9%), Florida (8%), North Carolina (7%), Virginia (6%), and Illinois (6%).

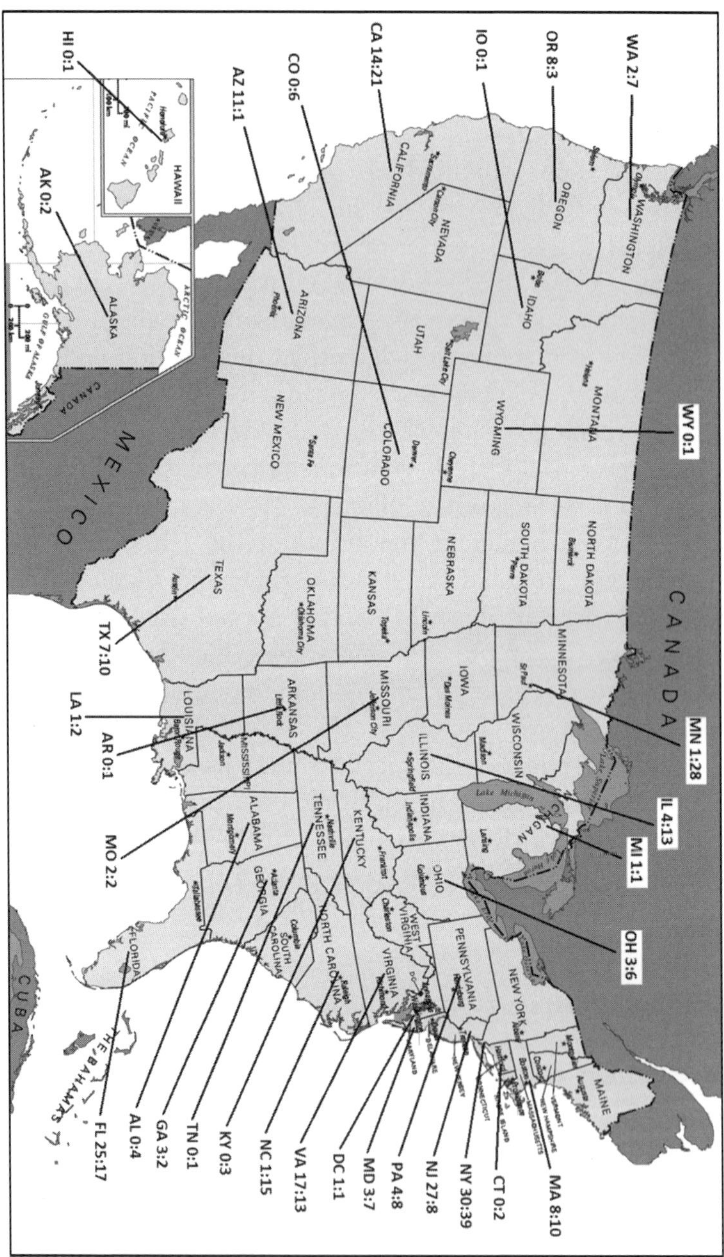

Figure 5.3. Geographical distribution of American residents/citizens involved in Islamist terrorism (1980s to September 11, 2013). Numbers indicate individuals who began offending before and after 9/11. Locations are approximate.[19]

Figure 5.4. Geographical distribution of British residents/citizens involved in Islamist terrorism (1980s to September 11, 2013). Numbers indicate individuals who began offending before and after 9/11. Locations are approximate.[20]

There has been even greater consistency in the UK, where the same four regions have produced most of the nation's jihadis over time. Number one, unsurprisingly, is London, which produced 62% of British jihadis before 9/11 and 42% afterwards. This is followed by the West Midlands, which produced 18% then 15%, Greater Manchester (4% then 8%), and West Yorkshire (4% then 6%).

Despite obvious differences of size and degree of concentration, the data thus reveal important similarities between both countries in the way that the geographic distribution of Islamist terrorists has varied over time. To begin with, there have clearly been hotspots of jihadi activity at the state or regional level and these have remained quite consistent from one time period to the next. Certain cities can also be considered hotspots.[21] In the US, New York City, and in particular Brooklyn, stands out while in the UK it has primarily been London (especially the East of the city), followed by Birmingham and Manchester.

These hotspots all have large, urban populations and are also home to relatively large numbers of Muslims. In the UK, the map of Islamist terrorism corresponds very closely to the map of the Muslim population in that the same four regions and three cities which produce the most jihadis are home to the most Muslims, and in the same rank order.[22] This should not come as a surprise since Islamist terrorists — as small a minority as they are — emerge from within these larger populations. That said, the correlation is far from perfect and it seems unlikely that the same degree of correspondence exists on the other side of the Atlantic where jihadis have been far more dispersed.[23] Moreover, focusing at the level of inner-city districts and local communities, the relationship between the distribution of jihadis and Muslims becomes much less clear. For example, according to the UK Office of National Statistics, the London districts with the most Muslims are Newham, Tower Hamlets, and Redbridge, none of which individually stand out as having produced particularly high numbers of known terrorists.[24]

Given that larger Muslim populations can only partially and indirectly explain greater numbers of jihadi terrorists, there must be other factors involved. Cities like New York and London of course hold a certain symbolic value for terrorists, which means that they are more likely to be targeted for attack. But, all things considered, this does not explain very much. A more important dynamic is that radicalization and recruitment for terrorism largely rely upon the localized social transmission of ideas. Accordingly, the original distribution of Islamist terrorism prior to 9/11 is expected to persist over time to the extent that lasting, pro-jihadi subcultures were established in those locations. The historical consistency observed in both countries thus lends a degree of support to the 'social transmission' hypothesis discussed in Chapter 2. Nevertheless, it is far from inevitable that lasting hotspots will form. For example, in the US, there has been significant decline in New Jersey and Arizona, while in the UK, at a more local level, fewer jihadis over time have come from North West London and the Finsbury Park area. This has likely occurred for a combination of reasons including successful dismantling of jihadi networks, the independent departure of influential individuals, loss of control over certain institutions, or a failure to generate sufficient support in the first place.

This brings us to the second broad similarity in terms of the geographic distribution of cases: despite considerable continuity, there has also been change. Certain hotspots have endured in both countries, but they also now account for a smaller proportion of each sample. This is not because traditional hotspots have necessarily tended to produce fewer jihadis — in fact, all in the UK and two in the US have produced more. Rather, it is an indication of the fact that more cases have occurred outside of these areas after 9/11, resulting in more geographically dispersed and less predictable patterns of activity, especially in the US. This has almost certainly been driven at a fundamental level by heightened awareness of the global jihadi cause since 2001, combined with increased exposure to the ideology via the Internet. This 'virtual' transmission of ideas of course means that potentially anyone, anywhere can become radicalized and take it upon themselves to commit acts of terrorism. Even so, the Internet cannot be held entirely responsible. Political events around the world and the movement or migration of groups and individuals from one location to another have also played significant roles. For instance, it was these factors combined which resulted in Minnesota becoming the number two jihadi hotspot in all of America, whereas prior to 9/11 Islamist militancy in the state had been practically non-existent.

What is clear from this discussion is that there are competing influences working towards geographic stability versus expansion of

Islamist terrorism in both countries. Jihadi hotspots in the UK, however, are stronger and more stable overall than in the US, and although we will continue to see cases occurring outside of those hotspots, we can expect them to remain dominant overall. This is a direct result of established, pro-jihadi subcultures within these areas, the formation of which was likely facilitated by the fact that Britain's Muslim population occupies relatively limited and somewhat segregated space on an island of little more than 240,000 km^2. By contrast, America's Muslims are spread across a country of more than 9 million km^2 and jihadi subcultures (as promoted by the likes of the now-defunct Revolution Muslim) also appear to be less well developed. In accordance with this, hotspots in the US are weaker and more susceptible to change.

A final, related observation is that the findings here for the UK are very much in conformity with previous research, while there is some disparity for the US.[25] Specifically, London and New York are confirmed as jihadi hotspots while Minnesota in particular was not highlighted in the much-publicized report by Simcox and Dyer. The reasons for this are methodological. These authors did not take into account changes before and after 9/11 and focused only on either convicted terrorists or those who were killed in suicide attacks between 1997 and 2011. The findings here thus highlight the need to analyze both changes over time as well as (reliable) reports of terrorist activity that have not necessarily resulted in conviction or a suicide attack.

Demographic Profiles

Age

As described in the tables above, and as expected, the vast majority of Islamist terrorists from/living/offending in the US and UK have been young males. More precisely, the average age in the US prior to 9/11 ranged from 27.6 to 31.3 (corresponding to when individuals began and ended their jihadi careers). After 9/11, this remained fairly constant at 28.0 to 29.3. In the UK, the average ages before 9/11 were very similar at 27.7 to 31.9, but since 2001 they have dropped slightly to 25.9 to 27.2. A reduction in average age over time has been found before in Canadian,[26] Australian,[27] and global[28] samples of Islamist terrorists, so this is not unexpected. Today, more and more young people are exposed to jihadi ideology over the Internet and they are also far more likely to be detected and apprehended at an earlier stage in their militant careers. Based on this, it would have been quite reasonable to anticipate similar, even larger changes occurring in both countries. The fact that this has not occurred casts some doubt on the theory that jihadis are getting younger on the whole. Furthermore, it is worth noting that while the youngest person in both samples was just 15 years of age, the oldest was 73 in the US and 65 in the UK.[29] Overall, these findings are very much in line with previous research, confirming that while young males predominate, even pensioners may become involved in terrorism.

Sex

Women, although very much in the minority, are also not exempt from involvement. Indeed, their role appears to be growing. In the pre-9/11 period, just three women were included in the US sample, all of whom played *ad hoc* or supporting roles and none of whom were obviously radicalized.[30] No female jihadis were confirmed in the UK during the same period. Since then, another 12 females were detected in the US plus 13 in the UK, amounting to 4–5% of each sample. Most of them have played facilitation or support roles, however many of them were clearly radicalized and some have actively participated in violence. Perhaps the most infamous among these is Aafia Siddiqui, who first became involved with Islamist extremists while living in the US during the 1990s, before eventually being apprehended in Afghanistan in 2008 and later convicted for trying to kill American servicemen.[31] Others include Colleen LaRose, otherwise known as 'Jihad Jane', who conspired with a number of others to assassinate the Swedish cartoonist Lars Vilks;[32] Roshonara Choudhry, who attempted to murder a British member of parliament in May 2010;[33] Shasta Khan, who was convicted in 2012 along with her husband for planning to bomb Jewish areas in Manchester;[34] Samantha Lewthwaite — the widow of 7/7 bomber Jermaine Linsday — who is accused of planning terrorist attacks in Kenya;[35] and Nicole

Mansfield, originally from Flint, Michigan, who was killed in Syria in May 2013 while apparently out on a reconnaissance mission for the Islamist organization Ahrar al-Sham.[36] Cases like these will remain the exception rather than the rule, but we should expect to see continuing confirmation of female support for, and participation in violent jihad. Indeed, since the end of the sampling period (post-September 2013), a handful of Americans and more than two dozen females from the UK have either been arrested or publicly accused of involvement in terrorism, mostly in relation to Syria/Iraq.

Place of Birth and Residency Status

Additional demographic information summarized in Tables 5.1 and 5.2 relates to whether individuals in each sample were born in the US or UK, or whether they emigrated there. This is of particular interest, because it gives some indication of the extent to which Islamist terrorism is actually home-grown. In the US, before September 2001, 32% of individuals were Americans by first nationality[37] and 64% were foreigners, but 32% overall were also naturalized citizens or held permanent residency status.[38] After 9/11, the number of Americans rose to 42% while the number of foreigners dropped to 58%, and 42% overall had been granted citizenship or permanent residency. The pattern of development in the UK, although more pronounced, is remarkably similar. Prior to 9/11, 32% of the sample was British compared to 65% foreign (including 25% overall who were naturalized citizens or permanent residents). After 9/11, 56% of individuals were British, 40% foreign, and 18% had been awarded British citizenship or the right to remain in the country indefinitely. These figures show that in both countries, there has been a clear, sizeable increase in the number of indigenous jihadi terrorists.

This change is even more pronounced when we consider the average length of time that foreigners have spent living in each country before becoming involved in terrorism. In the US, this increased from 4.1 years to 10.7, and in the UK it increased from 2.4 years to 9.1. This implies that over time, foreign jihadis operating in or out of either country are more likely to have radicalized there as opposed to having come with the pre-existing intention of conducting terrorist activities.[39] In line with this analysis, the number of individuals entering each country using illegal means dropped from 8% to 4% in the US, and from 17% to 4% in the UK.[40] Combined, these results clearly demonstrate a much greater home-grown component to Islamist terrorism. That said, it is also apparent that British jihadis are comparatively more likely to be born and raised in the UK compared to their American counterparts, who are more likely to have been born overseas and to be naturalized citizens or permanent residents.[41] In both cases it appears that the majority of individuals are radicalizing within their respective home/host countries but the overall balance in the domestic versus overseas origins of home-grown jihadis is different. This appears to be at least a partial reflection of the respective Muslim populations and may also be related to the presence of more well-established jihadi subcultures in Britain, but it is an issue that will require further research to untangle.

Nationality

Another question which arises relates to ethnicity or nationality. Aside from American and British, what other nationalities are represented?[42] The pre-9/11 sample in the US includes a total of 24 different nationalities. Aside from American, the greatest numbers of individuals were Egyptian (15%), Saudi (13%), and Palestinian (10%). After 9/11, a total of 39 nationalities were included, with most individuals being of South Asian (including Pakistani, Bangladeshi, and Indian) (17%) or Somali (16%) heritage. In the UK before 9/11 a total of 22 nationalities were represented, including 25% Algerians, another 25% who were of South Asian heritage, and 12% who were Libyans. The post-9/11 sample includes 36 nationalities, yet it is also more dominated by South Asians (especially Pakistanis) who account for 49% of all British jihadis within this period.[43] In both countries, the ethnic composition of the samples is reflective of patterns of immigration and has become more diverse over time. The greater ethnic diversity of jihadis in the US is thus a reflection of its seemingly more varied Muslim population.[44] By contrast, 68% of British Muslims are of Asian background, with Pakistanis alone making up 38%.[45] Moreover, the ethnic make-up of American and

British jihadis has clearly also been sensitive to shifts in the global jihadi landscape. This explains the increase in the number of Somalis in the US, the decrease in the number of Algerians in the UK, and also the rising number of South Asians in both countries as Pakistan took on greater significance in the global jihad after 9/11.

Education

The next variable of interest is education. In line with the discussion in Chapter 2 and with previous research findings, the available data here do not support the contention that home-grown jihadis are simply a bunch of uneducated thugs. In the US, prior to 9/11, at least 24% had obtained university qualifications (including six Master's degrees and two PhDs), 19% had completed high school, and only 1% had failed to do so. After 9/11, these figures were 16% (including seven Master's, three MDs and a degree in pharmacy), 21%, and 11%, respectively. In the UK, at least 17% of the earlier sample had completed university (including three Master's, two PhDs, one MD, and a degree in dentistry), 19% had completed high school, and none had failed to do so.[46] After 9/11, 10% had graduated from university (including at least one Master's, two MDs, and another degree in dentistry) and 17% graduated from high school, with just 1% failing to complete basic education.

Although a great deal of information was missing,[47] it is relatively safe to assume that most individuals in both samples are likely to have at least a foundational high school education.[48] Certainly, the data here confirm that several American and British jihadis are very highly educated, meaning that this is by no means a form of fail-safe protection against radicalization. Furthermore, there is nothing to suggest that lack of education is a causal factor for involvement in Islamist terrorism. None of this is particularly surprising. What is of greater interest is the fact that British jihadis appear to have been consistently less likely to obtain university qualifications, while their American counterparts are more likely to fail to complete high school.[49] Even more interesting is the fact that overall levels of education in both countries seem to have decreased somewhat over time. In the absence of obvious and compelling explanations for these observations,[50] we must not forget that the observed changes are relative — in both cases the number of people with university qualifications actually increased slightly from one time period to the next, and yet they accounted for a smaller proportion of each sample. It is also quite possible that the picture here is obscured by the large amounts of missing information and further exploration is therefore necessary.

Occupation

Following on from levels of education, additional insight into who becomes an Islamist terrorist in each country can be gained by looking at occupations. As summarized in Table 5.1, 17% of American jihadis who became active before September 11, 2001 were in skilled occupations such as senior manager, engineer, or computer programmer; another 19% were in semi-skilled occupations such as truck driver, construction worker, or car salesman; 20% were in unskilled occupations such as cab driver, factory worker, or retail salesperson; 13% were students; and 6% were unemployed. In the more recent period, only 8% of individuals were classed as holding skilled occupations; 19% were semi-skilled; 20% were unskilled; 18% were students; and 13% were unemployed. In the UK prior to 9/11, 7% of individuals were in skilled occupations; 11% were in semi-skilled jobs; 12% were unskilled; 7% were students; and 14% were unemployed. After 9/11, the number of individuals in skilled occupations decreased further to just 3%; the semi-skilled category stayed constant at 11%; the number of individuals in unskilled occupations rose to 16%; 10% were students; and 18% were unemployed.

There are two findings of note here. First of all, in both countries there has been a relative decrease in the number of jihadi terrorists in skilled occupations and a rise in the number of unemployed (with little change in between). This is consistent with the finding that there has been a relative decrease in the number of individuals who have successfully completed university education. Together, these results are in alignment with the notion that violent jihad has become an established counterculture which appears to resonate somewhat more among the socioeconomically disadvantaged. This in turn lends support to the argument that feelings of disillusionment and marginalization, *while unlikely to be primary causal factors*, can nevertheless raise the level of pre-disposing risk for radicalization. The second finding with regards to occupation again appears to support the results for education and corresponds with previous research.[51] Hence, it appears that British jihadis are much less likely to hold skilled or semi-skilled occupations compared to those in the US, and across time they have shown a stronger tendency to be unemployed.[52] The true picture is once again likely to have been distorted by missing information (particularly in the UK), and yet it reinforces the suggestion that British jihadis on the whole are somewhat less well-off than their counterparts on the other side of the Atlantic. This may go some way to explaining higher rates of mobilization in the UK, although it should be remembered that the connection between socioeconomic status and involvement in terrorism is indirect. Indeed, as Simcox and Dyer have also highlighted, radicalization is clearly occurring in the US as well despite the relative advantages afforded American Muslims, thus reinforcing the argument that socioeconomic factors play a secondary role at best.[53,54]

Faith

Given the significance of religious affiliation as a marker of identity and a point of reference for beginning to unravel the mystery of Islamist terrorism, it is important to inspect this in greater detail. Before 2001 in the US, 78% of individuals were classed as 'born' Muslims, 17% were converts, and 1% (just one individual[55]) was a non-Muslim. Since then, 65% of individuals were classed as born Muslims, 22% were converts, 2% were non-Muslims, and another 2% were classed as 'religious offshoots' who combined elements of Islamist ideology with other theological concepts.[56] By comparison, 91% of individuals who were active before 2001 in the UK were classed as born Muslims and 9% were converts. After 9/11, the number of confirmed, born Muslims decreased to 75%, converts increased slightly to 12%, and 1% (two individuals) were classed as non-Muslims.

In reality, the observed decrease in the number of born Muslims in both countries is unlikely to have been quite so large. This is because there were additional unknowns for whom there was insufficient information to be able make a judgment but, based on names and the overall balance of probabilities, were most likely Muslims from birth, if only nominally so. Indeed, it is also important to note that very few jihadis in either sample were reported to have been devout practitioners from an early age, thus reinforcing the notion that popular interpretations of Islam are essentially incompatible with the violent ideology of Islamist terrorists.

The most interesting finding here, however, is that the percentage of converts to Islam among US jihadis has been consistently close to double that in the UK. This is a consistent but somewhat larger difference than detected in earlier research; however, as discussed below, the findings regarding converts are otherwise markedly different.[57] Moreover, in both countries there has been a slight proportional increase — and a large increase in absolute terms — in the number of converts over time. The latter trend can again be explained by heightened awareness of jihadi ideology and its consolidation as a counterculture after 9/11. However, the difference between the two countries is more difficult to explain. On the one hand, the number of American converts is larger than the UK both proportionally and in absolute terms (50 versus 34). On the other hand, as Simcox and Dyer have noted, the percentage of converts involved in Islamist terrorism in the US appears to correspond with the estimated proportion of converts within the American Muslim population as a whole, while converts in the UK appear to be over-represented among British jihadis.[58] Although an immediate, comprehensive explanation for these differences is elusive, it would appear that British converts are more likely to be exposed to pro-jihadist attitudes as a result of the greater physical presence of related social networks. Furthermore, as the discussion below reveals there are some rather intriguing qualitative differences between jihadi converts in each country, particularly in relation to criminality and mental illness.

As for the presence of a small number of non-Muslims involved in Islamist terrorism, this is a reminder that there will always be exceptions to the rule. So although the vast majority of jihadis are ideologically engaged to some extent, there are others who are willing to assist them or to try to use them for their personal gain. Typically, this refers to criminal opportunists who are seeking to profit in some way by providing terrorists with goods or services. For example, in 2004 one Gale Nettles (dubbed 'Ben Laden') was arrested at the age of 66 in a sting operation in Chicago, attempting to sell fertilizer to al-Qaeda.[59] Others have offered to train operatives, obtain weaponry, provide false documents, and launder money. In a rather bizarre case in the UK, a man named Malcolm Hodges once tried to incite Islamist terrorist attacks against the Association of Chartered Certified Accountants more than a decade after failing his accountancy exam.[60] In Hodges' case — and in several others involving criminal opportunists — he is perhaps best described as a troubled individual, with social and possible psychological problems (see 'Ideological Classification' below). It is also frequently the case that such individuals are older and in the context of the US they are likely to have significant criminal records and to be caught in sting operations.[61] Thus, while small numbers of non-Muslims do seek involvement in Islamist terrorism for non-ideological reasons, they are unlikely to have actual connections to genuine jihadis and are very much on the outer fringes of the phenomenon, if not society in general as well.

Marital Status

After faith, the next variable of interest is marital status. Just as Western jihadis are not lacking in education, nor are they desperate singletons incapable of forming relationships with the opposite sex. In the US, 51% of individuals in the sample before 9/11, and 30% afterwards were married or co-habiting at the time they took up violent jihad. In the UK, the corresponding figures were 40% and 32%. In both countries, many of these individuals also had children. These findings are again very much in line with previous research where this variable was recorded and although it is impossible to comment on the quality of these relationships, the idea that jihadis by-and-large are socially inept, sexually frustrated loners driven by the promise of virgins in heaven is not supported.[62] Nevertheless, it is certainly interesting to note that the relative percentage of those who are married appears to have declined in recent years, which might be seen as yet further evidence of a growing appeal of violent jihad as a counterculture among marginalized young men.

Criminality

If this is indeed the case, we might also expect to see a rise in levels of criminality. This certainly appears to have been the case in the US, where before 9/11 only 13% of individuals were known to have a previous criminal record, compared to 28% since.[63] In particular there have been increases in the relative number of individuals with convictions for violence, weapons offenses, drugs, and dishonesty. The picture in the UK, however, is almost the complete opposite, where prior convictions were confirmed in 31% of the earlier sample but only 19% of the latter. This apparent reduction in criminality is largely due to the dismantling of the jihadi networks of the 1990s, which included significant numbers of illegal immigrants from North Africa who were prolific fraudsters and dealt extensively in false documents. This interpretation is supported by the fact that there were notable decreases in the proportion of dishonesty and immigration offenses in the UK. Returning to the US, it seems that the higher rates of criminality since 9/11 are related to the greater number of converts, 56% of whom have criminal records compared to just 20% of the rest of the sample during this period. British converts also account for a significant amount of criminality after 9/11 (29% had criminal records versus 17% of the rest of the sample) although it is a much smaller proportion and less of a difference compared to non-converts than in the US.

Mental Health

The final demographic variable of interest listed in Tables 5.1 and 5.2 relates to mental health. Just 3% of American jihadis who began their careers prior to 9/11 are known to have suffered from a history of mental health problems, compared to 11% since then (plus an additional 1% whose mental health was questioned at trial). Meanwhile, the respective figures in the UK are 6% and 5%.[64] What is immediately obvious from these findings is that — as discussed in Chapter 2 — psychopathology does not generally explain involvement in terrorism.[65] As in other categories though, it is the differences between countries that are of interest and yet again American converts in particular appear to be playing a role. Thus, while there is no compelling reason for the variance prior to September 11, 2001, the post-9/11 difference is partially explained by the fact that 24% of US converts (versus 9% in the UK[66] and 8% of the rest of the US sample) have a documented history of mental health issues. Moreover, when we re-examine educational achievement, we also find that US converts who mobilized after 9/11 are much more likely to have failed to complete high school (26% after 9/11, compared to 7% of the rest of the US sample during this period[67]) and are also less likely to hold a university level qualification (10% versus 17%). Likewise, they were far more likely to be unemployed (28% versus 4% of the rest of the sample). This is in direct contrast to Simcox and Dyer's findings which suggested that US converts were *more* likely to hold a college degree compared to non-converts as well as more likely to be either employed or currently undergoing education.[68] Again this difference is explained by the methodology employed. Firstly, by grouping together people who mobilized to violent jihad before and after 9/11, changes over time are obscured. For instance, in the current sample 28% of pre-9/11 converts in America had obtained a college or university qualification and therefore were much more highly qualified than those who mobilized after 9/11. In addition, the current research utilized a somewhat wider sampling frame, allowing for people who were still facing legal allegations, were killed overseas (not necessarily just in suicide attacks), or were prosecuted for non-terrorism offenses, such as Jose Pimentel, Troy Kastigar, and Justin Singleton, respectively. Once again, this highlights the need to measure changes over time and when the findings here in relation to mental health, education, and occupation are viewed together with the above findings in relation to criminality, it is clear that a sizeable minority of home-grown jihadis in the US consists of a disadvantaged 'underclass' that is quite distinct from the rest of the sample. British converts are also clearly marginalized. In addition to the findings noted above, 31% were unemployed after 9/11 compared to 16% of non-converts, and only one individual (accounting for 3%) had completed university compared to 11% of the rest of the sample. It is thus converts more than anyone else that conform to stereotypical descriptions of jihadis as disenfranchised. However, the disparity in the UK, while substantial, is much less than in the US and British converts still account for a smaller proportion of the sample overall.[69]

Radicalization

Having addressed *who* becomes an Islamist terrorist in the US and UK, let us now turn our attention to the question of *how* they get involved. Given that this is such an important question both for understanding and potentially combating extremist mobilization, there is remarkably little information available that would enable a reliable, systematic analysis at the aggregate level. The reason for this, of course, is that we only find out that people are violent extremists *after* they have already radicalized,[70] meaning that their journeys up until that point in time must be pieced together after the fact, and all too often that simply is not possible in any real detail.

In light of these challenges, the focus of investigation here is deliberately restricted to a single, key issue which continues to preoccupy academics, practitioners, and policymakers alike — the role of the Internet in home-grown radicalization.[71] Radicalization was thus classified as either 'social' (involving face-to-face interaction), 'virtual' (involving downloaded material and sometimes interaction online), or 'mixed' (consisting of a combination of the two). Although relatively simplistic, this enabled a quantitative assessment of the relative balance of social and online behaviors. By way of example, groups that seemingly radicalized primarily by way of social interaction include the Los Angeles cell begun by Kevin James and Levar Washington in prison, and the 7/7 London bombers. Examples of 'virtual' radicalization are Colleen LaRose in the US and Andrew 'Isa' Ibrahim in the UK, while instances of 'mixed' radicalization include a small group centered around Tarek Mehanna in Massachusetts and the Operation Guava groups in Britain.

Despite this approach, the relative lack of information remained a serious problem both before and after 9/11.[72] With this limitation in mind, the Internet was still in its infancy during the 1990s and so it is no surprise that the available information pointed almost exclusively to socially driven processes of radicalization prior to 2001.[73] Certainly this seems to have been the case for the many acolytes of influential figures such as Omar Abdel Rahman and Abu Hamza al-Masri, for instance. The only individual for whom the Internet seemingly played a role during this period was Adam Gadahn. However, this was at the very outset of Gadahn's pathway to extremism when he was first learning about religion, and it was only later that he truly radicalized after falling under the influence of veteran jihadis.[74]

After 9/11, the picture is more varied. In the US, 4% of individuals were classed as having radicalized by way of social interaction, another 4% were classed as having radicalized purely online, and 13% were judged to have undergone a mixed process. The corresponding figures in the UK were 6%, 3%, and 7%. On its own this is not enough to draw conclusions with a great deal of confidence, other than that it confirms that all three types of radicalization seem to exist (and therefore the Internet has indeed increased in significance since 2001). More tentatively, these figures also suggest that contemporary radicalization in the US and UK is most likely to involve social and virtual elements combined. This observation is supported by the fact that the majority of people in both samples offended in groups, rather than on their own, and use of the Internet for accessing and downloading propaganda was also relatively widespread (see Chapter 6). Based on this analysis and what we know about radicalization more generally, it would thus appear that social interaction acts as the engine of radicalization, while online propaganda provides the fuel.

At face value, this is really not so different to the pre-9/11 era, when group interaction was also supplemented by physical materials such as books, magazines, and videos. What is different, of course, is that the Internet is much more widely available and also enables online interaction, which presents opportunities for networking and in some cases may reduce the need for actual physical contact. Hence, the precise balance of social and virtual processes appears to vary within different groups. As indicated by the above figures, a small number of individuals also radicalized entirely online. We should not, however, interpret this as meaning that the Internet is *replacing* in-person social interaction as the primary mechanism of radicalization. People who radicalize entirely online are very much the exception to the rule and also tend to be atypical in a number of other ways. In particular, although some of them do go on to take part in group-based extremist activities (such as Colleen LaRose and Jamie Paulin-Ramirez), many of them are more-or-less isolated loners. Moreover, in the US, seven of nine virtually radicalized individuals were converts[75] and in the UK, four of nine were 'troubled individuals', two of whom had documented mental health problems. Thus, although the Internet clearly plays a significant role in radicalization in both countries, there is little reason to believe that this process is transitioning entirely to the virtual realm.[76]

Nevertheless, this does not necessarily mean that the balance of social and virtual radicalization in America is identical to that in Britain. An additional, even more tentative implication of the above figures is that the Internet may be playing a bigger role in the US. Thus, when we add the virtual and mixed cases of radicalization, this accounts for 17% of individuals in the US versus 10% in the UK. Of course, the large amounts of missing data prohibit firm conclusions and the known difference here is hardly vast. However, it would indeed make sense in light of the above discussions relating to the geographical distribution of cases and the relative lack of socially ingrained jihadi subcultures in the US. It may also help explain the greater involvement of American converts, since the Internet played a role in the radicalization of at least 26% of these individuals, compared to 14% of the rest of the US sample and 11% of converts in the UK (see also 'The Role of the Internet' in Chapter 6). Given the potential ramifications for counterterrorism, this is a worthwhile avenue for future exploration.

Beyond understanding how the Internet has impacted upon processes of radicalization after 9/11, questions remain about the quality of interactions, where these interactions take place, specific materials which jihadis find most appealing, the arguments they use to justify their actions, and possible indicators or outward signs of increasing extremism.[77] Although macro-level quantitative analysis of these issues was again thwarted by a lack of data,[78] a number of them are touched upon in the following chapter under the headings of group characteristics, the (operational) role of the Internet, and stated motivations. The implications of these findings are also discussed in the closing chapter of the book. Suffice it to say that they are congruent with the earlier discussion of radicalization and motivations for Islamist terrorism in Chapter 2.

Ideological Classification

The final variable summarized in Tables 5.1 and 5.2 explores the issue of ideological commitment. During the course of this research, three main types of individuals were identified based on their behavior, verbal expressions of belief and additional information about their personal circumstances and motivations: (1) Jihadists — people who were clearly engaged with jihadi ideology to some extent; (2) Criminal opportunists who were willing to provide criminal services for personal gain; and, (3) Troubled individuals for whom personal, social, or psychological problems appeared to play a significant role, perhaps more so than true ideological commitment.[79]

Before 9/11, 97% of individuals in the US sample were classed as jihadists, just one person was judged to be a criminal opportunist, and there were no troubled individuals. Similarly, 99% of the UK sample consisted of jihadists and no other ideological types were detected.

In accordance with many of the other variables examined in this study, what we find after 9/11 is more variety. In the US, 82% of individuals were classed as jihadists — a notable drop from the earlier period — while the remainder consisted of 7% criminal opportunists, 4% troubled individuals, and 3% ideological offshoots[80] (plus 7% who could not be classified due to lack of information). Meanwhile, in the UK 91% of individuals were classed as jihadists, 2% were troubled individuals, and there was one criminal opportunist (with another 7% who defied classification).

These results echo the earlier discussion (above) in relation to the greater number of converts and the related increases in criminality and mental illness in the US. Hence, the increased involvement of criminal opportunists and troubled individuals is an added indication that Islamist terrorism is attracting a small yet significant number of highly marginalized Americans who perceive violent jihad as an opportunity for financial gain and/or expression of personal grievances and a fascination with violence. An illustrative example is Joseph Brice, a drug-abusing college drop-out from Asotin County in Washington who was arrested in May 2011 and later convicted for planning to supply jihadi terrorists — in reality the FBI — with improvised explosives. Previously, Brice had been a right-wing extremist before transitioning to violent jihad, which he actively promoted online. But according to investigators his real motives were simply 'violence and chaos'[81] and although he claimed to 'fight for the cause of Allah'[82] he still drank alcohol on a daily basis.[83] Indeed, it is important to point out that many criminal opportunists and troubled individuals are non-Muslims, or of unknown faith, meaning that the 'underclass' of Islamist terrorism in America includes more than just converts.

These developments have been comparatively lacking in the UK. The only criminal opportunist in the British sample was a Hindu named Hemant Lakhani who was actually caught in a US sting operation in August of 2003.[84] There were also fewer troubled individuals, all but two of whom were converts (suggesting that there is less 'outsider appeal' to violent jihad in Britain). The main difference in the UK before and after 9/11 was thus the rise in the number of 'unknowns' where there was insufficient information to be able to make a judgment. This included a couple of 'odd' individuals whose motives could not be determined,[85] plus a handful of people who knew about terrorist plots but chose not to disclose it to authorities, or who assisted terrorist offenders on an *ad hoc* basis (and were thus seemingly motivated by friendship, loyalty, and/or disdain for authorities). Most of them, however, were most likely jihadists (based upon what they are known or alleged to have done) meaning that the difference in the UK from one time period to the next is smaller than the above figures suggest.

Ultimately, although home-grown jihad in the US appears to have been slightly more ideologically diluted than in the UK, we should not lose sight of the fact that the vast majority of people in both samples are indeed jihadists who are mentally engaged with extremist ideology, including a few particularly dedicated individuals. This lends support to the motivational model proposed in Chapter 2 which suggests that exposure to jihadi ideology — with some exceptions — is a necessary condition for involvement in Islamist terrorism.

Concluding Remarks

The question of who becomes an Islamist terrorist in the US and UK is by no means straightforward. Generally speaking, the findings here are very much in conformity with established theoretical and empirical observations of Western jihadis, confirming that the primary candidates are young, Muslim males, typically from quite unremarkable backgrounds. In that sense, we see a great deal of similarity between the two countries as well as consistency over time. However, looking past such superficial and rather bland observations, there are also important differences and significant aspects of change.

Jihadis in the US are more geographically dispersed, ethnically varied and on average appear to be slightly better off than in the UK. However, the data also suggest that a relatively large jihadi 'underclass' exists in the US, largely consisting of converts and criminals who are comparatively uneducated as a group and frequently suffer from social and psychological problems. This is likely to have been facilitated by the growth of the Internet as a vehicle for propaganda and a mechanism of radicalization, which was observed in both countries but which may have occurred to a greater extent in the US. As a result, Islamist terrorism in America has suffered from a degree of 'ideological dilution', whereby a small, yet significant minority has become involved for primarily non-ideological reasons.

By contrast, UK jihadis are more geographically confined within certain hotspots; they are dominated by South Asians (although more likely to be born in the UK) and they are more likely to lie at the lower-to-middle end of the socioeconomic spectrum. This includes a relatively large number of converts compared to estimates for the UK Muslim population as a whole, but — while still a distinct subgroup — they are somewhat closer to the rest of the British sample and are fewer in number compared to the US. The available information suggests that while the Internet has indeed become more important to radicalization, localized, pro-jihadi subcultures appear to be the most significant factor in the UK. Perhaps because of this, there are fewer truly marginalized individuals within the UK sample and the jihadi movement in Britain seems to be more ideologically homogenous overall.

Differences notwithstanding, there are three fundamental points of similarity in the way that Islamist terrorism has developed in the US and UK: After 9/11, jihadi terrorist activity has increased, it has become more home-grown, and it has become more diverse in terms of who becomes a terrorist and how. But what, precisely, have these individuals been doing? Do American and British jihadis engage in the same activities? Has their behavior evolved over time? These are the questions which are addressed in the following chapter.

Notes

[1]367 is the US sample total including 2 repeat offenders (Daniel Boyd and Hysen Sherifi). Minus repeat offenders the true US sample total is 365.

[2]435 is the UK sample total including 7 repeat offenders (Abdul Rehman Saleem, Ibrahim Abdullah Hassan, Shah Jalal Hussain, Abdul Muhid, Umran Javed, Nicholas Roddis, and Zohaib Kamran Ahmed) plus 1 control order absconder (BX) who was later identified as Ibrahim Magag. The true UK sample total is 427.

[3]US population figures from 1980 to 2013 were obtained from the United States Census Bureau ('U.S. and World Population Clock', available at: www.census.gov/popclock). UK population figures were obtained from the Office for National Statistics ('Age Structure of the United Kingdom, 1971–2085', available at: http://www.ons.gov.uk/ons/interactive/uk-population-psyramid—dvc1/index.html).

[4]The average yearly rate of Islamist terrorism (individuals beginning their jihadi careers) in the US was 0.0000000378634127 In the UK it was 0.0000002127156243.

[5]Pew Research Center, *The Future of the Global Muslim Population* (Pew Research Center, 2011), available at: www.pewforum.org/2011/01/27/the-future-of-the-global-muslim-population/, accessed February 4, 2014.

[6]Other features of the Muslim population that might be important include, for example, the precise religious composition (different 'sects'), age distribution, gender, and proportion of first/second/third generation immigrants.

[7]Jonathan Bronitsky, 'Crescent Over the Thames', *War on the Rocks*, September 3, 2014, available at: http://warontherocks.com/2014/09/crescent-over-the-thames/#_, accessed September 3, 2014.

[8]Note that this calls into question the argument that different rates of Islamist terrorism in each country can be primarily explained by differences in the socioeconomic standing of the respective Muslim populations. If America's Muslims are indeed much better off than those in the UK, why have the rates of jihadi mobilization relative to Muslim population size seemingly been so similar?

[9]Note that this refers to overt behavior and does not capture earlier processes of radicalization which are mostly impossible to reliably determine.

[10]Note that for practical reasons the 1980s are represented as a whole decade in Figures 1 and 2, rather than being broken down year by year. Meanwhile the point on each graph for the 1990s records those individuals who are known to have begun their jihadi careers in the 1990s but where the precise year is unknown.

[11]In addition, there are numerous individuals within the UK sample (among them, for example, Abu Qatada) whose first known or clearly alleged involvement in terrorism did not occur until the 1990s even though we may reasonably suspect that they were involved much earlier than this. The picture is also somewhat confused by the fact that some individuals who offended in the US (e.g. Omar Abdel Rahman) began their careers in terrorism before they entered the country.

[12]This analysis is supported by the fact that militants beginning their careers at this time in the UK had far more known domestic connections than their American counterparts.

[13]Jennifer Pinto, 'Public's Views of Afghanistan War Have Turned Sour', *CBS News*, October 5, 2009, available at: http://www.cbsnews.com/news/publics-views-of-afghanistan-war-have-turned-sour/, accessed February 13, 2014; Dalia Sussman, 'Poll Shows View of Iraq War Is Most Negative Since Start', *New York Times*, May 25, 2007, available at: http://www.nytimes.com/2007/05/25/washington/25view.html?_r= 2&oref=slogin&, accessed February 13, 2014.

[14]'Terror Charges Unsealed in Minnesota Against Eight Defendants, Justice Department Announces', *US Department of Justice*, November 23, 2009, available at: http://www.justice.gov/usao/mn/major/major0459.pdf, accessed June 11, 2010.

[15]The reasons for this lull are not immediately obvious, although one possible explanation is that British jihadists were laying low or simply experiencing collective fatigue following the extremely high profile arrests of the liquid bomb plotters in August of 2006. In any case, we should not expect a constant rate of jihadist mobilization.

[16]See, for example, 'Ali Twins Jailed for Funding Terrorism Abroad', *BBC News*, August 1, 2012, available at: http://www.bbc.co.uk/news/uk-england-london-19079802, accessed August 1, 2012.

[17]Including ten prosecutions in Yemen; seven in France; two in Egypt; and one each in Algeria and the US.

[18]Note that Table 5.2 lists the total percentage of legal allegations (and special sanctions). It does not distinguish between foreign and domestic measures due to limitations of space.

[19]This map was adapted using the following original source: http://commons.wikimedia.org/wiki/File:US_map_-_states_and_capitals.png, accessed February 20, 2015.

[20]This map was adapted using the following original sources: http://upload.wikimedia.org/wikipedia/commons/1/11/United_Kingdom_administrative_areas.svg and http://upload.wikimedia.org/wikipedia/commons/4/45/United_Kingdom_NUTS_location_map.svg, accessed February 20, 2015.

[21]The top three US cities for jihadist activity before 9/11 were New York City, NY (15%), Jersey City, NJ (13%), and Lackawanna, NY (6%). After 9/11 they were New York City, NY (13%), Minneapolis, MN (10%), and Chicago, IL (4%).

[22]Based on data from the 2011 UK Census (see '2011 Census: KS209EW Religion, Local Authorities in England and Wales' (2012), *Office for National Statistics*, available at: http://www.ons.gov.uk/ons/rel/census/2011-census/key-statistics-for-local-authorities-in-england-and-wales/rft-table-ks209ew.xls, accessed April 29, 2014).

[23]Unfortunately, there is much less reliable information available to be able to assess the situation in the US.

[24]'2011 Census: KS209EW Religion, Local Authorities in England and Wales'.

[25]Robin Simcox and Emily Dyer, *Al-Qaeda in the United States: A Complete Analysis of Terrorism Offences* (The Henry Jackson Society, 2013), available at: http://henryjacksonsociety.org/wp-content/uploads/2013/02/Al-Qaeda-in-the-USAbridged-version-LOWRES-Final.pdf, accessed April 7, 2013; Robin Simcox, Hannah Stuart, and Houria Ahmed, *Islamist Terrorism: The British Connections* (London: The Centre for Social Cohesion, 2010).

[26]Sam Mullins, '"Global Jihad": The Canadian Experience' (2013), *Terrorism and Political Violence*, 25(5), 734–776.

[27]Sam Mullins, 'Islamist Terrorism and Australia: An Empirical Examination of the "Home-Grown" Threat' (2011), *Terrorism and Political Violence*, 23(2), 254–285.

[28]Marc Sageman, *Leaderless Jihad: Terror Networks in the Twenty-First Century* (Philadelphia: University of Pennsylvania Press, 2008).

[29]Reported ages at time of first known jihadi offense.

[30]They were: Evelyn Cortez, who assisted Matarawy Saleh's attempt to evade arrest; Lynne Stewart, who allowed Omar Abdel Rahmen to smuggle messages out from his prison cell; and October Lewis, who sent money to her husband, Jeffrey Battle, while he pursued jihad overseas.

[31]'Aafia Siddiqui Found Guilty in Manhattan Federal Court of Attempting to Murder U.S. Nationals in Afghanistan and Six Additional Charges', *Federal Bureau of Investigation*, February 3, 2010, available at: http://www.fbi.gov/newyork/press-releases/2010/nyfo020310a.htm, accessed February 3, 2010; Farah Stockman, 'Activist Turned Extremist, US Says: Ex-Hub Woman

Tied to Al Qaeda', *The Boston Globe*, August 12, 2008, available at: http://www.highbeam.com/doc/1P2-17002360.html, accessed June 30, 2006.

[32]'Federal Judge Sentences "Jihad Jane" to Serve 10 Years in Prison for Role in Plot to Commit Murder Overseas', *Federal Bureau of Investigation*, January 6, 2014, available at: http://www.fbi.gov/philadelphia/press-releases/2014/federal-judge-sentences-jihad-jane-to-serve-10-years-in-prison-for-role-in-plot-to-commit-murder-overseas, accessed January 6, 2014.

[33]'Woman Jailed for 15 Years for Attempting to Murder MP', *The Telegraph*, November 3, 2010, available at: http://www.telegraph.co.uk/news/uknews/terrorism-in-the-uk/8107344/Woman-jailed-for-15-years-for-attempting-to-murder-MP.html, accessed November 3, 2010.

[34]'Oldham Wife Shasta Khan Guilty of Jewish Jihad Plan', *BBC News*, July 19, 2012, available at: http://www.bbc.co.uk/news/uk-england-manchester-18882619, accessed July 19, 2012.

[35]Mike Pflanz, 'July 7 Bomber Widow Samantha Lewthwaite Charged With Planning Explosions', *The Telegraph*, May 11, 2012, available at: http://www.telegraph.co.uk/news/worldnews/africaandindianocean/kenya/9260206/July-7-bomber-widow-Samantha-Lewthwaite-charged-with-planning-explosions.html, accessed May 11, 2012.

[36]Ruth Sherlock, 'Syria: From Acton to Idlib, the British Jihadi Who Died Fighting Assad', *The Telegraph*, June 1, 2013, available at: http://www.telegraph.co.uk/news/worldnews/middleeast/syria/10093474/Syria-from-Acton-to-Idlib-the-British-jihadi-who-died-fighting-Assad.html, accessed June 1, 2013.

[37]The number of people who were specifically reported to have been born in each country was lower than the number who were reportedly American or British as their first nationality. Both sets of figures were recorded separately, although the latter is used to describe the sample since it strongly implies place of birth.

[38]Note that Tables 5.1 and 5.2 show the percentage of foreigners who held US/UK naturalized citizenship or who had permanent residency. This, of course, is different to the overall percentage of each sample.

[39]An alternative explanation would be that we have seen an increase in so-called 'sleeper cells'; however there is nothing to support this interpretation and plenty to suggest that the majority of Western jihadis of foreign origin have indeed radicalized within their host countries.

[40]This also disputes the myth that terrorists generally infiltrate America and Britain using false passports or other illegal means. The data acquired for this study suggest that they are far more likely to enter the country using legitimate passports and visas, although numerous individuals then violated the terms of their visa (e.g. by overstaying or working on a student visa) or fraudulently obtained permanent residency or citizenship (e.g. via marriage).

[41]This is also in accordance with studies of convicted terrorists (see Robin Simcox and Emily Dyer, 'Terror Data: US vs. UK', *World Affairs Journal*, July/August 2013, available at: http://www.worldaffairsjournal.org/article/terror-data-us-vs-uk, accessed December 10, 2013).

[42]This is regardless of whether individuals were domestic or foreign-born, i.e. it includes first and second nationalities.

[43]Note that the Percentage of South Asians in the British sample is very much in line with the research conducted by Simcox *et al.* (*The British Connections*). However, they detected just 14 nationalities in their sample compared to 36 here. This again highlights the significance of methodology and the need to constantly update research.

[44]Pew Research Center, *Muslim Americans: Middle Class and Mostly Mainstream* (Pew Research Center, 2007), available at: http://pewresearch.org/assets/pdf/muslim-americans.pdf, accessed April 29, 2009.

[45]'What Does the Census Tell us About Religion in 2011?', *Office for National Statistics*, May 16, 2013, available at: http://www.ons.gov.uk/ons/rel/census/2011-census/detailed-characteristics-for-local-authorities-in-england-and-wales/sty-religion.html, accessed May 9, 2014.

[46]Note that levels of education in the US and UK are not always directly comparable. Numerous individuals in the UK sample achieved only a basic high school education, leaving at the age of 16. In the US, the age at which people can leave high school varies depending on the state and the specific ages of individuals in the sample were not reported. Moreover, 'college' in either country can mean different things — for this study it was generally classed as the equivalent of university, except in cases where the qualifications appeared to be closer to the level of high-school. These judgements, however, were not always easy to make.

[47]Information about level of education was unavailable for 48% of the combined US sample, and 72% of the total UK sample.

[48]Of course this assumption is far from certain, but is supported by the fact that the majority of American and British jihadis have lived much of their youth in the US/UK and in both cases high school education is compulsory. Moreover, when terrorism suspects have particularly low or high levels of education it tends to be reported in the news, whereas the average (completing high school) is much less likely to be considered worthy of public interest.

[49]These findings are broadly compatible with those of Simcox and Dyer, although they measured the level of educational *attendance* rather than qualifications and of course the methodological differences noted also apply (see Simcox and Dyer, 'Terror Data: US vs. UK').

[50]For example, a decline in educational achievement could feasibly be related to a decrease in average age; this might apply in the UK (although the age differential over time was small) but is seemingly less applicable in the US, where age appears to have remained relatively constant.

[51]Simcox and Dyer, 'Terror Data: US vs. UK'.

[52]Across time, a total of 31% of individuals in the US sample were in either skilled or semi-skilled occupations and 10% were unemployed. The respective figures for the UK are 15% and 16%.

[53]Simcox and Dyer, 'Terror Data: US vs. UK'.

[54]In addition, the dramatic increase in Islamist militancy in the West in response to Syria suggests that there must be other, much more relevant factors involved than socioeconomic status of domestic Muslim populations, since this is unlikely to be subject to such rapid change.

[55]This was Lynne Stewart, the lawyer of Omar Abdel Rahman, who was convicted for helping him smuggle messages out from his prison cell.

[56]This refers to members of the 'Liberty City 7' from Miami, who combined Islam with teachings of the Moorish Science Temple.

[57]Robin Simcox and Emily Dyer, 'The Role of Converts in Al-Qa'ida-Related Terrorism Offenses in the United States', *CTC Sentinel*, 6(3), available at: https://www.ctc.usma.edu/posts/the-role-of-converts-in-al-qaida-related-terrorism-offenses-in-the-united-states, accessed April 2, 2013.

[58]*Ibid.*

[59]Rudolph Bush, '160-Year Sentence in Bomb Scheme: FBI had Tracked Plan to Blow up Courthouse', *Chicago Tribune*, January 13, 2006, available at: http://www.highbeam.com/doc/1G1-140830975.html. Accessed December 7, 2011.

[60]'Man Urged Terror Attacks on Accountancy Institutes — 10 Years after Failing Professional Exams', *The Daily Mail*, February 19, 2008, available at: http://www.dailymail.co.uk/news/article-516448/Man-urged-terror-attacks-accountancy-institutes-10-years-failing-professional-exams.html, accessed July 1, 2010.

[61]This may therefore have affected the average age of US jihadis after 9/11, which did not demonstrate the expected, modest decline observed in the UK.

[62]See Mullins, '"Global Jihad": The Canadian Experience'.

[63]Note that the problem of missing information is particularly acute regarding criminal records since it is very rare that an *absence* of previous criminality is reported (the total percentages of 'unknowns' were thus 63% in the US and 76% in the UK).

[64]As with information about criminal records, missing data are especially acute when it comes to mental health because there is little reason to report on the absence of a condition.

[65]This is reinforced by the fact that no single type of mental health problem dominated in either sample. Rather, a wide range of issues were represented, including depression, schizophrenia, bipolar disorder, Asperger's syndrome, drug addiction, and low IQ among others.

[66]Compared to 6% of the rest of the UK sample.

[67]Just one individual, equating to 3% of British converts is known to have failed to complete high school after 9/11.

[68]Simcox and Dyer, 'The Role of Converts in Al-Qa'ida-Related Terrorism Offenses in the United States'.

[69]As noted above, British converts may be over-represented among jihadi terrorists compared to estimates for the UK Muslim population. Although troubling, it is important to bear in mind that there is no national register of converts and so further research is necessary in order to verify and explain this.

[70]Note that this does not mean that there is a fixed sequence of events or a clear separation of processes of radicalization from operational activity. Indeed, radicalization (sometimes countered by 'de-radicalizing' factors) must be considered an ongoing process. From this perspective, processes of

radicalization are continuing (though not necessarily escalating) even as a group of individuals is planning a terrorist attack.

[71] For operational uses of the Internet, see Chapter 6.

[72] Data pertaining to social vs. virtual radicalization were missing in 69% of the total US sample, and 84% of the total UK sample. Expressed the other way around, data *were* available for 115 American and 71 British jihadis.

[73] 36% of American and 14% of British jihadis prior to 9/11 were judged to have radicalized as a result of face-to-face social interaction. While in reality these figures should almost certainly be much higher than this, the scarcity of information does not allow reliable judgments to be made without speculation.

[74] Raffi Khatchadourian, 'Azzam the American: The Making of an Al Qaeda Homegrown', *The New Yorker*, January 22, 2007, available at: http://www.newyorker.com/reporting/2007/01/22/070122fa_fact_khatchadourian?currentPage=all, accessed March 5, 2010.

[75] Three out of nine virtually radicalized individuals in the UK were converts. Although this is lower than in the US, it is still proportionally higher than average.

[76] This view is also confirmed by previous research, for example Ines von Behr, Anaïs Reding, Charlie Edwards, and Luke Gribbon, *Radicalisation in the Digital Era: The Use of the Internet in 15 Cases of Terrorism and Extremism* (Brussels: RAND, 2013).

[77] For a lengthier discussion of many of these issues see Angel Rabasa and Cheryl Benard, *Eurojihad: Patterns of Islamist Radicalization and Terrorism in Europe* (New York, Cambridge University Press, 2015).

[78] Not to mention practical limitations relating to the size and scope of the current study.

[79] Note that the 'criminal opportunist' and 'troubled individual' categories also sometimes overlapped with one another and with the 'jihadi' classification, and were *not* treated as mutually exclusive in the analysis (therefore some individuals were counted more than once).

[80] This refers again to the 'Liberty City' group arrested in Miami in June 2006, plus Mohammed Reza Taheri-Azar, who ran people over at a North Carolina college campus in March of the same year. In both cases, elements of Salafi-jihadi ideology were combined with other beliefs — in Miami with teachings of the Moorish Science Temple, while in the case of Taheri-Azar (who was also classified as a troubled individual), it was incorporated into his own idiosyncratic worldview.

[81] Bill Morlin, 'From White Supremacist to Muslim Jihadist', *Salon*, June 13, 2013, available at: http://www.salon.com/2013/06/13/islamic_jihadists_tie_to_white_supremacists_partner/, accessed June 13, 2013.

[82] Thomas Clouse, 'Clarkston Bomb-Maker Linked to Jihad Training Website', *The Spokesman-Review*, September 25, 2012, available at: http://www.spokesman.com/stories/2012/sep/25/local-man-guilty-national-security-case/, accessed September 27, 2012.

[83]Bill Morlin, 'Washington Bomb-Maker Pleads Guilty', *Salon*, September 26, 2012, available at: http://www.salon.com/2012/09/26/washington_bomb_maker_pleads_guilty/, accessed September 27, 2012.

[84]'Briton Sentenced to 47 Years in Missile-Smuggling Plot', *North County Times*, September 13, 2005, available at: http://www.nctimes.com/news/local/military/article_993b2bac-93b3-5773-ba2b-f8c41a4e890a.html, accessed June 6, 2013.

[85]These were Saeed Ghafoor, who repeatedly made a point of informing prison officials that he was planning terrorist attacks upon his release from jail, and Clive Dennis, who showed up at Mogadishu airport in March of 2012 in a somewhat bizarre bid to join al-Shabaab.

Chapter 6

What Exactly Have American and British Jihadis Been Doing?

Collectively, American and British jihadis have engaged in the entire spectrum of behavior that constitutes terrorism, from simply possessing propaganda and instructional materials to successfully conducting attacks. On the whole, this behavior is still quite poorly understood though, and there are many important questions, yet few satisfactory answers. This chapter presents the findings of an in-depth exploration of jihadi activity in the US and UK, including group characteristics, offense periods, operational activities and roles, sources of funding, international dimensions and associations, the role of the Internet and stated motivations (see Tables 6.1 and 6.2).

Group Characteristics

Group Size

The investigation begins with a deceptively simple-sounding question: how big is the average jihadi terrorist group in each country? Prior to 9/11, the average group in the US consisted of 2.2 people, with a minimum of 1 and a maximum of 19. After 9/11, the average was 2.3 (including undercover operatives, or 1.9 excluding them), the minimum was again 1, and the maximum was 7. The respective figures for the UK were 1.4 (with a range of 1 to 10) and 2.2 (with a range of 1 to 13). This suggests that groups were smaller in the UK prior to 9/11, but roughly the same size as in the US since then. These calculations, however, must be treated with caution. Jihadis in Western countries operate in largely informal, semi-clandestine and

Table 6.1. Operational behaviors of American jihadis beginning their careers before and after 9/11 (1980–2013).

	Pre-9/11	Post-9/11
Group characteristics	Average known group size 2.2; 92% of cases an integral part of wider networks; Leadership linked to foreign terrorist organizations in 67% of cases, though little evidence of outright control	Average known group size 2.3; 41% of cases an integral part of wider networks (6% connected; 48% discrete); Leadership tied to foreign terrorist organizations in 32% of cases; 26% of cases 'leaderless'
Offense period	Average: 3.4 years	Average: 1.1 years
Operational activity/roles	55% overseas training/combat (+ 4% attempted); 31% facilitating jihad; 27% domestic training; 19% conducted attacks; 15% planning attacks; 13% fundraising; 7% promoting jihad; 58% focused overseas; 69% traveled overseas	33% facilitating jihad; 27% planning attacks; 22% fundraising; 19% overseas training/combat (+ 18% attempted); 18% promoting jihad; 14% domestic training; 6% conducted attacks; 51% focused overseas; 40% traveled overseas
Sources of funding	21% charity/donations; 20% organizational support; 8% legitimate means; 6% online (61% unknown)	17% crime; 9% charity/donations; 8% friends/family; 5% org. support; 4% legitimate means (58% unknown)
International dimensions and associations	85% of cases linked to foreign terrorists; 49% of individual links to militants in Afghanistan; 43% to Pakistan; 13% linked to Bosnia; 6% to Sudan, 4% to Egypt; 43% of individuals linked to al-Qaeda; 57% of individuals have named overseas associations; 46% have named domestic associations	46% of cases linked to foreign terrorists; 14% of individual links to militants in Somalia; 13% linked to Pakistan; 4% to Yemen, 3% to Iraq; 8% of individuals linked to al-Qaeda; 24% of individuals have named overseas associations; 29% have named domestic associations
The role of the Internet	Internet used for operational purposes in 29% of cases beginning before 9/11 (71% unknown)	Internet used for operational purposes in 60% of cases beginning after 9/11 (40% unknown)
Stated motivations	Motives primarily expressed in terms of a combination of religion, altruism, and anger at foreign policy (46% unknown)	Primary motivational themes unchanged (30% unknown)

Table 6.2. Operational behaviors of British jihadis beginning their careers before and after 9/11 (1980–2013).

	Pre-9/11	Post-9/11
Group characteristics	Average known group size 1.4; 97% of cases an integral part of wider networks; Leadership linked to foreign terrorist organizations in 76% of cases, though little evidence of outright control	Average known group size 2.2; 59% of cases an integral part of wider networks (17% connected; 18% discrete); Leadership linked to foreign terrorist organizations in 36% of cases; 25% of cases 'leaderless'
Offense period	Average: 4.9 years	Average: 1.2 years
Operational activity/roles	48% overseas training/combat (+ 1% attempted); 43% facilitating jihad; 32% fundraising; 25% planning attacks; 25% promoting jihad; 6% conducted attacks; 83% focused overseas; 72% traveled overseas	25% facilitating jihad; 24% overseas training/combat (+12% attempted); 22% planning attacks; 18% promoting jihad; 15% fundraising; 10% possession of terrorist materials; 9% domestic training; 8% conducted attacks; 38% focused overseas; 42% traveled overseas
Sources of funding	15% crime; 7% charity/donations; 6% organizational support; 3% online; 2% friends/family (69% unknown)	4% friends/family; 3% crime; 3% charity/donations; 2% organizational support; 1% online (87% unknown)
International dimensions and associations	92% of cases linked to foreign terrorists; 48% of individual links to militants in Afghanistan; 33% to Pakistan; 17% linked to Algeria; 11% to Bosnia, Chechnya, Libya; 41% of individuals linked to al-Qaeda; 59% of individuals have named overseas associations; 69% have named domestic associations	53% of cases linked to foreign terrorists; 15% of individual links to militants in Pakistan; 6% to Afghanistan; 5% linked to Somalia, 4% Syria, 3% Iraq; 9% of individuals linked to al-Qaeda; 19% of individuals have named overseas associations; 46% have named domestic associations
The role of the Internet	Internet used for operational purposes in 23% of cases beginning before 9/11 (77% unknown)	Internet used for operational purposes in 41% of cases beginning after 9/11 (59% unknown)
Stated motivations	Motives primarily expressed in terms of a combination of religion, altruism, and anger at foreign policy (59% unknown)	Primary motivational themes unchanged (54% unknown)

often very fluid networks, meaning that it is frequently extremely difficult to define the boundaries of group membership and sometimes even impossible to assign certain individuals to specific groups.[1] So, although the most common group size in both countries and across all time-periods was 1, this is purely a reflection of analytical challenges and does not mean that people mostly offended by themselves.

Connectivity

In order to compensate somewhat for this deficiency, each group or individual was further classified as either 'discrete' (meaning socially isolated and operationally autonomous[2]), 'connected' (part of wider extremist networks but operationally independent[3]), or 'networked' (operating as an integral part of a larger, collective effort[4]). Of the Islamist terrorism cases that began before September 11, 2001, 92% in the US were classed as networked, compared to just 41% since then, while discrete cases rose from 5% to 48% (including 2 discrete *individuals* — 'lone actor' terrorists — in the earlier period and 22 in the latter).[5] In the UK, 97% of cases beginning prior to 9/11 were networked, compared to 59% since then, plus 17% which were connected and 18% which were discrete (including 24 lone actors compared to just 2 in the preceding period).

These findings confirm that there is much more to immediate group size than meets the eye. They also show support for the general assumption that home-grown Islamist terrorism has become more autonomous over time, and for the observation that there has been an increase in lone actor terrorism (which accounts for 17% of cases[6] in both countries after 9/11). However, the degree of autonomy in each country is quite different. Jihadis operating in the UK are much more likely to be networked or at least connected to other groups and individuals as compared to the US, where there is a stronger tendency for cases to be discrete and little evidence for a 'middle ground' (i.e. very few 'connected' cases).[7] This ties in with the results discussed in Chapter 5, which point to the existence of established jihadi subcultures and therefore interconnections between cases in the UK, but a comparative lack thereof in the US.

Leadership

A related variable of interest — and one of the most vigorously debated issues in terrorism research — is group leadership. As indicated in the tables above, leadership was tied to foreign terrorist organizations (FTOs) in 67% of US jihadi cases prior to 9/11 and 32% of cases since then;[8] 'within-group leadership only'[9] cases rose from 14% to 23%, and cases where there was no apparent leadership[10] rose from 6% to 26%.[11] By comparison, leadership was tied to FTOs in 76% of UK cases before 2001 versus 36% afterwards;[12] 'within-group leadership only' applied to 1% and then 8% of cases,[13] while leaderless cases[14] increased from 1% to 25%.

Before and after 9/11, there has evidently been a significant degree of autonomy in both countries even where leadership has been linked to FTOs, and although operatives are sometimes dispatched to fulfill a certain mission (such as 9/11 or the 7/7 bombings) there is little evidence of issuing direct orders to be found. Rather, groups and individuals seem to have largely been free to interpret and fulfill the 'commander's intent' as they see fit, and even to choose their own operational roles and goals. Furthermore, the degree of autonomy varies according to context. Whilst operating overseas, individuals function within the relatively formal hierarchical structures which govern training camps and paramilitary terrorist/insurgent organizations operating in conflict zones. Those who then return home and conduct operations on behalf of the organization are more often semi-autonomous, with significant freedom of action, whilst those who fail — or simply do not try — to establish contact with FTOs in the first place are completely self-organized and self-financing.

Moreover, in line with the less networked nature of jihadi terrorism in both countries over time, the proportional influence of FTOs has declined in the post-9/11 era. Surprisingly, there is little apparent difference between the two countries on this dimension. However, when we break the FTO-linked category down further into cases that were directly part of FTO hierarchies versus semi-autonomous cases, we find a stronger tendency towards the latter type in the UK.[15] This is an indication of greater influence of FTOs within Britain itself as compared to the US, where direct FTO influence has rarely extended beyond individual jihadi fighters in conflict zones. Thus, for example, the young men who made their way from Minnesota to Somalia joined al-Shabaab but — with the exception of a small number of recruiters — did not attempt to carry out actions on behalf of the group in America. By comparison, Irfan Naseer and Irfan Khalid (the leaders of the Operation Pitsford group arrested in Birmingham in September 2011) received training in Pakistan before returning to the UK where they recruited others with the intention of conducting domestic attacks.[16]

In accordance with the general decline in FTO influence, exclusively within-group leadership has become more common in both countries, although the available data suggest that this has been more pronounced across time in the US. This is partially explained by the slightly stronger tendency of UK jihadis to have links to foreign terrorists (see 'International Dimensions and Associations' below) and also resonates with the above finding that US groups are more likely to be operationally discrete.[17]

Finally, the rise in leaderless cases in both the US and UK mostly corresponds to the above-mentioned increase in lone actor terrorism (including non-violent cases) while the remainder consists of a handful of groups where leadership was not seemingly a factor. For instance, the friends of Boston bomber Dzhokhar Tsarnaev, who were accused of obstructing the investigation on an *ad hoc* basis, were not following orders, nor did they have a group leader.[18] Such cases are unusual however, and on the whole groups of jihadis in both countries, whilst generally lacking clearly defined structures, do tend to possess their own internal order whether or not they are connected to FTOs. Past research has suggested that two roles in particular are a universal feature of groups of Western jihadis — namely 'spiritual sanctioners' or ideologues, and operational leaders.[19] Although this claim is not supported,[20] it is true that some form of internal leadership does tend to exist — just as it does in everyday social groups — as a product of mutual understanding, individual personalities and initiative, knowledge, experience, abilities, and connections. In some cases specific group *emirs* or leaders and other roles were identified,[21] but above all, the groups examined for this research are best described as informal and collaborative.

Offense Period

How long do jihadi careers typically last? Again, this is more complex than it sounds. Offense periods here are based on the first known, overt behavior in support of violent jihad up until the last known involvement (usually coinciding with arrest or death). However, this does not capture earlier periods of radicalization and almost certainly underestimates the beginning of many individual careers. Conversely, people are not necessarily continuously engaged in terrorist activity from start to finish, but sometimes drift in and out or are incarcerated for periods of time, meaning that the duration of some careers is arguably exaggerated. With these complications in mind, the tables above show that the average offense period of US individuals who began their careers before 9/11 was 3.4 years, compared to 1.1 year since then. The corresponding figures for the UK are 4.9 years and 1.2.[22] These results are evidence of vastly expanded counterterrorism capabilities after 9/11, confirming that jihadi careers are likely to be cut short much sooner than in the past.

Operational Activity/Roles

We now turn our attention to what exactly American and British nationals have been doing in support of global jihad. The various activities and roles are listed in ranked order for each country and time period in Tables 6.1 and 6.2, but due to the variation involved they will be discussed here in a fixed order, ranging from membership in a terrorist network where no other specific activities could be determined, to conducting attacks. Unless otherwise stated, these classifications are not mutually exclusive and are primarily defined based upon known *behavior* rather than specified legal *offenses*, although the two are clearly related.[23] This allows a more direct comparison of what exactly individuals from each country are known to have *done*, rather than what they have necessarily been prosecuted for.

Membership in a Terror Network

Although many individuals in both samples were part of terror networks, this particular category was reserved for peripheral group members whose behavior could not be otherwise classified (e.g. failing to disclose information about associates' activities) or where information was simply insufficient to be able to determine anything more about what exactly they did. It applied to 1% of individuals in the US before and after 9/11, compared to 1% and then 6% of the UK sample.

Possession of Terrorist Materials

'Terrorist materials' include documents and/or other articles which are judged to have been collected for purposes of terrorism.[24] For the most part, this refers to possession of violent, provocative propaganda and instructions on bomb-making and other techniques as contained for example in the 'al-Qaeda manual' and more recently in *Inspire* magazine. A smaller number of individuals in this category also possessed items that could be used for constructing improvised explosive devices,[25] but had not taken sufficient, additional steps which might clearly demonstrate planning a specific attack. Even more so than membership in a terror network, possession of propaganda and instructional materials was practically ubiquitous throughout both samples. However, this category refers exclusively to those individuals where this was their *primary* offense (and for 25 of 32 individuals in total, this was their *only* known offense).

No-one in the US, either before or after 9/11, was classified this way. In the UK, it applied to 2% of individuals who began offending before, and 10% who began after 9/11 (although all of these individuals were actually prosecuted in the latter period). The reason for the disparity between countries is simple. Terrorist possession offenses (proscribed in the Terrorism Act of 2000) are illegal in the UK but not in the US. Hence, if this is the only known behavior there is no prosecution and therefore no public record of it in the US. Notably, this gives UK authorities the option of intervening at an earlier stage in a person's involvement in jihadi activity, meaning that he/she can be prosecuted for what is usually a relatively low-level offense before they have the opportunity to progress to more serious crimes (which of course is by no means inevitable). As discussed further in Chapter 7, these legislative differences have a number of practical implications for counterterrorism in each country.

Promoting Violent Jihad

Promoting jihad involves the incitement or glorification of terrorism in order to encourage others to take part by way of production and dissemination of propaganda and/or face-to-face interaction. This applied to 7% of individuals who began their jihadi careers in the US prior to 9/11, and 18% afterwards. The respective figures for the UK sample are 25% and 18%. The apparent difference between the two countries before 9/11 is consistent with the fact that the UK emerged as a hotspot for jihadi activity during this time, while the US — though targeted for attack — never took on the same significance. The greater number of 'promoters' in Britain can be considered both a cause and a consequence of the growth of jihadi subcultures in London and elsewhere, as influential figures such as Abu Qatada created a sort of snowball effect, attracting new followers and creating additional promoters and recruiters who in turn exerted their own influence. Not all promoters are equal of course — some, such as Hassan Butt, are now viewed as braggarts and liars;[26] others have been subject to control orders and have never been named in public;[27] while others still have done little more than pass out leaflets in the street.[28] Nevertheless, the accumulation of all this activity surely exacerbated the situation in Britain and the effects of this are still being felt today.

The above figures suggest that after 9/11 things have changed. In particular, there has been a rather substantial increase in the number of jihadi promoters in the US. Although this is true, there has also been a qualitative change. The majority of post-9/11 promoters in the US have been active online as opposed to recruiting people face-to-face, and with the exception of Anwar al-Awlaki and perhaps a handful of others,[29] none of them can be considered particularly influential. More recently (outwith the sampling time-frame of this research) a Michigan-based preacher called Ahmad Musa Jibril was named as one of the most popular spiritual influencers among jihadis in Syria.[30] However, he has so far avoided explicit incitement to terrorism and the fact remains that the majority of jihadi promoters in the US since 9/11 have been amateurish and lacking in authority. The observed increase in promotional activity is a concern, but it is hardly indicative of the same type of growth that occurred in the UK during the 1990s.

In Britain, the transformation since 2001 has been more subtle. To begin with, there has been a slight proportional decrease, rather than an increase in this type of activity, which is not easily explained. Furthermore, only a third of UK promoters who began their careers after 9/11 are known to have disseminated material online, compared to 60% of those in the US. Instead, they have been more active as face-to-face recruiters, protestors and 'street preachers'. For example, from at least 2004 to 2006 one Mohammed Hamid (a student of Abu Hamza and Abdullah el-Faisal) hosted Islamic discussion groups at his home and organized a series of domestic training camps in preparation for violent jihad.[31] Several individuals have also been prosecuted in the UK for inciting murder and terrorism at public rallies organized by Omar Bakri Mohammed's successor, Anjem Choudary and other members of the al-Muhajiroun network.[32] More recently, Michael Adebolajo and Michael Adebowale (who had also attended protests with Choudary) were known as aggressive *dawa* preachers on the streets of East London before brutally murdering Lee Rigby in May of 2013.[33]

Britain has not been without its fair share of amateurs and bedroom-based jihadi promoters, and — similar to in the US — there have been fewer truly influential figures in recent years. But promotion of jihad has still maintained a gritty, street-level presence in the UK that is lacking in the US, yet again pointing to the existence of enduring, self-perpetuating jihadi subcultures within Britain.

Facilitating Violent Jihad

In this context, facilitation encompasses a range of activities aimed at enabling others to fulfill their goals *vis-à-vis* violent jihad. At the lower end of the spectrum it consists of various forms of bottom–up (sometimes *ad hoc*) assistance, while more serious cases involve top–down planning and organization of things such as recruitment, overseas travel and training. In both countries, this was the second most common form of behavior overall (bearing in mind that facilitation is not mutually exclusive of other activities). In the US, it accounted for 31% of pre-9/11 starters and 33% of post-9/11 starters, while the respective figures for the UK were 43% and 25%.

As with promoting jihad, the greater number of facilitators active in the UK prior to 9/11 is a reflection of the rather more established networks that existed at that time. Furthermore, there yet again appears to have been something of a qualitative difference. Very significant and well-connected operatives can be found in each sample during this period, such as Ali Mohamed and Wadih el-Hage in the US, and Anas al-Liby, Abu Doha, Abu Hamza, and Mohammed Ajmal Khan in the UK. However, there were more low- to mid-level facilitators in the US, and more upper-level facilitators in the UK. What is more, if we exclude cases of *ad hoc* assistance and failed attempts at facilitation to leave only 'genuine' facilitators, the observed quantitative gap is even wider (26% vs. 43%). This reinforces the notion that while jihadis in the US were focused on conducting domestic attacks, British-based operatives were dedicated to consolidating and expanding networks.

If this assessment is accurate, why then, do we see a slight increase in facilitation in the US after 9/11 and a sizeable decrease in the UK? There have certainly been some significant facilitators active in the US since 2001, most notably David Headley, who played a key role in the planning stages of the Mumbai attacks.[34] But such individuals have become scarcer in recent years, while the proportion of 'pseudo-facilitators' has grown substantially. More than a quarter of US facilitators after 9/11 either voluntarily offered their services to, or in some cases accepted requests from organized jihadists;[35] however, most of them were caught in sting operations and were not in contact with actual terrorists. Removing these individuals and other *ad hoc* helpers from the equation reveals that the number of actual facilitators has dropped to 23%.

A small number of *ad hoc* and peripheral facilitators have also been active in the UK after 9/11,[36] and excluding them from the analysis gives an adjusted figure of 21%, down from 43% in the previous period. Given that facilitation is necessarily dependent on the existence of groups and especially networks of people, the apparent decline in this type of activity is perhaps related to the less networked nature of jihadi cases in Britain over time (see 'Connectivity' above and 'International Dimensions and Associations' below). There have still been some very capable, well-connected British facilitators after 9/11 (more so than in the US),[37] but it would appear that there have been fewer opportunities for this type of activity to flourish.

Fundraising

Fundraising is a vital component of terrorism, yet also particularly challenging for law enforcement and still greatly under-researched insofar as Western jihadis are concerned. The different sources and amounts of funding are discussed in greater detail below, but suffice to say that it involves a very broad spectrum of activities, from one-off, small-time individual efforts to large-scale organized endeavors. In the US, 13% of the pre-9/11 sample engaged in fundraising, compared to 22% of the post-9/11 sample. The figures for the UK were 32% and 15%. The larger proportion of jihadi fundraisers beginning their careers in Britain before 2001 was primarily a result of the expansive network of North Africans centered around Abu Doha and Abu Qatada. It is also consistent with the above findings in relation to facilitation, since the two activities are often combined. We should, however, be cautious about reading too much significance into this because although fewer fundraisers were identified in the US prior to 9/11, the available information suggests that they were even more productive than their British counterparts (see 'Sources of Funding' below).

Along similar lines, the apparent changes after 9/11 must also be examined more closely. Although there was an increase in the number of individuals involved in fundraising activities in support of violent jihad in the US, most of these were small-scale and relatively insignificant compared to the previous period. Moreover, one of the most sophisticated fundraising networks in the UK was set up by the Libyan Islamic Fighting Group (LIFG), which began in 1999 but continued to grow for several years *after* 9/11.[38] So while the quantitative analysis superficially suggests that there was a rather dramatic decrease in fundraising activities in Britain, the difference in reality is less than it would appear. Ultimately, (as was the case for facilitation) there has not been a vast difference in the popularity of fundraising in the US and UK since 2001; whether or not there are differences in terms of methods and amounts involved is discussed below.

Domestic Training

Overseas paramilitary-style training with FTOs represents the ultimate experience in preparation for violent jihad. Western-based jihadis also sometimes engage in domestic training exercises in order to ready themselves for the harsh conditions overseas or to prepare for missions at home. Of the pre-9/11 US sample, 27% engaged in domestic training, compared to 14% of the post-9/11 cohort, while in the UK the respective figures were 2% and 9%.

The relatively large number of individuals involved in training in the US prior to 9/11 included members of the World Trade Center conspiracy; numerous followers of Omar Abdel Rahman; the 9/11 pilots who learned to fly in the US; and the two jihadi groups from Virginia and Portland. Only three people were identified by name as having undergone training in Britain before 2001. In November 1999 the *Sunday Telegraph* ran a story on 'Muslim fundamentalist' training camps organized by Omar Bakri Mohammed and Anjem Choudary in which Choudary was quoted as saying: 'Before they go abroad to fight for organizations like [al-Qaeda[39]], the volunteers are trained in Britain. Some of the training involve[s] guns and live ammunition'.[40] Two volunteers were also interviewed — one who simply went by the name 'Abdullah', the other who was named as Abdul Wahid Majid.[41] The third person known to have attended training camps in Britain before 9/11 was future 7/7 bomber Mohammed Siddique Khan. These were not, of course, the only people attending these camps, nor were they one-off affairs.

Majid claimed to have trained at least ten times in Britain before also training with militants in Pakistan; West Yorkshire Police spotted Khan training with approximately 40 other men;[42] and as Bakri Mohammed bragged to the *Telegraph* back in 1999, 'Last week, we sent 38 people to Chechnya'.[43] It would thus appear that in all likelihood domestic training was even more widespread in the UK than it was in the US before 9/11.

In light of this, the post-9/11 figures therefore suggest a reduction in this type of activity in both countries (not just the US). However, it is more accurately viewed as a reduction in *organized* domestic training camps, rather than training *per se*, which of course is a natural response to heightened levels of security since 2001. Hence — with the exception of Mohammed Hamid's camps in Britain — domestic training after 9/11 has generally been smaller-scale, less formally organized and more covert. For example, preparing for jihad in the US often involves little more than a couple of friends going to a shooting range, while in the UK it largely consists of jogging and visits to the gym.

Overseas Training and Combat

To become a *mujahid* and fight for Allah against infidel soldiers is the number one ambition of jihadis worldwide. Of the individuals who mobilized in the US before 9/11, 55% engaged in overseas training and/or combat, and another 4% attempted to do so. After 9/11, this was achieved by 19% and attempted by another 18%. The corresponding figures for the UK were 48% (plus 1% attempted) and 24% (plus 12% attempted).

On the whole, there is a great deal of similarity here. Overseas training and combat was clearly the most popular type of activity in both countries overall and although the (known) rate was slightly higher in the US before 9/11, this is largely because trained operatives were sent there to attack it, rather than because more Americans succeeded in making their way to conflict zones. Indeed, if the above-mentioned claims of Bakri Mohammed and others are truthful then many more jihadis from the UK were successful in this regard. Another striking similarity is that there has apparently been a substantial decrease in overseas training and combat since 9/11. There are two main reasons as to why this may have occurred: (1) reduced opportunities due to enhanced counterterrorism measures and/or a lack of necessary connections, and (2) an increased willingness to act at home (see below). It is also possible that the observed reduction in overseas activities could be a reflection of a gradual loss of interest in long-running conflicts such as in Afghanistan, Somalia, or Yemen. Whether or not this is true, the war in Syria and the rise of the 'Islamic State' (IS) in Iraq have undoubtedly reignited this interest and the number of British and American jihadis with overseas training and combat experience has risen significantly since the end of the sampling period for this book.

One final, yet important observation here is that these results — in addition to those below regarding connections to terrorists overseas — again contradict the work of Simcox and Dyer, who found that US jihadis in their sample were much more likely to have trained and fought overseas compared to their British counterparts and were more often connected to designated terrorist organizations.[44] This is yet another reflection of difficulties which can arise if we (a) do not account for changes over time, and (b) utilize relatively narrow sampling criteria.[45] Crucially, when we focus exclusively on the post-9/11 period and take a more inclusive approach to sampling we find a very different reality and the suggestion that 'the terror threat in America appears to be greater than that in the UK'[46] is simply not supported.

Planning and Conducting Attacks

Intentionally lethal attacks against non-combatant targets are one of the defining features of contemporary terrorism. It is this tactic in particular which rightly earns jihadis the 'terrorist' label. In the US, 15% of individuals who began offending before 9/11 were involved in planning attacks, and another 19% actually conducted attacks.[47] After 9/11 the figures were 27% and 6%. Meanwhile in the UK, 25% of the pre-9/11 sample planned, and 6% conducted attacks. The respective figures post-9/11 were 22% and 8%. Overall, these figures are remarkably consistent, showing that over time approximately a

Table 6.3. Confirmed planned and conducted terrorist attacks by US and UK jihadis before and after 9/11 (1980–September 11, 2013). Numbers refer to *cases*, not individuals.

	Planned domestic	Conducted domestic	Planned overseas	Conducted overseas	Total
US pre-9/11	6	4	2	0	12
US post-9/11	38	8	1	5	52
UK pre-9/11	1	1	6	2	10
UK post-9/11	19	7	14	8	48

third of jihadis in the US and the UK have been involved in planning or conducting attacks, and for the most part they have been unsuccessful. The only major deviation to this overall pattern is the fact that before 9/11 more individuals in the US were successful in bringing their plans to fruition (and of course this mostly consists of the 9/11 hijackers themselves).

Things become more interesting, however, when we examine the attacks in greater detail. Table 6.3 shows the number of planned and conducted attacks at home and abroad involving jihadis from each country according to when the offenses in question actually occurred (as opposed to when the perpetrators first mobilized). Although the totals for each country before and after 9/11 are almost identical, the balance between domestic versus overseas targets is quite different. Specifically, although domestic operations have clearly become more popular since 9/11 in both cases, British jihadis have shown a much stronger propensity to plan and conduct attacks abroad. Given that the US tops the jihadi wish-list of targets worldwide, it is perhaps only natural to find that Islamist terrorists operating in that country are chiefly concerned with domestic attacks.[48] This also partially explains the British preference for overseas targets, since they too have sought to attack the US on a number of occasions. In addition, British jihadis — such as the Iraqi–Swede Taimour Abdul-Wahab al-Abdaly — have added opportunities and motivation to conduct attacks elsewhere in Europe. More importantly, UK-based planners and perpetrators of attacks have been much more successful at establishing contact with foreign terrorists, including designated FTOs. So although the overall difference between the two samples is not dramatic in terms of connections to foreign terrorists (see below), the disparity for this particular activity is substantial. Specifically, 75% of US cases involving planning or conducting attacks prior to 9/11 had links to foreign terrorists.[49] After 9/11, this figure reduced to just 23%. In contrast to this, the figures in the UK before and after 9/11 were 80% and 73%.

It is the domestic plots that are of particular interest though, since they reveal the extent to which the respective countries have become viable targets in the eyes of their residents and also show how successful the terrorists have been against the authorities. Of the 10 domestic plots in the US prior to (and including) 9/11, 4 were successful: the assassination of Meir Kahane in November 1990; the murder of two CIA employees by Mir Aimal Kasi in January 1993; the first World Trade Center bombing; and the 9/11 attacks.[50] In the UK, there were just two domestic plots during this period. One (the firebombing of an army barracks) was successful but very minor; the other was the rather more serious attempt by Moinul Abedin to create what would have been a much more destructive explosive device.

The picture after 9/11 is rather more complex. Of the 46 domestic plots in the US between 2001 and 2013, 38 were thwarted, 4 were completed but were essentially failures,[51] and 4 were successful.[52] This means that 17% of plots were not detected prior to execution, while 9% were outright successes. In the UK there were 26 domestic plots during the same period. Nineteen were thwarted; four were completed;[53] and three were successful.[54] Of the domestic plots, 27% went undetected and 12% were outright successes. The numbers of completed and successful attacks are thus practically identical, with the major difference lying in the number of (publicly disclosed) plots that have been thwarted. As discussed above, there are certain reasons why Americans may be more likely to choose domestic targets as compared to jihadis in the UK. In addition, it is worth noting that 48% of domestic plots in the US were investigated using sting operations. These are discussed at greater length in the following chapter, but given that it is far more difficult to run such operations overseas, this also helps explain the domestic focus of American jihadis. If we were to remove these cases from the analysis, the total number of planned and conducted attacks would be 27, which brings the two samples into almost exact alignment in terms of thwarted compared with successful domestic attacks.

Continuing the focus on post-9/11 domestic plots (planned and conducted), it is important to examine specific *modi operandi.* Both countries showed a similar preference for exclusively civilian (46% vs. 54%) or government targets (28% vs. 27%). However, US jihadis were more likely to choose mixed targets (20% vs. 4%), while British jihadis' targets were more likely to be unknown at the time of arrest (7% vs. 15%). British militants also showed a stronger preference for explosives as the sole method of attack (48% vs. 62%) and for alternative weaponry, including knives in particular (4% vs. 19%). Meanwhile, American jihadis were more likely to choose firearms (17% vs. 12%) or mixed methods of attack, which generally included firearms in addition to explosives (26% vs. 8%). British jihadis were more likely to plan or commit suicide as part of domestic attacks (9% vs. 19%), although in absolute terms the numbers were similar (4 vs. 5 cases where intent was clearly demonstrated[55,56]). Similarly, there was no real difference in the percentage of *genuine* lone actor jihadis planning or conducting attacks (26% vs. 23%),[57] but in absolute terms the number in the US was double that in the UK (12 vs. 6).[58]

Above all, these results suggest a pragmatic approach to terrorist attacks at home. Thus, in addition to the traditional preference of terrorists to use explosives (which are much more difficult to make than many people realize), jihadis in both countries are clearly willing to make use of whatever is available to them.[59] Intriguingly, the slightly stronger tendency of British jihadis to select civilian targets and to choose suicide tactics furthermore suggests a more 'hardcore' commitment to violent jihad within the UK after 9/11. This was not readily detected in the ideological classification discussed in Chapter 5; however, it is congruent with the assessment that jihadi subcultures are more established in the UK and is also supported by the fact that from 2001 to 2013, British jihadis planned or conducted at least 11 suicide attacks overseas, compared to just 3 confirmed American cases during the same period.

Overseas vs. Domestic Focus and Theater of Operations

The final variables of interest in relation to operational activity (regardless of specific roles) are the focus/target, and theater of operations. Of the individuals who mobilized in the US before 9/11, 58% were focused on directing their efforts exclusively overseas and 69% of the sample traveled abroad. After 9/11, 51% of American jihadis were focused overseas but only 40% actually traveled outside the US. By comparison, 83% of British jihadis before 9/11 were focused exclusively overseas and 72% of them engaged in international travel. After 9/11 these figures dropped to 38% and 42% respectively. These results confirm that over time jihadis from each country have become more willing to focus their efforts on achieving domestic outcomes and are also less likely to travel abroad.[60] It is also not surprising to find similar rates of overseas travel in light of the findings in relation to overseas training and combat (see above).

Sources of Funding

Having discussed the relative popularity of fundraising (above), it is important to learn what we can about the sources and scale of those activities. Based on the limited information that was available, the most common methods of fundraising among US cases beginning prior to 9/11 included organized charities or personally collected donations (21% of cases), direct FTO support (20%), legitimate means (8%), and online collections (6%). After 9/11, the most common methods were crime (17% of cases), charity or donations (9%), support from friends or family (8%), FTO support (5%), and legitimate means (4%). In the UK, the known methods of fundraising before 9/11 included crime (15% of cases), charity or donations (7%), FTO support (6%), online collections (3%), and friends or family (2%). After 9/11, they have included friends or family (4%), crime (3%), charity or donations (3%), FTO support (2%), and online methods (1%).

Due to the particularly large amounts of missing information about fundraising activities, particular caution must be exercised in interpreting these results. With that in mind, there are several tentative findings of note. To begin with, the evidence for financial support provided by FTOs to individuals coming from and/or operating in the US or UK, has been scant. Of course, this applied to the 9/11 hijackers and to a number of other previous cases in the US especially, but given that this was the 'golden age' of bin Laden's organization, it would not have been surprising to find a heavier financial footprint from al-Qaeda. What *is* surprising is that the data suggest that American jihadis have enjoyed the financial backing of FTOs more often than those in Britain. This is plausible enough for the pre-9/11 era since the US was targeted for attack to a far greater extent than the UK. Overall, however, it is most likely a product of missing information rather than anything else. For example, there were several individuals in the British sample after 9/11 (such as Rashid Rauf and Rangzieb Ahmed) who were almost certainly supported by al-Qaeda and/or similar organizations, but the available information fell short of providing confirmation. Nevertheless, it seems that FTO support in both countries has become less common over time. The most notable examples after 9/11 were Uzair Paracha, who agreed to perform certain 'favors' for al-Qaeda in return for a $200,000 loan (although Paracha played a minor role and it is unclear whether the money ever materialized);[61] David Headley, whose handlers gave him more than $25,000;[62] and Faisal Shahzad, whose efforts to attack New York were bankrolled by the Pakistani Taliban to the tune of $17,000.[63] More recently, it has emerged that recruits who have joined with jihadist groups in Syria and Iraq are paid a salary for their services and it is quite possible that the potential for handouts from FTOs will increase as a result of the resurgence of violent jihad in the Middle East. However, the apparent decline in FTO funding during the sampling period is entirely consistent with the gradual decimation of al-Qaeda after 9/11 and before the conflict in Syria escalated. Ultimately, the open source data indicate that American and British jihadis are more likely to give money to FTOs, rather than to receive it.

A second trend that may have occurred is a reduction in the use of organized charities to fund Islamist terrorism in either country. As already mentioned, there were some extremely lucrative initiatives of this sort that were established prior to 9/11, especially in the US (see Chapter 3). However, since these large-scale, relatively out-in-the-open enterprises were closed down after 9/11 there have not been any similar cases uncovered of the same magnitude. So while organizations like the Benevolence International Foundation were able to raise millions of dollars, the most successful case in the US after 9/11 so far has been that of Hafiz Muhammad Sher Ali Khan, a Florida imam who managed to raise around $50,000 which he personally collected and transferred to Tehrik e-Taliban Pakistan (TTP).[64]

Similarly, the most successful instance of this after 9/11 in the UK was the Operation Pitsford case in Birmingham where members of the group, posing as charity workers, collected an estimated £33,000 (around $56,000).[65] Previously, another Birmingham-based group led by Parviz Khan used almost identical tactics to gather at least £20,000 ($34,000), claiming that they were collecting for humanitarian aid.[66] Hence, it seems that there has been a shift towards apparently down-scaled and comparatively covert practices, which would be a natural response to the increased scrutiny of charities since 2001. That said, there is also reason to believe that charities are playing a much more significant role than can be currently verified. For example, in September 2012 it was alleged — but not proven — that the Al Muntada Trust, headquartered in London, had provided funds to Boko Haram in Nigeria.[67] At the time of writing there have also been several warnings that charities are being used to finance terrorists in Syria, and numerous individuals have been arrested and charged accordingly in Britain. As the Chairman of the UK Charity Commission remarked in April of 2014, '[t]he problem of Islamist extremism and charities ... is, alas, growing'.[68] It is therefore quite possible that evidence will emerge in the future of renewed efforts to utilize charities as a means of fundraising for terrorism.

A third point of interest relates to criminality (which is inclusive of fraudulent collections for 'charity'[69]). In line with the discussion of criminal records in Chapter 5, we see an increase in criminal fundraising for jihad in the US, but an apparent decrease in the UK. This provides additional evidence of a criminal 'underclass' of American jihadis, who rely on their illicit skills (such as they are) to fund their operations. It includes several small-time criminals who were not particularly successful, such as Ahmed Ferhani, who managed to raise the princely sum of $100 from the sale of drugs, which he then gave to an undercover agent as a down-payment for three handguns and a grenade.[70] However, there have also been a few rather more capable individuals, in particular Khaled Ouazzani, who donated more than $23,000 to 'al-Qaeda',[71] which he raised by defrauding banks and laundering money through an auto-parts business that he ran in Kansas City.[72]

Meanwhile, the apparent reduction in criminal fundraising for jihad in the UK is yet another reflection of the extinction of North African fraud and counterfeiting networks which were rampant during the 1990s. Comparable criminal-jihadi networks have not been exposed since, although there is reason to fear that jihadi fundraisers are exploring more sophisticated and lucrative possibilities. Indeed, the highest-grossing terrorism financing scheme in the UK to date — uncovered in 2005 — netted £1.8 million (more than $3 million) by way of online credit card fraud.[73] However, this is not to suggest that British jihadis in general have graduated to more complex and profitable criminal endeavors. The remaining criminal fundraising cases that were detected consisted of fraudulent charity collections which took place at street level and although the Pitsford group tried investing their takings in the foreign exchange market, this was a resounding failure.[74,75] Nevertheless, we cannot assume that more ambitious efforts will always fail and what is clear is that both American and British jihadis will exploit any opportunities that they are capable of in order to fund their activities.

In line with this observation, it is noteworthy that support from friends or family and legitimate means (including employment, collection of social benefits, and use of credit cards or loans) also account for a considerable proportion of known sources of funding. In fact, these are probably much more common than is explicitly confirmed by the data since the lack of an identifiable *scheme* is of little interest to reporters and for many people it is their regular source of income or their family and friends that are the most readily available financial sources. This is furthermore supported by the fact that the majority of American and British jihadis do not have criminal records and on top of this the amount of money needed to buy a plane ticket or to be able to access material online is not significant. In all likelihood the vast majority of cases examined for this research cost well under $10,000, with many working out at just a fraction of that amount.[76] Indeed, most individuals seemed to scrape their funds together from wherever they could, rather than necessarily entering into a separate conspiracy in order to make money.

Finally, as a caveat, it is worth reiterating that information about the sources and amounts of funding was simply not available for the majority of cases. It is quite probable that in addition to legitimate means, charities, crime, and online fundraising methods are more widespread than we currently know. This lack of information, along with the relatively few convictions for this particular type of activity suggests that there is a need for added investment in measures to counter terrorist financing. Certainly, there is a great need for more detailed research.

International Dimensions and Associations

The degree to which home-grown terrorism cases are connected to FTOs or likeminded individuals abroad is a major topic of interest since it is often assumed that such connections are lacking.[77] As summarized in Tables 6.1 and 6.2, 85% of US cases which began prior to 9/11 were connected to foreign terrorists, compared to just 46% of cases since then. In the UK, the respective figures were 92% and 53%. On the whole — and perhaps somewhat surprisingly — there is not a vast difference between the two countries at first glance.[78]

Nevertheless, we cannot assume that the *quality* or *type* of contact is necessarily the same. For instance, as already noted above, British jihadis involved in planning and conducting attacks are more likely than their American counterparts to have overseas connections and this is likely to raise their potential capabilities in terms of domestic assaults.[79] This is confirmed when we compare the most significant foreign-supported plots in the US since 9/11 (Bryant Vinas, the Zazi plot, and Shahzad) with those in the UK (the Operation Crevice case; Dhiren Barot and cohorts; the 7/7 bombings; the attempted 21/7 attack; the 2006 airlines plot; the Operation Pathway case; and Operation Pitsford). Moreover, we find that the non-violent cases most likely to have foreign connections after 9/11 in the US are jihadi fundraisers (71% compared to 58% in the UK), which indicates more of an external flow of support. Meanwhile in the UK it is facilitators who are most likely to have international connections among non-violent cases (66% versus 45% in the US). These results support the observation that American jihadis are more focused overall on overseas objectives in comparison to British militants, while reinforcing the notion that UK jihadis are more likely to function as relatively integrated actors within an international system.

A further point of interest relates to the location of overseas connections. Across time, jihadis from the US and UK have been linked to foreign terrorists in more than 20 different nations spread throughout Asia, the Middle East, Africa, Europe, and elsewhere. More specifically, among US jihadis who mobilized prior to 9/11, the most common overseas connections were to Afghanistan (49%), Pakistan (43%), Bosnia (13%), Sudan (6%), and Egypt (4%), and at least 43% of individuals were connected to al-Qaeda core in the Afghanistan–Pakistan region (AQC).[80] For those who began their careers after 9/11, the most common connections were to Somalia (14%), Pakistan (13%), Yemen (4%), and Iraq (3%), and only 8% of individuals had links to AQC. By comparison, the numbers in the UK before 9/11 were Afghanistan (48%), Pakistan (33%), Algeria (17%), Bosnia, Chechnya, and Libya (11% each), with 41% of individuals linked to AQC. After 9/11, the most common overseas connections were to Pakistan (15%), Afghanistan (6%), Somalia (5%), Syria (4%), and Iraq (3%), with just 9% of people linked to AQC.

As expected, prior to 9/11 the majority of connections to foreign terrorists were to Afghanistan and/or Pakistan.[81] Both samples also showed significant connections to Bosnia as a result of the war there and most of the remaining links were to Africa, although the specific locations varied according to individual and historical circumstances. Hence, the US connections to Sudan and Egypt are a reflection of the fact that several individuals went to Khartoum with bin Laden during the early 1990s and/or were members of the Egyptian Islamic Jihad and Gamaa' Islamiyah. Meanwhile the UK links to Algeria and Libya are a result of the significant presence in Britain of the Armed Islamic Group (GIA), the Salafist Group for Preaching and Combat (GSPC) and the Libyan Islamic Fighting Group (LIFG). Thanks to its proximity and the deliberate efforts of domestic fundraising and recruitment networks, the UK also had stronger connections to Chechnya (which accounted for just 3% of the US sample).

What we see after 9/11 is a shift in the location of overseas connections, which has occurred as existing conflicts gradually subsided only to be replaced by new ones. Hence, Bosnia, Chechnya, and Algeria are no longer the hubs of militancy they once were, while Somalia, Iraq, Yemen, and Syria have emerged in their place. Of course, the war in Afghanistan has dragged on and some connections continue to be made there (more so in the UK), but as al-Qaeda crept across the border and levels of militancy escalated in Pakistan, the locus of foreign connections followed. Indeed, for jihadis from America, Pakistan is second only to Somalia as a point of contact with foreign militants, thanks to the recruiting pipeline that was established in Minnesota. Meanwhile British jihadis — many of whom have origins in South Asia — are more likely to establish links with terrorists in Pakistan than anywhere else.

Nevertheless, it is somewhat surprising to find that the percentage of American jihadis with links to Pakistan is almost the same as in the UK.[82] On the one hand, there seems to have been something of a qualitative difference, with British militants more often succeeding in acquiring training and receiving ongoing support. On the other hand, it is another reminder that — despite the 'underclass contingent' discussed in Chapter 5 — American jihadis on the whole are more internationally connected than is often assumed. This is also reflected in terms of connections to AQC, which are strikingly similar in both samples before and after 9/11. The fact that such connections have sharply reduced since 2001 is certainly a positive development, although other branches of the AQ network have picked up some of the slack. For instance, after 9/11 connections were also established with al-Qaeda in the Arabian Peninsula (3% of US; 1% of UK); al-Qaeda in Iraq (2% US; 1% UK); and al-Shabaab (14% US; 5% UK). At face value, these figures even suggest that American jihadis have been in contact with formal AQ affiliates more often than British;[83] however, it is important to note that information about specific organizations — as opposed to general location — is often lacking, meaning that organizational affiliation could frequently not be determined.

Despite limitations in the data it is clear that the foreign connections of jihadis from both countries have become rather more thinly spread, both as a result of an increasingly complex militant landscape and reduced opportunities. That said, the situation is extremely dynamic and since the end of the sampling period for this research there has been a pronounced shift to Syria in particular as well as Iraq as the current hotspots for global jihad. Indeed, it is estimated that 'more than 100'[84] Americans and somewhere between 300 and 700[85] British nationals have gone to Syria, with most of them seemingly joining IS, Jabhat al-Nusra (JN), or smaller groups loosely affiliated with one or the other (this is discussed further in Chapter 8). As time goes on and more information becomes available we will be able to compile more accurate figures and to assess with greater certainty whether or not there any differences in the precise affiliations and actions of American and British jihadis in relation to this conflict. For the time being, it is safe to say that violent Islamist extremists from both countries have pivoted to Syria and Iraq along with the rest of the world.

Returning our attention to the sampling time-frame, additional insight can be gained into the balance of international versus domestic connections by examining *named* associations, i.e. where terrorist associates are explicitly identified. For individuals who mobilized prior to 9/11 in the US, 57% had named international associations, and 46% had named domestic associations outside of their immediate group. After 9/11, the respective figures dropped to 24% and 29%. In the UK, 59% of individuals who mobilized before 9/11 had named international associations, compared to 69% with named domestic associations. After 9/11, these figures also dropped to 19% and 46%.

What we find here is a great deal of similarity in terms of international associations (which have become less common and more likely anonymous over time), but a consistent and sizeable difference in terms of domestic associations. More than any of the previously discussed indicators, this provides the strongest evidence yet of the interconnected nature of Islamist terrorism cases in the UK as compared to the US, thereby reinforcing the notion that domestic jihadi subcultures are playing a key role in Britain.

This is likewise confirmed when we look at domestic organizational or network affiliations. Prior to 9/11 in the US, 29% of the sample was directly connected to the World Trade Center/Omar Abdel Rahman network, while after 9/11 the Minnesota–Somali network accounted for 11% of the sample and a further 3% of individuals were connected to Revolution Muslim. By comparison, before 9/11 at least 45% of the UK sample was directly connected to the Finsbury Park and/or Abu Doha/Abu Qatada networks and 7% of individuals were connected to al-Muhajiroun (AM). Then in the post-9/11 sample, another 11% had direct connections to AM, while 6% of individuals were linked to Mohammed Hamid (himself a product of the Finsbury Park scene). Comparing the two countries, the quantitative differences here are magnified when we take into account the overlap and the persistence over time of jihadi networks in Britain (particularly AM), which has not been seen in the US.

Nevertheless, there is also an important similarity in the sense that domestic organizations or identifiable networks account for a much smaller proportion of each sample than they used to. This is in line with the observed reduction in named domestic associations and suggests that Islamist terrorism networks have become more fragmented in the post-9/11 era.

The Role of the Internet

The role of the Internet for radicalization was discussed in Chapter 5. This section will focus on more 'operational' uses.[86] As indicated in

Tables 6.1 and 6.2, specific information about use of the Internet was often lacking, but with this in mind it is obvious that such activities have increased over time in both countries. Hence, reported use of the Internet rose from 29% to 60% of jihadi cases beginning before and after 9/11 in the US, and from 23% to 41% of cases in the UK. These increases are even more dramatic if we divide the samples according to when the offenses actually occurred rather than when the cases began: use of the Internet in the US thus rose from 15% to 61% of cases, while the UK rose from 7% to 37%.

These findings lend additional support to the earlier suggestion that the Internet appears to be playing a somewhat more substantial role within processes of radicalization in the US as a result of fewer opportunities for pro-jihadi social interaction in person (see Chapter 5). But we also need to look more closely at exactly *how* the Internet is being used. Focusing on post-9/11 activities,[87] individual uses of the Internet included communication (37% US; 17% UK), accessing propaganda, forums and/or instructional material such as *Inspire* magazine[88] (35% US; 24% UK), disseminating material (16% US; 8% UK), researching attacks (12% US; 11% UK), researching logistics/making purchases (5% US; 1% UK), group/network formation (22% US; 4% UK), and fundraising (2% US; 1% UK). Of course many, if not all of these activities are likely to have been more widespread than the available data suggest. However, we are still able to gain a sense of their relative distribution. To begin with, it is clear that interactive and consumerist behaviors are most common, while more aggressive and technical behaviors are comparatively rare. Furthermore, it is noteworthy that double the percentage of American jihadis or more as compared to the UK are known to have communicated or distributed material online, which is consistent with participation in a virtual jihadi world in lieu of a real one.

Likewise, a much larger percentage of Americans appeared to use the Internet as the initial basis for group or network formation, i.e. transforming online relationships into collaborative virtual or physical alliances. This applied to 13 cases in the US versus just 3 in the UK and included a variety of different circumstances and types of activity including promoting jihad,[89] fundraising and facilitation,[90] attempted overseas training and combat,[91] and planning attacks.[92] In some cases collaborators worked together exclusively online, while in others individuals or groups were willing to travel both domestically and internationally in order to physically meet with one another and look for ways to combine resources. These efforts were not always successful. In three of the US cases, physical meetings were attempted but failed or else turned out to be unproductive, and in another six, the 'terrorist' contacts turned out to be undercover FBI agents. Nevertheless, it is evident that compared to their British counterparts, American jihadis are more likely to seek contact with others online as a means of expanding networks and creating opportunities which are otherwise unavailable to them.

Finally, as a caveat, it is important to yet again acknowledge the significance of recent developments in relation to the conflict in Syria and Iraq. Specifically, although Islamist militants have been using social media for several years now, this has expanded quite dramatically to become the focal point of online jihadi activity. Platforms such as Facebook, Youtube, Twitter, Instagram, Ask.fm, and others are now being used extensively for propaganda, recruitment, facilitation, fundraising, and networking. Organizations such as IS are investing more and more in this technology and the use of social media by foreign fighters in Syria and Iraq has been prolific. As a result, we should expect to find an increase in use of the Internet for 'operational' purposes in the future.

Stated Motivations

Although we have now examined operational behaviors quite extensively, one last question remains: how do people understand and justify their actions once they are actively participating in terrorist activity? In both countries and across time the primary motivational themes that have been expressed have been politics and religion, combined with altruism and revenge.[93] The desire to defend and/or avenge fellow Muslims and anger at Western foreign policy are thus consistently repeated along with pervasive references to religious identity, principles, and goals. Thus, for example, the killing of two

CIA personnel in 1993 was explained as 'just revenge for the deaths of "Muslim brethren"',[94] while the 1998 petrol bombing of army barracks in the UK was 'clearly prompted by the resumption of the bombing on Iraq'.[95] More than a decade later the Boston bombing is believed to have been 'payback for US wars in Muslim lands',[96] and British soldier Lee Rigby was murdered, according to his killers, 'because Muslims are dying daily by British soldiers... It is an eye for an eye and a tooth for a tooth... we swear by the almighty Allah we will never stop fighting you until you leave us alone'.[97]

As these examples demonstrate, the revenge element in particular tends to be emphasized when offering justification for domestic attacks. Those who choose to fight abroad are more likely to stress altruistic motivations, a sense of personal obligation, and sometimes the desire to live in a 'real' Islamic state but the central themes remain the same. Hence, when asked why he wanted to go to Bosnia during the 1990s, Clement Rodney Hampton-El responded: 'I think it was a disgrace in the sight of humanity that these people [were]... raping women... killing children... So I thought it was my duty to try to do something as an individual'.[98] Similarly, Ibrahim al-Mazwagi — Britain's first known casualty of the war in Syria — proclaimed that 'We can't accept enemies of Allah for our religion — killing us, abusing our religion, belittling it, taking our lands. This is not something we stand for. So the Mujaheddin [sic], those who practice jihad, are those who defend the Muslims'.[99]

Of course, these are all examples of *ex post facto* public justifications. However, similar themes emerge from covert recordings. For instance, during the course of plotting to attack an Illinois mall in 2006, Derrick Shareef swore 'by Allah' that he was 'down for the cause' and complained that 'Kafirs don't give a damn about us, niggers don't care what happens to the Umma, about sisters getting raped... '.[100] Around about the same time Parviz Khan was being recorded in the UK as he explained his own perverse rationale for wanting to behead a British Muslim soldier: 'At least we can stop [Muslims] from doing the Haram... Don't join the army, it is haram. Wait till you go into Kuffar. They're not listening. So now we have to use force'.[101]

In addition to these core themes, there are other motives which although less often explicitly stated have become increasingly evident after 9/11. This includes specifically anti-American/anti-Western attitudes, sometimes combined with domestic grievances. For instance, Quazi Nafis — a young Bangladeshi student arrested in 2012 for planning to attack the New York Federal Reserve — repeatedly expressed his hatred for the US. In an article he wrote intended for *Inspire* magazine, he elaborated:

> all I had in my mind [was] how to destroy America...I came up to this conclusion that targeting America's economy is [the] most efficient way to draw the path of obliteration of America as well as the path of establishment of [the] Khilapha [Caliphate].[102]

Disdain for life in the West — as opposed to foreign policy — is also sometimes apparent. Irfan Naseer, the leader of the Operation Pitsford group, made this abundantly clear as he ranted, 'They wanna...have sex like donkeys on the street, they wanna club, act like animals and why shouldn't we terrorise them, tell me that?'[103]

Another motivational theme that appears to have gained traction in recent years involves the expression of bravado, 'macho' attitudes towards violence, adventure and death, and in some cases the deliberate adoption of a villainous role. These sentiments were exemplified by New Jersey native Mohamed Alessa, who was convicted for attempting to join al-Shabaab. In a recorded conversation with his co-conspirators, he declared that:

> A lot of people need to get killed bro, swear to God...I have to get [an] assault rifle and just kill anyone that looks at me the wrong way, bro...my soul cannot rest until I shed blood. I wanna, like, be the world's [best] known terrorist...Freaking Major-Nidal-shaved-face-Palestinian-crazy-guy; he's not better than me. I'll do twice what he did.[104]

Overt statements such as these were not widespread in either sample, but were detected more often in the US (9% of individuals versus 2% in the UK). This is likely to be at least partly due to the fact that these types of motives tend to be expressed more often in private conversations, which are frequently described in US indictments and other legal documents but are much less publicly available for UK cases.[105] Another reason, however, could be the greater presence of highly marginalized individuals in the US sample who seem to be drawn to violent jihad for non-ideological reasons (see Chapter 5).

Others from both the US and UK have expressed motives of redemption from a life of crime and a search for meaning and self-worth, while others still have expressed social, nationalistic, anti-Semitic, and even financial and personal motives. Thus, although motivations are primarily expressed in terms of ideological goals shaped by the belief in an existential war between Islam and the West, it is clear that — as discussed in Chapter 2 — there is a variety of other contributing factors. Moreover, it is also clear that jihadis themselves recognize this and are deliberately appealing to a range of motivational 'needs' in their efforts to attract new recruits. By way of example, a recent online video featured a British jihadi proudly showing off his Glock 19 handgun while simultaneously offering advice on 'how to leave that "gangster life" behind and join the life of jihad'. '"Where are you when they are slaughtering our children and our fathers, not to say our women after they get raped?" he asked, "Where are you when we need to start taking heads off? ... Come on!"'[106]

Concluding Remarks

Overall, there has been a great deal of similarity in the operational behavior of American and British jihadis, in particular the apparent decrease in foreign influence and the corresponding increase in levels of autonomy. Related trends that emerged in both countries included an increased domestic focus of activities, a decrease in the proportion of individuals engaging in international travel, and a shift in the location of overseas connections according to changes in the global jihadi landscape combined with historical developments unique to each country. Additional broad similarities were seen in terms of leadership, group size, career lengths, independent financing activities and motives. Moreover, it is noteworthy that overseas training and combat was the most popular type of activity overall in each country, while planning or conducting attacks accounted for about a third of each sample. Finally, there has also been a sizeable increase in the number of lone actor jihadis in both the US and UK.

Nonetheless, there were also important differences. Cases in the US were more often operationally discrete and there were much fewer connections between jihadis on the domestic stage. In accordance with this, there was evidence that the Internet has played a greater role for American jihadis, as reflected in increased online promotional activities, communication, dissemination of material, and — perhaps most significantly — group or network formation. In addition, the US has seen an increase in pseudo-facilitators who are lacking real connections or capabilities, an increase in criminal fundraising, and in the number of domestic attack plotters caught in sting operations, all of which are related to the existence of a highly marginalized underclass of jihadis in America, as discussed in Chapter 5.

By comparison, jihadis in the UK functioned more often as integrated components within a wider network, or were at least connected to similar individuals. Domestic connections were especially prevalent as compared to the US and promotional activities frequently occurred at street level. This reaffirms the observation that jihad in the UK is sustained by persistent subcultures of jihad, manifest by way of interpersonal networks of likeminded individuals. In terms of international connections (and in contrast to previous research), British jihadis have benefited more substantially from overseas leadership and support, in particular when it comes to planning and conducting attacks. As a result of this they have been more active in conducting terrorist attacks overseas and more competent and potentially deadly in planning and conducting attacks at home.

These differences in terms of operational behavior are related to interacting historical, domestic, and international circumstances and to *who* becomes a jihadi terrorist in each country. Events have also been shaped to some extent by the counterterrorism activities of the American and British authorities, which are examined in the following chapter.

Notes

[1]Naturally, missing information also contributes to these problems.

[2]For example, James Cromitie *et al.* in the US and Kevin Gardner in the UK.
[3]For example, Ramy Zamzam *et al.* in the US, Michael Adebolajo and Michael Adebowale in the UK.
[4]For example, Anwar al-Awlaki in the US and Ibrahim al-Mazwagi in the UK.
[5]In classifying 'lone actor' terrorists it is important to note that the author does not consider individual offenders who were caught in sting operations to qualify. In their minds, they were not acting alone and this distinguishes them from genuine lone actor terrorists who are willing to conduct attacks without any social or operational support. Furthermore, this classification is not restricted to individuals who planned or conducted attacks but includes any such individuals regardless of their operational activity.
[6]Note that this is *cases*, not individuals. Lone actors account for 10% of US individuals and 8% of UK individuals after 9/11.
[7]Connected cases in the US accounted for just 2% before 9/11 and 6% afterwards.
[8]Pre-9/11 examples include Wadih El-Hage and Jose Padilla; post-9/11 examples include Ahmed Omar Abu Ali and Omar Hammami.
[9]Pre-9/11 examples include Imran Mandhai and Shueyb Mossa Jokhan, and Emadeddin Muntasser *et al.*; post-9/11 examples include Raees and Sheheryar Qazi, and the Tsarnaev brothers.
[10]For example, Ghazi Ibrahim Abu Maizar before 9/11 and Yonathan Melaku afterwards.
[11]14% of US cases before 9/11 and 19% afterwards were classed as 'unknown'. In the UK, these figures were 18% and 31%.
[12]For example, Anas al-Liby and Khalid al-Fawwaz before 9/11, and Rashid Rauf and Bilal al-Berjawi after 9/11.
[13]This included 'D' (a government alias) who was subordinate to Abu Qatada and Abu Doha prior to 9/11; and Munir Farooqi *et al.* after 9/11.
[14]Mohammed Abdullah Azam before 9/11, and — among others — Bilal Zaheer Ahmed after 9/11.
[15]Before 9/11, leadership in 52% of US and 45% of UK cases was classed as being directly related to FTO hierarchies. After 9/11 these figures were 23% and 19%, respectively. Meanwhile, 12% of US cases and 30% of those in the UK were classed as semi-autonomous before 9/11, compared to 9% and 17% afterwards.
[16]'The Joker Who Wanted to be a Bomber', *BBC News*, February 21, 2013, available at: http://www.bbc.co.uk/news/uk-21414518, accessed February 21, 2013.
[17]Note that more definitive conclusions here are prevented by missing information. 17% of the total US sample versus 26% of the total UK sample was classed as 'unknown' in terms of leadership.
[18]It also does not appear that Tsarnaev's friends were radicalized themselves. In that sense they are not jihadis and could even be excluded from the sample. However, by including peripheral cases and those who aid and abet on an *ad hoc* basis, we gain a more complete understanding of Islamist terrorism in each country.

[19]Mitchell Silber and Arvin Bhatt, *Radicalization in the West: The Homegrown Threat* (New York: New York City Police Department, 2007).

[20]Sanctioners or ideologues were identified in 9% of US cases before 9/11 and 5% afterwards. The figures for the UK were 4% and 0%. It appears to be much more common for groups to draw spiritual inspiration and knowledge from well-known, established ideologues such as Anwar al-Awlaki — with whom they generally have no connections — rather than to appoint such a figure internally. Operational leadership of some description was much more common but was rarely formally acknowledged or personified by a single individual, making it difficult to identify any one person as the clear, overall leader of a group.

[21]See, for example, *United States of America v. Abu Khalid Abdul-Latif and Walli Mujahidh*, Complaint, United States District Court Western District of Washington at Seattle, Case No. MJ11-292, June 23, 2011, ¶22, available at: http://nefafoundation.org/newsite/file/US_v_WalliMujahidh_complaint.pdf, accessed July 26, 2011.

[22]The shortest known offense period in both countries was 1 day, while the maximum was 17 years in the US and 21 years in the UK for individual who mobilized prior to 9/11 (reduced to 9 years in both cases after 9/11).

[23]This is especially the case regarding possession of terrorism-related materials.

[24]More than any other terrorist-related behavior this is tied directly to legislation — specifically sections 57 and 58 of the UK Terrorism Act (2000).

[25]Krenar Lusha — arrested in the UK in August 2008 — is an illustrative case. Lusha had stockpiled more than 70 liters of petrol along with instructional materials relating to the manufacture of explosives and other suspicious materials. However, he was convicted only of possession of articles connected to purposes of terrorism rather than preparing or conspiring to commit a specific violent offense. His known behavior therefore falls short of providing confirmation that he was clearly planning a terrorist attack, despite a legal ruling that there must be a clear connection between items possessed and intended future acts of terrorism (see Susan Hemming, 'The Practical Application of Counterterrorism Legislation in England and Wales: A Prosecutor's Perspective' (2010), *International Affairs,* 86(4), 962–3, cited in Frank Foley, *Countering Terrorism in Britain and France: Institutions, Norms and the Shadow of the Past* (Cambridge: Cambridge University Press, 2013), Kindle Edition, Chapter 4).

[26]Vikram Dodd, 'Al-Qaida Fantasist Tells Court: I'm a Professional Liar', *The Guardian*, February 9, 2009, available at: http://www.guardian.co.uk/uk/2009/feb/09/uksecurity-july7, accessed February 15, 2013.

[27]See, for example: *AJOUAOU and A, B, C and D and Secretary of the State for the Home Department*, Special Immigration and Appeals Commission, Appeal Nos: SC/1/2002, SC/6/2002, SC/7/2002, SC/9/2002, SC/10/2002, October 29, 2003, ¶136, available at: http://www.siac.tribunals.gov.uk/Documents/outcomes/documents/sc92002b.pdf, accessed April 22, 2012.

[28]'Muslim Guilty of Inciting Racial Hatred', *BBC News*, May 30, 2002, available at: http://news.bbc.co.uk/2/hi/uk_news/england/1966839.stm, accessed May 19, 2010.

[29]The only US promoters aside from Awlaki who might be considered to have been influential individuals within the sampling time-frame are Samir Khan (who helped produce *Inspire* magazine until being killed in September 2011); Abd al-Moeed bin Abd al-Salam (a lead figure in the Global Islamic Media Front who was killed in Pakistan in December 2011); and Omar Hammami (who joined al-Shabaab and appeared in numerous promotional videos until his death in September 2013).

[30]Joseph Carter, Shiraz Maher, and Peter Neumann, *#Greenbirds: Measuring Importance and Influence in Syrian Foreign Fighter Networks* (London: International Centre for the Study of Radicalisation and Political Violence, 2014), available at: http://icsr.info/wp-content/uploads/2014/04/ICSR-Report-Greenbirds-Measuring-Importance-and-Infleunce-in-Syrian-Foreign-Fighter-Networks.pdf, accessed April 19, 2014.

[31]'Profiles: The Terror Gang Members', *The Independent*, February 26, 2008, available at: http://www.independent.co.uk/news/uk/crime/profiles-the-terror-gang-members-787469.html, accessed June 28, 2010.

[32]Fran Yeoman, 'Four Jailed for Hate Crimes at Cartoon Protest', *The Times*, July 18, 2007, available at: http://www.timesonline.co.uk/tol/news/uk/article 2097883.ece, accessed July 2, 2010.

[33]Sean O'Neill, 'Butchery Fuelled by Skunk Cannabis and a Doctrine of Hatred', *The Times*, December 20, 2013 (accessed December 30, 2013 via Lexis Nexis Academic).

[34]'David Colemen Headley Sentenced to 35 Years in Prison for Role in India and Denmark Terror Plots', *Federal Bureau of Investigation*, January 24, 2013, available at: http://www.fbi.gov/chicago/press-releases/2013/david-colemen-headley-sentenced-to-35-years-in-prison-for-role-in-india-and-denmark-terror-plots, accessed January 24, 2013.

[35]Examples include Tarik Shah, Michael Reynolds, and Uzair Paracha.

[36]Mostly, these individuals provided assistance to the failed 21/7 bombers.

[37]Notable examples include Rashid Rauf, Parviz Khan, Rangzieb Ahmed, Omar al-Brittani, and (allegedly) Mohammed Qayum Khan, among others.

[38]'QE.S.124.06. SANABEL RELIEF AGENCY LIMITED', *United Nations Security Council Committee*, August 13, 2009, available at: http://www.un.org/sc/committees/1267/NSQE12406E.shtml, accessed May 31, 2014.

[39]The article in question refers to al-Qaeda as 'the International Islamic Front (IIF), founded by bin Laden'.

[40]Chris Hastings and Jessica Berry, 'Muslims in Britain Train for Bin Laden', *The Washington Times*, November 7, 1999, available at: http://www.nl.newsbank.com, accessed June 3, 2014.

[41]Based on similarity of names and background information, it is quite possible that this is the same person as 'Abdul Waheed Majeed' who blew himself up in Syria on February 6, 2014 (see Kiran Randhawa, Justin Davenport, and David Churchill, 'EXCLUSIVE: Suicide Bomber Brit Worked as Driver for

Hate Cleric Omar Bakri', *The Evening Standard*, February 13, 2014, available at: http://www.standard.co.uk/news/crime/exclusive-suicide-bomber-brit-worked-as-driver-for-hate-cleric-omar-bakri-9125787.html, accessed February 13, 2014).

[42]Kim Howells, *Could 7/7 Have Been Prevented? Review of the Intelligence on the London Terrorist Attacks on 7 July 2005* (London: Intelligence and Security Committee, 2009), 17, available at: http://www.cabinetoffice.gov.uk/media/210852/20090519_77review.pdf, accessed May 20, 2010.

[43]Hastings and Berry, 'Muslims in Britain Train for Bin Laden'.

[44]Robin Simcox and Emily Dyer, 'Terror Data: US vs. UK', *World Affairs Journal*, July/August 2013, available at: http://www.worldaffairsjournal.org/article/terror-data-us-vs-uk, accessed December 10, 2013.

[45]The appeal of stricter sampling criteria is of course understandable and entirely defensible from an academic standpoint: the greater certainty attached to the data, the greater the confidence in the conclusions drawn. However, as the current comparison between the two sets of research repeatedly show, narrow sampling can also have misleading repercussions.

[46]Simcox and Dyer, 'Terror Data: US vs. UK'.

[47]Note that planning and conducting attacks were treated as mutually exclusive. In other words, 'planning' refers to cases where conspirators did not get a chance to put their plans into action. There were three exceptions to this rule where individuals planned attacks in addition to the ones they conducted (Ramzi Yousef and El Sayyid Nosair in the US, and Kamel Bourgass in the UK).

[48]Note — in addition to the five attacks recorded in Table 6.3 which were conducted by American jihadis overseas, at least two others were (possibly) committed during the same time-frame by Abdisalan Hussein Ali and Mohanad Shareef Hammadi). However, Ali's attack has not been confirmed, and Hammadi's offenses occurred during the Iraqi insurgency before he came to the US.

[49]This refers to any form of documented contact or communication and does not necessarily indicate overseas training or foreign support of operations.

[50]Note that two additional attacks occurred prior to 9/11 but were excluded from the sample due to a lack of information confirming jihadist motivations. These were Rashid Baz's shooting of Jewish school children on the Brooklyn Bridge on March 1, 1994, and Ali Hasan Abu Kamal's shooting attack on the Empire State Building on February 24, 1997. Also excluded were murders committed by jihadists as part of in-fighting rather than for purposes of terrorism. Likewise, after 9/11, the July 4, 2002 attack on an El Al ticket counter at Los Angeles airport by Hesham Mohamed Hedayat was also excluded.

[51]These were Charles Bishop's suicide attack in Tampa in 2002; Mohammed Taheri-Azar's attempt to run people over at a North Carolina college campus in 2006; Faisal Shahzad's attempt to bomb Times Square in May of 2010; and the shooting of several government targets in Virginia by Yonathan Melaku from October 2010 to June 2011.

[52]Successful jihadi attacks in the US included Naveed Haq's attack on a Seattle Jewish center in 2006; Abdulhakim Mujahid Muhammed's assault on an Army and Navy recruiting center in Little Rock in June 2009; Nidal Malik Hasan's shooting spree at Ford Hood in November 2009; and the Boston bombings in April 2013.

[53]Completed, yet unsuccessful attacks in the UK since 9/11 include the 21/7 attempted bombings in London in 2005; the attempted bombing of a London nightclub and Glasgow airport in June 2007; Nicky Reilly's attempted suicide bombing of an Exeter restaurant in 2008; and the stabbing of an MP by Roshonara Choudhry in May 2010.

[54]Successful attacks in the UK after 9/11 included the spur-of-the-moment murder of a policeman by Kamel Bourgass in January 2003; the 7/7 bombings in 2005; and the murder of Lee Rigby in Woolwich in May 2013.

[55]The domestic cases after 9/11 in the US which involved planned/actual suicide attacks were Charles Bishop's attack on the American Bank Plaza building in Tampa in 2002; Najibullah Zazi *et al.*'s New York subway plot of 2008–2009; Sami Osmakac's plans to wreak havoc in South Tampa in January 2012; and Amine el-Khalifi's bid to attack the US Capitol building in February 2012. The UK cases were the 7/7 London bombings of 2005; the 21/7 attempted bombings; the attempted bombing of Glasgow airport in 2007; Nicky Reilly's attempted suicide bombing of 2008; and the Operation Pitsford plot that was disrupted in 2011.

[56]This excludes individuals who said they were willing to die but did not clearly plan or actually commit suicide themselves (such as Nidal Hasan in the US, and Lee Rigby's killers in the UK). Bryant Vinas was excluded from the count of planned suicide attacks in the US because he had not done anything other than say that he was willing to commit such an attack. Also excluded from the count of planned suicide attacks in the UK was the case of Andrew Ibrahim, who had begun making two suicide vests but whose intention to wear one himself cannot be reliably demonstrated.

[57]Lone individuals only, excluding pairs, groups, and sting operations.

[58]Note — this does not contradict the earlier statement that there were 22 lone actors in the US and 24 in the UK after 9/11. Although the focus tends to be only on lone actor terrorists who are planning attacks, they can of course be engaged in other behaviors.

[59]This is consistent with recent analysis, which found that 'jihadi terrorism in Europe is becoming more discriminate in its targeting while attacks types and weapons are becoming progressively more diverse' (Petter Nesser and Anne Stenerson, 'The Modus Operandi of Jihadi Terrorists in Europe', *Perspectives on Terrorism*, 8(6), available at: http://www.terrorismanalysts.com/pt/index.php/pot/article/view/388/771, accessed December 12, 2014.

[60]At first glance these results might seem to contradict the finding that US jihadis are more involved in planning and conducting attacks at home, compared to the UK. However, the analysis of focus of operations is inclusive of all activities, not just attacks, and refers to individuals rather than cases. Moreover, American jihadis have maintained a slightly stronger tendency towards exclusively

domestic foci of operations (27% and 30% before and after 9/11, compared to 5% and 26% in the UK), while British militants have shown more of a mixed focus, i.e. an interest in both domestic *and* overseas activities (this applied to 13% and then 15% of US individuals before and after 9/11, compared to 12% and 25% in the UK).

[61]'U.S. Convicts Pakistani of Providing Support to Al Qaeda', *United States Attorney Southern District of New York*, November 25, 2005, available at: http://www.justice.gov/usao/nys/pressreleases/November05/parachaconvict-ionpr.pdf, accessed June 18, 2014.

[62]Jason Burke, 'Rogue Operator — David Coleman Headley on LeT', *Jane's Intelligence Review*, January 13, 2011.

[63]Andrea Elliott, 'Militant's Path From Pakistan to Times Square', *The New York Times*, June 22, 2010, available at: http://www.nytimes.com/2010/06/23/world/23terror.html?tntemail1=y&emc=tnt&pagewanted=all, accessed June 23, 2010.

[64]Curt Anderson, 'Fla. Imam Gets 25 Years Prison for Taliban Support', *ABC News*, August 23, 2013, available at: http://abcnews.go.com/US/wireStory/fla-imam-25-years-prison-taliban-support-20051002, accessed August 23, 2013.

[65]'Terrorists Ordered to Hand Back Stolen Charity Money', *West Midlands Police*, January 12, 2014, available at: http://west-midlands.police.uk/latest-news/press-release.asp?ID=5710, accessed January 12, 2014.

[66]'British-Born Muslims Supply Equipment to al-Qaeda', *The Telegraph*, March 9, 2009, available at: http://www.telegraph.co.uk/news/worldnews/asia/afghanistan/4962802/British-born-Muslims-supplied-equipment-to-al-Qaeda.html, accessed March 9, 2009.

[67]Jamie Doward, 'Peer Raises Fears over UK Charity's Alleged Links to Boko Haram', *The Telegraph*, September 9, 2012, available at: http://www.theguardian.com/world/2012/sep/09/uk-charity-boko- haram?INTCMP=SRCH, accessed June 22, 2014.

[68]'Charity Commission Warns of Islamic Extremism Threat', *BBC News*, April 20, 2014, available at: http://www.bbc.com/news/uk-27092885, accessed April 20, 2014.

[69]Note that the different fundraising types often overlap with one another (i.e. they are not mutually exclusive), and groups are not necessarily restricted to a single method.

[70]'First Terrorist Convicted on State Terror Charges Sentenced to Decade in Prison for 2011 Plot to Attack Manhattan Synagogues', *New York Police Department*, March 15, 2013, available at: http://www.nyc.gov/html/nypd/html/pr/pr_2013_03_15_terrorist_convicted_on_state_terror_chages.shtml, accessed March 16, 2013.

[71]The credentials of the 'al-Qaeda operatives' who took Ouazzani's money have since been called into question, although it does not detract from his demonstrated intent and capability.

[72]Mark Morris and Tony Rizzo, 'In Federal Court, Kansas City Man Admits Sending Money to al-Qaida', The *Kansas City Star*, May 19, 2010, available

at: http://www.kansascity.com/2010/05/19/1957858/kc-man-admits-sending-money-to.html, accessed May 20, 2010.

[73] Nicola Woolcock, 'Three Students Jailed for Inciting Terrorism on "Holy War" Websites', *The Times*, July 6, 2007, available at: http://www.timesonline.co.uk/tol/news/uk/crime/article2034011.ece, accessed July 25, 2010.

[74] An additional, potentially significant case involved illegal shipments of the stimulant khat, which were sent from the UK and sold in the US for a substantial profit. However, initial reports of ties to terrorism were not confirmed and the perpetrators were prosecuted for criminal offenses only. This case was therefore excluded from the analysis.

[75] Tom Whitehead, 'Fundraiser of Terror Gang Lost £9000 in Bad Trading', *The Telegraph*, October 23, 2012, available at: http://www.telegraph.co.uk/news/uknews/terrorism-in-the-uk/9627456/Fundraiser-of-terror-gang-lost-9000-in-bad- trading.html, accessed October 23, 2012.

[76] A recent report which analyzed the funding of 40 jihadist terrorism plots in Western Europe reached an almost identical conclusion: 'three quarters of the plots studied estimated to cost less than $10,000', (Emilie Oftedal, The Financing of Jihadi Terrorism Cells in Europe (*Norwegian Defence Research Establishment*, 2015), available at: http://www.ffi.no/Rapporter/14-02234.pdf, accessed January 26, 2015).

[77] Note that this does not necessarily imply leadership from abroad, which was analyzed separately.

[78] This is confirmed when we examine individuals rather than cases. Before and after 9/11, 76% and then 40% of US jihadis had some form of connection to foreign terrorists, compared to 90% and then 37% in the UK. Although the actual numbers remain higher in the UK after 9/11 (90 individuals versus 109), to find such proportional similarity is quite unexpected. As noted above, these results also conflict with those of Simcox and Dyer.

[79] Note that this difference persists when we include only *domestic* plots and attacks (before and after 9/11, 70% and then 20% of such cases in the US had overseas connections, compared to zero and then 54% in the UK).

[80] 'Al-Qaeda' is defined here as individuals located in Afghanistan and/or Pakistan who are reportedly members of that organization. The regional branches of al-Qaeda were counted separately.

[81] Note that overseas connections are not mutually exclusive and it was especially common prior to 9/11 to find that individuals had connections to militants in both Afghanistan and Pakistan. If we eliminate this overlap, the figures for the Afghanistan–Pakistan region are as follows: before and after 9/11 in the US: 62% and 13%; before and after 9/11 in the UK: 58% and 19%.

[82] Although the confirmed numbers in absolute terms were 29 (US) and 45 (UK).

[83] Note that Simcox and Dyer also found this difference (Simcox and Dyer, 'Terror Data: US vs. UK').

[84] Eli Lake, 'Exclusive: Al Qaeda's American Fighters Are Coming Home — And U.S. Intelligence Can't Find Them', *The Daily Beast*, May 20, 2014, available at: http://www.thedailybeast.com/articles/2014/05/20/exclusive-more-than-100-americans-are-waging-jihad-in-syria-u-s-intelligence-says.html, accessed May 20, 2014.

[85]Tom Whitehead, 'Up to 700 Britons Feared Fighting in Syria', *The Telegraph*, April 24, 2014, available at: http://www.telegraph.co.uk/news/uknews/law-and-order/10785316/up-to-700-Britons-feared-fighting-in-Syria.html, accessed April 24, 2014.

[86]Note that as always there is no clear dividing line between analytical concepts. Processes of radicalization (and associated use of the Internet) therefore overlap with operational behaviors, in particular downloading of propaganda.

[87]That is, when the offenses actually occurred rather than when the offenders mobilized.

[88]*Inspire* magazine was specifically mentioned as having played a role in 8 US cases and 13 UK cases beginning after 9/11 (or 6% and 9% respectively).

[89]For example, Zachary Chesser and Jesse Morton in the US and Younis Tsouli *et al.* in the UK.

[90]Most notably, Gufran Ahmed Kauser Mohammed from the US sample, and Aabid Khan from the UK.

[91]Cases include Syed Haris Ahmed and Ramy Zamzam *et al.*, both from the US.

[92]For instance, Colleen LaRose *et al.* from the US and the Operation Guava case in the UK.

[93]Missing information was, as ever, quite significant but references to a combination of religious, altruistic, and political motives were recorded for 59% and then 54% of individuals in the US sample, and 39% and 43% of the UK sample before and after 9/11. The differences are primarily due to availability of information and are not likely to reflect real differences in the way that jihadis in the US and UK justify their actions.

[94]Gretchen Lacharite, 'Group Threatens to Keep Killing Americans: Links Pakistan Murders to Kasi Sentencing', *The Washington Times*, November 14, 1997, available at: http://www.highbeam.com/doc/1G1-56779808.html, accessed July 30, 2011.

[95]'Iraq Protest Student Jailed for Petrol Bomb Attack', *The Press Association*, March 5, 1999, accessed via *Lexis Nexis Academic*, June 5, 2013.

[96]Susan Candiotti, 'Suspect: Boston Bombing was Payback for Hits on Muslims', *CNN*, May 16, 2013, available at: http://edition.cnn.com/2013/05/16/us/boston-bombing-investigation/index.html, accessed May 16, 2013.

[97]'Woolwich Attack: The Terrorist's Rant', *The Telegraph*, May 23, 2013, available at: http://www.telegraph.co.uk/news/uknews/terrorism-in-the-uk/10075488/Woolwich-attack-the-terrorists-rant.html, accessed May 23, 2013.

[98]*United States of America v. Omar Ahmad Ali Abdel Rahman et al*, Testimony of Clement Hampton-El, United States District Court Southern District of New York, S5 93 CR 181 (MBM), August 2, 1995, 15628, available at: http://hurryupharry.org/wp-content/uploads/2010/05/US-vs-Omar-Ahmad-Ali-Abdel-Rahman.pdf, accessed August 11, 2012.

[99]'Britons Fighting with Syria's Jihadi "Band of Brothers"', *Channel 4 News*, June 14, 2013, available at: http://www.channel4.com/news/syria-war-rebels-jihadi-ibrahim-al-mazwagi, accessed June 14, 2013.

[100]*United States of America v. Derrick Shareef*, Affidavit, United States District Court Northern District of Illinois, Case No. 06CR0919, December 8, 2006, 4, 6,

available at: http://nefafoundation.org/miscellaneous/FeaturedDocs/U.S._v_Shareef_Complaint.pdf, accessed June 10, 2010.

[101] Duncan Gardham, 'Transcript of Parviz Khan Discussing the Plot', *The Telegraph*, February 18, 2008, available at: http://www.telegraph.co.uk/news/uknews/1579023/Transcript-of-Parviz-Khan-discussing-the-plot.html, accessed May 9, 2010.

[102] *United States of America v. Quazi Mohammad Rezwanul Ahsan Nafis*, Complaint, United States District Court Eastern District of New York, Case No. :12-CR-00720, October 15, 2012, available at: http://cbsnewyork.files.wordpress.com/2012/10/nafis-complaint.pdf, accessed February 10, 2013.

[103] Tom Whitehead, 'Non-Muslims Have "Sex like Donkeys" and Deserve to be Blown-Up, Said "Terror Plot" Leader', *The Telegraph*, October 25, 2012, available at: http://www.telegraph.co.uk/news/uknews/terrorism-in-the-uk/9633060/Non-Muslims-have-sex-like-donkeys-and-deserve-to-be-blown-up-said-terror-plot-leader.html, accessed October 25, 2012.

[104] *United States of America v. Mohamed Alessa and Carlos E. Almonte*, Complaint, United States District Court District of New Jersey, Case No. 2:11-CR-00133, June 4, 2010, available at: http://nefafoundation.org/file/US_v_Almonte_complaint.pdf, accessed December 12, 2011.

[105] Certainly overt expressions of 'jihadi cool' and bravado have become more common over the past 2–3 years with the rise of social media in Syria and Iraq.

[106] 'YouTube Jihadist Urges Brits to Quit "Gangster Life"', *Al Arabiya News*, June 29, 2014, available at: http://english.alarabiya.net/en/perspective/features/2014/06/29/YouTube-jihadist-urges-Muslim-Brits-to-quit-gangster-life.html, accessed June 29, 2014.

Chapter 7

How Have Jihadis Been Dealt With?

Terrorism and counterterrorism are opposite sides of the same coin; it is hard to imagine one without the other. The actors on either side of the equation reaffirm one another's existence and shape each other's behavior in an endless cycle of action and reaction. It is therefore important that we examine not only the terrorists and how they behave, but also the counterterrorism tools that are used against them. In contrast to the former, the latter is still greatly under-researched and gaining access to 'counterterrorists' for research purposes can be difficult.[1] Moreover, we are not always privy to the details of how and when exactly formal criminal/counterterrorism investigations are initiated, the techniques that are used or the evidence that is utilized. As a result, the following analysis is therefore very much exploratory and the judgments made are inherently tentative, based on the information that is publicly available. Nevertheless, there is still sufficient information to allow meaningful insights and to illuminate areas in need of further exploration, thereby adding to our understanding of the murky world of counterterrorism as it relates to American and British jihadis. We begin by looking at the investigative process in each country, followed by sources of evidence, legal processing times, and an examination of judicial outcomes, concluding with a discussion of ways in which jihadis in each country have reacted to the measures used against them (see Tables 7.1 and 7.2 below).

Table 7.1. Investigative and legal processes for jihadi terrorism cases in the US before and after 9/11 (1980s–2013).

	Pre-9/11	Post-9/11
Investigative process*	15% of domestic investigations initiated overseas; 56% initiated domestically (29% unknown); Investigations initiated by: domestic offences (32%), international offences (12%), tip-offs (12%), domestic CT (6%), domestic law enforcement (6%), international law enforcement (3%). Average length of domestic investigations 40.7 months; 26% of domestic cases involved informants/undercover operatives	10% of domestic investigations initiated overseas; 57% initiated domestically (33% unknown); Investigations initiated by: tip-offs (21%), domestic CT (17%), domestic offences (9%), domestic law enforcement (8%), international CT (7%), international offences (3%), OSINT (3%), COIN (1%). Average length of domestic investigations 16.2 months; 42% of domestic cases involved informants/undercover operatives
Primary sources of evidence**	Primary sources of evidence (15 domestic cases): Combined sources (10 cases, 67%); Offender confessions (2 cases, 13%); 1 case (7%) where offender apprehended at time of offense; 1 case based on HUMINT; 1 on SIGINT	Primary sources of evidence (149 domestic cases): 34% combined sources; 32% sting operations; 7% offender confessions; Other sources include SIGINT, electronic, personal/public records, offender apprehension, HUMINT, physical/forensic evidence and OSINT (10% unknown)
Legal processing times (individuals prosecuted)**	Average time from arrest to conviction 22.7 months; Average time from conviction to sentencing 17.4 months	Average time from arrest to conviction 17.5 months; Average time from conviction to sentencing 9.4 months
Legal outcomes (individuals prosecuted)**	35 individuals prosecuted domestically; 70% convicted, 27% pleaded; Average custodial sentence 42 years; 14% life sentences	207 individuals prosecuted domestically; 37% convicted; 62% pleaded; Average custodial sentence 15.2 years; 9% life sentences

*Sample divided by when investigations began.
**Sample divided by when investigations ended.

Table 7.2. Investigative and legal processes for jihadi terrorism cases in the UK before and after 9/11 (1980s–2013).

	Pre-9/11	Post-9/11
Investigative process*	33% of domestic investigations initiated overseas; 29% initiated domestically (38% unknown); Investigations investigated by: domestic CT (21%), international offences (17%), international CT (13%), domestic offences (8%), international law enforcement (4%). Average length of domestic investigations 27.5 months; No reported uses of informants or undercover operatives	6% of domestic investigations initiated overseas; 35% initiated domestically (58% unknown); Investigations initiated by: domestic CT (12%), domestic offences (12%), domestic law enforcement (8%), international CT (5%), tip-offs (3%), international offences (1%), OSINT (1%). Average length of domestic investigations 5.5 months; 4 domestic cases involving undercover operatives
Primary sources of evidence**	Primary sources of evidence (7 domestic cases): Physical/forensic (2 cases, 29%); HUMINT (2 cases, 29%); 1 case (14%) based on combined evidence; 1 offender apprehended at time of offense; 1 case unknown	Primary sources of evidence (152 domestic cases): 36% secret; 17% combined sources; 16% physical/forensic; 10% electronic; Other sources include offender apprehension, surveillance, offender confessions, HUMINT, SIGINT, undercover agents, OSINT and personal/public records (8% unknown)
Legal processing times (individuals prosecuted)**	Average time from arrest to conviction 17.5 months; Average time from conviction to sentencing 3 months	Average time from arrest to conviction 17.7 months; Average time from conviction to sentencing 1.8 months
Legal outcomes (individuals prosecuted)**	3 individuals prosecuted domestically; 3 convicted, Average custodial sentence 10.3 years	190 individuals prosecuted domestically; 48% convicted, 51% pleaded; Average custodial sentence 7.2 years; 15% life sentences

*Sample divided by when investigations began.
**Sample divided by when investigations ended.

Investigative Process

As the previous chapters have illustrated, jihadist terrorism in the US and UK has become increasingly home-grown over time and yet it also retains a significant, albeit diminished international element. At the same time, there has been an unrelenting emphasis on international cooperation in counterterrorism (CT), which intensified after 2001. In light of these developments, it makes sense to examine the domestic vs. international balance of CT investigations (CTIs). Before 9/11, a total of 34 Islamist terrorism cases are known to have been investigated by US authorities.[2,3] Of those 34 cases, 19 (56%) were initiated domestically and 5 (15%) were initiated in response to overseas events. In the UK, 24 CTIs were initiated during the same period, of which 7 (29%) were initiated at home and 8 (33%) were initiated abroad.[4] After 9/11, 144 US CTIs were recorded, 82 of which (57%) were initiated at home, compared to 15 (10%) abroad.[5] The corresponding figures for the UK were 144 CTIs in total, comprised of 51 (35%) domestic and 8 (6%) overseas.[6] The remainder in all instances is unknown.

The available data suggest a similar pattern over time in both countries in that the number of CTIs has vastly increased since 2001 in order to cope with the rising threat (and of course these figures include only the investigations that we know of). Moreover, it would appear that while the number of investigations initiated in response to overseas events has increased ever so slightly, proportionally it has declined. This suggests that CTIs are now more likely to begin at home, which would certainly make sense in light of the much larger and more capable CT machinery constructed in both nations after 9/11. It is also very much consistent with the observed increase in domestic radicalization and the proportional decrease in connections to terrorists abroad (see Chapters 5 and 6). So while international cooperation in CT has undoubtedly expanded over the last 14 or more years, domestic authorities still retain primary ownership over their respective terrorist populations. More revealing insights are gleaned from an examination of the particular activities, events, or sources of information that gave rise to investigations.

Responding to Domestic Offenses

Responding to an overt terrorist offense, in particular if it is an attack, is generally seen as a failure in counterterrorism since the goal is to prevent them from happening in the first place. Before and after 9/11, 32% and then 9% of US CTIs were initiated in response to domestic offenses, while in the UK the respective percentages were 8% and 12%. The disparity between countries prior to 9/11 is particularly striking. However — as always — we need to take care in interpreting these results. The much larger percentage of cases initiated in response to domestic offenses in the US during this period is not a reflection of many more incidents of terrorism actually taking place; rather it is explained by the fact that multiple investigations were initiated in response to one major event — namely the bombing of the World Trade Center in 1993, which led to the prosecution of another eight connected cases. In addition to Omar Abdel Rahman *et al.* this included a number of peripheral individuals who were prosecuted for relatively ordinary criminal offenses, such as Ibrahim Ahmad Suleiman (an alleged fundraiser for the Afghan *mujahideen* living in San Antonio, Texas who was prosecuted for perjury and naturalization fraud[7]) and Kelvin Smith, who provided paramilitary-style training to some of Rahman's followers and later pleaded guilty to making false statements and disposing of firearms and abseiling equipment that the group had left at his property in Pennsylvania.[8] Only two other domestic incidents occurred in the US during this period that qualify as acts of jihadi terrorism and which prompted investigations: the assassination of Meir Kahane in 1990 and the shooting of CIA personnel in Virginia in 1993.

Meanwhile, just two incidents in total took place in the UK prior to 2001: the 1998 petrol bombing of a Territorial Army base and the distribution of anti-Semitic leaflets at an al-Muhajiroun (AM) event in 2000, which resulted in convictions for attempted arson and incitement of racial hatred, respectively. In contrast to the US these were relatively trivial events and although conceivably they might have led to other investigations — since both were linked to the same extremist organization — there is no evidence that this was the case.

After 9/11 there has been greater similarity between the two countries since both experienced significant domestic attacks which prompted multiple, additional investigations. In the US, the 9/11 attacks led more-or-less directly to the investigation of three additional cases included in the sample,[9] while the Boston marathon bombing also led to the investigation of Dzhokar Tsarnaev's friends who acted as *ad hoc* accomplices after the fact. In the UK, the 7/7 bombings in turn led to another two successful CTIs,[10] while the 21/7 attempted bombings led to the investigation and prosecution of another ten individuals who helped the perpetrators escape and/or failed to disclose information. Major attacks, whilst tragic and to be avoided at all costs, thus tend to reinvigorate counterterrorism operations — sometimes facilitated by the introduction of new legislation — and lead to the dismantling of wider networks.

There were also some important differences after 9/11 in terms of the number and type of incidents which prompted investigations. In the US there was a total of nine actual incidents, all of which were terrorist attacks. By comparison, 14 incidents took place in the UK but only 6 were attacks while the remaining 8 were much less serious offenses including hoaxes and incitement of terrorist activity at demonstrations and on the Internet.[11] Hence, American authorities have initiated CTIs more often in response to actual attacks taking place, while British authorities have also actively responded to a range of relatively petty overt offenses, a number of which would potentially be protected as freedom of speech under American law.

Responding to International Offenses

Domestic investigations can of course be initiated in response to international events as well.[12] Prior to 9/11 this applied to 12% of US CTIs and 17% of UK CTIs, which translates into four cases apiece. One individual — Rachid Ramda — was investigated in the UK in response to the 1995 metro bombings in France, but all of the remaining cases in both countries were investigated in response to the East African embassy bombings in 1998. Intelligence agencies may well have been aware of the individuals in question already but it was not until after the attacks that law enforcement agencies really pursued them. In the US, they included Wadih el-Hage, Essam al-Ridi, Ihab Ali, and Ziyad Khaleel.[13] In the UK they included Khalid al-Fawwaz, Ibrahim Eidarous, and Adel Bari, who were promptly detained pursuant to US extradition requests;[14] Anas al-Liby, who was also charged by the Americans but fled from his home in Manchester before British police could arrest him; and Saad al-Faqih, who was first implicated in the bombings during a trial in New York in 2000 and was finally subject to UN and UK financial sanctions for ties to al-Qaeda in December of 2004.[15]

After 9/11 the percentage of domestic CTIs which were initiated in response to overseas offenses diminished in both countries, dropping to 3% in the US and 1% in the UK. US cases included Hasan Akbar, who attacked and killed two fellow American soldiers in Kuwait in March 2003; Ahmed Ali, who was arrested in Saudi Arabia following the assault on a housing compound in Riyadh in May 2003 and was later convicted of plotting to kill George W. Bush; David Headley, who was eventually tracked down due to his role in the Mumbai attacks of November 2008; and Omar Mohamud, who blew himself up in Mogadishu in September 2009.[16] The only UK case that was included in this category was that of Richard Reid and Saajid Badat, with specific reference to Badat who was prosecuted in the UK after Reid's failed attempt to down an airliner in December 2001.[17] Interestingly then, all but one of the cases that were initiated overseas and led to significant legal action in the UK, both before and after 9/11, originated with American investigators.

As per the previous analysis of international behavior (see Chapter 6), other overseas offenses certainly occurred during this period (3 involving Americans and 13 involving British jihadis) but were handled primarily by the countries concerned.

Domestic Counterterrorism

Proactive detection of terrorist activity represents the apex of counterterrorism since it enables the prevention of more serious offenses before they can take place. At face value, the figures here are not particularly encouraging: before and after 9/11, this applied to 6% and then 17% of cases in the US, compared to 21% and then 13%

in the UK. However, this should not necessarily be seen as failure on behalf of the respective authorities. For starters, the percentages before 9/11 are easily skewed due to the small sample sizes and the actual numbers involved have increased in both countries — from 2 to 24 in the US and from 5 to 18 in the UK. More importantly, this is certainly not the entire picture. In reality domestic CT agencies have for the most part effectively managed nearly all of the cases identified for this research — as well as many more where details are simply not publicized — regardless of how they were first detected.[18]

Things become more interesting when looking a little more closely at exactly how and why CTIs were initiated. Before 9/11, both cases in the US that were classed as 'domestic CT' were actually fairly straightforward criminal investigations which were initiated as 'offshoots' to the investigation into the so-called 'Day of Rage' plot to attack New York City landmarks in 1993 (which was itself a response to the attack on the World Trade Center earlier that year). In the first case, one of the suspects in the plot, an Egyptian named Matarawy Saleh, had gone on the run and was found in hiding in a New Jersey motel along with one Ashraf Mohammed and Evelyn Cortez, who were both then prosecuted for harboring a fugitive.[19] In the second case, Omar Abdel Rahman's lawyer, Lynne Stewart and two others were prosecuted for relaying messages from the 'Blind Sheikh' in his prison cell to his followers on the outside, including a *fatwa* mandating the 'killing [of] Jews wherever they are found'.[20] Although hardly dramatic examples of counterterrorism,[21] they nevertheless demonstrate a phenomenon that has reoccurred multiple times after 9/11 in both the US and UK (see below), whereby CTIs tend to 'snowball' as loose ends are tied up and one investigation leads to another based on associations between suspects.

By contrast, the five cases investigated in the UK before 9/11 were all seemingly part of a much broader CT effort aimed at gathering intelligence on the luminaries of 'Londonistan' and their followers. This included Abu Qatada, Abu Hamza, and Omar Bakri Mohammed, plus two individuals who were later subject to control orders and were assigned the government aliases 'P' and 'A'. Although specific information is lacking, many more individuals who were part of these networks undoubtedly came to the attention of British authorities at this time. Thus, while US CTIs prior to 9/11 were prompted by specific offenses and were therefore more tightly focused *criminal* investigations, the more exploratory efforts in the UK were initiated in response to the growth of highly visible extremist networks whose true criminal intent was yet to be determined.

After 9/11, proactive CTIs have begun in response to a wider range of initial sources of information. In the US, the most popular sources have included covert informants or undercover operatives (nine cases[22]), monitoring of online activity (eight cases[23]), and 'snowballing' from one investigation to the next (six cases[24]), with one additional case identified by way of financial irregularities.[25] In the UK, snowballing of investigations also appears to be a common occurrence, accounting for 7 of 17 cases,[26] while routine observation of convicted terrorist offenders on parole led to two new CTIs[27] and monitoring of online activity led to the initiation of just one investigation that we know about.[28] Details are scarce in the remaining seven domestic CT cases in the UK but they appear to have been initiated by way of ongoing monitoring of known extremist networks since all of them had been involved for some time with other jihadists within Britain, including one or more of the following high-profile individuals: Abu Doha, Abu Qatada, Abu Hamza, Abdullah el-Faisal, Abu Izzadeen, and Anjem Choudary.

By way of example, the nine individuals arrested in December 2010 under Operation Guava had been actively plotting for no more than a few months but had been known to security services for several years. Several of them were associated with 'Islam4UK' (a reincarnation of AM) and had been involved in activism on behalf of the group including protests, handing out leaflets promoting jihad, and picketing mosques.[29] Moreover, some of their homes had been searched as early as 2008, others had been involved in tensions between local Islamists and members of the English Defence League, and at the time of their arrests they were found to have contact details stored in their phones for el-Faisal, Izzadeen, and Choudary.[30] This tends to suggest a more-or-less continuous process of monitoring persons of interest and their associations, with criminal investigations commencing in response to specific intelligence (the source of which is rarely revealed) and/or such factors as suspicious travel and established contact with known terrorists either at home or abroad.

Although the data here provide only glimpses into how CTIs are initiated in each country, they are nevertheless consistent with what we know about other aspects of investigative practice and the nature of the threat. For instance, it is worth noting that the seemingly more prominent role of informants for identifying cases in the US is consistent with their widespread use in CTIs there more generally and as sources of evidence used at trial (see below).[31] Furthermore, the greater use of online surveillance in order to identify terrorism suspects in the US is congruent with the suggestion that the Internet plays a more significant role for American jihadis (see Chapter 6). Finally, the central importance of domestic extremist associations as a means of identifying suspects in the UK supports the observation that British jihadis are the product of extremist subcultures consisting of fairly extensive and still quite visible human networks. Indeed, while arrests in the UK are carefully targeted,[32] as many as 8,000 al-Qaeda sympathizers were under investigation by 2006 as part of a nationwide operation known as Project Rich Picture, which aimed 'to drill down and identify those who may be coming into contact with radical sources'.[33] CTIs in the UK today are clearly carrying on in the same vein although the process appears to have become more refined. For instance, following the Woolwich attack in 2013, MI5 introduced a program named Operation Danube in order to 'manage the level of risk posed by low level subjects of interest' on the periphery of terrorism investigations, and established a dedicated team to monitor '"self-starters" who are outside the ... usual terror networks and [identify] recurring "subjects of interest" who feature in more than one extremist network'.[34] Nevertheless, there were still 'at least 3,000' suspected Islamist extremists being monitored in the UK as of February 2015.[35]

International Counterterrorism

Domestic CTIs are also sometimes initiated as a result of activities or information received from international partners. In the US, this did not apply to any cases before 9/11 but applied to ten afterwards (amounting to 7% of known CTIs for that period), while the respective figures for the UK were three (13%) and seven (5%). Notably, although the proportion of 'international CT' cases is small, the actual numbers have increased somewhat over time in both countries.

In all instances, these have either involved American/British residents being detained overseas, or else being identified by way of their connections with foreign terrorists. Examples include Operation Magnesium, which led to the dismantling of a terrorism financing and facilitation network based in Leicester in the UK after the arrest of Djamel Beghal in Dubai in July 2001;[36] Daniel Maldonado, who was arrested in Kenya in January 2007 after joining al-Shabaab;[37] and Younis Tsouli and his confederates who were arrested in London and Kent after evidence was discovered linking them to suspects in Bosnia.[38]

In some cases (such as Maldonado and Jose Padilla before him) the individuals concerned were known to authorities already; however, they were not apparently the focal point of existing investigations and certainly no decisive action was taken against them until after they were clearly implicated as a result of overseas developments. This is suggestive of a problem which has intensified in recent years in relation to Syria and Iraq, whereby it is very difficult to prevent someone from traveling abroad for violent jihad unless criminal intent can be clearly demonstrated in advance.

Domestic Law Enforcement

In addition to specific counterterrorism investigations, routine law enforcement also plays a role in the identification of terrorist offenders. Two cases (6%) were detected this way in the US before 9/11 and 11 cases (8%) were detected afterwards, compared to no such cases in the UK in the former period and 11 cases (8%) in the latter. A more detailed examination reveals that terrorist offenders were brought to the attention of law enforcement officers as a result of a diverse range of criminal behavior.

The two cases in the US before 9/11 involved border control (which led to the arrest of Abdelghani Meskini in New York[39]) and a routine traffic stop[40] (eventually leading to the discovery of a plot to establish a jihadi training camp in Oregon and the arrest of Earnest Ujaama[41]). After 9/11, two CTIs resulted from ordinary criminal investigations relating to illegal money transfers (Saifullah Ranjha[42]) and bank fraud (Ruben Shumpert[43]); two connected cases were discovered after reports of noise from weapons being fired (the 'Portland 7' and an associate named Khaled Steitiye[44]); and other cases were identified by way of threats to the President made from within prison (Clifton Cousins[45]), armed robbery (Kevin James *et al.*[46]), trying to purchase drugs from an informant (Ronald Grecula[47]), setting off explosives (Joseph Brice[48]), airport security (Raja Lahrasib Khan[49]), a traffic stop (Ahmed Abdellatif Sherif Mohamed[50]), and a parole violation (Michael Finton[51]).

In the UK, all such cases occurred after 9/11. They included two CTIs as a result of immigration offenses (Abbas Boutrab[52] and Pa Madou Jobe[53]), two investigations stemming from border control (Yassin Nassari[54] and Houria Chentouf[55]), the chance discovery of incriminating material during a rape investigation (Abdullah el-Faisal[56]), a drug inquiry (Mohammed Azam[57]), and others identified by way of money laundering (Omar Altimimi[58]), offenses committed in prison (Kevin Gardner[59]), a burglary inquiry (Asim Kauser[60]), a domestic dispute (Mohammed and Shasta Khan[61]), and a traffic stop (Operation Alva[62]).

Although there are no discernible systematic differences between the two countries in terms of the particular types of law enforcement action that lead to CTIs, the variety of cases listed above is striking. Contrary to popular belief, few terrorism cases are uncovered by border control or airport security. In fact, this might be expected, given that most of the individuals included in this research were either American or British citizens, legal residents, or were in possession of at least temporarily valid visas. However, given that terrorists quite often violate the terms of their visas having entered the country, it is surprising that more cases are not uncovered as a result of immigration offenses. The remaining cases are of course testament to the importance of having appropriately trained and alert law enforcement officers who are able to identify possible signs of terrorist activity during the course of their everyday duties. This is reinforced by the fact that the individuals named above were not always responsible for the crimes that were being investigated at the time (e.g. the rape and burglary cases) and were sometimes discovered essentially by chance.

International Law Enforcement

International law enforcement actions have played only a very small role in the identification of American and British jihadists and were responsible for the initiation of just one CTI apiece before 9/11 and none since then. In the US, the case in question was Ali Mohamed who was placed under surveillance by the FBI after he was questioned by Canadian authorities regarding his relationship with one Essam Marzouk, an illegal immigrant later convicted for terrorism offenses in Egypt who was detained at Vancouver airport in June of 1993.[63] The British case was Haroon Rashid Aswat[64] who was actually arrested in 2005 as the result of a US extradition request for his role in the Oregon training camp six years earlier, which was first uncovered by way of the same routine traffic stop that proved to be fateful for Earnest Ujaama.

Both of these cases are rather more complex than the brief descriptions above might suggest. By 1993 Mohamed had been playing a dangerous game as a double agent for some time, although from what is publicly known this was the point when he finally became a terrorism suspect. Nevertheless it was not until after the embassy attacks five years later that he was actually arrested. Similarly, Aswat had surely been known to British authorities for several years as Abu Hamza's right-hand man but it was not until after the London bombings in 2005 that any real effort was made to detain him. In both cases then, the individuals in question were 'persons of interest' already and their brushes with law enforcement in other countries were apparently insignificant at the time but proved to be crucial years later during the aftermath of successful terrorist attacks.

In today's world it seems likely that leads like this would be followed up immediately, but consideration must be given to the often limited resources available to law enforcement agencies amidst competing priorities, and of course being able to gather enough evidence to establish a case in a court of law. For example, in March 2012 a Londoner of Jamaican origin named Clive Everton Dennis was detained at Mogadishu airport on suspicion of planning to join Islamist militants. Despite his claims to simply be looking for 'somewhere sunny' to 'relax' with fellow Muslims and no 'violent stuff' he was found in possession of knives and other suspicious materials and was promptly deported.[65] No legal action has been taken against him in the UK (and he is thus excluded from the count of domestic CTIs initiated abroad). Whilst somewhat unusual, such cases always have the potential to come back and haunt us in the future.

Tip-Offs

Tip-offs from members of the public can provide vital information in the fight against terrorism and are a sign of some degree of cooperation between members of the public and the authorities. In the US, tip-offs led to the initiation of 4 CTIs (12%) before 9/11 and 30 (21%) afterwards. In stark contrast to this, publicly available information suggests that there were no public tip-offs before 9/11 in the UK and only five (3%) since then.

Based on this, it would appear that authorities in the US enjoy a much greater — or at least more *useful* — level of assistance from the American people than their British counterparts do from the UK population. However, the US results are somewhat inflated by the fact that seven cases in the sample were all part of the Operation Rhino investigation into Minnesota Somalis joining al-Shabaab and all therefore originated from the same initial reports, which came from concerned family members.[66]

There are also reasons to believe that cooperation from the British public is likely to be better than the figures here suggest: first, there has been at least one other case in the sample where a tip-off contributed to a CTI even if it did not initiate it;[67] second, more recent reports indicate that tip-offs from parents and others are helping to identify suspects who have gone to Syria and Iraq;[68] third, there is generally quite a strong emphasis on community policing in Britain whereby a great deal of effort is invested in building good community relations and encouraging people to come forward with information; and fourth, the more guarded approach to publishing details of CTIs in the UK suggests that tip-offs — as with everything else — are simply less likely to become public knowledge. In connection with this, the observed difference here may also be related to the different legal tools available in each country. In the US, a number of tip-offs came from people who were either already acting as a paid informant or else became one and in that capacity played a central role in the case. Whilst it would be naïve to think that British authorities do not also rely on informants (or 'covert human intelligence sources' (CHISs)), they are kept very much in the shadows. Finally, just because the British public are not seemingly identifying terrorism suspects to begin with does not mean that they do not cooperate once an investigation has begun.

In spite of all this, there is a degree of speculation involved here and the relatively small contribution from public tip-offs in Britain that we know about is still cause for concern. In fact it should be noted that one of the tips received by UK authorities actually came from the US after an American website moderator alerted them to threatening remarks made online by Ishaq Kanmi from Lancashire, who was later imprisoned for disseminating terrorist propaganda.[69] The *known* degree of assistance provided by the British public in identifying terrorism cases is therefore even less than the above figures suggest and is at least worthy of a more in-depth review.

Looking at the particular sources of tip-offs, the only real noticeable difference between the two countries relates to the aforementioned role of informants in identifying terrorism suspects in the US, which has not been seen in the UK. Aside from this, there has been considerable variation. Information has been supplied by members of the Muslim community, businesses and online contacts in both countries. In one case in the UK, the former work colleagues of an offender called the police after he showed up claiming to be in possession of landmines,[70] while in the US friends or associates have come forward in a number of cases, as have family members, anonymous tipsters, room/cell-mates, Internet 'vigilantes',[71] and once, in 1996, a member of al-Qaeda handed himself in at an American embassy in Africa.[72] Together, this variety is encouraging and indicates a growing awareness of terrorism in society.

Other Sources of Investigations

Other sources which have given rise to domestic CTIs after 9/11 have included open source intelligence (OSINT) and overseas counterinsurgency operations (COIN).[73] OSINT led to the initiation of four CTIs (3%) in the US and one in the UK. In all instances, investigations were seemingly initiated in response either to jihadi propaganda and/or media coverage of individual activities. The US cases include Adam Gadahn, Omar Hammami, Samir Khan, and Eric Harroun, while the UK case involved Hassan Butt, a self-confessed Taliban recruiter.[74] More recently, social media has risen to new heights of popularity among jihadis in Syria and Iraq and we should therefore expect OSINT to become increasingly important both for identifying suspects and as a form of evidence at trial. Indeed, social media records played a key role in securing the conviction of Mashudur Choudhury in the UK in May 2014, making him the first British national to be prosecuted for terrorism offenses in relation to Syria.[75]

As for COIN, this of course took place exclusively in conflict zones and for the most part the individuals involved were dealt with primarily by the relevant overseas military forces (including numerous British nationals detained at Guantanamo). As a result, most of these cases[76] are therefore excluded from the count of domestic CTIs, despite efforts made to confirm individual identities and piece together background information after the fact. The one exception to this, where an individual was captured abroad and then prosecuted at home was John Walker Lindh, the so-called 'American Taliban'. The popularity of fighting abroad of course means that many more American and British jihadis will likely be captured or killed by foreign militaries in years to come, and although the culprits at that point — if still alive — might not be prosecuted at home, it seems likely that we will see more concerted efforts by domestic authorities to track down and dismantle recruitment and facilitation networks in connection with these cases.

Length of Investigations

The length of counterterrorism investigations is very difficult to determine, not just due to a lack of information but also because investigations are not necessarily always continuous. CTIs sometimes appear to begin, only to discontinue or to be kept going with relatively few resources until such time as something significant occurs and the case reaches a turning point which leads to an increase in activity. Length of investigation here was judged according to the first known investigative action up until the point of arrest and includes domestic CTIs only. In the US, before 9/11 the average length of CTIs was calculated to be 40.7 months (close to three-and-a-half years), with a range of 0 to 144 months.[77] After 9/11, the average CTI length decreased to 16.2 months, with a range of 0 to 64.[78] Results for the UK show a similar pattern but with quite different values. Before 9/11, the average CTI length was 27.5 months (just over two years) with a range of 3 to 62 months,[79] while after 9/11 the average time decreased to 5.5 months with a range of 0 to 23.[80]

In both cases there appears to have been a rather substantial decrease in the average length of CTIs, which is consistent with the observed decrease in average jihadi careers (see Chapter 6) and with previous research.[81] The lengthier investigation times in the US are explained by several factors. Before 9/11, there were of course some very significant CTIs in relation to planned or actual attacks on the homeland. In addition, a number of investigations into fundraisers and facilitators were initiated in the early 1990s but it was not until after the embassy attacks and then 9/11 that these cases were finally wrapped up. Regarding investigations beginning after 9/11, the different time-frames involved in each country are explained at least in part by different legislation. In the US, the preference is to prosecute individuals for a specific plot or conspiracy (usually under charges of conspiring/attempting/providing material support to terrorists[82]), which of course often takes time to unfold. By contrast, legislation in the UK also allows for the prosecution of offenses which are comparatively easy to prove and enable swifter intervention in many cases (in particular the possession of terrorist-related materials and engaging in conduct in preparation for acts of terrorism[83]).

Notably, the British recourse to prosecution of more straightforward and sometimes minor offenses appears to have been driven to some extent by the failure to secure high-end convictions in major terrorism trials that took place between 2004 and 2010.[84] Indeed, 'preparing for acts of terrorism' (which has since taken over from possession offenses as the most popular terrorism charge in the UK[85]) was introduced in 2006 and carries a lower burden of proof than needed to convict for conspiracy.[86] American investigators meanwhile have suffered their own setbacks and criticisms but on the whole appear to take confidence in having found a reliable and effective — albeit comparatively lengthy — investigative formula which relies on offenses first laid out in 1994.

Informants and Undercover Operatives

It is no secret that informants (CHISs[87]) and undercover operatives (UCs), usually deployed in the context of sting operations, are central to the American approach to counterterrorism within the US. Moreover, these tactics have become increasingly prevalent over time. CHISs and/or UCs were involved in 9 CTIs (24%) before 9/11, compared to 61 (44%) afterwards. By contrast, no British CTIs that were known to have involved CHISs or UCs before 9/11 and only four (3%)[88] have made use of them since then.

The reason for this disparity again largely comes down to differences in legislation.[89] The sanctity of 'freedom of speech' enshrined in the American constitution makes it difficult — though not impossible[90] — to prosecute people for offenses such as incitement of violence. Similarly, it would be much more difficult to prosecute someone for possession of 'terrorist' materials such as *Inspire* magazine (a popular approach in the UK), even though it is produced by a proscribed organization and contains bomb-making instructions and clear incitement to hatred and violence. Such restrictions leave few alternatives but to seek prosecution for conspiracy offenses and/or overt acts in support of proscribed terrorist organizations. Furthermore, the American legal system allows for more aggressive use of CHISs and UCs to include sting operations, which enable law enforcement to control the progress of the investigation and thereby minimize the risk to public safety whilst still being assured of a successful conviction.

By way of illustration, a 'typical'[91] sting unfolds in the following manner: (1) a suspect is identified, for example by expressing a desire to commit a jihadist-inspired terrorist attack, at which point a CHIS makes contact and befriends him; (2) the suspect and the CHIS conspire together to conduct a domestic attack; (3) the CHIS will then introduce the suspect to a UC who is posing as an al-Qaeda facilitator; (4) the UC will repeatedly test the suspect's commitment, including offers to opt out, and the suspect will pledge a 'formal' oath of allegiance; (5) the suspect will conduct surveillance of targets, sometimes accompanied by the CHIS, and will record a video explaining his rationale; (6) the UC will supply (inert) explosives and/or other weaponry; (7) the suspect will either be arrested at the point of accepting weapons or immediately after attempting to execute the planned attack, e.g. by trying to detonate the explosives. Throughout the investigation, conversations involving the suspect will be recorded, thus clearly establishing motivation and intent, which are then actively demonstrated when they 'push the button'.

In addition to ensuring public safety, this approach has a number of advantages, the most important being that there is rarely any doubt that the individual(s) involved actually intended to commit a terrorist attack. By contrast, in cases involving domestic attack plots in the UK, the authorities must play a delicate balancing act between collection of evidence and public safety. Moreover, intervention by necessity takes place before the attack is attempted, meaning that the legal case is dependent on sufficient evidence of intent. Suspects of course deny that they were actually going to harm anyone, which in the past has resulted in a number of lengthy and costly trials. As noted above, this helps to explain the British proclivity for earlier intervention based on lesser offenses (although 'preparation for acts of terrorism' still carries a maximum sentence of up to 30 years[92]).

Nevertheless, there are also significant downsides to the use of sting operations and they have become a matter of controversy in the US. Critics often object to the fact that the informants (who are paid for their services) are themselves often quite serious criminal offenders with dubious motives and significant incentive to *try* to lure suspects into a plot. The broader allegation — which is aimed primarily at the FBI and their partners — is that suspects are effectively manipulated into incriminating themselves and without assistance from the authorities (e.g. in supplying weapons or money) the individuals involved would never commit such offenses. This of course is the entrapment defense, which is invariably mounted at trial but has so far been struck down every time. Indeed, partly as a response to this criticism, the practice of sting operations has become more refined over time. For instance, the fact that suspects are now given multiple chances to back out of the plot appears to have been designed specifically to counter any claims that suspects were coerced, and although there are still potential problems with this from a psychological perspective,[93] it has proven to be effective from a legal standpoint.[94]

Meanwhile in the UK, stricter regulations governing the use of CHISs and UCs mean that the US approach would almost certainly fail to stand up in a British court of law which, combined with the ability to press charges for lesser offenses, explains their far more limited application. Furthermore, while the majority of US investigations involving CHISs and UCs are sting operations, only one of four such cases in the UK could be described in those terms and none of them have involved paid informants. In November 2005, Kazi Nurur Rahman — who had trained in Pakistan with Mohammed Siddique Khan and Omar Khyam, among others — was arrested after he tried to buy firearms and grenades from undercover officers posing as arms dealers.[95] The other relevant cases have involved two instances of infiltration of terrorist groups by undercover police officers,[96] and one case where a female officer posed as the receptionist at a storage facility where fertilizer was being kept.[97] Interestingly, one of the infiltration cases — the investigation of Munir Farooqi and two others who were attempting to recruit people in Manchester for violent jihad abroad — was given the 'Detective Investigation of the Year' award in 2012.[98] Nevertheless, such tactics are still used sparingly in the UK.

Primary Sources of Evidence

Turning the attention to domestic legal cases which *concluded*[99] before and after 9/11, it is instructive to examine the primary sources of evidence relied upon by authorities to press charges, secure convictions, or otherwise justify punitive action.[100] Too few legal cases concluded before 9/11 to be able to make meaningful comparisons, therefore the discussion will focus on developments since 2001. That said, it is worth noting that both before and after 9/11 the largest proportion of cases in the US (67% and 34% respectively) were classified as 'combined', meaning that no single type of evidence stood out as being key to the case.

For example, the prosecution in the World Trade Center bombing drew upon a variety of physical and forensic evidence as well as financial records and eyewitnesses.[101] In the investigation of David Headley and Tahawwur Rana, it was a combination of Headley's confession, signals intelligence (SIGINT, including wiretaps, listening devices, and electronic surveillance), plus financial records.[102] In another case, Betim Kaziu — who was arrested in August 2009 after making multiple attempts to join Islamist terrorist organizations overseas — the evidence against him included human intelligence (HUMINT, in the form of confederate testimony) plus travel records and a martyrdom video that he had recorded while in Kosovo.[103] In the Boston bombings investigation, the evidence includes CCTV footage, items found in the alleged offenders' possession and places of residence, and incriminating remarks made by Dzhokhar Tsarnaev shortly after he was apprehended.[104]

Of cases investigated in the UK, 17% were classified the same way, utilizing varying combinations of different types of evidence. For instance, Sohail Qureshi — arrested in 2006 en route to Pakistan — was convicted on the strength of online SIGINT, surveillance, financial records, and items in his possession (including night vision goggles and £9,000 in cash), all of which made it abundantly clear that he was preparing to join a terrorist organization.[105] Although the precise mixture of evidence varies from case to case, in the UK it has often included electronic evidence in the form of computer files and downloads as well as physical possessions. Khalid Baqa, for example, was prosecuted in April 2013 for disseminating terrorist publications after he was found in possession of more than 300 CD-ROMs featuring extremist material downloaded from the Internet.[106]

In other cases, however, prosecutions seemed to rest upon particular sources/types of evidence more than others. In the US, 32% of cases have been based primarily on evidence gathered by CHISs and UCs in sting operations, thus confirming how crucial they have become to the American approach to counterterrorism.[107] By comparison, undercover operatives were the primary source of evidence on just two occasions in the UK, where more than a third of cases were based on information that remains secret. This is explained by the use of 'special' administrative sanctions in Britain, including control orders, terrorism prevention and investigation measures (TPIMs), deportations, exclusions and revocation of citizenship in cases handled by the Special Immigration and Appeals Commission (SIAC), and freezing of financial assets by HM Treasury.[108]

Control orders in particular were designed to enable restrictive capabilities in cases where there is either insufficient evidence to prosecute and/or it would be detrimental to national security to disclose the sources of intelligence/'evidence'. As a result, although the level of detail in the allegations that are made public in such cases varies immensely, the sources of information are always kept secret, even from the accused.[109] Even so, a careful reading of publicly available documents in these cases suggests that a variety of sources come into play including surveillance, travel records, SIGINT, and — perhaps most important of all — HUMINT, which in all likelihood comes from informants and undercover operatives.

For instance, the government's case against 'CC' and 'CF' — who stand accused of being key figures in a UK-based network tied to al-Shabaab, taking part in terrorist training, and planning attacks on Western targets in Somalia — provides a fairly specific timeline of events including details of travel plus names of associates both at home and abroad, and even refers to differing levels of participation and motivation.[110] This would not be possible without a range of fairly intrusive investigative measures being in place in addition to significant international cooperation. In light of the recent surge of 'foreign fighters' going to Syria and Iraq, and the associated difficulties of managing and prosecuting these individuals, it is quite possible that special sanctions will play an even greater role in the UK over the next few years, meaning that evidentiary sources will be kept secret more often. Indeed, in August 2014 the national terrorism threat level was elevated to 'severe' and plans were put in place to expand disruptive counterterrorism powers, including strengthening of TPIMs.

In cases where the source of evidence *could* be determined, two particular types stand out as having been significant in the UK, but apparently less so in the US. Physical/forensic evidence was the primary source in 16% of UK cases compared to 1% in the US, and electronic evidence was central in another 10% of cases in the UK but only 3% in the US. Examples of physical evidence include offender-made records such as written attack plans, martyrdom videos, and notes on bomb-making, as well as weapons, precursor explosive materials, and books. These kinds of incriminating materials have proven to be crucial in a variety of prosecutions ranging from relatively low-level to extremely serious offenses. In October 2007, for example, a minor named Abdul Muneem Patel was sentenced to six months in juvenile detention after being found in possession of a US explosives manual.[111] At the other end of the spectrum, physical evidence consisting of firearms, knives, an improvised explosive device (IED), and leaflets addressed to 'the enemies of Islam' constituted the crux of the prosecution's case against the six individuals who were convicted for planning what would have been a deadly assault on members of the English Defence League in July 2012.[112]

Physical evidence is thus particularly important in the UK for two key reasons — the fact that the legislation allows for prosecution of possession of materials likely to be of use for terrorism, and because it is often crucial for establishing malicious intent in cases involving preparation for terrorist attacks. In the US, nascent plots to conduct attacks are typically turned into sting operations, while terrorism 'possession offenses' do not exist in law. As a result, physical evidence was central on just one occasion — the prosecution of Paul Rockwood, who had drawn up a 'hit-list' of people he believed should be executed for insulting Islam.[113] However, although he was given eight years in prison he was actually convicted of nothing more than making false statements in a terrorism investigation.[114]

As for electronic evidence, this refers to illegal materials such as bomb-making instructions and incitements to terrorism which were either downloaded and stored on computers or other devices, and/or were uploaded and disseminated online. For example, in June 2013 an aeronautical engineering graduate named Norman Faridi was convicted in the UK for possessing information likely to be of use for terrorism after a downloaded copy of '39 Ways to Serve and Proceed in Jihad' was found stored in his home.[115] In May 2013 Ibrahim Abdullah Hassan and Shah Jalal Hussain (both repeat offenders and affiliates of AM) were arrested for uploading a series of audio files entitled 'In Pursuit of Allah's Governance on Earth', resulting in convictions for encouraging acts of terrorism.[116]

Electronic evidence was also central in five cases in the US (compared to 15 in the UK) and sometimes for very similar offenses. Notably, Emerson Begolly was convicted for soliciting acts of terrorism within the US,[117] while Zachary Chesser was convicted for communicating threats and soliciting others to engage in violent or threatening felony conduct.[118] In other cases, however, the result has been quite different. Mohammad Radwan Obeid, who was evidently trying to recruit people for terrorism online, was convicted for immigration offenses and lying to the FBI;[119] Jubair Ahmed received a 12-year prison sentence for providing material support to a Foreign Terrorist Organization after supplying Lashkar e-Taiba (LeT) with a propaganda video which he uploaded to YouTube;[120] and Samir Khan — one of the original creators of *Inspire* magazine — was killed in the same drone strike that targeted Anwar al-Awlaki in September 2011.[121]

The reasons for the apparent difference in the significance of electronic evidence in the US and UK are similar to those for physical evidence. In particular, the ability to prosecute for possession offenses in the UK, as well as disseminating terrorist publications and/or encouraging terrorism mean that materials which are either downloaded or shared online become the *primary* evidence in building a prosecution. Although the cases of Begolly, Chesser, and his accomplice Jesse Morton demonstrate that there is a line that can be crossed in the US which enables prosecution for things that are said or posted online, convictions for such offenses are rare and are not necessarily dealt with under CT legislation. Moreover, it would appear to be extremely difficult — if not impossible — to prosecute someone for merely possessing much of the material which leads to convictions in the UK. However, this is not to suggest that electronic evidence is not important in the US. Far from it, in fact. Electronic communications using email or other platforms — which were recorded under the heading of SIGINT for this research — were central in another three cases in the US (and two in the UK). More importantly, electronic evidence — especially material disseminated via social media — is still used to identify persons of interest who may then be targeted for further investigation, and may still be used in combination with other forms of evidence (as was the case, for example, with Joseph Brice[122]). The key difference is that it is more likely to be the *primary* form of evidence in cases in the UK.

Aside from the differences already described, there is little else of note. Offender confessions have been a primary source of evidence more often in the US (ten cases or 7% versus two cases or 1% in the UK), although it is not a vast disparity and there is no single reason that explains it. Other forms of evidence have included HUMINT, SIGINT, OSINT, offender apprehension at the time an offense was committed, surveillance, eyewitnesses, and personal/public records; however, none of these have featured prominently as primary sources of evidence in either country. They are either relatively rare (as with apprehension and eyewitnesses) or else appear more likely to be combined with other forms of evidence rather than standing out as central to a case.

Legal Processing Times

In cases where suspects are charged with a criminal offense, the time (not to mention cost) that it takes to convict and then sentence them generally exceeds the preceding investigation. In the US, before 9/11 the average time from arrest to conviction was 22.7 months and the average time from conviction to sentencing was 17.4, giving a combined total of 37.1 months of post-charge legal processing time (excluding appeals). After 9/11, the respective figures were 17.5 months and 9.4, giving a total of 26.9. In the UK, the average time from arrest to conviction before 9/11 was 17.5 months, with an additional 3 months for sentencing, giving a total of 20.5. After 9/11, the respective averages were 17.7 and 1.8, adding up to 19.5.

In the US there has been a rather substantial decrease in legal processing times, mostly in relation to the time it takes from conviction to sentencing. There has been a slight reduction in the same area in the UK although the difference is marginal. Of greater interest is the fact that legal processing times have been considerably longer in the US compared to the UK, both before and after 9/11. While this suggests a more efficient legal process in Britain, it is also likely related to the more frequent prosecution of relatively minor and therefore more straightforward crimes such as terrorist possession offenses. The larger reduction over time in the US has brought the two countries considerably closer in this area, with a difference of just 7.4 months in total legal processing times after 9/11. Nevertheless, with averages of more than two years in the US and more than a year-and-a-half in the UK to arrive at a sentencing date from the time of arrest, the post-charge phase of CTIs remains lengthy and no doubt expensive.[123]

Legal Outcomes

Part of the reason for the observed decrease in legal processing times in the US may be the fact that terrorist offenders are more likely to plead guilty than in the past. Of the 35 individuals who were prosecuted in the US before 9/11, 70% were convicted; yet after

9/11 the balance was reversed, with 62% of 207 individuals pleading guilty. Only three individuals were prosecuted in the UK before 9/11, although all were convicted, and of 190 individuals prosecuted after 9/11, 51% pleaded guilty.[124] Given that there are so few acquittals on charges of terrorism, the shift over time towards pleading guilty might be expected as offenders now realize that the odds are stacked against them and that they will receive a lengthier sentence if convicted.[125] Nevertheless, a sizeable minority of jihadi offenders in the US and half of those in the UK are still willing to take their chances at trial.

In both countries there has been a reduction in the average prison sentence since 9/11: in the US, from 42 years to 15.2, and in the UK from 10.3 to 7.2. The much shorter average sentences in the UK are yet another reflection of the outlawing and prosecution of lesser offenses, in particular possession and dissemination of terrorist materials. Meanwhile reduced penalties over time can be explained by a combination of factors: the small number of convictions, yet including some very lengthy sentences prior to 9/11;[126] a general shift toward pre-emptive prosecution before acts of violence can take place; a flexible approach to sentencing whereby the same offenses are met with varied punishments depending on the circumstances; and the prosecution of a wider range of offenses, sometimes using 'ordinary' legislation for relatively trivial crimes. Indeed, regarding the latter, a handful of 'alternate', often non-custodial sentences were also handed out in both countries, including probation, deportation, and time served on three occasions in the US, and a formal caution, community work order, rehabilitation, and one suspended sentence in the UK.

At the more serious end of the spectrum, life sentences were handed out to 14% of individuals in the US before 9/11 and 9% afterwards, compared to zero of just three prosecutions and then 15% in the UK, plus an additional three indeterminate sentences, including one in hospital. Although the slightly higher percentage of life sentences in the UK is worth noting, there is a significant difference in practice. In the US, life means life, but offenders in the UK are still eligible for parole after serving a minimum term.[127] In the sample this ranged from just 7.5 to 40 years with an average of 23.2.

Ultimately then, the results consistently show that the penalties for terrorism are much harsher in the US.

Postscript: Repeat Offenders and Forensic Awareness

Having examined the way that terrorist offenders are dealt with in each country, it is important to consider some of the ways in which this impacts upon their behavior. As we have seen, legislation shapes terrorism insofar as it dictates what is proscribed and how the authorities can intervene. In the US, the large number of domestic attack plots is at least partly a product of the use of sting operations, while the greater number of low-level offenders in the UK is a reflection of a broader range of prohibited activities. Arguably then, the legislation in the US makes the threat appear more severe than it might be, while legislation in the UK makes it appear larger, at least in comparison to American definitions of terrorist activity.[128] In either case, there is no way of telling if the individuals in question would progress to violent behavior in the absence of intervention.

Putting aside these more philosophical questions, one area where we are beginning to see a difference is in recidivism. The longer sentences in the US mean that terrorist offenders there generally have fewer opportunities to re-offend compared to the UK where 'terrorists' may be back out on the streets within a matter of months. As a result, there are just two repeat offenders within the US sample — Daniel Boyd and Hysen Sherifi. Both were prosecuted along with several others in 2011 in relation to a plot to attack US military bases in Virginia. Boyd had also been briefly imprisoned in Pakistan back in 1991 when he and his brother — who had been training together with *mujahideen* for several months — were accused of robbing a bank.[129] Sherifi meanwhile hatched a plot *after* his conviction in October 2011 to kidnap and behead three witnesses who had testified against him.[130] In Boyd's case, there was a long period of inactivity following a brush with the law in a foreign country where the primary concern was criminal activity as opposed to militancy, while Sherifi's second offense was closely tied to the first and was prosecuted under 'ordinary' legislation.[131]

By comparison, the UK sample includes seven repeat offenders, many of whom also offended together.[132] These were Abdul Muhid and Abdul Rehman Saleem,[133] who were convicted for inciting terrorism overseas during an AM event in 2004,[134] and for stirring up racial hatred at another AM event in 2006;[135] Ibrahim Abdullah Hassan and Shah Jalal Hussain, who were convicted for their role in the 2004 event and then again for encouraging terrorism online in 2013;[136] Umran Javed, who had been convicted for his part in the 2006 protest and was prosecuted again in 2012 for possession of documents likely to be of use for terrorism;[137] Nicholas Roddis, who was imprisoned in 2008 for perpetrating a bizarre hoax and then charged again in 2012 having been released and apparently caught in possession of bomb-making manuals and a variety of related components;[138] and finally, Zohaib Kamran Ahmed, who was charged with possession of *Inspire* magazine in July 2011 and was re-arrested a year later in relation to the plot to attack the EDL, eventually receiving a sentence of 19.5 years.[139] Several others are known to have engaged in multiple offenses but where no legal intervention took place at the time,[140] another eight individuals included in the sample absconded from control orders,[141] and another three repeat offenders have so far been recorded since the end of the sampling period.

Although there are some caveats here it is nevertheless quite clear that the shorter prison sentences in the UK provide opportunities to re-offend and that an unknown percentage of terrorist convicts remain motivated to take advantage of such opportunities.[142] The very tentative good news is that most repeat offenders have so far only committed low-level offenses rather than escalating towards violence. That said, Zohaib Ahmed was clearly not deterred by his first arrest, instead proceeding with several others to plan a domestic terrorist attack and most of those who fled their control orders are believed to have joined terrorist organizations overseas. Moreover, there are others still who have stopped short of breaking the law since completing prison sentences but are still active in spreading extremist ideas which perpetuate and expand jihadi subcultures. For instance, in September 2014 it was reported that at least three former terrorism convicts in the UK — Abdullah el-Faisal, Atilla Ahmet, and Mizanur Rahman — had organized an online conference where they voiced their support for the 'Islamic State' (IS) in Iraq and Syria.[143] Continued activism and recidivism therefore present potentially serious problems that are particularly relevant in the UK.

A second issue of some concern relates to the build-up of knowledge about counterterrorism tools and techniques — referred to as 'forensic awareness' or 'security consciousness'. Jihadi terrorists of course know that they are breaking the law and take various steps to try and avoid detection, such as communicating in code, exchanging messages using email 'drop-boxes', mislabeling, hiding and encrypting computer files, changing their physical appearance or sometimes wearing disguises, and employing counter-surveillance measures. Skill-levels vary considerably but overall tradecraft is rarely sophisticated. Code systems, for example, usually do little more than substitute certain words — typically names of locations or sometimes weapons or explosives — and make references instead to things such as girls, weddings, food, sports, business transactions, or the weather. Although the exact meaning may be difficult to decipher, unnatural delivery or nonsensical phrases can raise suspicion. Once it is established that some form of code is indeed being used, it provides evidence of deliberate deception and is thus self-incriminating.[144]

Nevertheless, there have been a number of cases where terrorist offenders demonstrated considerable resourcefulness, dedication, and skill in their efforts to avoid detection. For instance, in 2004 Junade Feroz and Abdul Aziz Jalil (who were part of Dhiren Barot's plan to attack the UK) drove several hundred miles just to use an Internet café.[145] In another case, a pair of al-Qaeda operatives from Manchester named Rangzieb and Habib Ahmed were found in possession of an address book containing a multitude of terrorists' contact details written in invisible ink.[146] Two particularly skilled individuals were David Headley and Tahawwur Rana. Thanks to their connections with a Pakistani intelligence officer, they used a relatively complex code system and were able to create an elaborate cover to mask the nefarious nature of Headley's international travel.[147]

Others have been lacking in skill but have nevertheless been well aware of the likelihood of coming under surveillance and have taken sometimes quite innovative steps to try and outfox security services. For instance, a British group arrested in July 2012 had taken to typing their conversations on a laptop which they passed around between them before deleting the text when they were finished — mistakenly believing that incriminating details would be impossible to recover.[148] In another case involving a plot to bomb the London Stock Exchange, conspirators met in public spaces and were so careful about speaking openly that they sometimes struggled to understand what each other was trying to say.[149]

Perhaps of greater concern are advances in encryption technology, allowing individuals to communicate, store, and delete information securely. Rajib Karim, a former British Airways employee arrested in February 2010, used a particularly sophisticated encryption system and although police were able to decipher enough to secure a conviction, the chief forensic investigator admitted that it was 'so complex and layered' that at the time of the trial most of the messages contained on Karim's hard-drive were still unreadable.[150] Although Karim apparently made use of commercially available software, jihadi terrorist organizations are also producing their own encryption and mobile communications applications such as 'Asrar al-Mujahideen', 'Asrar al-Dardashah', and 'Tashfeer al-Jawwal', which they make available to download in multiple languages including user-friendly tutorials.[151] There has yet to be a reported case of American or British jihadis using such software, but there can be little doubt that promotion of these programs in *Inspire* magazine and other platforms aimed at Western recruits is steadily raising forensic awareness. Moreover, mobile phones are using increasingly secure encryption, as are readily available applications such as Kik and Surespot, which jihadists are known to use.

Another area where forensic awareness is increasing relates to the continued use of sting operations in the US. This was something that al-Qaeda drew attention to in the second edition of *Inspire*, which was published online back in 2010. In an article entitled

'Tips for our Brothers in the United Snakes of America', the author advised to:

> Beware of informants: If the Feds suspect you are up to something, they may try to set you up through an informant. There were quite a few brothers who were arrested using this method...Learn your lesson: beware of individuals who are unknown to you and do not put your trust in those who pose as mujahidin.[152]

Paying even scant attention to mainstream media coverage of terrorism cases in the US would lead to the same conclusion. Indeed, the arrest of Mohamed Osman Mohamud in Oregon in November 2010 nearly derailed the investigation of Antonio Martinez, who was caught in a separate sting operation on the other side of the country less than two weeks later. Having seen Mohamud's arrest on the news, Martinez — who was planning to attack an armed forces recruitment center in Maryland — became worried that he was being set up and had to be reassured that his contacts were genuine before pressing ahead.[153] The general awareness of sting operations in the US may also go some way to explaining why they often seem to ensnare less capable individuals, since more savvy operators are less likely to fall for such tactics.

A final phenomenon worth mentioning involves the deliberate promotion of activities aimed at disrupting counterterrorism, along with sharing of advice and information in order to raise others' forensic awareness and operational security. Zachary Chesser, a convert from Virginia who was imprisoned in 2010 was particularly vocal on the subject. In April 2010 he penned a series of short online articles (more than 30 pages in total, posted on the 'Revolution Muslim' website) entitled 'Counter Counter-Terrorism', in which he gave quite detailed — albeit amateur — advice on operational security in communications, meetings, and use of transport, among other issues.[154] Shortly before his arrest in July, he also posted a message on the Al Fallujah Islamic Forums website entitled 'Desensitizing Federal Agents', where he called on jihadis to leave inert suspicious packages in public places in order to desensitize and overwhelm law enforcement and thereby increase the chances that a real explosive device would go undetected in the future.[155]

Also of note is Bilal Zaheer Ahmad, who was arrested in the UK just a few months later than Chesser for attempting to instigate terrorism online. In October 2011, from inside prison, he wrote six pages of 'Advice on Security', in which he highlighted CT methods and capabilities and suggested various steps to protect oneself against the law.[156] This was apparently sent to a group of German jihadists and subsequently posted on the Internet so that others could also learn from his experience.[157]

Neither Chesser's, nor Ahmad's publications are likely to keep security services awake at night and there is no evidence that they have been influential among their peers. Their writings confirm that Western jihadis are concerned about their own security — as well they should be — and that they are attempting to learn from each other's experience. Nevertheless, translating this into effective practice is a challenge that very few have been able to overcome. More recently, a great many jihadis fighting in Syria and Iraq — including British nationals in particular — have shown that they are willing to sacrifice operational security in favor of their own personal 'fame' and the opportunity to promote the cause.

Concluding Remarks

Certain developments have been common to both the US and UK — in particular an increase in the sheer number of CTIs, the fact that they are more likely to begin at home than abroad, 'snowballing' of investigations (especially in response to successful attacks when they have occurred), a decrease in investigation and legal processing times, an increase in guilty pleas, and a reduction in average sentences. There also appears to have been a general increase in forensic awareness, leading to some innovation but ultimately so far having a negligible impact on terrorists' operational security overall.

Observed differences between the two countries are a result of different legislation, established law enforcement practices and differing manifestations of the threat. Specifically, monitoring of the Internet seems to be more important for identifying terrorism suspects in the US, where offenders are far more geographically dispersed and less likely to be part of a physical extremist 'community'. CHISs and UCs clearly play a much greater role in the US both in terms of initiating investigations and in providing evidence used at trial. The American preference, or 'need' to identify specific conspiracies also appears to relate to the need for multiple, combined sources of evidence, longer legal processing times, and to longer sentences compared to the UK.

Meanwhile, CTIs in the UK seem more likely to begin as a result of continuous monitoring of known extremists and their associations and — based on the available information — are less likely to arise from public tip-offs. Sources of evidence are more likely to be kept secret in the UK thanks to the implementation of special sanctions including control orders and TPIMs. On the other hand, the existence of lesser terrorism offenses in UK law also means that physical/forensic and electronic evidence are more likely to feature as the *primary* basis of successful prosecutions. The prosecution of such offenses also no doubt relates to shorter investigation and legal processing times and shorter sentences, but also to more repeat offenders and continued extremist activism. The implications of these findings, along with those from previous chapters, are discussed in Chapter 8.

Notes

---

[1]A particularly notable contribution in this area is Frank Foley's comparison of the evolution of counterterrorism in the UK and France (Frank Foley, *Countering Terrorism in Britain and France: Institutions, Norms and the Shadow of the Past* (Cambridge: Cambridge University Press, 2013) Kindle Edition).

[2]Note that it is not presumed that the numbers of CT investigations identified for this study are exhaustive. In reality, they no doubt represent just a fraction of investigations conducted.

[3]An additional six cases were dealt with almost entirely overseas with little apparent American involvement other than the suspects. Such cases (which were generally in response to offenses committed abroad, or were conducted in the context of counterinsurgency (COIN) operations) were excluded from the analysis of US/UK CTIs since they were handled primarily by the 'host' countries and do not tell us anything about American or British counterterrorism processes.

[4]Before 9/11 another 23 cases involving British suspects were handled almost entirely by foreign authorities.

[5]After 9/11 an additional 21 CTIs focused on US suspects took place almost entirely overseas.

[6]An additional 61 CTIs focused on British suspects took place overseas.

[7]Steve McGonigle and Gayle Reaves, 'Ties to Terror: Texas Linked Network of Suspects in World Trade Center Bombing', *The Dallas Morning News*, June 8, 1997. Accessed November 23, 2011 via http://www.dallasnews.com/archive/.

[8]'Former Agent Kelvin Smith Pleads Guilty' (1998), *The Federal Wildlife Officer*, 11(3), 1–2, available at: http://web.archive.org/web/19990528131525/http://www.fwoa.org/news/fwoanws15a.html, accessed November 16, 2011.

[9]These were Enaam Arnout; Nabil al-Marabh, and Ali Saleh Kalah al-Marri, all of whom were separately arrested within months of the attacks taking place. Many more people were certainly investigated as a direct result of the 9/11 attacks, however these are the only three cases within the sample where this was judged to be the case.

[10]These were Khalid Khaliq, an associate who was prosecuted for possession of the al-Qaeda manual; and Mohammed Shakil, Waheed Ali, and Sadeer Saleem, three associates who had all previously trained in Pakistan and were accused — but acquitted — of providing assistance to the London bombers (although Shakil and Ali were convicted of conspiring to attend another overseas training camp at the time of their arrest). Note that the latter three individuals were counted as separate cases in the sample since they led quite distinct jihadi careers but were classed as a single CTI since they were investigated together.

[11]Note that although seven attacks took place during this period, one was the murder of a police officer by Kamel Bourgass in 2003. This is not classed as having initiated a CTI since Bourgass was already a wanted man based on intelligence received from Algeria.

[12]Note that not all international incidents necessarily prompt a domestic investigation, other than to perhaps identify a body and piece together information about the individual(s) in question. For the purposes of this analysis, cases such as this which were — as far as is known — primarily dealt with overseas were not included in the present calculations so as to avoid 'contaminating' the findings (see notes 2–5).

[13]Excluded from this list is Ali Mohamed who played a key role in orchestrating these attacks and was arrested in the US in September 1998 after being subpoenaed to testify before a grand jury. However, Mohamed had apparently been under fairly consistent FBI surveillance (including monitoring of his phone calls) since approximately June of 1993 after he was arrested in Canada with an associate of bin Laden's named Essam Marzouk. The embassy bombings were thus the 'final straw' in Mohamed's case as opposed to being the initial reason for investigation (see Benjamin Weiser and James Risen, 'The Masking of a Militant: A Special Report.; A Soldier's Shadowy Trail In U.S. and in the Mideast', *The New York Times*, December 1, 1998, available at: http://www.nytimes.com/1998/12/01/world/masking-militant-special-report-soldier-s-shadowy-trail-us-mideast.html, accessed August 13, 2011).

[14]Eidarous died from leukaemia in mid-2008 while al-Fawwaz and Bari were finally extradited to stand trial in the US in October 2012.

[15]'Bin Laden Connected to London Dissident', *BBC News*, March 10, 2002, available at: http://news.bbc.co.uk/2/hi/uk_news/1862579.stm, accessed May 11, 2010; 'UK Freezes Saudi Group's Assets', *BBC News*, December 24, 2004, available at: http://news.bbc.co.uk/2/hi/uk_news/4123807.stm, accessed May 11, 2010.

[16]Note that as far as is known, when Mohamud blew himself up in Somalia it was the first time that authorities became aware of him. This distinguishes him from the numerous Somali–Americans from Minnesota who also joined al-Shabaab, since law enforcement agencies knew of their whereabouts already since they had received information from the families.

[17]Note that other, similar cases were not included in this category. For example, Umar Abdulmutallab was classed as having been investigated overseas rather than in the UK since he was dealt with primarily in the US. This is not to say that there was no British investigation whatsoever, but that it would have been very much secondary to that of the lead country.

[18]For instance, in November 2014 it was revealed that 40 terrorist plots had been disrupted in Britain during the nine years since the London bombings in 2005 — compared to a total of 33 foiled plots involving British nationals both at home and abroad which were identified for this research from 2001–2013 (Loulla-Mae Eleftherious-Smith, 'Theresa May: British Security Services Foiled 40 Terror Plots Since 7/7 Attacks', *The Independent*, November 24, 2014, available at: http://www.independent.co.uk/news/uk/crime/theresa-may-british-security-services-foiled-40-terror-plots-since-77-attacks-9879712.html, accessed November 24, 2014).

[19]'Couple Go to Prison for Aiding Suspect', *The New York Times*, December 9, 1994, available at: http://www.nytimes.com/1994/12/09/nyregion/couple-go-to-prison-for-aiding-suspect.html, accessed November 11, 2011.

[20]Julia Preston, 'Defendant Tells of His Role in Edict Urging Killing of Jews', *The New York Times*, December 9, 2004, available at: http://www.nytimes.com/2004/12/09/nyregion/09stewart.html, accessed May 13, 2010.

[21]Some observers might argue that the case of Mohammed and Cortez does not involve acts of terrorism and should not be included in the sample. Although such cases are indeed criminal, rather than 'terroristic', they are still relevant to understanding terrorism because they illustrate how terrorists may benefit from associations with individuals who are not themselves part of an extremist conspiracy but are nevertheless willing to assist. Another question that might arise in relation to this case is over how it could be considered different to that of Dzhokhar Tsarnaev's friends, who provided *ad hoc* assistance after the Boston bombings. The CTI into Tsarnaev's friends was classified as a 'response to a domestic offense' because it stemmed directly from that attack. The investigation of Mohammed and Cortez was classified differently because they were another step removed from the World Trade Center attack (though still a direct result of a CTI).

[22]There are many more cases involving informants/undercover operatives but where they did not actually initiate the investigation (see the discussions of sting operations and primary sources of evidence).

[23]Note that two of these cases were allegedly first identified using the National Security Agency's PRISM electronic surveillance and data mining program. Specifically, PRISM was reportedly used to first identify Khalid Ouazzani and also Wesam el-Hanafi and Sabirhan Hasanoff (who were in communication with Ouazzani but counted as a distinct case). US officials have also claimed that PRISM was used to identify Najibullah Zazi *et al.*; however, earlier information suggests that Zazi had already been identified as a result of information-sharing with the UK and Pakistan due to his connections with suspected terrorists in those countries.

[24]These included: (1) Nuradin Abdi, who was identified by way of Iyman Faris; (2) Hassan Abu Jihaad, who came under investigation after incriminating material was found on the computer of Babar Ahmad in the UK; (3) Mahmud Faruq Brent, who was linked to the investigation of Tarik Shah *et al.*; (4) Ahmed Hussein Mahamud, who was linked to the Operation Rhino investigation; (5) Nima Ali Yusuf, who also came under investigation as a result of Operation Rhino; and (6) Abdella Ahmad Tounisi, who was identified as a result of the investigation into Adel Daoud.

[25]This was the case of Hafiz Muhammad Sher Ali Khan, convicted of sending money to Tehrik e-Taliban Pakistan.

[26]These were: (1) The Operation Crevice investigation, which grew out of the investigation into Mohammed Qayum Khan; (2) Kazi Nurur Rahman, who was identified by way of Operation Crevice; (3) 'AM' who was identified by way of Operation Overt; (4) Aabid Khan *et al.*, who were linked to the investigation of Younis Tsouli; (5) 'AY', who was also linked to Operation Overt; (6) Lamine and Ibrahim Adam, who were linked to Operation Crevice; and (7) Abdul Muneem Patel, another individual linked to Operation Overt.

[27]Namely Umran Javed and Nicholas Roddis.

[28]The offender in question is Umer Farooq who had accessed extremist websites and was prosecuted for downloading terrorist materials including *Inspire* magazine and *The Terrorist Handbook of Explosives*. Two other cases (Bilal Zaheer Ahmad and Royal Barnes) were also initiated in response to online activities; however, they were classed as 'responding to an offense' since they both uploaded material which amounted to overt criminal acts.

[29]Rebecca Camber, 'Big Ben Bomb Gang Out in Six Years: Outrage as Terror Plotters Plead Guilty in Turn for Light Sentences', *The Daily Mail*, February 2, 2012, available at: http://www.dailymail.co.uk/news/article-2094799/London-Stock-Exchange-bomb-plot-4-radical-Muslims-planned-target-Boris-Johnson.html, accessed February 2, 2012.

[30]Camber, 'Big Ben Bomb Gang Out in Six Years'; Duncan Gardham, 'How the MI5 Watchers Trapped the Home-Grown Terrorists', *The Telegraph*, February 1, 2012, available at: http://www.telegraph.co.uk/news/uknews/terrorism-in-the-uk/9055705/How-the-MI5-watchers-trapped-the-home-grown-terrorists.

html, accessed February 1, 2012; 'Terrorism Gang Jailed for Plotting to Blow up London Stock Exchange', *The Telegraph*, February 9, 2012, available at: http://www.telegraph.co.uk/news/uknews/terrorism-in-the-uk/9072455/Terrorism-gang-jailed-for-plotting-to-blow-up-London-Stock-Exchange.html, accessed February 9, 2012.

[31] It would of course be naïve to think that UK authorities *do not* use informants, but they clearly keep them more secret and tend not to build legal cases around them.

[32] See Foley, *Countering Terrorism in Britain and France*, Chapter 5, Kindle Edition.

[33] Jason Bennetto, 'MI5 Conducts Secret Inquiry into 8,000 Al-Qa'ida "Sympathisers"', *The Independent*, July 3, 2006, available at: http://www.independent.co.uk/news/uk/crime/mi5-conducts-secret-inquiry-into-8000-alqaida-sympathisers-406435.html, accessed October 7, 2014.

[34] Alan Travis, 'MI5's Battle to Identify Radicalised Britons Likely to Turn to Terrorism', *The Guardian*, February 27, 2015, available at: http://www.theguardian.com/uk-news/2015/feb/27/mi5-struggle-identify-people-britain-likely-turn-terrorism-isis, accessed February 27, 2015.

[35] *Ibid.*

[36] Steve Bird, 'Quiet Existence in Leicester Suburb Masked Complex Terrorist Network', *The Times*, April 2, 2003, available at: http://www.timesonline.co.uk/tol/news/uk/article1125944.ece, accessed June 22, 2010.

[37] Cindy George, 'Former Houston Man Charged with Aiding Terrorists', *The Houston Chronicle*, February 13, 2007, http://www.chron.com/disp/story.mpl/metropolitan/4550991.html, accessed November 6, 2010.

[38] Brian Krebs, 'Terrorism's Hook into Your Inbox', *The Washington Post*, July 5, 2007, available at: http://www.washingtonpost.com/wp-dyn/content/article/2007/07/05/AR2007070501153_pf.html, accessed June 25, 2010.

[39] Sam Skolnik, 'Longtime Con Man Admits to Aiding Ressam in Bomb Plot', *The Seattle Post-Intelligencer*, March 30, 2001, available at: http://www.highbeam.com/doc/1G1-72551570.html, accessed January 18, 2012.

[40] Sean O'Neill and Daniel McGrory, *The Suicide Factory: Abu Hamza and the Finsbury Park Mosque* (London: HarperCollins, 2006), 186–200.

[41] Note that the traffic stop in the Ujaama case was not followed up until after 9/11. However, without that stop having occurred it is doubtful whether the investigation would have taken place.

[42] Nick Madigan, 'Global Sting Nets 16 in Md.: 39 are Indicted in Bribery and Money Laundering', *The Baltimore Sun*, September 21, 2007, available at: http://www.highbeam.com/doc/1G1-168915619.html, accessed June 7, 2010.

[43] Paul Shukovsky, '14 Arrested in Raids by Terror Task Force', *The Seattle Post-Intelligencer*, November 19, 2004, available at: http://www.seattlepi.com/local/200337_raid19.html, accessed June 13, 2010.

[44] Mike Lewis, 'Vigilant Officer Noticed More Than Target Practice', *The Seattle Post-Intelligencer*, October 5, 2002, available at: http://www.highbeam.com/doc/1G1-92514643.html, accessed December 5, 2011.

[45] *United States of America v. Clifton L. Cousins*, Opinion, United States District Court Northern District of Ohio Eastern Division, 05-3228, May 17, 2007, available at: http://oh.findacase.com/research/wfrmDocViewer.aspx/xq/fac.20070517_0000586.NOH.htm/qx, accessed July 5, 2012.

[46] Rob Harris, 'Kevin James and the JIS Conspiracy, *Frontline*, October 10, 2006, available at: http://www.pbs.org/wgbh/pages/frontline/enemywithin/reality/james.html, accessed June 8, 2010.

[47] *United States of America v. Ronald Allen Grecula, Sr.*, Superseding Indictment, United States District Court Southern District of Texas, 4:05-CR-00257, August 8, 2006, available at: http://www.investigativeproject.org/documents/case_docs/336.pdf, accessed June 8, 2010.

[48] Mike Carter, 'Man Injured in Bomb Blast Suspected of Terrorism Ties', *The Seattle Times*, May 13, 2011, available at: http://seattletimes.com/html/localnews/2015050211_bombwarrant14m.html, accessed January 6, 2013.

[49] *United States of America v. Raja Lahrasib Khan*, Complaint, United States District Court Northern District of Illinois Eastern Division, March 25, 2010, ¶15, available at: http://nefafoundation.org/file/US_v_LahrasibKhan_complaint.pdf, accessed December 18, 2011.

[50] *United States of America v. Ahmed Abdellatif Sherif Mohamed*, Sentencing Memorandum, United States District Court Middle District of Florida, Case No. 8:07-CR-342-T-23MAP, November 4, 2008, available at: http://www.nefafoundation.org/miscellaneous/FeaturedDocs/US_v_Mohamed_SentencingMemo.pdf, accessed June 12, 2010.

[51] Bruce Rushton, 'Man Accused in Bombing Plot Known for Strong Stance on Islam', *The Journal Star*, September 24, 2009, available at: http://www.pjstar.com/archive/x1800826354/Man-accused-in-bombing-plot-known-for-strong-stance-on-Islam, accessed December 17, 2011.

[52] '"Terrorist" Manual Found in House', *BBC News*, November 6, 2003, available at: http://news.bbc.co.uk/2/hi/uk_news/northern_ireland/3247919.stm, accessed March 13, 2012.

[53] Ross McCarthy, 'Illegal Immigrant Working in Birmingham Jailed for Terrorism Offence', *The Birmingham Post*, April 21, 2009, available at: http://www.birminghampost.net/news/west-midlands-news/2009/04/21/illegal-immigrant-working-in-birmingham-jailed-for-terrorism-offence-65233-23430498/, accessed July 3, 2010.

[54] 'Man Jailed Over Terror Blueprints', *BBC News*, July 17, 2007, available at: http://news.bbc.co.uk/2/hi/uk_news/6902942.stm, accessed July 2, 2010.

[55] 'Airport Woman Hid Terror Manual', *BBC News*, November 2, 2009, available at: http://news.bbc.co.uk/2/hi/uk_news/england/manchester/8337754.stm, accessed July 6, 2010.

[56] 'Cleric Supporter Jailed for Rape', *BBC News*, July 4, 2003, available at: http://news.bbc.co.uk/2/hi/uk_news/england/london/3045904.stm, accessed August 21, 2014.

[57] 'Briton Jailed for 12 Months for Amassing Library of Books on Terrorism', *The Associated Press*, March 19, 2003, accessed via *Lexis Nexis Academic*, June 5, 2013.

[58]'Man Jailed over Terror Cell Plan', *BBC News*, July 6, 2007, available at: http://news.bbc.co.uk/2/hi/uk_news/england/manchester/6277384.stm, accessed May 6, 2010.

[59]'"Sick" Bomb Planner is Locked Up', *BBC News*, July 28, 2009, available at: http://news.bbc.co.uk/2/hi/uk_news/8172933.stm, accessed June 29, 2010.

[60]'Man Who Downloaded Recipes on How to Make Explosive Devices Jailed', *The Bolton News*, January 27, 2012, available at: http://www.theboltonnews.co.uk/news/districtnews/districtatog/9498382.Man_who_downloaded_recipes_on_how_to_make_explosive_devices_jailed/, accessed April 14, 2012.

[61]'Muslim Pair Linked to Bradford "Planned Anti-Jewish Jihad at Home"', *The Yorkshire Post*, June 21, 2012, available at: http://www.yorkshirepost.co.uk/news/at-a-glance/main-section/muslim-pair-linked-to-bradford-planned-anti-jewish-jihad-at-home-1-4667864, accessed July 20, 2012.

[62]Tom Whitehead, 'EDL Attack: The Terror Plot Foiled by Luck', *The Telegraph*, April 30, 2013, available at: http://www.telegraph.co.uk/news/uknews/terrorism-in-the-uk/9972367/EDL-attack-the-terror-plot-foiled-by-luck.html, accessed May 7, 2013.

[63]Weiser and Risen, 'The Masking of a Militant'.

[64]Alan Cowell, 'Briton Sought on U.S. Terror Charges Appears in London Court', *The New York Times*, August 9, 2005, available at: http://www.nytimes.com/2005/08/09/international/europe/09london.html, accessed April 30, 2010.

[65]Mike Pflanz and Abukar Albadri, 'Brit Wanted to Join al-Qaeda but Wanted None "of the Violent Stuff"', *The Telegraph*, March 28, 2012, http://www.telegraph.co.uk/news/worldnews/al-qaeda/9171769/Brit-wanted-to-join-al-Qaeda-but-wanted-none-of-the-violent-stuff.html, accessed April 18, 2012.

[66]David Hanners, 'Minneapolis Man on Trial, Accused of Aiding Somali Terrorists', *Twin Cities.com*, September 30, 2012, available at: http://www.twincities.com/ci_21669306/minneapolis-man-trial-accused-aiding-somali-terrorists, accessed August 23, 2014.

[67]Ian Cobain and Richard Norton-Taylor, 'The Phone Call That Asked: How Do You Make A Bomb?', *The Guardian*, May 1, 2007, available at: http://www.theguardian.com/uk/2007/may/01/terrorism.politics1, accessed August 23, 2014.

[68]Liz Hull and Mia De Graaf, 'Teenage Twin Sisters from Manchester Crept Out of Their Bedrooms in The Middle of The Night and Flew to Join ISIS in Syria', *The Daily Mail*, July 6, 2014, available at: http://www.dailymail.co.uk/news/article-2682120/Teenage-twin-sisters-Manchester-crept-bedrooms-middle-night-flew-join-Isis-Syria.html, accessed July 6, 2014.

[69]Sally Henfield, 'Blackburn Man "Posted Terror Message on US Website"', *The Lancashire Telegraph*, June 18, 2009, available at: http://www.lancashiretelegraph.co.uk/news/4445648.Blackburn_man____posted_terror_message_on_US_website___/, accessed July 3, 2010.

[70]'Hoax Bomb Left on Maltby Bus as "Practical Joke"', *Dinnington Today*, July 15, 2008, available at: http://www.dinningtontoday.co.uk/news/Hoax-bomb-left-on-Maltby.4289230.jp, accessed July 3, 2010.

[71]For example, Jeremy Reynalds, 'Terror From Hartford (Part I)', *The Global Politician*, August 15, 2005, available at: http://www.globalpolitician.com/21090-terrorism-america, accessed July 12, 2011.

[72]Johanna McGeary, 'A Traitor's Tale', *Time*, February 11, 2001, available at: http://www.time.com/time/printout/0,8816,98939,00.html, accessed July 11, 2011.

[73]For the purposes of this study, COIN operations were distinguished from 'international CT' by virtue of being conducted by military forces in the context of conflict zones such as Afghanistan.

[74]Note that Greater Manchester Police ultimately concluded that Butt was lying about much of his activities and elected not to charge him; however, his stories are at least partially corroborated by way of his associations and at least one British jihadi admitted that he had stayed at a Pakistani guesthouse run by Butt before crossing the border into Afghanistan (Armadeep Bassey, 'Taliban Scot: I'll Fight On', *The Sunday Mirror*, November 11, 2001, available at: http://www.highbeam.com/doc/1G1-79940380.html, accessed February 13, 2013).

[75]Sandra Laville, 'First British Conviction for Syria-Related Terror Offence', *The Guardian*, May 20, 2014, available at: http://www.theguardian.com/uk-news/2014/may/20/briton-convicted-terror-offence-syria-jihadist-training-camp?CMP=twt_gu, accessed May 20, 2014.

[76]In the US, this applied to 4 cases before and 5 cases after 9/11, compared to 8 and then 14 in the UK.

[77]This was the investigation of Kiffah Wael Jayyousi, Adham Amin Hassoun, and Mohamed Hesham Youssef, who ran a fundraising and facilitation network and were responsible for the recruitment of Jose Padilla. Wiretaps began in this case in 1993 and Jayyousi was finally arrested in 2005.

[78]Although Aafia Siddiqui was first questioned in April/May of 2002 after a suspicious banking report was filed, it was not until March of 2003 that a global alert for her was issued and she was eventually captured in Afghanistan in July 2008

[79]Saad al-Faqih became a terrorism suspect in 1998 and was finally subject to financial sanctions in 2004.

[80]The investigation that led to the arrest of Saajid Badat in 2003 began after Richard Reid was arrested in 2001.

[81]Sam Mullins '"Global Jihad": The Canadian Experience' (2013), *Terrorism and Political Violence*, 25(5), 734–776.

[82]As defined under the United States Code Title 18, Sections 2339A and 2339B.

[83]Proscribed under the Terrorism Act (2000) and (2006), respectively.

[84]See Foley, *Countering Terrorism in Britain and France*, Chapter 4, Kindle Edition.

[85]For the period 1999–2009 it was found that the most popular terrorism charge in the UK was possession of documents/records likely to be of use for terrorism (Terrorism Act 2000, section 58; n =19). A further nine people had been charged with possession of articles for purposes of terrorism (Terrorism Act 2000, section 57), and only eight people had been charged with engaging in

conduct in preparation for acts of terrorism (Terrorism Act 2006, section 5) (Robin Simcox, Hannah Stuart and Houria Ahmed, *Islamist Terrorism: The British Connections* (London: The Centre for Social Cohesion, 2010), 246). In the current sample, for the period 2001–2013 a total of 48 individuals had been charged with preparing for acts of terrorism (including 43 convictions at the time of writing). This compares to 44 people charged (including 42 convictions) with possession of documents or articles likely to be of use for terrorism (i.e. section 57 and 58 offenses combined).

[86]Foley, *Countering Terrorism in Britain and France*, Chapter 4.

[87]American investigators often use the abbreviation CHS, or sometimes refer to informants as 'cooperating witnesses' (CWs). For the sake of consistency the British acronym CHIS will be used.

[88]These were: Operation Crevice; Kazi Nurur Rahman; Mohammed Hamid *et al.*; and Munir Farooqi *et al.*

[89]As demonstrated in Foley's analysis of counterterrorism in the UK and France, the development and practical application of legislation is also tied to threat perceptions, societal norms, and institutional routines (see Foley, *Countering Terrorism in Britain and France*).

[90]For example Zachary Chesser was prosecuted for making online threats and soliciting others to engage in violent or threatening felony conduct as well as conspiring to join al-Shabaab.

[91]Of course, not all stings follow the exact same pattern. The example here is simply used to illustrate the basic process.

[92]Foley, *Countering Terrorism in Britain and France*, Location 5773, Kindle Edition.

[93]From the point of view of psychology, merely being in the presence of another individual alters the social reality. Furthermore, although the frequent offers of a way out for suspects do indeed provide a chance to walk away from the situation, the individuals involved could equally interpret this as a test of their commitment and therefore feel even more motivated to proceed. This is especially in light of the fact that they usually believe that they are talking to a real member of al-Qaeda who is in a *de facto* position of authority. There is, however, no easy solution to this — rather it seems inherent to the nature of these operations and at the point that a person attempts to detonate explosives, believing that they will be killing dozens of people in the process, there are few opportunities for redemption. That said, as is discussed in Chapter 8, it is important that sting operations are carefully reviewed, used only selectively, and that alternatives are sought.

[94]However, not all investigations are equal. There have been a few cases where investigators have come under significant criticism, most notably the 'Newburgh Four' case involving James Cromitie *et al.* More recently, an apparent attempted sting operation involving a Tunisian student named Ahmed Abassi was deemed by prosecutors to be too flawed to pursue at trial, resulting in a plea deal for minor immigration offenses (Adam Goldman, 'In New York Counterterrorism Sting, a Setback for Federal Law Enforcement', *The Washington Post*, August 14, 2014, available at: http://www.washingtonpost.com/

world/national-security/in-new-york-counterterrorism-sting-a-rare-setback-for-the-fbi/2014/08/14/6179d5b2-0dc2-11e4-8c9a-923ecc0c7d23_story.html?wpmk= MK0000203, accessed August 14, 2014).

[95]Nicola Woolcock, 'Plumber "Planned to Bring Down Jet" in Rocket Attack', *The Times*, May 1, 2007, available at: http://www.timesonline.co.uk/tol/news/uk/crime/article1729047.ece, accessed June 29, 2010.

[96]Lucy Bannerman, Sean O'Neill, and Michael Evans, 'How the Terror Camp Gang Were Bugged and Caught', *The Times*, February 26, 2008, available at: http://www.timesonline.co.uk/tol/news/uk/crime/article3437865.ece?print=yes&randnum=1269826722148, accessed June 28, 2010; 'Greater Manchester Police "Infiltrated" Terror Gang', *BBC News*, May 10, 2011, available at: http://www.bbc.co.uk/news/uk-england-manchester-13354270, accessed May 31, 2011.

[97]Cobain and Norton-Taylor, 'The Phone Call That Asked: How Do You Make A Bomb?'.

[98]Martin Beckford, 'Undercover Anti-Terror Operation Wins National Award', *The Telegraph*, October 4, 2012, available at: http://www.telegraph.co.uk/news/uknews/terrorism-in-the-uk/9586867/Undercover-anti-terror-operation-wins-national-award.html, accessed October 5, 2012.

[99]'Concluded' here refers to 'post-charge' or the equivalent.

[100]All investigations of course make use of multiple sources/types of evidence; however, specific types of evidence also sometimes stand out as being critical to the overall case.

[101]'The Case Against 7 Suspects', *The Chicago Sun-Times*, March 6, 1994, available at: http://www.highbeam.com/doc/1P2-4217669.html, accessed November 22, 2011.

[102]'Tahawwur Rana, Canada Consultant, Guilty, 2 Terror Charges Stemming From Mumbai Attack', *The Huffington Post*, June 9, 2011, available at: http://www.huffingtonpost.ca/2011/06/09/tahawwur-rana-guilty-mumbai-attack_n_874561.html, accessed September 13, 2011; *United States of America v. Tahawwur Hussein Rana*, Complaint, United States District Court Northern District of Illinois, Case No. 09 CR 849, October 27, 2009, available at: http://www.justice.gov/usao/iln/pr/chicago/2009/pr1027_01a.pdf, accessed August 29, 2014.

[103]Tom Hays, 'Betim Kaziu Guilty Of Supporting Overseas Terror', *The Huffington Post*, July 7, 2011, available at: http://www.huffingtonpost.com/2011/07/08/betim-kaziu-guilty-of-sup_n_893082.html, accessed December 18, 2011.

[104]Scott Wilson, Greg Miller, and Sari Horwitz, 'Boston Bombing Suspect Cites U.S. Wars as Motivation, Officials Say', *The Washington Post*, April 23, 2013, available at: http://www.washingtonpost.com/national/boston-bombing-suspect-cites-us-wars-as-motivation-officials-say/2013/04/23/324b9cea-ac29-11e2-b6fd-ba6f5f26d70e_print.html, accessed April 23, 2013.

[105]Sean O'Neill, 'Dentist Sohail Qureshi Jailed Over Terror Charge', *The Times*, January 8, 2008, available at: http://www.timesonline.co.uk/tol/news/uk/crime/article3153554.ece, accessed May 11, 2010.

[106] Jaymi McCann, 'Council Worker, 48, Jailed After Being Found With Hate Rants by Convicted Terrorist and Footage of Beheadings On 352 Discs', *The Daily Mail*, April 26, 2013, available at: http://www.dailymail.co.uk/news/article-2315394/Hackney-council-worker-Khalid-Baqa-jailed-352-discs-terrorist-material-beheadings.html, accessed June 7, 2013.

[107] Note that this does not contradict the earlier assertion that 42% of US cases after 9/11 involved CHISs/UCs. Other sources of evidence may also come into play and hence several cases involving undercover operatives were classed as utilizing 'combined' evidence. In addition, the sample was divided differently to make these calculations.

[108] It also includes four individuals who were detained in Guantanamo where the primary source of evidence could not be determined from open source materials. Nevertheless, the use of secret evidence in counterterrorism is very much a British phenomenon.

[109] The alleged offenses also vary in cases involving special sanctions, ranging from fundraising and facilitation activities to joining terrorist organizations abroad and planning domestic terrorist attacks.

[110] *Secretary of State for the Home Department v. CC and CF*, Special Immigration and Appeals Commission, EWHC 2837 (Admin), October 19, 2012, available at: http://www.bailii.org/cgi-bin/markup.cgi?doc=/ew/cases/EWHC/Admin/2012/2837.html&query=CF+and+v+and+Secretary+and+of+and+State+and+for+and+the+and+Home+and+Department&method=boolean, accessed January 5, 2013.

[111] 'Explosives Manual Teenager Jailed', *BBC News*, October 26, 2007, available at: http://news.bbc.co.uk/2/hi/uk_news/7063727.stm, accessed June 30, 2010.

[112] Krista Kennedy, 'Islamic Extremists who Targeted EDL Face Years in Jail', *The Evening Standard*, June 6, 2013, available at: http://www.standard.co.uk/news/crime/islamic-extremists-who-targeted-edl-face-years-in-jail-8646743.html, accessed June 6, 2013.

[113] 'Alaskan Jailed for Eight Years Over Islam "Hit List"', *BBC News*, August 24, 2010, available at: http://www.bbc.co.uk/news/world-us-canada-11078443, accessed December 12, 2011.

[114] Technically speaking, the 'hit-list' was not in fact the evidence used to convict Rockwood — rather it was the lies he told during interview. However, without the list there would not have been a case to investigate.

[115] Shenai Raif, 'Student Found With "Terrorism Manual" Norman Idris Faridi Facing Jail After Being Turned Down Job At London 2012', *The Independent*, March 13, 2014, available at: http://www.independent.co.uk/news/uk/crime/student-found-with-terrorism-manual-norman-idris-faridi-facing-jail-after-being-turned-down-job-at-london-2012-8535137.html, accessed March 15, 2014.

[116] Tom Whitehead, 'Friend of Lee Rigby's Killer Jailed for Distributing Terrorism Material', *The Telegraph*, June 6, 2014, available at: http://www.telegraph.co.uk/news/uknews/terrorism-in-the-uk/10882441/Friend-of-Lee-Rigbys-killer-jailed-for-distributing-terrorism-material.html, accessed June 6, 2014.

[117]'Pennsylvania Man Pleads Guilty to Terrorist Solicitation and Firearms Offense', *Department of Justice*, August 9, 2011, http://www.justice.gov/opa/pr/2011/August/11-nsd-1028.html, accessed August 17, 2011.

[118]'Virginia Man Sentenced to 25 Years in Prison for Providing Material Support and Encouraging Violent Jihadists to Kill U.S. Citizens', *Department of Justice*, February 24, 2011, available at: http://www.justice.gov/opa/pr/2011/February/11-nsd-238.html, accessed June 28, 2011.

[119]Rob Modic, 'Jordanian Faces More Time in Jail, Deportation Man Sentenced for Lying to FBI Agents About an E-Mail Account He Had', *The Dayton Daily News*, July 8, 2006, available at: http://www.highbeam.com/doc/1P2-11976278.html, accessed December 7, 2011.

[120]'Woodbridge Man Sentenced to 144 Months for Providing Material Support to Terrorist Organization', *United States Attorney's Office*, April 13, 2012, available at: http://www.justice.gov/usao/vae/news/2012/04/20120413ahmadnr.html, accessed July 2, 2012.

[121]Suzanne Kelly, 'Samir Khan: Proud to be an American Traitor', *CNN*, September 30, 2011, available at: http://articles.cnn.com/2011-09-30/middle-east/world_meast_analysis-yemen-samir-khan_1_samir-khan-aqap-inspire-magazine?_s=PM:MIDDLEEAST, accessed December 20, 2011.

[122]'Clarkston Man Sentenced to Federal Prison for Attempting to Provide Material Support to Terrorists', *Federal Bureau of Investigation*, June 12, 2013, available at: http://www.fbi.gov/seattle/press-releases/2013/clarkston-man-sentenced-to-federal-prison-for-attempting-to-provide-material-support-to-terrorists, accessed June 17, 2013.

[123]Indeed, the post-charge phase generally lasts longer than the investigation up until the point of arrest. Using the same sample division (i.e. individuals prosecuted before and after 9/11) the figures are as follows: pre-9/11 US — 35.6 months average investigation until arrest versus 37.1 months post-charge legal processing time until sentencing; post-9/11 US — 18.2 months investigation versus 26.9 months post-charge processing; pre-9/11 UK — 9.8 months investigation versus 20.5 legal processing; post-9/11 UK — 6.9 months investigation versus 19.5 legal processing.

[124]48% were convicted, while the outcome (conviction versus plea) was unknown for two individuals.

[125]Overall, this is confirmed by the statistics. After 9/11, the average sentence for individuals convicted in the US was 25.7 years, compared to 14.0 for those who pleaded guilty. Convicted individuals were also much more likely to be sentenced to life in prison (19% versus 2%). In the UK, the average sentence for people who were convicted was actually *less* than for those who pleaded guilty (6.7 versus 7.4 years) however, they were still much more likely to receive a life sentence (29% versus 3%).

[126]Thereby skewing the average.

[127]Note that as of February 2015, British courts will have the option of imposing whole-life sentences ('British Courts can Impose Whole-Life Prison Sentences', *BBC News*, February 3, 2015, available at: http://www.bbc.com/news/uk-31110814, accessed February 5, 2015).

[128] This also has implications for comparative rates of terrorism. Many individuals convicted under terrorism legislation in the UK would probably not be prosecuted in the US.

[129] *The North Carolina Jihad Cell and the Quantico Marine Base Plot* (The NEFA Foundation: November 2009), available at: http://www.orgsites.com/va/asis151/QuanticoJihadCellPlot.pdf, accessed September 9, 2014.

[130] 'Jury in North Carolina Finds Convicted Terrorist Guilty of Murder-for-Hire Plot', *Federal Bureau of Investigation*, November 8, 2012, available at: http://www.fbi.gov/charlotte/press-releases/2012/jury-in-north-carolina-finds-convicted-terrorist-guilty-of-murder-for-hire-plot, accessed May 31, 2013.

[131] Note that plotting to murder witnesses as an act of revenge is not, on the face of it, an act of terrorism. However, this case was still included in the sample as directly related to terrorism and an example of continued recruitment and criminal activity by a terrorist offender.

[132] In addition, Qasim Abukar was acquitted on one occasion, only to later be subject to special sanctions, at which point he was given a government alias. Several others are known to have been involved in jihadist activity, though not convicted, only to be prosecuted for new offenses years later.

[133] Note that Saleem was also reported to have fought for the Taliban in 2001 along with Abu Waheed (also known as 'Waheed Mahmood') who was later convicted for his role in the Operation Crevice plot ('British Muslims Survived', *Sky News*, November 18, 2001, available at: http://news.sky.com/home/article/1035593, accessed January 18, 2012). Though technically not re-offending, since there was no legal intervention, this nevertheless provides evidence of lengthy and intermittent jihadi careers.

[134] Fran Yeoman, 'Four Jailed for Hate Crimes at Cartoon Protest', *The Times*, July 18, 2007, available at: http://www.timesonline.co.uk/tol/news/uk/article2097883.ece, accessed July 2, 2010.

[135] 'Six Guilty of Terrorism Support', *BBC News*, April 17, 2008, available at: http://news.bbc.co.uk/2/hi/uk_news/7352969.stm, accessed March 30, 2010.

[136] Tom Whitehead, 'Friend of Lee Rigby's Killer Jailed for Distributing Terrorism Material', *The Telegraph*, June 6, 2014, available at: http://www.telegraph.co.uk/news/uknews/terrorism-in-the-uk/10882441/Friend-of-Lee-Rigbys-killer-jailed-for-distributing-terrorism-material.html, accessed June 6, 2014.

[137] 'Umran Javed: Jailed for Terror Material Found on Computer', *BBC News*, September 19, 2012, available at: http://www.bbc.co.uk/news/uk-england-derbyshire-19645280, accessed September 20, 2012.

[138] Tom Whitehead, 'Hoax Bomber "Researched Real Bombs Just Months After Leaving Prison"', *The Telegraph*, January 30, 2013, available at: http://www.telegraph.co.uk/news/uknews/terrorism-in-the-uk/9837261/Hoax-bomber-researched-real-bombs-just-months-after-leaving-prison.html, accessed February 3, 2013.

[139] 'English Defence League Rally Bomb Plotters Jailed', *BBC News*, June 10, 2013, available at: http://www.bbc.co.uk/news/uk-22841573#TWEET784179, accessed June 10, 2013; Tom Whitehead, 'EDL Attack: The Terror Plot Foiled by Luck', *The Telegraph*, April 30, 2013, available at:

http://www.telegraph.co.uk/news/uknews/terrorism-in-the-uk/9972367/ED L-attack-the- terror-plot-foiled-by-luck.html, accessed May 7, 2013.

[140]In addition to Abu Waheed (note 115 above), others included Mohammed Siddique Khan, Omar Khyam, and Michael Adebolajo. There are doubtless many others.

[141]Control order absconders included in the sample were AD (Zeeshan Siddiqui), AB and AC (Lamine and Ibrahim Adam), K (Mohamed Azmir Khan), CF, CC (Mohammed Mohamed), BX (Ibrahim Magag), and HH. In addition, A (Mohammed Jabar Ahmed) fled the UK despite being designated under a Treasury Order, and Cerie Bullivant also absconded from a control order but was excluded from the sample because the order was subsequently quashed on the grounds that it would not have been upheld in light of new material.

[142]Abdul Saleem and Abdul Muhid were prosecuted for the 2006 offense *first*, meaning that they did not re-offend following legal intervention. Similarly, Zohaib Ahmed was re-arrested *before* pleading guilty to his first offense.

[143]Shiv Malik, 'Radical Preachers Praise Isis in Online Conference', *The Telegraph*, September 8, 2014, available at: http://www.theguardian.com/uk-news/2014/sep/08/radical-preachers-isis-islamic-state-online-conference, accessed September 9, 2014.

[144]For example, see *Abid Naseer, Ahmad Faraz Khan, Shoaib Khan, Abdul Wahab Khan and Tariq Ur Rehman v. Secretary of State for the Home Department*, Special Immigration and Appeals Commission, Appeal No. SC/77/80/81/82/83/09, May 18, 2010, available at: http://www.siac.tribunals.gov.uk/Documents/outcomes/1_OpenJudgment.pdf, accessed April 12, 2012.

[145]'UK al-Qaeda Cell Members Jailed', *BBC News*, June 15, 2007, available at: http://news.bbc.co.uk/2/hi/uk_news/6755797.stm, accessed June 5, 2013.

[146]'UK Prosecutor: Man had Terrorist Contact Book', *MSNBC News*, September 24, 2008, available at: http://www.msnbc.msn.com/id/26875545, accessed March 31, 2010.

[147]*United States of America v. Tahawwur Hussein Rana*, Complaint, United States District Court Northern District of Illinois, Case No. 09 CR 849, October 27, 2009, available at: http://www.justice.gov/usao/iln/pr/chicago/2009/pr1027_01a.pdf, accessed August 29, 2014.

[148]'UK Trio Jailed for Preparing Acts of Terrorism', *BBC News*, April 25, 2013, available at: http://www.bbc.co.uk/news/uk-22294720, accessed April 25, 2013.

[149]Duncan Gardham, 'How the MI5 Watchers Trapped the Home-Grown Terrorists', *The Telegraph*, February 1, 2012, available at: http://www.telegraph.co.uk/news/uknews/terrorism-in-the-uk/9055705/How-the-MI5-watchers-trapped-the-home-grown-terrorists.html, accessed February 1, 2012.

[150]Alistair MacDonald and Cassell Bryan-Low, 'U.K. Case Reveals Terror Tactics', *The Wall Street Journal*, February 7, 2011, available at: http://online.wsj.com/articles/SB10001424052748704570104576124231820312632, accessed September 20, 2014.

[151]'GIMF Releases Mobile Encryption Program for Android, Symbian Devices', *SITE Monitoring Service*, September 4, 2013.

[152]Yahya Ibrahim, 'Tips for our Brothers in the United Snakes of America' (2010), *Inspire*, 2, 55–57, available at: http://jihadology.net/2010/10/11/al-qa%e2%80%99idah-in-the-arabian-peninsulas-al-mala%e1%b8%a5im-media-releases-inspire-magazine-issue-2/, accessed October 12, 2014.

[153]*United States of America v. Antonio Martinez*, Complaint, United States District Court for the District of Maryland, Case No. 10-4761-JKB, December 8, 2010, 12–13, available at: http://s3.amazonaws.com/nytdocs/docs/536/536.pdf, accessed December 21, 2011.

[154]What seems to be the full series of Chesser's 'Counter Counter-Terrorism' articles (written using the pseudonym Abu Talhah) were reproduced on the following site: 'Islamic Instruction Manual — Detailed Read — Religion of Peace', *Terror News Briefs*, April 15, 2011, available at: http://terrornews-briefs.blogspot.com/2011/04/islamic-instruction-manual-detailed.html, accessed November 28, 2011.

[155]*United States of America v. Zachary Adam Chesser*, Criminal Information, United States District Court for the Eastern District of Virginia, Case 1:10-CR-00395-LO, October 20, 2010, 15, available at: http://nefafoundation.org/newsite/file/US_v_Chesser_information.pdf, accessed January 10, 2011.

[156]Bilal Zaheer Ahmad, 'Bilal Ahmad: October 1, 2011 (Some Advice on Security)', *Islamic Awakening*, March 7, 2012, available at: http://forums.islamicawakening.com/f18/some-advice-on-security-brother-bilal-zaheer-56985/, accessed October 16, 2014.

[157]'Inmate Put Terrorism Advice on Internet', *Express and Star*, February 1, 2012, available at: http://www.expressandstar.com/news/2012/02/01/inmate-put-terrorism-advice-on-internet/, accessed April 13, 2012.

Chapter 8

Conclusion

Having analyzed the background and behavior of more than 300 American and more than 400 British jihadists, as well as the law enforcement response in each country up to September 2013, let us now consider theoretical and practical implications of results. The chapter begins with a brief summary of findings followed by a discussion of the impact of events in Syria and Iraq, with a particular focus on the issue of 'foreign fighters'. Next, the general and theoretical implications of this research are considered, as well as country-specific implications for counterterrorism in light of the current situation.

Summary of Findings

Common Trends

Findings are summarized in Table 8.1 below. Although the precise manifestation is never the same, several broad trends have developed over time which are common to both countries and which generally confirm some of our assumptions about home-grown Islamist terrorism (HGIT). In particular, results indicate that the phenomenon has become increasingly home-grown since 9/11 in the sense that offenders are more likely to have been born and/or raised in the US/UK and to have radicalized there as opposed to being sent from abroad with the *a priori* intention of committing acts of terrorism. Rates of terrorist activity have also increased since 2001 and offenders have become more diverse in terms of ethnicity and socioeconomic background. Motives are generally expressed in terms of a mixture

Table 8.1. Comparative summary of findings in relation to Islamist terrorist activity in the US and UK (1980s–2013).

	Common trends	US-specific	UK-specific
Jihadi offenders	Increased mobilization after 9/11; More 'home-grown'; Greater variety; Mostly young males, but more females getting involved; Varied socioeconomic backgrounds; Motives expressed in terms of religion, political grievances, altruism, and revenge; Radicalization is both social and 'virtual'	Geographically dispersed; Ethnically varied; On average better off, although there is a relatively large jihadi 'underclass', largely consisting of converts and criminals, often with social/psychological problems; Internet appears to play a larger role in radicalization	Geographically confined to 4 regional hotspots; Dominated by South Asians (mostly born in UK); Lower to middle-class but fewer clearly marginalized individuals; Radicalization primarily driven by localized jihadi subcultures
Terrorist activity	Proportional decrease in foreign connections and influence; Increase in operational autonomy; Increased domestic focus; Reduced and more varied international travel; Informal leadership; Small groups; Shorter careers; Independent financing; 'Foreign fighting' most popular activity; Increase in lone actors	More often operationally discrete; Few domestic connections; Greater 'operational' use of Internet, including promoting violent jihad and group/network formation; Rise in 'pseudo-facilitators', criminal fundraising, and domestic plotters caught in stings (related to jihadi underclass)	More often networked or connected to likeminded others, especially in the UK; Street-level promotional activities (related to jihadi subcultures); More likely to have foreign support, especially for planning/conducting attacks; More overseas attacks and more competent domestic operations

(*Continued*)

Table 8.1. (*Continued*)

	Common trends	US-specific	UK-specific
Counter-terrorism	Increased and enhanced counterterrorism activities; Most CT investigations (CTIs) begin at home; 'Snowballing' of CTIs is common; Multiple sources of evidence utilized; Decreased investigation and legal processing times; Increased guilty pleas; Reduced average sentences; Signs of increasing forensic awareness of offenders	Monitoring of Internet more important for identifying suspects; Public tip-offs quite common; Far greater role of informants/ undercover operatives and use of stings; Preference for prosecuting serious offenses using combined sources of evidence; Longer CTIs, legal processing times and sentences compared to UK	CTIs more likely to begin as result of continuous monitoring of known extremists; Few public tip-offs; Evidence often kept secret; Minor offenses often prosecuted based on physical or electronic evidence; Shorter investigation, legal processing times and sentences; More repeat offenders

of religion, political grievances, altruism, and a desire for revenge against the perceived 'enemies of Islam'.

Although the impact of the Internet has not been identical in either country, broadly speaking it appears to have *supplemented*, rather than *replaced* face-to-face interaction as a source of radicalization.

There are also a number of operational indicators which are consistent with assumptions about the general nature of HGIT. In particular, the proportional decrease in connections with foreign terrorist organizations (FTOs) corresponds with an increase in autonomy as well as domestically focused operations, thus reinforcing the notion that home-grown terrorists are often independent amateurs willing to attack their own country. Likewise, international travel in furtherance of violent jihad has decreased proportionally speaking and jihadi careers are usually shorter than in the past. Offenders also tend to operate in small, self-funded groups (although lone actors have become more common in recent years) and leadership appears to be mostly informal. All of this is consistent with the general concept of loosely affiliated, autonomous terrorism. Nevertheless, it is important to take note of the fact that international travel in pursuit of violent jihad has continued and has become more varied over time in accordance with shifting hotspots of jihadi activity around the globe. Moreover, overseas training and combat, i.e. becoming a 'foreign fighter', remains the most sought-after goal for both American and British jihadis, and approximately half of all cases still have international terrorist connections.

Counterterrorism (CT) activities have naturally expanded in order to cope with the increasing number of people mobilizing to violent jihad in each country. American and British authorities retain primary responsibility for their respective residents and citizens and CT investigations (CTIs) are more likely to begin at home than abroad despite advances in international cooperation. It is also quite common for CTIs to 'snowball' in the sense that one investigation will lead to others, with investigators drawing upon multiple sources of evidence in combination rather than relying on any one particular type more than others. CT in each country has also become more efficient over time — average investigation and legal processing times have decreased and offenders are more likely to plead guilty. Average prison sentences have also reduced as authorities have taken a flexible approach to prosecutions. Although there are signs of increasing forensic awareness among terrorist offenders in both the US and UK, this awareness is unevenly spread and has not so far been matched in terms of capability.

US-Specific Findings

American jihadis are far more geographically dispersed than their counterparts in the UK. They are also more ethnically varied and — on average — slightly better off socioeconomically speaking. However, it is also clear that a jihadi 'underclass' of highly marginalized individuals exists in the US, which is less apparent in the UK. This largely consists of converts and criminals who are less well educated and well off, are much more likely to have a history of social and psychological problems compared to other jihadists, and are also more likely to be caught in sting operations. It furthermore appears that the Internet is somewhat more important to processes of radicalization in the US, seemingly as a result of the comparative lack of physical jihadi subcultures.

Operationally speaking, American jihadis are more often 'discrete' actors who are not part of a wider network and tend not to have connections to other jihadi terrorists within the US. In line with the apparent greater role of the Internet for radicalization, jihadis in the US also seem to utilize this more often for 'operational' purposes, in particular for promoting jihadi ideology and for group/network formation. This is indicative of the construction of virtual subcultures in lieu of real ones. Moreover, there has been a rise in 'pseudo-facilitators' (or aspiring jihadis), criminal fundraisers, and domestic plotters caught in stings, all of which are largely connected to the above-mentioned jihadi underclass.

In accordance with the significant online presence of jihadi offenders, the Internet also seems to be more important in the US for identifying terrorism suspects. Public tip-offs are also relatively common, which partially relates to the far greater use of informants and undercover operatives for identifying suspects as well as gathering evidence in investigations. These tactics are utilized for a variety of reasons, not least of which being the relative inability to prosecute individuals for more minor offenses, meaning that specific plots or conspiracies must usually be identified.[1] Informants and undercover agents are frequently the primary source of evidence within stings, but the general norm is to combine multiple sources of evidence together. These trends seem to contribute to the fact that CTIs, post-charge legal processing times, and sentences are all longer in the US compared to the UK.

UK-Specific Findings

British jihadis are relatively confined to four regional hotspots of activity, namely London and surrounding areas, the West Midlands, Greater Manchester, and West Yorkshire. There is a great deal of ethnic diversity but offenders of South Asian heritage dominate. Compared to the US, British jihadis are slightly worse off on average and typically come from low-to-middle-class backgrounds. They are not, however, poor, socially isolated, or obviously marginalized on the whole. There is nothing to indicate that they typically come from broken homes, that they have no friends or that they are serious criminals, and people who knew them before they radicalized often describe them as 'normal'. Their transformation seems to take place primarily among groups of friends situated within broader, pro-jihadi subcultures which are now well established within parts of the UK.

In connection with these observations, British jihadis are also more likely to operate as part of larger terrorist networks, and in particular are more likely to have connections to other UK-based Islamist terrorists outside their immediate group. Jihadi ideology is certainly promoted online, but more significant still — and not apparently seen in the US — are street-level promotional activities such as extremist *dawa* stalls and sometimes quite aggressive 'protests', which are manifestations of underlying subcultures. British jihadis have also been more successful in making meaningful contact with foreign terrorist organizations (FTOs) and in particular have received greater levels of external support for planning and conducting attacks. In relation to this they have taken part in more terrorist attacks overseas and have presented a more serious threat in domestic operations.

It appears that British authorities must monitor a large number of potentially violent jihadis on a more-or-less continuous basis and that criminal CTIs are then initiated in response to specific intelligence (the source of which is rarely disclosed) that often relates to known persons-of-interest or their associates. In this context, the available information suggests that public tip-offs are rarely forthcoming and informants are conspicuous by their apparent absence, although it would be naïve to think that human intelligence sources are not being exploited. Indeed, fewer details of CT practice in the UK are publicly disclosed and the introduction of control orders, succeeded by terrorism prevention and investigation measures (TPIMs), mean that sources of intelligence/evidence are often kept secret. UK legislation does, however, enable the prosecution of lesser offenses such as the possession or dissemination of terrorist materials and the encouragement or glorification of terrorism, which tend to rely primarily on physical or electronic evidence. The prosecution of such offenses also relates to shorter investigation and legal processing times as well as shorter average prison sentences compared to the US. The downside to this is that there have been more repeat offenders in the UK, as well as former terrorism convicts who remain active within extremist circles.

Syria and Iraq: A New Era in Jihadi Terrorism?

Although this book represents one of the largest empirical studies of jihadi terrorist activity in the US and UK to date, the findings are nevertheless limited by the sampling timeframe which ended in September 2013. Much has happened since then as the war in Syria has escalated and the situation in Iraq has gone from bad to worse. Indeed, the increasingly interrelated conflict in these two countries is widely seen as one of the most significant developments in the history of 'global' jihad. The fight against Assad in particular is perceived around the world as a legitimate struggle against an evil tyrant. Simultaneously, we have witnessed the incredible rise of the 'Islamic State' (IS) which, having split from al-Qaeda in February 2014, went on to seize control over much of Iraq and Syria and boldly announced the re-establishment of the 'Caliphate' in June. IS in particular has proven to be adept at utilizing social media to amplify its successes and promote its cause, and the conflict has played out online in excruciating detail.

A variety of factors have thus combined to create a 'perfect storm' which is attracting unprecedented numbers of foreign jihadi fighters from around the world. At the time of writing, as many as 25,000 foreign fighters from as many as 100[2] different countries are believed to have gone to Syria and Iraq within a three-year period, with most of those volunteers joining either Jabhat al-Nusra (JN) or IS.[3] Although most of these volunteers come from the Middle East and North Africa, between 2,000 and 5,000 are thought to come from Western nations including the US and UK.[4]

More specifically, current estimates of American foreign fighters in Syria/Iraq range from 12 to 300, with 'around 100' being the most-often cited figure.[5] Meanwhile, estimates for the UK range from 300 to 700.[6] These are, of course, approximations which vary widely and are inherently unreliable. Nevertheless, since the end of the sampling period for this research, more than 50 individuals have been added to the US database and more than 300 have been added in the UK. The vast majority of these cases are related to Syria/Iraq in some way, and many of the British suspects especially appear to have acquired first-hand combat experience. A more detailed picture will of course emerge over time, but what is clear even at this early stage is that (a) there has been a significant increase in mobilization to violent jihad in both countries, and (b) rates of mobilization are much higher in the UK. Given that the *confirmed* numbers of jihadi terrorists relative to Muslim population sizes were found to be much closer than expected (see Chapter 5), this is the clearest, verifiable evidence yet of the disparity between these two nations.

In addition to quantitative changes, the Syria/Iraq conflict is also having a qualitative impact on the nature of the threat. To begin with, jihadi use of the Internet has greatly expanded so that mainstream social media including Facebook, YouTube, and Twitter in particular are now the go-to places for jihadi propaganda. This would suggest that we are likely to see an increase in online radicalization and there have already been claims that Western jihadis are now 'radicalized via Twitter' rather than, for example, in mosques.[7] However, although there is some truth to this, we should be wary of binary, all-or-none explanations, and avoid jumping to premature conclusions. Jihadi messages are indeed far more visible than they have ever been before, and this means that more people are being exposed to their ideas. However, this does not automatically mean that face-to-face interaction in physical places (which does not take place in the public eye) has suddenly become irrelevant. In-person interaction with one's peers is likely to be a more powerful mechanism — and perhaps more often a barrier — of radicalization and many of the latest generation of British jihadis appear to have radicalized and joined up together with friends. Based on currently available information, the same cannot be said for the handful of Americans whom we *know* have fought in Syria/Iraq, which reinforces the notion that the Internet plays a more important role in sustaining HGIT in the US compared to the UK. Moreover, the fact that far fewer Americans are signing up for jihad, despite having access to the same online propaganda, seems at least partially related to the lack of physical, pro-jihadi subcultures which lie at the heart of the problem in Britain.

While the jury is still out on the extent to which processes of radicalization have become 'virtualized', there is greater certainty that the Internet has taken on a renewed operational significance. As well as distributing propaganda and providing updates on events on the ground, the fact that many fighters now maintain their own personal social media accounts has made it much easier for aspiring *mujahideen* to make contact with a FTO. Fighters clearly relish the attention and have taken it upon themselves to play advisory roles, scheduling question-and-answer sessions on Ask.fm and other platforms, where they provide practical and logistical advice on how to reach the conflict zone and what to expect if/when people get there (the more sensitive issues dealt with in private). As a result of this, we are seeing an increased use of the Internet for communication, group/network formation, and facilitation. That said, terrorist organizations such as IS clearly recognize that the Internet is a double-edged sword and have made numerous attempts at reigning in the online behavior of their recruits.[8] Moreover, as time has gone on and jihadis have repeatedly violated user guidelines, thousands of accounts have been shut down and it is unclear whether they will have the same level of online freedom that they once had, or that social media will be as significant on the domestic stage once the current conflict eventually dies down.

Another change taking place in response to the Syria/Iraq conflict is an increase in non-violent domestic support operations — most notably fundraising — in the UK. There are almost certainly dedicated recruitment and facilitation networks operating in Britain and there have been numerous arrests aimed at disrupting these activities. Moreover, there seems to have been a rather dramatic rise in suspected cases of fundraising for terrorism. In August 2014, Amal El-Wahabi — a mother of two from London — was found guilty of trying to send €20,000 to her jihadist husband who had gone to fight in Syria the previous year.[9] More worrying still, the North West Counter Terrorism Unit reported in October that they had seized £250,000 in cash from IS supporters attempting to travel to Syria, most of which was seized at Manchester airport.[10] Given that there are many other points of departure from Britain — and that many people are no doubt successful in evading detection — the amount of money currently being raised for terrorism in the UK is clearly significant. Although it remains to be seen whether these types of activities have increased on a similar scale in the US, six individuals were charged with sending several thousand dollars' worth of money and equipment to Islamist terrorists overseas (including both al-Qaeda and IS) in February 2015.[11]

Yet another new development has been the rising number of females traveling to Syria/Iraq, now believed to account for up to 10% of foreign jihadi volunteers.[12] Again, this has been much more obvious in the UK than the US, but there are examples of this from both countries. For instance, in September 2014 Shannon Conley, from Colorado, became the first female to be prosecuted in America for attempting to join IS after apparently being seduced by one of their fighters whom she met online.[13] There have been numerous cases like this in the UK, including girls as young as 15, and many have actually been successful in joining terrorist organizations. IS especially is deliberately targeting females for recruitment and the Internet seems to be a key part of this process, perhaps even more so than for males. Although their motivations surely vary, most appear to travel with the expectation of becoming a 'jihadi bride' and as such they are generally not allowed to fight even though they may be given a gun. Nevertheless, several British women reportedly formed an all-female 'police force' known as the 'al-Khanssaa brigade', which patrols the streets of Raqqa enforcing *sharia*.[14] At present, it is an open question whether or not females within IS will graduate to more violent roles, and whether women's collective fascination with the jihad in Syria/Iraq will outlast the current conflict. Both of these outcomes are very real possibilities though, as the female appetite for violence appears to be growing. The arrest of Noelle Velentzas and Asia Siddiqui (charged with conspiracy to use a weapon of mass destruction) in New York in April 2015 is a clear indication of this.[15] The problem of female radicalization therefore needs to be addressed as a matter of some urgency.

The primary concern of Western governments, however, is the issue of returning foreign fighters. In particular, the fear is that these individuals, now 'professionally' trained and hardened by combat, will return home determined to conduct attacks. In order to assess the likelihood of this, we need to examine the historical record. For the time period 1990–2010, using estimates of jihadi foreign fighter numbers from Europe, the US, Canada, and Australia, Hegghammer found that approximately 11% of veteran fighters went on to plan or conduct domestic attacks.[16] The author's own calculations for the US and UK from 2001 to 2013 are quite different, although there are also important methodological differences. Based on the current samples, 20% of American and 17% of British jihadis who received overseas training and/or combat experience also planned or conducted domestic attacks. These figures then rise to 28% and 35%, respectively, if we also consider terrorist attacks abroad. However, it is important to note that this research only included offenders who could be individually identified, meaning that the total number of foreign fighters is likely to be lower than in reality and the risk of attack is therefore exaggerated. We should thus treat these as high-end estimates and we can expect the number of jihadis returning from Syria/Iraq and then planning domestic attacks to be *considerably less* than a fifth of the overall (estimated) total.

Even so, small numbers of veteran jihadis can still be highly dangerous and we cannot necessarily assume that these percentages will remain constant in the face of contextual and environmental changes. Although coalition airstrikes against IS and JN weaken these organizations militarily, they also give them and their supporters added incentive to conduct terrorist attacks in retaliation. Indeed, there has been an outpouring of threats and incitements to terrorism from jihadis worldwide and IS has called upon sympathizers to 'kill any disbeliever, whether he be French, American, or from any of their allies' using any means available.[17] Even before this statement was made, returning jihadis were beginning to make their presence felt, most notably with the attack on the Jewish Museum in Brussels in May 2014 which left four people dead. Since then, the number of domestic terrorism plots allegedly linked to, or inspired by IS has been steadily increasing, and several related arrests were made in London in October with five people subsequently charged (at least one of whom is believed to have spent time in Syria).[18] Perhaps in recognition of this, al-Qaeda also appears to be stepping up its efforts to strike against the West, with its branch in Yemen claiming responsibility for the *Charlie Hebdo* attack in Paris in January 2015.[19]

In addition to all this, veteran jihadis (those who have trained and/or fought overseas) have a well-deserved reputation for radicalizing and recruiting others as well as facilitating connections to FTOs and providing financial and other forms of support. They thus play an important role in sustaining and expanding jihadi networks and they may well *create* domestic terrorists even if they do not engage in violence themselves. The bottom line, then, is that even though the majority of returning foreign fighters are unlikely to pose a direct terrorist threat, a small number of hardcore individuals will plan to carry out attacks themselves and an unknown additional number will carry on non-violent subversive activities which are more of a long-term risk.

Furthermore, we should also bear in mind that veteran jihadis are not the only problem. Although veterans are generally more capable and influential, they still account for a minority of home-grown jihadis (19% in the US; 24% in the UK) and the majority of Islamist terrorist attacks in Western countries are carried out by people who do not have overseas experience. By way of illustration, just 13% of domestic attack cases (planned or conducted) in the US included one or more veteran jihadis, compared to 38% in the UK. Although there is an obvious disparity here (again largely explained by differences in investigative practice) it is clear that the *quantitatively* greater threat in both countries comes from ideologically inspired but untrained individuals. In today's context, these people cannot be overlooked.

In summary, the conflict in Syria/Iraq has, and is continuing to impact upon the nature of HGIT in the US and especially in the

UK in a variety of ways — most notably in levels of radicalization and mobilization, the numbers of experienced foreign fighters with connections to FTOs, the growing role of the Internet, greater numbers of female jihadis, and, ultimately, an increased risk of domestic attack, which may or may not involve veteran fighters. We will now consider the practical and theoretical implications of the findings from this research in light of these developments.

General/Theoretical Implications of Findings

This research has empirically examined who becomes an Islamist terrorist and how, what they do, and how they have been dealt with in the US and UK. One of the most important contributions of this is that it helps us to appreciate what HGIT is and what it involves. The term 'home-grown terrorism' emerged in the West in recognition of the fact that Islamist terrorists had become an internally generated threat, rather than being a problem of foreign infiltration. Although it is otherwise loosely defined, there is not necessarily any need to dwell on this. It is more important to recognize that although there are certain tendencies associated with this type of terrorism (citizens/long-term residents radicalized in the West, frequently lacking substantial organizational support), it cannot be artificially separated from 'international' or 'global' jihadi terrorism and it involves a wide spectrum of actors, operational configurations, and capabilities. Links to FTOs — though reduced — are by no means a thing of the past in either country, and we are currently witnessing a quantitative if not qualitative resurgence of this phenomenon, which may well transform the nature of the threat in coming years. We should not, therefore, assume too narrow or rigid definitions that cloud our thinking on what is an incredibly varied and dynamic issue.

Unfortunately, there is still a tendency for people to try and oversimplify things by boiling them down to singular issues whilst ignoring other factors that are just as important. For instance, there are some who believe that religion lies at the heart of the problem, while others still will claim that this has nothing to do with it and the real issues are the marginalization of Muslims in the West, a youthful desire for adventure and meaning, or simply the primordial allure of violence. None of these explanations by themselves is helpful. Islam in general is not the problem, but the *specific* jihadist interpretation of it is certainly a major contributing factor and we should not ignore this. Concepts of 'marginalization' or 'disenfranchisement' imply financial, educational, occupational, and social deprivation. Whilst this does apply to some American and British jihadis, it does not describe either sample on the whole. Moreover, there are too many people who experience the same — and worse — conditions but are *not* drawn to jihadi terrorism, and too many people who *do* become involved but come from quite comfortable, even sometimes highly successful backgrounds. To claim then that socioeconomic conditions are the real underlying causes here is to ignore a multitude of other factors which have more direct explanatory power. Likewise, to say that jihadi terrorism is *really* all about adventurism or violence — or any other singular issue — is to apply blinkers which only narrow and constrain our understanding of the problem.

This does not mean that these issues are irrelevant — rather that they are each a piece of a much larger and more complicated puzzle. As previously noted, jihadis themselves clearly recognize this and deliberately try to appeal to a range of different motivations. For instance, Rayat al-Tawheed (a primarily British group currently active in Syria) has produced a variety of motivational posters including such slogans as 'Real struggles need real men'; 'The shortcut to Jannah [Paradise] is Jihad'; 'This is our call of duty'; 'Sometimes people with the worst pasts create the best futures'; 'It won't be easy but it'll be worth it'; and 'Sometimes you just got to get up and go'. All of these are accompanied by suitably inspiring images and collectively they seek to strike a chord on multiple levels.

If we are to become more effective in countering this threat, we need to be equally accepting of the fact that this is not about any one issue alone. That said, it may still be useful to prioritize certain issues over others. The findings from this research give broad, albeit tentative support for the motivational model described in Chapter 2 and so it is worth considering some of the implications of this for CT.[20] To begin with, there are two elements of specific pre-disposing risk that stand out as being particularly important. First, the occurrence of conflicts involving Muslims creates such a widespread sense of grievance, empathy, and desire to help that it creates fertile ground for terrorist recruitment. This is very clearly demonstrated by the fact that rates of mobilization consistently spike when conflict breaks out and has never been more obvious than with the current situation in Syria/Iraq. This relationship must be formally acknowledged and incorporated into domestic CT strategies and risk assessments with the aim of enabling a more proactive and flexible mobilization of resources when necessary. It should also be noted that these conflicts — whilst centered around religious identity — are fundamentally political in nature (more on this below).

A second element of pre-disposing risk that stands out is the fact that there are geographical hotspots of jihadist activity, especially in the UK but also in the US. Practically speaking, hotspots should of course be closely monitored at national, regional, and local levels and used to prioritize resources. Although this may seem self-evident, there are indications that this is poorly appreciated, or at least not being given the attention it deserves. For example, higher-risk states such as New York and Minnesota receive less money in homeland security grants on a *per capita* basis than states such as Alaska, South Dakota, and Delaware.[21] Fewer people of course means more spending per person, but the fact that South Dakota — a state in which there has been zero terrorist activity to date — received $100 million over an 11-year period still raises the question whether that money could be spent more wisely. Meanwhile on a theoretical note, the existence of geographical hotspots provides some support to the 'social transmission' hypothesis (see Chapter 2) and to the notion that radicalization and recruitment are being driven by pro-jihadi subcultures in the UK where these trends are more pronounced.

This brings us to a second important aspect of the model that was supported, i.e. that the necessary conditions for almost all involvement in HGIT are ideological exposure, social contact, and opportunity. With relatively few exceptions,[22] American and British jihadis were found to be in contact with likeminded others (either in person or online), to be in possession of jihadist propaganda, and to be ideologically engaged to some extent. Although they did not necessarily exploit every opportunity available to them, there were certainly times when practical barriers constrained their behavior. It follows that sufficient disruption of one or all of these three overlapping elements would severely reduce the likelihood of mobilization to violent jihad, meaning that they should be targeted for intervention as a matter of priority. Naturally, this is easier said than done and involves a range of different methodologies, all of which are already employed to some extent, including a variety of 'hard' and 'soft' measures.

Countering Ideology

This is arguably the most challenging task ahead of us and it is evident that existing efforts to counter the appeal of jihadi propaganda in both the US and UK have so far been insufficient. Collectively, we must therefore both expand and refine the 'war of ideas' and although this is hardly an earth-shattering revelation it is an argument that must be repeated *ad nauseam* until it is fully embraced. There are three issues in particular that need to be addressed: (1) the scale/scope of counter-messaging; (2) the type of arguments used; and (3) coordination with other efforts.

Regarding the scale and scope of counter-messaging, there is a need to utilize both broad and individually targeted approaches as part of comprehensive strategies for countering violent extremism (CVE). Indeed, CVE initiatives were recently recognized by the UN as being an essential component in the struggle to reduce the risk of jihadi foreign fighters, and both the US and UK are taking steps in this direction (see country-specific discussions below). With this in mind, there is still plenty of room for improvement. In particular, it is generally accepted that for too long jihadis have been allowed to run rampant on the Internet and that more must be done to disrupt and counter online propaganda. The fact that the Internet has markedly grown in significance for American and British jihadis since 2001 clearly supports this argument. However, governments should also take greater advantage of the fact that they have easy access to mainstream media, including both national and local television, radio, and newspapers. At present, all of these tools are under-utilized by governments yet exploited at every opportunity by extremists.

The arguments used against Islamist terrorists must also be more comprehensive. There seems to be a lingering assumption that to be truly effective against jihadi narratives, it is necessary to employ complex religious arguments which secular governments are unqualified to do.[23] But while theology has its place here, political motives are also important and yet for the most part largely unaddressed. For instance, foreign policy in relation to Syria (or similar, future conflicts) should be publicly explained as clearly and transparently as possible with potential jihadis in mind. Critical decisions such as those to launch airstrikes against IS — as obvious as they might seem — should also be explained with this audience in mind. The aim should be to persuade potential enemies rather than to defy or intimidate existing ones. Likewise, the central jihadist argument — that the West is at war with Islam — must be challenged far more openly and robustly. If our governments are unable to construct a more coherent *political* narrative than Islamist terrorists, it raises serious questions about their competency.

This leads in to a second gap/opportunity in the type of arguments that are used, i.e. the need to construct and sell a compelling *positive* counter-narrative. It is one thing to discredit and undermine a flawed ideology championed by bloodthirsty thugs, but quite another to provide an appealing alternative. To that end, more effort must be made to create and promote Western/American/British narratives that offer more than simply vague concepts like 'freedom', 'tolerance', or 'equality'. If they are to really be competitive, they must address all of the motivational needs which jihadi narratives do, including desires for meaning, significance, and excitement, and must also counter the perception that Western society and capitalism in general are morally bankrupt and spiritually empty. This is no small task, but one that must be attempted.

Finally, to address the third issue in relation to counter-ideology, there is a need for greater strategic coordination in CT. If we are saying one thing but appear to be doing another, then our words will not merely fall on deaf ears but will generate resentment and anger.

Simply put, actions speak louder than words. Particularly sensitive issues here include civilian casualties, real or perceived violations of law and abuse/misuse of power by military, intelligence, or police personnel at home or abroad. Addressing any such issues in as timely a manner as possible with an emphasis on openness and accountability will go some way to reducing negative repercussions. Likewise, perceptions of global inequality and economic exploitation — which are largely grounded in reality — must be more actively addressed if positive counter-narratives are to truly carry any weight.

Countering Social Contact

With regards to social contact as a necessary condition for radicalization and involvement in terrorism, the most obvious implications are to prioritize the disruption and, if necessary, prosecution of extremist ideologues, recruiters, and organizations. This has been a policy in the UK for some time, as exemplified by the prosecution of various 'hate preachers' and the banning of al-Muhajiroun and its offshoots. Similarly, the need to disrupt extremist networks led to the recent strengthening of powers to subject terrorism suspects to locational constraints, meaning that certain individuals can (again) be forced to move to a new area and/or be banned from certain parts of the country.[24] There are also plans to introduce so-called 'extremism disruption orders' (EDOs) which would severely curtail the ability of designated extremists to speak in public and online.[25] However, such measures are likely to face significant legal challenges and based on past experience are hardly a guarantee of success. Similar restrictions on freedom of speech and movement would also be far more difficult, if not impossible to implement in the US. Nevertheless, there is still a need to make it more difficult for extremists to organize, form networks, and spread their ideas. Alternative, soft interventions such as mentoring programs might serve a similar purpose by exerting positive social influence in individuals' lives (thus countering extremist influences) whilst reducing the potential for additional grievances against the State.

Virtual connections between extremists in cyberspace are another ongoing challenge. It is now well known that online platforms are increasingly used for networking and facilitation in addition to simply broadcasting propaganda, and yet jihadists continue to exploit this technology. Governments have relatively little control over this and although companies including Facebook, YouTube and Twitter have to some extent attempted to limit the posting of certain material, they have been reluctant to take more decisive action and are still allowing terrorists to make use of their services. Counterterrorism authorities must therefore continue to pursue closer cooperation with a wider range of relevant online companies, with a view to establishing a collaborative approach towards the joint disruption of online terrorist networks.

Reducing Opportunities

If extremist ideology and social connectivity are effectively suppressed, this in itself reduces opportunities for involvement in terrorism. More specific measures, such as reducing access to weapons or other dangerous materials and restricting people's ability to travel to jihadi conflict zones also fall into this category. The latter has become an international obsession in recent years and although progress is being made, the flow of foreign fighters heading to the Middle East has continued. Reports of Americans making the journey to Syria/Iraq have been sporadic and yet there are clearly still gaps in terms of monitoring and restriction of travel. For instance, Moner Mohammad Abusalha, who blew himself up in Syria in May 2014, had previously returned to the US for more than six months before making his way back to the conflict zone for the final time.[26] In another case, three teenage girls from Denver were prevented from joining IS, but had made it as far as Germany and were only stopped because their parents had not wasted any time in alerting the authorities.[27] That same month, British police reported that as many as five Britons per week were still traveling to join jihadists in the Middle East.[28]

It is therefore imperative that more is done to monitor and restrict the travel of suspected terrorists, utilizing all options available, including refusal or cancellation of passports and use of TPIMs or equivalent if necessary.[29] That said, it is not enough to simply prevent someone from traveling and leave it at that. There are now numerous examples from different Western countries where this has happened and the individuals in question have taken out their frustrations at home instead — Martin Couture-Rouleau, who ran down and killed a Canadian soldier in Quebec in October 2014, is a case in point.[30] Thus, even if there is insufficient evidence to prosecute or to apply other restrictive measures, something must be done to try and reduce the level of risk that these individuals pose. Again, soft interventions are a possibility and might include a variety of health or social services, educational assistance, vocational training, court-ordered or voluntary counseling, as well as specialized 'deradicalization' programs. Indeed, as of February 2015, deradicalization sessions became mandatory for terrorism suspects subject to TPIMs in the UK.[31] Such measures will not always be effective, but at the very least they will increase the visibility of potentially violent offenders.

Additional Matters of Concern

More specific matters which must also be addressed include the rising numbers of females and lone actor jihadis. Regarding the former, early indications are that online romances are at least part of the story, but religion, politics, and personal factors also come into play just as they do for males.[32] Nevertheless, this is an aspect of the threat that is still greatly under-researched. Both the American and British governments should therefore invest in projects aimed at understanding the similarities and differences between male and female jihadis and devising tailored strategies to combat radicalization among women.

As for lone actor terrorists, the primary concern is not only that we are seeing more of them, but that they are also harder to detect and therefore more likely to have an opportunity to conduct an attack. This is clearly demonstrated by the fact that lone actors have been responsible for the majority of completed attacks in Western countries since 2001 and the number of such attacks has increased in recent years (see Table 1.1, Chapter 1). Unfortunately, there is no simple solution to combating this particular threat. The more successful we are at combating the broader appeal of jihadist ideology over the long term, the fewer of these cases we are likely to see.

Conversely, effective disruption of extremist groups and networks may actually increase incidents of lone actor terrorism as individuals are 'forced' to act alone. In the short-term, it is primarily about raising awareness and encouraging people to come forward with information if they see/hear something suspicious. However, there is still the question of what to do if/when a potentially dangerous individual comes to the attention of the security services. If the person has not committed a crime, there is typically little that can be done and even if 24-hour surveillance was feasible it would still be extremely difficult to prevent an attack from happening. Given that lives are potentially at stake, this is a gap that needs to be addressed. Governments must therefore explore the full range of available options in order to ensure that there is a mechanism in place to allow early intervention, whether punitive or otherwise.

Implications for the US

There are two particular, interrelated issues that help to shape the size and nature of the threat from HGIT in the US: the existence of a jihadi underclass and the reliance on sting operations. Given that converts, criminals, and people with mental health problems are particularly prominent in the US sample and also tend to be the ones caught in stings, it is important that this subgroup is better understood.[33] At present, these individuals contribute significantly to the scale of the threat and especially to the number of domestic attack plots. They are an added burden on law enforcement and because they frequently receive lengthy prison sentences, they are also costly. This is not to suggest that these individuals are not potentially dangerous or that sting operations are inherently wrong — the FBI and their partners are dedicated, sincere professionals making the best use of the tools available to them in order to keep the public safe. However, if that same goal can be achieved more efficiently, much-needed resources may be freed up and all concerned will benefit.

To that end, American jihadis currently in prison should be systematically evaluated in order to better understand how and why highly marginalized individuals are sometimes attracted to violent jihad, and how they might be steered away from it. At the same time, although use of informants and sting operations has so far been effective, alternative options for dealing with these individuals should be explored. For instance, lesser offenses such as solicitation of acts of terrorism and distribution of information relating to explosives (the charges used to convict Emerson Begolly) could perhaps be used more often. The possibility of broadening such offenses and/or proscribing additional, relatively minor terrorism offenses should also be evaluated. This would mean that US investigators would be less reliant on conspiracy-type offenses (which are more time-consuming and invariably result in lengthy prison sentences) and would have a more appropriate set of tools for dealing with less serious or committed terrorism offenders. In some cases, soft interventions including for example, drug counseling, mental health treatment, or other forms of social support might be more appropriate and could potentially avoid the need for prosecution altogether. We should be under no illusion that such alternatives would always be applicable, as some individuals cannot be steered away from violence. But making more options available might help to improve the efficiency of CT in the US and weed out some of the 'misfits' who are currently adding to the American experience of violent jihad. Furthermore, given that sting operations are generally unpopular, use of alternative methods could go some way to enhancing trust between communities and law enforcement.

Indeed, improved cooperation with Muslim communities in America has been a goal of US CT efforts for some time. For example, the FBI has long placed an emphasis on this, as have police departments in Los Angeles and Minneapolis-St. Paul. 'Enhancing engagement with and support to local communities that may be targeted by violent extremists' was one of the stated goals of the 2011 'Strategic Implementation Plan for Empowering Local Partners to Prevent Violent Extremism in the United States'.[34] More recently, similar aims were again expressed by the US Attorney General with the announcement of a new 'Pilot Program to Counter Violent Extremists', which:

> will bring together community representatives, public safety officials, religious leaders, and United States attorneys to improve local engagement; to counter violent extremism; and — ultimately — to build a broad network of community partnerships to keep our nation safe.[35]

These, of course, are admirable goals and on paper very encouraging. However, the US government has been very slow to recognize the potential value that domestic CVE programs might have and to translate this into action. Existing efforts to build trust with Muslim communities have also had limited success and there is still 'deep suspicion that, despite all the meetings and the talk of outreach, the government's main goal is to recruit informants'.[36] Similar efforts in the UK have likewise been painted as an excuse to spy on Muslim communities, thereby adding to existing grievances against the government. CVE programs must therefore be implemented in a very careful and transparent manner if they are to fulfill their aims.

It is also crucial to realize that 'traditional' CT could potentially come into conflict with CVE in practice. For instance, when a potential suspect is identified a decision must be made about what type of intervention to employ — broadly speaking, criminal investigation or some form of support. Although these two pathways are not necessarily mutually exclusive, communities and families are likely to favor the latter option and may feel betrayed if a person is then prosecuted. It is thus important to identify any areas of potential conflict between CT and CVE, and between federal, state, and local authorities as well as non-governmental partners, and to have a plan in place for overcoming or minimizing such problems.

Another potential problem — again drawing from mistakes that were made in the UK — is that choosing partners in the community can be difficult and sometimes even counterproductive. American authorities will need to have a clear system in place for choosing who to work with so that they are empowering only those groups in society who can make a positive contribution to the stated aims of CVE and whose message is consistent with democratic values. On a related point, it is also fundamentally important that 'success' is clearly defined from the outset and that there is an ongoing commitment to the evaluation of programs. This will be vital to understanding program impact, learning from experience, and providing justification for funding, which will be necessary for program longevity.

There are two additional considerations raised by this research which are relevant to CT and CVE in the US. First is the importance of identifying and prioritizing hotspots of jihadi activity. The three cities where the CVE pilot program is being rolled out are Minneapolis, Boston, and Los Angeles. Minneapolis of course is an appropriate candidate for this, given that it currently ranks second among all US cities for number of jihadi terrorists produced since 9/11. It is even more appropriate in light of recent reports suggesting that a dozen or more Somali–Americans from the area have since gone to fight in Syria/Iraq.[37] This is significant not only because of the increased numbers, but because it suggests that a pro-jihadi subculture has been established in Minneapolis that is not limited to ethno-nationalist concerns with the conflict in Somalia. Boston and Los Angeles, however, are more curious choices as priorities for CVE. Boston was apparently chosen 'for the strength of ... existing relationships, community engagement and community oriented policing programs',[38] but combined with a very low number of jihadis since 9/11, these would appear to be better reasons *not* to prioritize it. In fact, the top three cities for jihadi activity since 9/11 have been New York City, Minneapolis, and Chicago. As with the allocation of homeland security grants (discussed above), it is thus apparent that empirically identified hotspots are not being given due consideration.

The second factor here — and the final point in relation to the US — is that although there are certain physical hotspots, the Internet appears to be particularly significant to HGIT in America. It thus follows that this should be a top priority for CVE in the US, just as it appears to be for CT. This will require more in-depth research into the online behavior of American jihadis to understand which websites and platforms they use most and how they radicalize, communicate and connect with one another. More effective counter-strategies can then be developed.

Implications for the UK

If HGIT in the UK is to be effectively crippled, the underlying subcultures that sustain it must be weakened. In order to achieve this it will be necessary to become more effective in countering extremist ideology, disrupting the organizations and networks which promote it, and reducing related opportunities, as discussed above. Although the British government has been trying to erode jihadi subcultures by way of the 'Prevent' strategy for several years now, both enthusiasm and funding for the project steadily diminished in the face of continuing difficulties and *increased* levels of mobilization to violent jihad in response to Syria/Iraq. As a result (and in spite of recent attempts at reinvigorating CVE in the UK[39]), the popular perception is that Prevent has failed.[40]

Given that this strategy was based to a large extent on empowering and engaging with local communities, this could also have serious implications for CVE plans in the US. However, despite the problems with Prevent (notably 'infiltration' by extremists and the seemingly widespread and erroneous perception that it was an excuse to spy on Muslims), it is far from clear that these problems characterized the entire strategy or that it was ineffective on the whole. The fact that jihadist mobilization has risen so sharply in recent years does not necessarily mean that Prevent failed altogether — it simply tells us that major conflicts involving Muslims are a far more influential factor. Negative perceptions of the UK's attempts at CVE appear to be driven at least in part by unrealistic expectations. To think that decades' worth of extremist social networking and mobilization to terrorism could be undone in a matter of five or six years, or that preventive mechanisms still in their infancy could stand up against the siren call of what is arguably the most significant jihadi conflict in modern history, is ludicrous.

We must therefore readjust our expectations and re-evaluate CVE in the UK once again, with the explicit understanding that this is a long-term commitment. It should also be recognized that this is not just about preventing specific individuals from becoming involved in terrorism or rehabilitating those who have already committed an offense. More fundamentally (and yet something which did not become a matter of policy until 2011), it is about undermining the extremist subcultures which enable violent jihadist ideology to thrive.[41] In addition to the various measures already discussed, there are several aspects of the situation in the UK which must be highlighted for special consideration.

First, although the Internet has grown in significance, pro-jihadi subcultures in the UK also appear to be sustained by street-level activism such as leafleting and inflammatory protests. More effective ways of preventing, disrupting, or undermining these activities must be found. Second, cooperation with Muslim communities needs to be improved. Police in the UK have made a number of public appeals to this end, and parents whose children have gone to fight in Syria/Iraq have increasingly come forward with information. Authorities must seek to capitalize on this in order to cultivate more positive, lasting relationships.

A third issue concerns the use of informants and undercover operatives in British CT, who play a much less prominent role in criminal investigations and prosecutions as compared to the US. There is not necessarily anything wrong with this (and of course it is closely tied to legal constraints), but it is worth considering that jihadis in the US are clearly wary of being infiltrated by law enforcement while the same fears do not appear to be as prevalent in the UK. If jihadi subcultures and related terrorist networks are to be undermined, it makes sense to sow distrust and to weaken internal cohesion. Cultivation of jihadi 'supergrasses', strategic disclosure of the use of undercover operatives, and limited use of misinformation could go some way to achieving this.

A fourth matter that is primarily relevant to the UK is jihadi recidivism. As increasing numbers of terrorism convicts are released from jail this becomes more of a concern, especially when we take into account not only overt violations of the law, but also continued contributions to the growth of extremist subcultures. The fact that such individuals are likely to have elevated status for having served time in prison 'for the cause' means that they are also likely to be particularly influential. This is a problem that must therefore be dealt with. Options might include greater investment in deradicalization programs within prison and continuing on release, combined with punitive measures such as the aforementioned EDOs, restrictions on group membership and associations, barring terrorism convicts from certain occupations or activities such as running schools or charities,[42] and enhancing prison sentences for repeat offenders.

Fifth, and finally, is the issue of foreign fighters in Syria/Iraq which the UK in particular has been struggling with. Although a range of preventive measures have already been discussed, such attempts have not so far been effective and newly introduced powers are primarily geared towards preventing or monitoring travel, or else temporarily barring terrorism suspects from returning to the UK.[43] It is therefore important to consider alternative possibilities for managing the problem whilst individuals are overseas, and mitigating the threat if/when they return home. As for managing foreign fighters, aside from gathering intelligence on individuals using social media and other methods, specialized family counseling programs may also be worth investing in. For example, the Hayat program in Germany appears to have had some success in persuading jihadi fighters overseas to stay in contact with their families and in some cases to abandon the fight.[44]

Another option here would be to extend an offer of amnesty or at least more lenient treatment for those who are willing to come home. Numerous British jihadis in Syria/Iraq have indicated that they want to return to the UK but are fearful of prosecution.[45] At the same time, IS has imprisoned and executed attempted defectors and made it clear that they will kill anyone else who tries to leave.[46] Such situations are ripe for exploitation. If the British government publicly indicated a willingness to bring these individuals home and treat them leniently, this could potentially be successful in acquiring human assets and demonstrating legitimacy over and above IS. This leads to another important point, which is the need for flexibility when fighters come home. Even more than jihadi ex-convicts, veteran fighters are key to sustaining supportive subcultures and for that reason must be treated as priority targets for intervention. However, while prosecution may be appropriate in some cases, a softer approach may be more productive in others. As noted above, deradicalization will be mandatory for terrorism suspects on TPIMs and there are plans to do the same for returning jihadi fighters,[47] but although the intention is good, anything that is framed as compulsory is likely doomed to fail. It seems it would be more fruitful to take a flexible approach, offering counseling and other forms of positive social support to those who appear to be lower risk and willing to engage, whilst prosecuting hardliners and more serious offenders. This would help to demonstrate that the government's goal is to target *terrorists* and not those who have been led astray.

Finally, it is important to realize that when the current conflict finally comes to an end, this will not necessarily mean that the immediate threat has diminished. On the contrary, there may be many battle-hardened, frustrated, and bored jihadi veterans who are unaccounted for and in the absence of overseas conflict, they may be more inclined to vent their anger at home.

Concluding Remarks

The aim of this book was to improve our understanding of jihadist terrorism involving people from, living, or offending in the US and UK. Hopefully that has been achieved. However, it is by no means the final word on the subject. This research was based exclusively on open source materials and missing information was a problem throughout, meaning that findings must be treated with caution. Future projects must therefore seek to test and verify the various hypotheses, theoretical models, and observations that have been put forward. The threat itself is also constantly evolving and we must therefore strive to keep pace.

One thing that is for certain is that Islamist terrorism — unfortunately — is not going away any time soon. Both the American and British people (regardless of faith or ethnicity) will therefore be facing this threat in one form or another for the foreseeable future. In doing so, it is vital that we stand together against those who have nothing to offer but hatred, intolerance, and violence.

Notes

[1]Compared to the UK.

[2]More than 25,000 Foreign Fighters Joining Islamists: UN, i24 News, April 3, 2015, available at http://www.i24news.tv/en/news/international/66457-150403-more-than-25-000-foreign-fighters-joining-islamists-un

[3]Peter Neumann, 'Foreign Fighter Total In Syria/Iraq Now Exceeds 20,000; Surpasses Afghanistan Conflict in the 1980s', *International Centre for the Study of Radicalisation*, January 27, 2015, available at: http://icsr.info/2015/01/foreign-fighter-total-syriairaq-now-exceeds-20000-surpasses-afghanistan-conflict-1980s/, accessed January 28, 2015.

[4]*Ibid.*; Michael Noonan, '15,000-plus for Fighting: The Return of the Foreign Fighters', *War on the Rocks*, October 8, 2014, available at: http://warontherocks.com/2014/10/15000-plus-for-fighting-the-return-of-the-foreign-fighters/, accessed October 8, 2014.

[5]Ken Dilanian and Eileen Sullivan, 'FBI: About a Dozen Americans Fighting in Syria', *Associated Press*, September 25, 2014, available at: http://mapnews.com/ap/db_355780/contentdetail.htm?contentguid=n8liAPTv, accessed September 25, 2014.

[6]Tom Whitehead, 'Up to 700 Britons Feared Fighting in Syria', *The Telegraph*, April 24, available at: 2014, http://www.telegraph.co.uk/news/uknews/law-and-order/10785316/Up-to-700-Britons-feared-fighting-in-Syria.html, accessed April 24, 2014.

[7]Tanveer Ahmed, 'Many of the Western Recruits to Jihad are Radicalised via Twitter', *The Australian*, October 11, 2014, available at: http://www.theaustralian.com.au/news/features/many-of-the-western-recruits-to-jihad-are-radicalised-via-twitter/story-e6frg6z6-1227086878745, accessed October 12, 2014.

[8]'IS Fighters Point to the Danger of the Misuse of Social Media', *SITE Intelligence Group*, September 26, 2014; Michel Moutot, 'Jihadists Increasingly Wary of Internet, Experts Say', *France 24*, January 31, 2015, available at: http://www.france24.com/en/20150131-jihadists-increasingly-wary-internet-experts-say, accessed January 31, 2015.

[9]Dominic Casciani, 'Woman Cleared of Smuggling Money for Syria in Underwear', *BBC News*, August 13, 2014, available at: http://www.bbc.com/news/uk-28778232, accessed August 13, 2014.

[10]Lizzie Dearden, 'Police Seize £250,000 of Cash Intended to Fund Isis at Manchester Airport and North-West Ports', *The Independent*, October 13, 2014, available at: http://www.independent.co.uk/news/uk/crime/police-seize-250000-of-cash-intended-to-fund-isis-at-manchester-airport-and-northwest-ports-9791703.html, accessed October 13, 2014.

[11]'U.S. Charges Six With Supporting Islamic Militant Groups: Justice Department', *Reuters*, February 6, 2015, available at: http://www.reuters.com/article/2015/02/07/us-usa-security-arrests-idUSKBN0LB01V20150207, accessed February 7, 2015.

[12]Harriet Sherwood, Sandra Laville, Kim Willsher, Ben Knight, Maddy French, and Lauren Gambino, 'Schoolgirl Jihadis: The Female Islamists Leaving Home to Join Isis Fighters', *The Guardian*, September 29, 2014, available at: http://www.theguardian.com/world/2014/sep/29/schoolgirl-jihadis-female-islamists-leaving-home-join-isis-iraq-syria, accessed September 29, 2014.

[13]'Arvada Woman Pleads Guilty to Conspiracy to Provide Material Support to a Designated Foreign Terrorist Organization', *US Department of Justice*, September 10, 2014, available at: http://www.justice.gov/opa/pr/2014/September/14-nsd-961.html, accessed September 11, 2014.

[14]Robert Mendick and Robert Verkaik, 'British Female Jihadis Sign up to the Islamic State's All-Women Police Force', *The Telegraph*, September 7, 2014, available at: http://www.telegraph.co.uk/news/uknews/terrorism-in-the-uk/11079386/British-female-jihadis-sign-up-to-the-Islamic-States-all-women-police-force.html, accessed September 7, 2014.

[15]'Two Queens, New York, Residents Charged with Conspiracy to Use a Weapon of Mass Destruction', *US Department of Justice*, April 2, 2015, available at: http://www.justice.gov/opa/pr/two-queens-new-york-residents-charged-conspiracy-use-weapon-mass-destruction, accessed April 3, 2015.

[16]Thomas Hegghammer, 'Should I Stay or Should I Go? Explaining Variation in Western Jihadists' Choice between Domestic and Foreign Fighting' (2013), *American Political Science Review*, 107(1), 1–15.

[17]Abdul Hameed Bakier, 'The Islamic State Issues Appeal to End Inter-Jihadist Rivalry (2014), *Terrorism Monitor*, 12(19), 3–4, available at: http://www.jamestown.org/programs/tm/single/?tx_ttnews%5btt_news%5d=42941&cHash=8e1947fb1f0d9df8b180a5a795319725#.VDjsna0cST8, accessed October 11, 2014.

[18]'Four Men from London Charged over "Terror Plot", Police Say', *BBC News*, October 17, 2014, available at: http://www.bbc.com/news/uk-29662245, accessed October 17, 2014.

[19]'AQAP Claims Responsibility for Charlie Hebdo Attack', *SITE Intelligence Group*, January 14, 2015.

[20]For instance, socioeconomic hardship appears to be a *general pre-disposing risk-factor*, given that offenders clearly come from all walks of life. Political grievance is a highly significant *specific pre-disposing risk-factor* in that rates of HGIT activity vary with overseas conflicts involving Muslims. The fact that certain geographical hotspots were found also supports the contention that location is a *specific pre-disposing risk-factor*. The proposed 'necessary conditions' were also supported in the sense that the vast majority of jihadi offenders were ideologically engaged, they were mostly in physical or virtual contact with likeminded others, and they had the opportunity to offend. Lastly, the examination of stated motivations reinforced the importance of ideological goals as a *direct motivating factor*.

[21]Joe O'Sullivan, 'Some Question Terrorism Funding Going to South Dakota', *Sioux City Journal*, June 13, 2014, available at: http://siouxcityjournal.com/news/local/state-and-regional/article_604ffae3-6893-550c-a3b8-1023fc540301.html, accessed June 14, 2014.

[22]These included a small number of criminal opportunists and 'troubled' individuals who were involved for primarily non-ideological reasons, and a few genuine lone actor terrorists with no discernible, relevant social contacts.

[23]Secular approaches to counter-ideology do exist. Notable examples include the US government's Center for Strategic Counter-Terrorism Communications (CSCC established in 2010) and the British Research, Information and Communications Unit (RICU, which began in 2007). Such efforts are commendable, however — criticisms aside — they are simply not enough.

[24]David Anderson, 'Relocation Relocation Relocation', *Independent Reviewer of Terrorism Legislation*, March 1, 2015, available at: https://terrorismlegislationreviewer/independent.gov.uk/relocation-relocation-relocation/, accessed March 4, 2015; 'Clegg: UK Can Tackle Terror Threat within the Law', *BBC News*, September 2, 2014, available at: http://www.bbc.com/news/uk-politics-29027995, accessed September 4, 2014.

[25]Holly Watt, 'Extremists to Have Facebook and Twitter Vetted by Anti-Terror Police', *The Telegraph*, September 30, 2014, available at: http://www.telegraph.co.uk/news/uknews/terrorism-in-the-uk/11129474/Extremists-to-have-Facebook-and-Twitter-vetted-by-anti-terror-police.html, accessed October 1, 2014.

[26]Adam Goldman and Greg Miller, 'American Suicide Bomber's Travels in U.S., Middle East Went Unmonitored', *The Washington Post*, October 11, 2014, available at: http://www.washingtonpost.com/world/national-security/american-suicide-bombers-travels-in-us-middle-east-went-unmonitored/2014/10/11/38a3228e-4fe8-11e4-aa5e-7153e466a02d_story.html?wprss=rss_world, accessed October 12, 2014.

[27]Lori Hinnant, 'U.S. Girls' Journey to Join Islamic State Shows Travel Flaws', *The Toronto Star*, October 23, 2014, available at: http://www.thestar.com/news/world/2014/10/23/us_girls_journey_to_join_islamic_state_shows_travel_flaws.html, accessed October 24, 2014.

[28]Ben Farmer, 'Five Britons a Week Joining Jihadists in Syria', *The Telegraph*, October 22, 2014, available at: http://www.telegraph.co.uk/news/worldnews/middleeast/syria/11178849/Five-Britons-a-week-joining-jihadists-in-Syria.html, accessed October 22, 2014.

[29]Significant steps were taken to address these issues in the UK with the Counter-Terrorism and Security Act (2015) which came into force on February 12.

[30]'Hit-and-Run Soldier Killer in Canada had Passport Seized', *BBC News*, October 21, 2014, available at: http://www.bbc.com/news/world-us-canada-29714300, accessed October 21, 2014.

[31]Anderson, 'Relocation Relocation Relocation'.

[32]Katherine Brown, 'Analysis: Why are Western Women Joining Islamic State?', *BBC News*, October 6, 2014, available at: http://www.bbc.com/news/uk-29507410, accessed October 6, 2014.

[33]This is not to suggest that British converts are not also worthy of more attention — rather that they are of comparatively greater importance in the US.

[34]*Strategic Implementation Plan for Empowering Local Partners to Prevent Violent Extremism in the United States* (White House: Washington DC, 2011), available at: http://www.whitehouse.gov/sites/default/files/sip-final.pdf, accessed May 1, 2012.

[35] 'Attorney General Holder Announces Pilot Program to Counter Violent Extremists', *US Department of Justice*, September 15, 2014, available at: http://www.justice.gov/opa/pr/attorney-holder-announces-pilot-program-counter-violent-extremists, accessed October 27, 2014.

[36] Eric Schmitt, 'U.S. Is Trying to Counter ISIS' Efforts to Lure Alienated Young Muslims', *The New York Times*, October 4, 2014, available at: http://www.nytimes.com/2014/10/05/us/us-is-trying-to-counter-isiss-efforts-to-lure-alienated-young-muslims.html?emc=edit_tnt_20141006&nlid=59679535&tntemail0=y, accessed October 4, 2014.

[37] Mukhtar Ibrahim, 'Jihad in Syria Lures Somalis from Minnesota', *MPR News*, June 12, 2014, available at: http://www.mprnews.org/story/2014/06/11/somali-americans-syria, accessed June 14, 2014.

[38] Shelley Murphy, 'Boston to Host Anti-Extremist Pilot Program', *The Boston Globe*, September 24, 2014, available at: http://www.bostonglobe.com/metro/2014/09/23/boston-site-program-prevent-residents-from-joining-extremist-groups/YpEpq2cYvITZ6u8AFkbarL/story.html?p1=Article_InThisSection_Bottom, accessed September 24, 2014.

[39] For example, educational institutions now have a statutory responsibility to play a more active role in Prevent, as outlined in the Counter-Terrorism and Security Act (2015).

[40] James Brandon, 'The UK's Counter-Radicalization Strategy Just Failed; What Now?', *War on the Rocks*, September 18, 2014, available at: http://warontherocks.com/2014/09/uk-attempts-to-create-moderate-islam-just-failed-what-now/, accessed September 21, 2014.

[41] Following a government review, the Prevent strategy has also focused on combating non-violent extremism since 2011 based on the recognition that 'what appear at first sight to be non-violent extremist ideologies are drawn upon by terrorists to justify violence' (see *Report to the Home Secretary of Independent Oversight of Prevent Review and Strategy* (London: HM Government, 2011), 5, available at: http://www.homeoffice.gov.uk/publications/counter-terrorism/prevent/prevent-strategy/lord-carlile-report?view=Binary, accessed August 21, 2011).

[42] Peter Dominiczak and Christopher Hope, 'Terrorists to be Banned from Running UK Charities', *The Telegraph*, October 22, 2014, available at: http://www.telegraph.co.uk/news/politics/david-cameron/11178444/Terrorists-to-be-banned-from-running-UK-charities.html, accessed October 22, 2014; Andrew Gilligan and Robert Mendick, 'Extremism in Britain: Now the Crackdown is Launched', *The Telegraph*, March 7, 2015, available at: http://www.telegraph.co.uk/news/uknews/terrorism-in-the-uk/11457174/Extremism-in-Britain-Now-the-crackdown-is-launched.html, accessed March 8, 2015.

[43] HM Government, *Counter-Terrorism and Security Act 2015 CHAPTER 6* (London: The Stationery Office, 2015), available at: http://www.legislation.gov.uk/ukpga/2015/6/pdfs/ukpga_20150006_en.pdf, accessed March 4, 2015.

[44] Stewart Bell, 'German Program that Reaches Out to Young Men Caught up in Radicalism Could be Template for Canada', *The National Post*, April 4, 2014,

available at: http://news.nationalpost.com/2014/04/04/german-program-that-reaches-out-to-young-men-caught-upin-radicalism-could-be-template-for-canada/, accessed April 4, 2014.

[45] Robin De Peyer, 'Disillusioned British Jihadists Stuck in Turkey Because They Are Too Scared to Come Back to UK', *The Evening Standard*, October 5, 2014, available at: http://www.standard.co.uk/news/world/disillusioned-british-jihadists-stuck-in-turkey-because-they-are-too-scared-to-come-back-to-uk-9775281.html, accessed October 5, 2014.

[46] Mark Townsend, 'Isis Threatens to Kill British Jihadis Wanting to Come Home', *The Guardian*, October 25, 2014, available at: http://www.theguardian.com/world/2014/oct/25/isis-threatens-kill-british-jihadis-wanting-to-come-home, accessed October 29, 2014.

[47] Tom Whitehead, 'British Jihadists to be Forced to Attend Deradicalisation Programmes, Says Cameron', *The Telegraph*, September 1, 2014, available at: http://www.telegraph.co.uk/news/uknews/terrorism-in-the-uk/11068878/British-jihadists-to-be-forced-to-attend-deradicalisation-programmes-says-Cameron.html, accessed September 2, 2014.

Glossary

Fatwa	A religious edict.
'Global' jihad	This refers to the concept of a violent struggle against the 'enemies of Islam' (particularly the United States and its allies), championed by al-Qaeda and subsequently adopted by numerous likeminded groups and individuals around the world (also see *jihad* below).
Islamism/Islamist	Islamism refers to politico-religious ideology which calls for the establishment of governmental rule based on the Islamic faith. Although Islamist *terrorists* readily resort to violence, this is not characteristic of Islamists on the whole.
Jihad	Although this has a much deeper religious meaning, the term is used here as Islamist terrorists themselves use it — to refer to the use of violence in defence of Islam (sometimes known as the lesser jihad).
Jihadi/jihadist	One who subscribes to militant Islamism. This is used interchangeably in this book with the terms 'militant', 'mujahid', 'terrorist', and 'offender'.

Mujahideen	Islamic fighters (singular: *mujahid*).
Radicalization	This is defined here are as the psychological, behavioral, and emotional process preceding involvement in terrorism. However, it is important to note that many people are radicalized to varying extents but do not become terrorists.
Salafism/Salafi/Salafist	Salafism is a strict, fundamentalist interpretation of Sunni Islam which is traditionally non-violent and apolitical. Contemporary Islamist terrorists share similar religious beliefs and are sometimes referred to as violent 'Salafi-jihadists'.
Terrorism/Terrorist	Despite the lack of a universally accepted definition, a 'typical' description of terrorism involves 'the use or threat of violence by non-state actors against non-combatant targets, intended to influence government policies and/or a wider audience by way of intimidation, in pursuit of political and/or religious objectives'. Notably, however, such definitions focus only on terrorist *attacks* and in reality 'terrorism' involves a wide range of non-violent activities and pre-cursor offences. In the interest of conducting as comprehensive an assessment as possible, this book therefore also includes people who have been accused or convicted of non-violent terrorism-related activities. People included in the sample are referred to collectively as Islamist terrorists, jihadis, militants, *mujahideen*, or offenders.
Ummah	A perceived global Muslim community.

Index